Parent Management Training

Parent Management Training

Treatment for Oppositional,
Aggressive, and Antisocial Behavior
in Children and Adolescents

Alan E. Kazdin, Ph.D.

OXFORD
UNIVERSITY PRESS

2005

OXFORD
UNIVERSITY PRESS

Oxford University Press, Inc., publishes works that further
Oxford University's objective of excellence
in research, scholarship, and education.

Oxford   New York
Auckland   Cape Town   Dar es Salaam   Hong Kong   Karachi
Kuala Lumpur   Madrid   Melbourne   Mexico City   Nairobi
New Delhi   Shanghai   Taipei   Toronto

With offices in
Argentina   Austria   Brazil   Chile   Czech Republic   France   Greece
Guatemala   Hungary   Italy   Japan   Poland   Portugal   Singapore
South Korea   Switzerland   Thailand   Turkey   Ukraine   Vietnam

Published by Oxford University Press, Inc.
198 Madison Avenue, New York, New York 10016
www.oup.com

Oxford is a registered trademark of Oxford University Press

Library of Congress Cataloging-in-Publication Data
Kazdin, Alan E.
  Parent management training : treatment for oppositional, aggressive, and antisocial
behavior in children and adolescents / Alan E. Kazdin.
    p.   cm.
  Includes bibliographical references and indexes.
  ISBN 978-0-19-515429-0

    1. Child psychotherapy—Parent participation. 2. Behavior disorders in children—
    Treatment. 3. Behavior disorders in teenagers—Treatment. 4. Child psychopathology.
    5. Adolescent psychpathology. 6. Parenting—Study and teaching. 7. Child rearing—
    Study and teaching. 8. Parent and child—Psychological aspects.   I. Title.
RJ505.P38K39 2005
618.92'8914—dc22   2004003627

9 8 7 6 5
Printed in the United States of America
on acid-free paper

This book is dedicated to parents, parenting, and parent training. Being a parent has been the most enjoyable and rewarding experience for me. Parenting, as is the case with most worthwhile activities, is enormously challenging to say the least. My situation has been eased by my children Nicole and Michelle, who trained their parents well and with the use of few aversive consequences.

Preface

Do professionals really need another book on psychotherapy for children and adolescents? The genre is already vast. Invariably "new and improved" techniques continue to appear, which is why we already have over 550 forms of therapy in use for children. It is as if inventing another therapy or a slight nuance of an existing treatment is one professional path to academic immortality. The impetus for this book is quite different. Parent management training (PMT) has rather special status as a form of psychotherapy or psychosocial intervention for clinical problems. In the context of child and adolescent psychotherapy, there is probably no other treatment with such strong evidence in its behalf. That alone would distinguish the treatment and lobby for its presentation. However, the importance of the focus is heightened by the ironic situation that PMT is rarely taught, discussed, or even mentioned in clinical training of child psychiatrists, clinical psychologists, school counselors, social workers, and psychiatric nurses. Thus, the people who provide direct services to children and adolescents rarely have opportunities to learn about this treatment, leaving aside formal supervised training that would develop the ability to administer the treatment in practice. Impetus for this book derives from the need to provide information about the treatment, its underpinnings, and concrete application in therapy.

Scholarly reviews of the research on PMT are widely available in journal articles and book chapters. In addition, treatment manuals and some self-help books for parents are available describing features of the intervention. There is a void between these two types of publications and in an effort toward their integration. This book is designed to redress this void by covering theory, research, and practice of PMT in a way that is clinically friendly and usable.

The book is presented in two integrated sections. The first section provides the background, principles, and concepts underlying PMT. This section highlights the key principles on which PMT is based and the techniques that derive from them. In addition, research on PMT is highlighted to support the claim that this is a well-studied intervention, to convey what we understand about how PMT works, and to identify what can be done to enhance the effects of treatment. No effort is made to cover all of the vast research that is available. Indeed, research on PMT continues to emerge and any updated report could be easily outdated if one attempted to cover nuances of this or that finding. Yet there is a fundamental body of research that is important to cover. Gaps in research and limitations of our understanding will also be mentioned to ensure that any hint that PMT is a panacea for outpatient treatment is explicitly countered. The first section of the book also discusses a range of issues that emerge in using PMT clinically. Variations of treatment, the content, sequence, and style of the sessions, ancillary procedures to add to PMT, obstacles that may emerge in treatment, and what to do if treatment is not working well are detailed. The first section of the book is not heavily burdened with concepts and terms. Even so, a glossary at the end of this section is provided to place all key concepts on one section.

The second section of this book provides a treatment manual of PMT, as applied in outpatient treatment for children and adolescents referred for oppositional, aggressive, and antisocial behavior. There are multiple variations of PMT. The variations differ in part as a function of the age of the children who are treated and the severity and scope of impairment they show. The common features pertain to the content and foci of the sessions and the key interventions that carry the burden of producing therapeutic change. This book includes a treatment manual that has been used with children and adolescents (2–14 years of age) for a period spanning 25 years. The manual has been revised based on findings of many investigators, our own research, and even more so from clinical application. The manual is not a substitute for supervised training. Yet, the manual conveys a detailed description of what is done to and by whom, what is said by the therapist in the sessions, and materials (e.g., handouts, aides for the parent) at each stage of treatment.

The first and second parts of the book are connected by more than a common binding from the printer. Rather, the initial part focuses not only on principles but issues and obstacles that emerge clinically and what can be done about them. An effort is made to move from the general (background, principles, theory) to the specific (e.g., techniques, dialogue of the therapist, parent, and child and materials used in treatment). Also, the first and second parts are designed to address clinically important issues. For example, PMT is very effective but may be weak or ineffective for any given clinical case. What can be done? Actually a great deal. PMT encompasses an extensive array of quite specific options of what to do to improve ailing programs. Also, PMT may work well if the parent carries out the procedures, but parent adherence can be a key problem. What can be done if the parents cannot or do not do the program at home? Here too, there is much to say and do to develop adherence in the parent. These and other questions are addressed; they are clinically critical questions but they are also informed by the principles and findings of PMT as well as by concrete strategies for use within the sessions. In short, the goal of this book is to provide a package that encompasses theory, research, and application in the confines of a readable book.

Research findings on PMT are excellent for establishing the effects of treatment and for answering facets about who responds. The book supplements the knowledge base with practical details about how to apply the treatment clinically. The details have benefited from the experience of several therapists who have applied this manual to families seen in short-term inpatient treatment and outpatient therapy. I have been very fortunate to have the opportunity to work with several therapists and clinic staff who have been directly involved in providing the treatment detailed in this book. At the University of Pittsburgh School of Medicine's Department of Psychiatry, a variation of the treatment described in this book was developed initially as treatment for inpatient children (ages 5–12) who were to be discharged to their parents. The treatment was also used for cases seen only on an outpatient basis. At Yale University's Department of Psychology and Child Study Center, the treatment has been provided in an outpatient service (Child Conduct Clinic) for children and adolescents (ages 2–14). At Yale, staff of the Child Conduct Clinic have included: Elif Attaroglu, Wayne Ayers, Justin Barsanti, Susan Breton, Elizabeth Brown, Susan Bullerdick, Erin Carrubba, Mary Cavaleri, Michael Crowley, Lisa Holland, Bernadette Lecza, Jennifer Mazurick, Molly McDonald, Michelle Ragozzine, Gloria Wassell, and Moira Whitley. Several graduate students have also worked at the clinic and contributed greatly including: Andres De Los Reyes, Jerusha Detweiler, Julie Feldman, Lori Hilt, Sara Lederman, Paul Marciano, Matthew Nock, and Francheska Perepletchikova. The extensive experience of these therapists and our daily interactions over cases has shaped the treatment as well as the research we were able to complete in applying the treatment clinically.

I am very pleased to acknowledge support that made this work possible. Support from the National Institute of Mental Health (Research Scientist and Senior Scientist Awards, and a MERIT Award), The William T. Grant Foundation, and Leon Lowenstein Foundation were pivotal to the work.

Contents

Parent Management Training

Introduction

Psychotherapy for children and adolescents is a fascinating topic that raises disturbing questions.[1] Do children really have problems that warrant psychotherapy? If so, can therapy really help? Parents, teachers, and mental health professionals have a strong interest in allaying children's miseries and improving their adjustment over the course of development. Also, treating a problem in childhood can reduce the likelihood of more severe problems in adolescence and adulthood. Advances in both treatment and prevention are needed because neither alone can address the scope of the problems that children, adolescents, and adults experience.

Children and adolescents may develop a vast array of social, emotional, and behavioral problems, and the number of youths who have such problems is large. Many interventions, including various forms of psychotherapy, medication, institutionalization (hospital, juvenile justice), special education, and assorted school programs, have been designed to address these problems. Psychotherapy is psychosocial intervention used to improve adjustment and functioning and to reduce maladaptive behaviors and various psychological and often physical complaints. Psychosocial intervention means that the treatments rely on interpersonal sources of influence, such as learning, problem solving, social support, and altering facets of the interpersonal environment (family interaction, how one approaches interactions with others). These sources of influence are distinct from biologically based interventions such as medication, surgery, and nutrition.

The focus of psychotherapy is how individuals feel (affect), think (cognitions), and act (behaviors). Psychological and biologically based interventions are not in competition; they are often combined. The key is not so much whether the treatment is based on a particular domain or derives from a psychological, biological, or other approach. Rather, the issue is whether a viable treatment can be provided that has evidence to suggest it will have an impact on the clinical problem. Health professionals (e.g., psychologists, pediatricians, psychiatrists, social workers, nurses) have a responsibility for helping children and families, many of whom are desperate for some assistance or care. In this context, we as mental health professionals are not too concerned whether an effective treatment comes from one approach or discipline rather than another. As an example, I work at a clinic for the treatment of aggressive and antisocial children.[2] Our clinic staff would be elated to learn about an easily deliverable effective treatment, whether it involved some yet to be identified herb, special diet, foot powder, drug, or therapy. I believe this view is widely shared.

The focus of this book is on parent management training (PMT), one of many psychosocial interventions that can directly address many of the problems that emerge during development. This chapter places PMT in context and highlights three areas: the scope of social, emotional, and behavioral problems that children and adolescents experience; the current status of psychotherapy and psychotherapy research; and the emergence of PMT as a treatment. These three topics provide background to the primary focus of the book—namely, presenting PMT and its procedures, evidence, strengths, and limitations.

Parent management training is one of many—indeed, hundreds—of interventions. We would not want to provide a new book on just any intervention. The contextual comments related to the current status of psychotherapy convey that PMT has features that warrant its special consideration and make it of special interest to researchers, mental health practitioners, trainees, and, perhaps most important, to potential consumers of research. This chapter clarifies what PMT is and the special features that make this technique unique among the many therapies for children and adolescents.

Problems That Warrant Treatment in Childhood and Adolescence

The need for effective treatments stems in part from the range of conditions that children and adolescents experience. This section has an overview of the range of problems to convey the scope of the challenges of identifying and developing treatments. For the purpose of presentation, the dysfunctions are grouped into three categories: social, emotional, and behavioral problems; problem and at-risk behaviors; and delinquency.

Social, Emotional, and Behavioral Problems

By social, emotional, and behavioral problems, I refer to a range of dysfunctions within the domain of mental health. These are delineated as "problems" because they are associated with impairment in functioning and often serve as the basis for treatment. Within this category are dysfunctions that are referred to as psychiatric or mental disorders, patterns of behavior that are associated with distress, impairment, or significantly increased risk of suffering, death, pain, disability, or an important loss of freedom. Critical to meeting criteria for a diagnosis is impaired functioning in everyday life. Thus, a few symptoms here or odd social behaviors are not enough to count as a disorder unless these also are reflected in difficulties in functioning at home, at work, at school, or in other contexts in which demands are made. Psychological dysfunctions or disorders are enumerated in various diagnostic systems. The dominant system

Table 1.1
Examples of Currently Recognized Psychiatric Disorders
Among Children and Adolescents Referred to Treatment

Attention-Deficit/Hyperactivity Disorder: A persistent pattern of inattention, impulsivity, and high and maladaptive levels of activity. These are often evident by difficulty in sustaining attention to tasks or play, often leaving one's seat in class, running around, or engaging in excessive activity in relation to developmental levels (e.g., same-age children) and contexts (e.g., classroom, day care).

Oppositional Defiant Disorder: A pattern of negativistic, defiant, and hostile behavior, including frequent arguing, temper tantrums, and noncompliance with adults. Stubbornness, resistance to directions, and seemingly intentional annoying of others are key characteristics.

Conduct Disorder: Aggressive or antisocial behavior in which the basic rights of others or social norms are violated. A pattern includes such behaviors as frequent fighting, lying, stealing, firesetting, cruelty to others (or to animals), and destroying property.

Major Depressive Disorder: The appearance of depressed mood or loss of interest in activities. Symptoms may include change in appetite or weight, sleep, and psychomotor activity; feelings of worthlessness or guilt; diminished energy; difficulty in thinking, concentrating, or making decisions; and recurrent thoughts of death or suicidal ideation, plans, or attempts.

Social Phobia: Symptoms of fear that emerge in social situations in which the person is exposed to unfamiliar people. Also, there may be performance demands in which the individual fears acting in ways that will be embarrassing or humiliating. The person is anxious in anticipating such situations and tries to avoid them.

Posttraumatic Stress Disorder: Development of symptoms of anxiety after exposure to an extreme traumatic event involving actual or threatened injury or witnessing an event that involves death, injury, or a threat to the physical integrity of another person. The events may be personal assault (e.g., sexual, physical, robbery), accidents, life-threatening illness, or a disaster (e.g., loss of one's home after a hurricane or tornado). Key symptoms are intense fear, helplessness, horror, reexperience of the event (e.g., thoughts, dreams), avoidance of stimuli associated with the event, and numbing of general responsiveness (e.g., detachment, restricted affect), and persistent symptoms of increased arousal (e.g., difficulty falling or remaining asleep).

---

is the *Diagnostic and Statistical Manual of Mental Disorders* (*DSM-IV*; American Psychiatric Association [APA], 1994), which delineates currently recognized disorders that may arise in infancy, childhood, adolescence, and adulthood. There are hundreds of clinical problems that have been identified in contemporary diagnosis, and children and adolescents can experience most of these.

From the hundreds of recognized psychiatric disorders, I have summarized several that are more common and more familiar among children and

Eating Disorders: The individual does not maintain minimal normal body weight (<85% of normal body weight), is intensely afraid of gaining weight, and exhibits a significant disturbance in the perception of his or her body. Many methods of weight loss may be adopted, such as self-induced vomiting, misuse of laxatives, and increased or excessive exercise.

Substance-Abuse Disorder: A set of disorders (depending on the substance) character-ized by a maladaptive use of the substance as evident in recurrent and significant adverse consequences (e.g., failure to fulfill role obligations at school, work, or home; social and interpersonal problems). The diagnosis is made on the basis of continued use after unto-ward consequences (e.g., in role performance, legal problems, school expulsion).

Schizophrenia: Symptoms include delusions, hallucinations, disorganized speech, grossly disorganized or catatonic behavior, and negative symptoms such as flat affect, poverty of speech (brief, empty replies), and inability to initiate or persist in goal-directed beha-vior. Significant dysfunction occurs in one or more areas of functioning, including inter-personal relations, work, school, or self-care.

Adjustment Disorder: Clinically significant emotional or behavioral symptoms in re-sponse to an identifiable psychological stressor or stressors. The symptoms include marked distress or a reaction in excess of what might be expected within the context or culture. The symptoms of many other disorders may emerge (e.g., anxiety, depressed mood, conduct problems).

Other Conditions: A set of problems that are not mental disorders but may serve as the focus of clinical attention, such as relational problems (e.g., between parent and child, between spouses), physical or sexual abuse of an adult or child, isolated antisocial beha-vior, bereavement, and many others that are not considered mental disorders but are brought to the attention of mental health professionals.

Note: Only summary characteristics of the selected disorders are presented here. Several specific inclusion criteria must be met related to symptoms, severity and duration, and patterns of onset for a diagnosis to be met (see *DSM IV*, APA, 1994). In addition, the symptoms must be associated with impairment in everyday functioning (e.g., school, home, community activities). Details of the diagnoses are beyond the scope of this chapter.

adolescents referred to treatment. Table 1.1 provides only a few of the disorders that are seen in clinical work and to which treatments are applied. Some of these disorders arise in childhood or adolescence (e.g., conduct disorder and attention-deficit/hyperactivity disorder in childhood), and others can arise at any time over the course of development (e.g., major depression, posttraumatic stress disorder).

The delineation and investigation of disorders are active areas of research with many fascinating subtopics. For example, a given disorder can vary over the course of development, there are subtypes of disorders, the criteria for saying that one has or does not have the disorder are not firmly established, and many disorders go together. For example, depression can emerge during childhood, adolescence, and adulthood and can be diagnosed based on symptoms common across the life span. Yet, some rather stark differences in depression are evident over the course of development. As one case in point, suicide attempt and completion, which sometimes accompany major depression, are rarely evident in children. The rates of attempt and completion increase significantly during adolescence and adulthood. Thus, a key feature associated with depression can change considerably over the life span. For present purposes, the developmental changes of various disorders, such as those illustrated here with depression, need not distract us from the broader point; namely, all sorts of clinical problems are recognized to occur in children and adolescents, and these serve as an impetus for seeking treatment.

To consider a broader range of children's dysfunctions, I have grouped various problems into five broad categories. These categories, presented in Table 1.2, summarize the types of problems children bring to treatment. Many of the currently recognized psychiatric disorders are encompassed by these categories. Of the categories listed in Table 1.2, externalizing disorders dominate as a basis for referral to clinical services (inpatient or outpatient treatment facilities). *Externalizing disorders* refer to problems that are directed toward the environment and others. Primary examples are oppositional, hyperactive, aggressive, and antisocial behaviors. *Internalizing disorders* refer to problems that are directed toward inner experience. Primary examples are anxiety, withdrawal, and depression.

There are hundreds of disorders, as I have mentioned, but how many children actually experience the dysfunctions these disorders reflect? *Prevalence* refers to the number of persons with the problem (e.g., psychiatric disorder) at a given point in time. Several studies spanning different geographical locales (e.g., the United States, Puerto Rico, Canada, and New Zealand) have yielded rather consistent results on the prevalence of disorders among children and adolescents (e.g., ages 4 to 18 years old). Between 17% and 22% suffer significant developmental, emotional, or behavioral problems (e.g., U.S. Congress, 1991; World Health Organization [WHO], 2001). There are approximately 70 million children and adolescents in the United States (Snyder, Poole, & Wan, 2000). Assume for a moment a prevalence rate of 20%; then, 14 million youths in the United States have significant impairments due to an emotional or behavioral problem.

Table 1.2
Broad Categories of Problem Domains and Disorders

Externalizing Disorders: Problems that are directed toward the environment and others or problems of "undercontrol" (impulsiveness, inattention, overreactions). Primary examples: oppositional, hyperactive, aggressive, and antisocial behaviors; encompassed by the psychiatric diagnostic categories attention-deficit/hyperactivity disorder, oppositional defiant disorder, and conduct disorder (see Table 1.1).

Internalizing Disorders: Problems that are directed toward inner experience or problems of "overcontrol" (inhibition, withdrawal, constraint). Primary examples: anxiety, shyness, withdrawal, and depression.

Substance-Related Disorders: Impairment associated with any of a variety of substances including alcohol, illicit drugs, and tobacco. These disorders, while important in their own right, are also associated with other psychiatric disorders.

Learning and Mental Disabilities: A range of problems related to intellectual and academic functioning, including mental retardation and learning disorders. Because of the more salient problems that serve as the basis for referral, such problems are probably underestimated in terms of both prevalence and impact on behavior among children and adolescents referred to treatment.

Severe and Pervasive Psychopathology: The more severe forms of psychopathology that have pervasive influences in the areas of functioning they affect and in their long-term course. Examples include schizophrenia and autism.

A prevalence rate of psychiatric disorders of approximately 20% is high. Surely this must be a vast overestimate. However, all indications are that this rate significantly *underestimates* the range of mental disorders and impairment. Prevalence rates are determined by identifying children who meet diagnostic criteria for a disorder. However, individuals who "miss" meeting the criteria but are close often show significant impairment and untoward long-term prognoses (Boyle et al., 1996; Lewinsohn, Solomon, Seeley, & Zeiss, 2000; Offord et al., 1992). For example, adolescents who come close to, but who do not meet, the criteria for major depression are much more likely to meet criteria for another disorder, to develop another disorder later, and to show impairment in psychosocial functioning when compared with individuals with few or no depressive symptoms.

Diagnostic criteria are intended to identify individuals with significant problems and impairment, but the bar has been set high. The criteria may not capture the range of individuals likely to have problems in their functioning. Many disorders are better represented as a continuum or set of continua based on the number and severity of symptoms and the degree of impairment, rather than as a condition achieved by a particular cutoff (Boyle et al., 1996; Flett, Vredenburg, & Krames, 1997; Kessler et al., 2003). Individuals who may not meet a specific cutoff point on the continuum may still suffer impairment in daily life and profit from psychological or other forms of treatment.

Overall, prevalence rates that are based on meeting criteria for diagnoses may be conservative. Those children identified with disorders are likely to be impaired, but many children who do not meet the criteria are also impaired and may have a poor long-term prognosis. The already high prevalence rate of mental disorders in children and adolescents clearly underestimates the scope of the problem.

Problem and At-Risk Behaviors

Currently recognized psychiatric disorders, particularly those included under externalizing and internalizing behaviors, are the primary focus of therapy with children and adolescents. Other problems warrant intervention because they are related to current and long-term functioning. These other problems partially overlap psychiatric disorders but can be distinguished from them.

During adolescence, there is an increase in *problem* or *at-risk behaviors* (DiClemente, Hansen, & Ponton, 1996; Ketterlinus & Lamb, 1994). Examples are use of illicit substances, truancy, school suspensions, stealing, vandalism, and precocious and unprotected sex. These are referred to as at-risk behaviors because they increase the likelihood of a variety of adverse psychological, social, and health outcomes. For example, alcohol abuse is associated with the three most frequent causes of mortality among adolescents: automobile accidents, homicides, and suicide (Windle, Shope, & Bukstein, 1996); approximately 90% of automobile accidents among adolescents involve the use of alcohol.

The problem behaviors obviously overlap with psychiatric diagnoses, and sometimes the distinction can be difficult to make. As a guide, the psychiatric disorders refer to a pattern of functioning, the presence of multiple symptoms, and impairment in everyday situations. Many youths with problem behaviors might well meet criteria for a disorder (e.g., substance abuse disorder). However, there is a larger group that would not; that is, they engage in problem behaviors, fit in with their peers, and manage daily functioning (e.g., at school).

The prevalence rates of problem behaviors are relatively high. For example, a survey conducted annually since 1975 has evaluated high school student use of substances. As an illustration of rates, in 2001, 49.8% and 25.7% of 12th-grade students reported alcohol use and illicit drug use, respectively, in the 30 days prior to the survey; 31.3% reported being drunk at least once; and 4.9% reported using marijuana daily or almost daily (http://www.nida.nih.gov/Infofax/HSYouthtrends.html). Other studies paint a similar picture, even though estimates of substance abuse vary as a function of the age of the sample, the types of substances (e.g., inhalants), the time frame (use in past week, month, year), the assessment method (e.g., self-report vs. medical emergency visits), and the impact of many other factors (e.g., social class, ethnicity, neighborhood). Even so, the rates of abuse and use are alarming. The direct and immediate health consequences and correlates of substance abuse (e.g., increased risk of death from overdose, injury and death while driving a vehicle, sexually transmitted disease through unprotected sex) are serious. The indirect and long-term consequences of substance abuse are problematic as well (e.g., school failure, poor occupational adjustment, crime, and mental disorders) (Newcomb & Bentler, 1988; U.S. Congress, 1991; World Health Organization [WHO], 2002).

Substance use is merely one example of at-risk behavior. Other examples are unprotected sexual activity and its risk for sexually transmitted diseases (including human immunodeficiency virus [HIV]) and teen pregnancy; delinquent, antisocial, and violent behavior; dropping out of school; and running away from home (DiClemente et al., 1996; www.cdc.gov/nchs/fastats/druguse.htm). Such behaviors are often associated with concurrent mental and physical health problems during adolescence, as well as with subsequent problems in adulthood.

Delinquency

Delinquency is a legal designation of behaviors that violate the law, such as robbery, drug use, and vandalism. Some of the acts are illegal for both adults and juveniles (referred to as *index* offenses), including homicide, robbery, aggravated assault, and rape. Other acts (referred to as *status* offenses) are illegal only because of the age at which they occur—namely, only for juveniles. Examples include underage drinking, running away from home, truancy from school, and driving a car.

Delinquency is a weighty subject in its own right, but it warrants additional mention for at least three reasons. First, delinquent acts overlap with psychiatric disorders and problem behaviors, as mentioned previously. Indeed, the distinction between delinquency and mental disorder is not always sharp, and individuals can readily meet criteria for both based on the same behaviors (e.g., conduct disorder symptoms). Second, individuals identified as delinquent often have high rates of diagnosable psychiatric disorders. Fifty to 80% of delinquent youths show at least one diagnosable psychiatric disorder—with conduct, attention deficit, and substance abuse disorders among the most common (see Kazdin, 2000a). Third, PMT is among the diverse types of psychotherapy used with delinquent youth, and hence this population is relevant to this book.

The prevalence rates of delinquency in the population at large vary as a function of how delinquency is measured. Arrest records, surveys of victims, and reports of individuals about their own criminal activities are among the most common methods. Because much crime goes unreported and undetected, self-report is often used and detects much higher rates than official records. Nevertheless, a few key points have widespread agreement. First, many adolescents (e.g., 70%) engage in some delinquent behavior, usually status rather than index offenses (Elliott, Huizinga, & Ageton, 1985; Farrington, 1995). Most of these individuals do not continue criminal behavior. Second, some (e.g., 20–35%) engage in more serious offenses (robbery and assault) and may be identified through arrest or contact with the courts. Third, a very small group of adolescents (e.g., 5%) are persistent or career criminals. Members of this smaller group engage in many different and more severe delinquent activities and are responsible for approximately half of the officially recorded offenses (Farrington, 1995; Tracy, Wolfgang, & Figlio, 1990).

Delinquency can be distinguished from psychiatric disorders and problem behaviors, but clearly there is overlap among the three ways of categorizing behaviors. The distinctions are often made because they refer to different problems, including whether the problem is circumscribed or part of a larger pattern and whether the problem violates the law. Yet, the arbitrariness of the distinctions is sometimes obvious and may even affect a child (or adult) in any given instance. For example, if a 10-year-old child sets a neighbor's house on fire, the agency first called to intervene (e.g., police, mental health services) may dictate the designation (emotional problem, delinquent act) and the intervention provided to the child (treatment, contact with the police, arrest).

General Comments

Psychiatric disorders, problem behaviors, and delinquency convey many but not all the social, emotional, and behavioral problems that children experience. Not all the adjustment woes are easily classified or diagnosable. For example, in response to stressors such as traumatic injury, divorce, loss of a sibling or parent, or entrance into a medical regimen (e.g., surgery, chemotherapy), there are often perturbations in adjustment among children, adolescents, and adults that may not fit into a diagnosable disorder but lead to distress and treatment or some intervention. The purpose here is not to catalogue every sort of problem that might be a candidate for treatment or that actually serves as a basis for intervening with children and families, but rather to convey the scope and prevalence of impairment and the need for interventions.

Psychotherapy and other interventions—social services; home, school, and community-based programs; residential and hospital treatment; and medication—that address the diverse social, emotional, and behavioral problems of children and adolescents are not in competition and share many of the same goals. A multipronged approach that involves all sorts of special services and interventions to meet the mental health needs of children and families is required. PMT is one form of psychotherapy. It is useful to place PMT in context by highlighting the broader topic of therapy for children and adolescents.

Current Status of Psychotherapy for Children and Adolescents

Traditionally, psychotherapy has been discussed in terms of approaches toward treatment. *Approach* refers to conceptual views, the general focus or emphasis of the interventions, and the domains that are viewed as central to the onset, course, and amelioration of the problem. Among the many approaches, psychodynamic, family, cognitive-behavioral, and experiential are familiar examples. Although there is still some focus on general approaches in writings about therapy and in graduate programs that train therapists, currently much greater attention is accorded to specific techniques of treatment.

Broad approaches have been largely abandoned for several reasons. First, they often attempt to account for clinical dysfunction in sweeping terms that apply to a wide range of problems. The accounts remain relatively general and fairly immune to empirical support or refutation. Second, research on various disorders has advanced greatly, and it is now recognized that multiple influences contribute to the development, maintenance, and amelioration of a particular clinical problem. A focus on any single level is incomplete and often just not very helpful or informative. Third, within a given approach (e.g., behavior therapy, family therapy), there are many competing conceptual views and treatment techniques. Thus, the coherence of an approach is much less clear today than in the history of psychotherapy. Fourth, treatment outcome research does not focus on "approaches" but rather on specific techniques. It may be helpful to write textbooks or to teach therapy in relation to approaches and broad conceptual views, but in clinical work and in research, it is specific interventions that are delivered.

More than 550 treatments can be documented to be in use for children and adolescents (Kazdin, 2000b). This number is conservative because it omits the combinations of treatments and variations under the broad rubric of "eclectic therapies" that are often used in clinical practice. The vast majority of these hundreds of treatments have never been studied empirically, and hence there is not even a morsel of evidence that they help children or families and lead to change.

Within the past 10 years, there has been heightened interest in identifying treatments that have evidence in their behalf. Different professional organizations and committees in several countries have made separate and somewhat independent efforts to identify such treatments (e.g., *Evidence-Based Mental Health*, 1998; Nathan & Gorman, 2002; Roth & Fonagy, 2005; Task Force on Promotion and Dissemination of Psychological Procedures, 1995). Many sources focus specifically on treatments for children and adolescents (e.g., Christophersen & Mortweet, 2001; Fonagy, Target, Cottrell, Phillips, & Kurtz, 2002; Kazdin & Weisz, 2003).

The various efforts have used different terms to delineate such treatments, including evidence-based treatments, empirically validated treatments, empirically supported treatments, evidence-based practice, and treatments that work. The different terms and the efforts they reflect are not completely interchangeable because the criteria of each of the groups have been slightly different. There are some commonalities. Treatments are identified as evidence based if:

- Treatment has been compared with either a no-treatment control group or some other intervention (e.g., standard, routine care, treatment as usual for the setting);
- Two or more randomized controlled studies attest to the effects of treatment;
- The studies include replication of the findings beyond the original investigator or originator of the treatment;
- The patient sample has been well specified (inclusion and exclusion criteria and perhaps diagnosis); and
- Treatment manuals were used for the intervention(s).

Table 1.3
Treatments for Children and Adolescents That Are
Empirically Supported for Key Problem Domains

Problem domain	Treatment
Anxiety, fear, and phobias	Cognitive-behavior therapy
	Modeling
	Reinforced practice
	Systematic desensitization
Depression	Cognitive-behavior therapy
	Coping with depression course
	Interpersonal psychotherapy for adolescents
Oppositional and conduct disorders	Anger control therapy
	Multisystemic therapy
	Parent management training
	Problem-solving skills training
Attention-deficit/hyperactivity disorder	Classroom contingency management
	Parent management training
	Psychostimulant medication

Notes: The techniques noted here draw from different methods of defining and evaluating evidence-based treatments. The information was derived from articles within special journal issues (Kendall & Chambless, 1998; Lonigan, Elbert, & Johnson, 1998) and edited books (Christophersen & Mortweet, 2001; Kazdin & Weisz, 2003; Nathan & Gorman, 2002). Psychostimulant medication is mentioned because this is the standard (and evidence-based) treatment for attention-deficit/hyperactivity disorder.

The criteria emphasize sound research methodology, including careful specification of who the clients are, precisely what is done in treatment, replication of the main finding, and replicability of the study, because critical features of treatment are well specified (e.g., use of treatment manuals) and used by other researchers. In developing clinical guidelines, occasionally authors combine evidence-based treatments with those that are probably effective but have not met all of these criteria (e.g., Wasserman, Ko, & Jensen, 2001). Criteria vary among different efforts to delineate evidence-based treatments, and criteria occasionally are debated. What is not as often debated is that a search through all of the available treatments in use for children and adolescents would find that only a small number would have evidence in their behalf by any rigorous or quasi-rigorous criteria. Table 1.3 lists evidence-based treatments that were culled from reviews by problem domain. Because these different sources do not invoke the same criteria, I have taken any treatment identified as evidence based from sources noted in the table. The list cannot be considered complete because at any time new treatments can meet the criteria and be added.

A few points are conspicuous from the list. First, there *is* a list of evidence-based treatments, and that in itself is reassuring and important for professionals, potential clients, and society at large. All treatments among the hundreds are not equal in the extent to which they have been studied and supported, a point that ought to be considered by professionals who provide services, those who receive services, and those who reimburse clinical services. Clearly, a child referred to treatment for severe anxiety ought to receive one of the evidence-based treatments as the intervention of choice. It is possible that other interventions, yet to be studied, would be very effective, but their use would be difficult to defend, based on current evidence.

Second, the list of evidence-based treatments is not that long, especially considering the more than 550 treatments mentioned previously. This raises the question of what *is* in use. Most of the treatments in use in clinical practice are not evidence based. Clearly, this fact raises concerns about disseminating research findings, training therapists, and changing the services delivered to patients.

Third, the list in Table 1.3 is dominated by cognitive-behavioral treatments. This is no coincidence; approximately 50% of child treatment studies investigate cognitive-behavioral techniques (see Durlak, Wells, Cotten, & Johnson, 1995; Kazdin, Bass, Ayers, & Rodgers, 1990). Also, to be counted as evidence-based treatments, studies must include several methodological features (e.g., use of treatment manuals, random assignment). These characteristics are much more likely among contemporary studies than in studies conducted 20 or 30 years ago, and cognitive-behavioral techniques are more popular in contemporary work. Although cognitive-behavioral treatments are heavily represented on the list, it would be an inappropriate leap to infer that cognitive-behavioral treatments in general are effective. There are many cognitive-behavioral treatments included in the hundreds of unevaluated treatments.

Overall, the identification of evidence-based treatment is not free from controversy. Although most mental health professionals probably are in favor of such treatments, there are concerns whether the findings demonstrated in controlled research settings can be extended to clinical practice (e.g., Chambless & Ollendick, 2001; Shadish, Navarro, Matt, & Phillips, 2000). This has led to empirical efforts to extend findings from research to clinical settings, where clinical problems, patients, therapists, and efforts to evaluate treatment depart from the comforts of controlled research. I mention evidence-based treatments here as a context for focusing on PMT.

Overview and Delineation of Parent Management Training

Definition and Core Features

PMT consists of an intervention in which parents are taught social learning techniques to change the behavior of their children or adolescents.[3] Parents are seen in many forms of treatment, and hence it is important to be clear about the scope of PMT. PMT does *not* include all treatments in which parents are seen or counseled as part of treatment or in which parents are trained to interact differently with their children. Most therapy includes contact and interactions with parents, at least when applied to children (rather than adolescents) (Kazdin, Siegel, & Bass, 1990). Also, variations of family therapy often entail exercises and tasks designed to change communication and interaction patterns in the home.

Whether a treatment falls under the rubric of PMT is based on four distinguishing but interrelated components: (a) a conceptual view about how to change social, emotional, and behavioral problems; (b) a set of principles and techniques that follow from that conceptual view; (c) development of specific skills in the parents through practice, role play, and other active methods of training; and (d) integration of assessment and evaluation in treatment and treatment decision making. Of course, given the vast array of treatments in clinical work, no doubt one could identify a treatment here or there at the margin and quibble about whether it *really* is or is not PMT. At the same time, there are many versions of PMT, and often these include many features other than those that define the treatment. Here, too, one can quibble about whether the intervention is really PMT only or PMT plus another treatment. These issues can be taken up later. At this point, it is more critical to be clear about the defining and core features.

First, the conceptual view is based on learning theory and research. Traditionally, three types of basic learning are often distinguished: respondent (or classical) conditioning, operant conditioning, and observational learning (or modeling) (see the glossary). Each type of learning has generated effective forms of psychotherapy for children, adolescents, and adults. PMT is based on operant conditioning, which focuses on antecedents, behaviors, and consequences as a way to develop and alter behavior. Operant conditioning is a well-developed area of basic and applied research and provides the underpinnings for many of the procedures used in treatment. The conceptual view emphasizes learning and experiences that can be provided to promote behavior change. The focus is on changing how individuals behave in everyday life. PMT entails changing parents and children at home and in other settings and contexts in which child behavior change is important. I refer to this as *social learning* to emphasize that the learning experiences are provided to the parents and children in the context of interpersonal interaction among multiple persons, including the family, therapist, teachers, and others in everyday life who may be involved in the treatment.

Second, PMT includes a variety of principles or general statements about relations between behaviors and events that precede or follow these behaviors. From the various principles, scores of techniques can be derived. For example, one key principle is *positive reinforcement*. From this principle, scores of variations of techniques can be generated (e.g., providing praise for the child). This example dangerously oversimplifies both the principles and techniques. Yet, at this point, I want to convey a structure of treatment that includes some small number of principles and many variations in the ways these can be translated to techniques. This point proves to be critical in clinical work. Occasionally a particular technique does not work or is difficult and cumbersome to implement. In such instances, it is quite common to make a change in the technique variation and achieve the desired treatment effects. Examples and explanations of how to do this are provided in later chapters.

Third, specific skills are developed in the parents through active training. This is accomplished by practice, role play, feedback, and modeling by the therapist of how to interact with the child, how to change child behavior, and how to implement the techniques introduced into treatment. Merely telling parents what to do cannot develop these skills. In developing the skills in the parents, the therapist uses many of the same techniques, such as positive reinforcement, shaping, and use of antecedents, that the parents will be using with their children.

Fourth, PMT integrates assessment and evaluation with treatment. A goal of treatment is to change child behavior and adaptive functioning. The goal is often approached or achieved during treatment, and hence new goals are selected. Alternatively, a particular goal may not be achieved, and hence changes are needed in what is done in treatment. The key to making decisions during treatment is having information about progress. PMT makes an effort to obtain this information while treatment is in effect by systematically monitoring progress.

The definition conveys that involving parents in treatment or merely trying to get parents to act in new ways is not sufficient to constitute PMT. The four components I have mentioned are central. Even with these, there are many variations of PMT that meet the definition and characteristics and are well studied. Thus, although there are defining characteristics and structure to the treatment, there are also many variations, as discussed later.

Along with the variations of treatment are the many different names other than PMT that are used. Some of the salient alternatives are behavioral parent training, parent training, parent behavior management training, and contingency management (in the home). Probably all are deplorable because they are nondescriptive or emphasize "management" of children, which is odd as a goal or concept and does not reflect the serious social, emotional, and behavioral problems (e.g., conduct disorder, autism) to which PMT is often applied. Also, the term is not likely to be attractive to parents or potential therapists because it does not sound very sensitive, relevant, or soft and mushy. Consider some other forms of treatment such as "play therapy," "family systems therapy," or "dynamic counseling." These terms sound so much better than parent *management* training. If they do not sound better, at least they are ambiguous so the consumer has little idea—positive or negative—about what is involved.

Status as an Evidence-Based Treatment

Parent management training is only one of several of the evidence-based treatments for children and adolescents listed in Table 1.3. At first blush, there might be no special reason to single out this technique in relation to others. However, there are very special features of PMT that make it unique among interventions. Some of the features that are highlighted here convey the rationale for presenting this technique by itself.

Perhaps the most salient characteristic is the research base. No other psychotherapy for children and adolescents has been as well investigated as PMT. I highlight the evidence later, but the point ought to be underscored now. I mentioned before that to be considered as an evidence-based treatment, two or more controlled studies must support the effects of the intervention. There are scores of studies of the effects of PMT and many reviews of the evidence as well, as discussed in chapter 6.

Of course, to say that PMT is the most investigated treatment does not mean that it is always effective or that all the critical questions that need to be asked about treatment can be answered. Analogously, for some forms of cancer, chemotherapy is by far the best and most studied treatment, but that says nothing about whether the treatment is as effective as we would like or, sadly, even if it is effective at all in any given case. The same holds for PMT as a treatment for many clinical problems or for many children referred for a problem for which PMT has been effective.

The special status of PMT as a treatment for children and adolescents is useful to consider in a relative and absolute sense. PMT *relative* to other treatments in use for children and adolescents has a very special status in light of the evidence. Other techniques do not approximate the evidence available on this intervention. Yet in some *absolute* sense—that is, without this comparison with other treatments—there remain critical questions about PMT. These are not trivial questions and include such weighty issues as why it is effective, for whom it is effective, and what the necessary, sufficient, and facilitative conditions are for its effective administration. Indeed, one might even be disappointed in the treatment in some ways because with all the vast research, there are some questions that probably should have been addressed long ago. I consider these issues later, but for now the standing of PMT in relation to other treatments is indeed special.

The research basis of PMT is much deeper than the studies of the treatment as applied to the clinical problems of children. I mentioned operant conditioning as the basis for the interventions that are used by the therapist to change parent behavior and by the parent(s) to change child behavior. The principles of operant conditioning and the techniques that derive from them have been used extensively outside the context of parent training. There is a vast body of research showing that the principles and techniques derived from them have been effective in:

- Developing academic behavior and improving classroom performance of students (from preschool through college)
- Developing prosocial behavior and adaptive functioning among individuals (children through adults) with developmental disabilities and mental retardation
- Preventing the development of deviant behavior among youths at risk for the onset of aggressive behavior, drug use, or problem behaviors more generally
- Improving adherence to medical regimens, including taking medication or engaging in activities that promote recovery
- Altering performance of athletes (amateur and professional), of employees in business and industry (job performance, accidents on the job, engaging in health-related activities), of men and women in the military (e.g., performance of specific activities, completion of training regimens), and of individuals in everyday life (e.g., recycling waste, conserving energy, using seatbelts).[4]

Parent management training is one area in which operant conditioning principles are applied in everyday life, and it is not necessarily the dominant application. This book focuses on PMT as a treatment for childhood and adolescent disorders, especially oppositional, aggressive, and antisocial behaviors. I mention these other applications because of their significance in relation to PMT. The procedures used in PMT have been applied to many populations from preschool to geriatric clients and in diverse settings including everyday life, community living facilities, business and industry, and treatment and rehabilitation institutions. Although the evidence in these other applications is well beyond the present focus, it is relevant. When we ask the general question, Do we really know that the procedures used in PMT are effective? the answer is yes, not only from the PMT literature but also from a rather large literature on the same techniques that have enjoyed widespread use beyond PMT.

A final point follows from what has been noted so far but is worth making explicit. PMT has been used in the context of treatment and prevention, but it is also used in everyday life to assist parents whose children are not experiencing special problems. Many parents wish further assistance in addressing the normal challenges of everyday life, such as having children comply with requests, bathe regularly, use utensils to eat, not throw food at meals, greet others in a reasonably friendly way, say "thank you," get along with a sibling, and scores of other such behaviors. Most of us have learned these personal and interpersonal behaviors without any special interventions. (Surprisingly, many adults have not learned these. The reader and one guest are invited to my annual Family-Reunion-Thanksgiving Gala for direct evidence of this point—and no cameras allowed.) At the same time, for those of us who are parents, we have often muddled through ways of interacting with our children that are wonderfully well intentioned but only mildly effective or ineffective. Moreover, some procedures routinely used (e.g., nagging, screaming, hitting) are not very effective and can have deleterious effects. PMT can help, whether or not there is a "problem." Brief variations of training (e.g., a few sessions) directed toward parents engaged in the routine challenges of parenting can be useful to them.

Underpinnings and Emergence of PMT

As a treatment, PMT began formally in the 1960s. The context for psychotherapy in general in the 1950s and 1960s certainly is relevant. All sorts of contextual influences can be identified, including changes in the diagnosis, assessment, and treatment of childhood and adult disorders; dissatisfaction with many current treatments in use in the 1950s and 1960s; research on the family as a possible contributor to clinical dysfunction, as well as a means of effecting change; and increased use of paraprofessionals, that is, individuals who were not professionally trained in therapy but who could serve as helpful adjuncts in everyday life (e.g., parents, teachers, and peers) (see Kazdin, 1978; London, 1986). Three historical streams that played a direct role in the emergence of PMT provide the background for contemporary work and further define what PMT is and how it is distinguished from other interventions: the development of operant conditioning, early applications of the principles and techniques of operant conditioning to change behavior in treatment settings as well as in everyday life, and the study of family interaction in relation to children's aggressive and antisocial behavior.

The Development of Operant Conditioning

PMT owes a great deal to the work of B. F. Skinner (1904–1990), who developed and elaborated operant conditioning. Operant conditioning is a type of learning that emphasizes the control that environmental events exert on behavior. The behaviors are referred to as *operants* because they are responses that *operate* (have some influence) on the environment. The environment—that is, what happens in relation to the response—has great influence on the responses that occur in the future. Operant behaviors are strengthened (increased) or weakened (decreased) as a function of the events that come before or immediately after them. The most familiar example is the use of positive reinforcement to increase behavior: A consequence that is "rewarding" immediately follows the behavior. There is much more to operant conditioning than behavior and consequences, but the example is a useful point of entry. Operants can be distinguished from reflex responses, such as a startle reaction in response to a loud noise or squinting in response to bright light. Reflex responses are unlearned and are controlled by eliciting stimuli. Most of the behaviors performed in everyday life—reading, walking, working, talking, nodding one's head, smiling, and other freely emitted responses—are operants. *Operant conditioning* is the type of learning that elaborates how operant behaviors develop and the many ways in which their performance can be influenced.

Beginning in the 1930s, Skinner's animal laboratory work elaborated the nature of operant conditioning, including the lawful effects of consequences on behavior and the many ways behavior responds to consequences, such as how they are presented and the conditions under which they are presented

Table 1.4
Summary of Key Principles of Operant Conditioning

Principle	Relation Between Environmental Events and Behavior
Reinforcement	Presentation or removal of an event after a response that increases the likelihood or probability of that response
Punishment	Presentation or removal of an event after a response that decreases the likelihood or probability of that response
Extinction	No longer presenting a reinforcing event after a response that decreases the likelihood or probability of the previously reinforced response
Stimulus control and discrimination	Reinforcing the response in the presence of one stimulus but not in the presence of another. This procedure increases the likelihood or probability of the response in the presence of the former stimulus and decreases the likelihood or probability of the response in the presence of the latter stimulus

(e.g., Skinner, 1938). These lawful effects generated the principles of operant conditioning (highlighted in Table 1.4), which provide general statements about the relations between behavior and environmental events. These principles and many techniques derived from them form the basis of PMT. Consequently, I return to them later in much more detail.

The brevity of my description of operant conditioning here should not misrepresent the scope of the impact of this type of learning on intervention research (treatment, prevention) and the applications in everyday life. Operant conditioning research has had enormous impact on basic and applied research (Kazdin, 1978). The experimental area of research, including both human and basic animal laboratory studies, has continued to flourish and is referred to as the *experimental analysis of behavior.*

Extensions and Applications of Operant Conditioning

Operant conditioning began as an area of experimental animal laboratory research designed to understand basic processes of learning. Laboratory work focused on overt behavior as a way of assessing learning, assessment of the frequency of behavior over time, and the study of one or a few organisms (e.g., rats, pigeons) at a time. The focus on one or two organisms over time permitted the careful evaluation of how changes in consequences influenced performance and the lawfulness of behavior under diverse circumstances. The experimental analysis of behavior refers not only to the study of operant conditioning but also this methodology of experimental control and research design.

Although the work began in the laboratory with animals (e.g., rats) as subjects, eventually the approach was extended to humans. These extensions had modest goals—namely, to see if the method was applicable to humans and whether the lawful relations demonstrated with various species in the laboratory could be replicated with humans. That is, would human behavior on laboratory tasks (e.g., lever pulling or pressing) be responsive to variations in reinforcement, and would there be any similarities to the relations demonstrated with animals (Lindsley, 1956, 1960)? There was no explicit interest at this time in developing therapeutic treatments to help people change.

Many of the lawful relations determined from years of animal research were replicated in human laboratory performance. Some of the early laboratory work produced intriguing and unexpected results that are relevant to our story. For example, laboratory studies were conducted with hospitalized patients with psychoses who performed on various apparatus daily to earn small rewards (e.g., money, pictures). Performance on the laboratory apparatus was often interrupted by pauses, when psychotic symptoms (such as vocal hallucinatory behaviors) could be observed. When these pauses took place could be seen graphically because responses on the apparatus did not occur. This observation suggested that the operant conditioning methods might be an objective way to study psychotic behaviors (e.g., when hallucinations occurred, their regularity, patterns) and factors that might influence their occurrence. Of greater significance for the present discussion was the unexpected finding that responding to laboratory tasks appeared to result in a reduction of symptoms (e.g., staring into space) both in the laboratory and on the hospital ward (King, Armitage, & Tilton, 1960; Lindsley, 1960). This finding clearly suggested that symptoms might be altered in important ways by increases in operant responding.

Laboratory studies of operant conditioning were extended to children with mental retardation and autism. At first, the goals were merely to use operant conditioning laboratory methods to investigate how these special populations learned and performed on tasks. Operant conditioning methods were soon extended to human behavior outside the laboratory to change behaviors that were more relevant to everyday life (Ullmann & Krasner, 1965). Several isolated demonstrations were simple by current standards and designed merely to see if environmental consequences could influence behavior beyond the context of a laboratory task.

Several demonstrations in the 1960s examined the extent to which environmental consequences could influence the behavior of hospitalized psychiatric patients. For example, one of these demonstrations involved a depressed patient who complained of sleeping difficulties and reported pains in her back, chest, head, and shoulders (Ayllon & Haughton, 1964). Medical evaluation revealed no identifiable physical problems to account for these difficulties. Perhaps these bodily (somatic) complaints were influenced by their consequences—namely, the reactions of the staff. The hypothesis that complaints in this person were operants—behaviors that operated on the environment and were maintained by the consequences—is rather interesting. As with any hypothesis, it might well be false.

Staff recorded the daily frequency of the patient's complaints for several days. After these observations (referred to as the baseline), they were instructed to ignore complaints rather than provide their usual consolation, sympathy, and attention. Perhaps attention had served as a reward (reinforcer) for the behavior, leading to its high levels; if so, cessation of the attention would reduce the behavior. Data continued to be collected on the frequency of complaints. After several days, staff were told to revert to their previous ways of responding to the patient's complaints. If staff attention really were influencing the complaints, the complaints would be expected to increase again. After several days of this, staff were finally told to withdraw their attention.

The effects of altering consequences for somatic complaints can be seen in Figure 1.1. The frequency of complaints is evident during baseline (staff behaving as usual), extinction (staff ignoring complaints), positive reinforcement (staff attention for complaints), and extinction (ignoring as before). The frequency of complaints changed dramatically as staff behavior changed. These results suggested that attention and consequences from others can greatly influence patient behavior.

This demonstration and many others like it indicated that human behavior in applied settings could be altered by changing the consequences. These demonstrations were unique because they included extensions of concepts of operant conditioning (e.g., various schedules of applying consequences) and the methodology (e.g., observing performance of individuals continuously over time to demonstrate experimentally what was responsible for behavior change). The findings consistently conveyed that applying consequences systematically could develop behavior and that assessing behavior carefully over time allowed evaluation of the effects of an intervention. Showing that behaviors could be increased and decreased established that it really was the environmental manipulations and consequences that were responsible for change.

By the late 1960s, the extensions of operant conditioning principles to human behavior had launched an area of research referred to as *applied beha-*

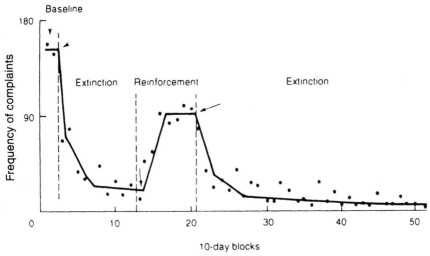

Figure 1.1 Frequency of complaints during the baseline, extinction, reinforcement, and extinction phases. During baseline, staff behaved as usual. During reinforcement, they provided attention when the patient complained. During the extinction phases, the staff ignored the patient's complaints. Reprinted from *Behaviour Research & Therapy, Vol. 2,* Ayllon et al., Modification of symptomatic verbal behavior of mental patients, 94, (1964), with permission from Elsevier.

vior analysis (Baer, Wolf, & Risley, 1968). Operant conditioning principles were increasingly applied to clinical, social, and educational problems. By the late 1970s, it was difficult to identify an area of everyday life (e.g., classroom learning, child rearing, medicine, sports, business), a setting (psychiatric hospitals, business, the home, college dormitories), or a sample (e.g., infants, nursing home residents, recruits in the armed forces) that was not included in operant conditioning programs (Kazdin, 1977). The applications, interventions, and research methods within applied behavior analysis have continued to develop and expand to this day.

Extensions to Child Rearing and Parenting

Extensions in the Home

As part of the extension of operant conditioning principles to everyday life, parenting and child rearing were obvious areas of work. Little frustrates parents more than the use of relatively ineffective and inefficient ways to promote child behaviors. Demonstration projects in the home were plentiful in the

1960s. I denote these as demonstration projects in part because they were early extensions that altered bothersome behaviors but were relatively narrow in their focus and designed, as often as not, to see if principles could be applied to change human behavior. For example, one of the earliest demonstrations was a carefully assessed and documented case showing that extinction (parent ignoring) of tantrums could greatly reduce a child's bedtime tantrums (Williams, 1959). The way in which the program was conducted—the documentation and explanation of successes and failures along the way, careful assessment of program effects on a continuous basis, and demonstration that tantrums were eliminated up to 2 years later—suggested that operant conditioning principles might well be extended in the home to address routine behaviors.

Throughout the 1960s, many additional demonstrations in the home indicated that parents could be trained to apply techniques that would alter child behavior. Many of these extensions focused on everyday concerns of parents (e.g., tantrums, thumbsucking, toileting, completing homework, complying with requests), but they soon encompassed children with significant impairment in these and related domains. Applications in the home, begun initially in the late 1960s and early 1970s (e.g., Hanf, 1969), stimulated a vigorous line of research that continues today.

These extensions of operant conditioning principles to the home were early efforts of PMT. In some ways, the demonstrations were not unique. From the 1960s through the 1970s, there were scores of demonstrations that training parents, teachers, hospital staff, peers, and others to deliver consequences contingently led to behavior change. The demonstrations often were rigorous in terms of the quality of the evidence and inferences that could be drawn.

Development of Aggressive and Antisocial Behavior

The work of Gerald Patterson, beginning in the 1960s, has had a special role in the development of PMT and extends beyond the application of operant conditioning principles to alter child behavior. Patterson was attracted to key features of applied behavior analysis, such as collecting data on clients continuously over time to see if change occurred and observing behaviors directly (rather than relying on self-report scales and questionnaires). Early applications in the 1960s were laboratory studies or demonstration projects (e.g., with hyperactivity, school phobia) that showed that reinforcement could alter important behaviors (Patterson, 1965a, 1965b). This work is in keeping with points I have made already. Patterson's exceptional contributions lay elsewhere.

In the 1960s, he began an extensive research program designed to understand the emergence and maintenance of aggressive child behavior in the home. The studies included directly observing child–parent interaction in the home. Meticulous observations (e.g., 29 different behaviors and interactions occurring from moment to moment in the home) were completed to evaluate parent–child interaction. For example, attention to and reinforcement of child deviant behavior, use of commands, delivery of harsh punishment, and failure to attend to appropriate child behavior, as well as the tone of different interactions, were all carefully observed (Patterson, 1982; Patterson, Reid, & Dishion, 1992; Reid, Patterson, & Snyder, 2002). Among the many interaction patterns, those involving coercion have received the greatest attention.

Coercion refers to a sequence of interactions between the child and parent (but this can be extended to other combinations of people). The sequence includes actions and reactions that increase the frequency and amplitude of angry, hostile, and aggressive behaviors. The sequence may begin with an argument over some action that has or has not been performed. It intensifies through verbal statements (e.g., yelling, screaming) to more intensive actions (e.g., hitting, shoving). Ultimately, one person in the interaction gives in or backs away from the interaction. In other words, the high-intensity interaction of one person (e.g., usually the child) ends the aversive behavior of the other person (e.g., usually the parent). This is the paradigm for the principle of negative reinforcement, which states that any behavior that terminates an aversive condition is likely to increase in frequency in the future. The high-intensity behavior of the child is reinforced (by termination of aversive parent behavior). Aggressive children are inadvertently rewarded for their aggressive interactions. Their escalation of coercive behavior is increased in the process, and they are likely to be more aggressive (more often, with higher intensity) in the future. The parent behaviors are part of the discipline practices that sustain aggressive behavior. The interaction does not place a single unidirectional causal relation between the parent and child. Rather, there is a dynamic interaction in which aversive behavior on the part of both parties escalates in a way that systematically programs, fosters, and develops greater deviance in the child.

The work was groundbreaking and sophisticated in several respects. First, the research showed that interactions can begin relatively simply with one person's irritability or anger but can increase in complexity as coercive interactions escalate to harsh and aggressive interactions. Second, coercion was proved not to be an abstract theory. Years of rigorous research while studying families in the home demonstrated and elaborated the sequences of interactions I have only highlighted here (Patterson, 1982; Patterson et al., 1992; Reid et al., 2002). In the process, the development of aggressive behavior and other influences (e.g., stress in the home, peer relations) were elaborated. How diverse facets of parents and the family are influenced by parent–child exchanges has been included in conceptual models and empirical tests of these models.

Third, the dynamic nature of parent–child interaction is worth mentioning insofar as it was a departure from the work on the development of child psychopathology that was in vogue at the time. During this period, the parent (usually the mother, such as the "schizophrenogenic mother") or the family was considered the source of the problem (e.g., schizophrenia, autism). Also, family therapy began to emerge, and in variants of it the child was viewed as the "identified patient" but not really the main or only patient in the home. Patterson's work actually studied interaction patterns and hence moved away from broad, reasonable, but largely unsupported theories. Also, he demonstrated what is now sometimes called reciprocal causation or bidirectional causes. This concept was nicely captured by referring to the aggressive child as "the victim and architect of a coercive system" (Patterson, 1976a).

Fourth, the work focused on conditional probabilities rather than causes; that is, rather than saying that a particular parent (or child) behavior caused the next behavior in a sequence of coercive interactions, the work noted that actions and reactions increased the probability that the behavior would move in one direction rather than another and toward some end rather than another. This is exactly what was shown in research: That is, probabilities change; given x (behavior of the parent), y (behavior of the child) is much more likely to occur. This is a much more careful analysis than rigidly expecting a single action to invariably have a single outcome.

There is much more to this work than can be mentioned here, including study of the influences of delinquent peers on child aggression and of parental stress on child-rearing practices, the stability of aggression and coercive practices over time, and the different types of aggressive behavior (early versus later onset, children who steal versus those who fight) (Reid et al., 2002). In relation to PMT, the program of research was critical in establishing that family interaction strongly influenced child aggression. From the perspective of the parent, the work emphasized "inept" parenting practices. The ways parents gave commands, ignored prosocial behavior, punished behavior, and other characteristics contributed to coercion and helped escalate aggression in the home.

Along with basic research on family interaction, Patterson and his colleagues developed PMT as an intervention to alter those practices that were shown to contribute to children's aggressive behaviors. Several studies showed that specific inept child-rearing practices contributed to aggressive behavior and that altering these practices significantly reduced aggressive behavior and related conduct problems (Dishion & Andrews, 1995; Dishion, Patterson, & Kavanagh, 1992; Forgatch, 1991). These were powerful demonstrations in the sense that parenting practices were shown to be causally related to aggressive behavior in children. The significance of this finding is difficult to overemphasize. Scores of studies showed that some feature (e.g., parenting) correlates with a particular child problem (e.g., anxiety). Most of such work is cross-sectional (demonstrated at one point in time) and correlational (merely showing an association). Patterson and his colleagues moved beyond this to develop a conceptual view (coercion theory), to demonstrate the time line between parenting practices and child deviance, and to show in clinical trials that changing parenting behaviors led to change in children's deviant behaviors. At least in relation to aggressive child behavior, PMT was not just another intervention that appeared to be effective. PMT was shown to operate on those domains of interaction that had been shown to foster aggressive child behavior.

General Comments

I have traced three influences leading to PMT. These influences are not exhaustive. It would be erroneous to imply that only the names and lines of work mentioned here had a direct impact on PMT. Once operant principles were extended beyond the laboratory, applications in the home, school, and various institutional settings proliferated and continued to convey that principles of operant conditioning and the methods used to evaluate the treatments were quite useful in changing behavior. Whether or not these methods focused on parenting, the emerging evidence supported the intervention approach. In addition, in the 1970s and 1980s, several investigators began programs of research on PMT. These programs, mentioned later, continued for an extended period, generated multiple outcome studies, and helped establish the intervention.

Overview of Remaining Chapters

The remaining chapters elaborate on different facets of PMT. Chapter 2 discusses the principles underlying PMT. The role of antecedents, behaviors, and consequences as the basis for changing children's (and parents') behavior is presented and illustrated with examples. Readers already conversant with operant conditioning and its applications in everyday life may wish to skip or skim this chapter.

Chapters 3 and 4 move from principles to techniques and identify a large set of interventions for application in the home. Also, essential ingredients to make the interventions effective are presented. The techniques are illustrated with examples that emphasize programs implemented in the home. Chapter 3 emphasizes positive reinforcement techniques and how they can be implemented effectively. Chapter 4 focuses on punishment and extinction techniques. Each chapter emphasizes application of the techniques, including obstacles that emerge, parents' concerns and issues, and when and how various techniques ought to be used.

Chapter 5 continues the movement of the text toward greater specificity and focuses on the characteristics of PMT: the content, tenor, and structure of the treatment sessions and the roles and tasks of the therapist and parents. Variations of PMT are presented as they have emerged in treatment of children of various ages and in different contexts.

Chapter 6 provides an overview of the evidence. Key areas that are reviewed include research on the effects of treatment; child, parent, family, and treatment factors that contribute to therapeutic change; and the mechanisms that are likely to be responsible for therapeutic change. Supplementary procedures occasionally used with PMT and their effects are noted. Finally, this chapter discusses the limitations of current research and what is not known that is important to know.

Chapter 7 discusses several issues that emerge in the clinical application of PMT pertaining to parent expectations and beliefs, adherence to treatment, and dropping out of treatment. Professional issues also are pertinent to treatment administration, including how PMT can clash with the training of mental health professionals and the various beliefs many professionals may bring to treatment. Perhaps the most central issue that can emerge in treatment is that the intervention may not work or work well enough for a given child and family. After all, one cannot tell the parents that PMT has to be working—the research says so. The program can have limited effects and indeed often does. However, there are many options for what to do to repair failing programs during the course of treatment. These options are discussed and illustrated in this chapter.

Chapter 8 discusses PMT in perspective. Based on findings, scope of the evidence, and applications, what can be concluded about treatment? Key challenges and limitations are also discussed, both in relation to research and in clinical application and extension of treatment. This is the final chapter of the first part of the book. A complete PMT manual follows.

Summary and Conclusions

This first chapter began with an overview of the social, emotional, and behavioral problems that children can experience. The problems and their prevalence provide a context for developing effective treatments. Unfortunately, most psychotherapies developed for children and adolescents that are in use in various clinics, schools, and institutional settings have never been studied in research. Recently, there has been an effort to delineate evidence-based treatments—therapies that do have evidence in their behalf. PMT is one of those treatments.

In PMT interventions, parents are taught social learning techniques to change the behavior of their children. Key features of PMT are its base in learning theory and research, a set of principles that describe the relations of events that precede and follow behavior, the focus on specific skills that are actively trained in the parents, and assessment and evaluation of progress as a basis of decision making over the course of treatment.

PMT features a strong research effort that derives from three sources. First, there has been extensive research on the technique itself. Indeed, probably no other psychotherapy for children has its strength of empirical support. Second, the procedures that form the basis of PMT have been studied extensively in many contexts beyond the family, such as day-care centers, schools, hospitals, and business and industry. Research in these and other areas attest to the effects of the procedures. Third, key principles of treatment have been developed from basic laboratory research, which has provided a strong scientific base for understanding the interventions and for applying them effectively. For example, a superficial rendition of PMT might be to reward positive, prosocial behavior. There is much more to the treatment. Moreover, how reinforcement is delivered very much dictates whether there will be any behavior change in the child. Much of this knowledge has been worked out in animal and human laboratory studies and confirmed by studies in applied settings.

The development of PMT was traced from three streams of influence: the emergence of operant conditioning, a type of learning that emphasizes the control that environment exerts on behavior; extensions of applications of operant conditioning to human behavior; and extensions specifically focused on child rearing and parenting. The careful study of family interaction in the context of children's aggressive behavior as part of this latter work had an enormous influence on PMT. Research identified sequences of parent–child interaction that predicted subsequent aggressive behavior and then showed that changing these sequences reduced children's aggressive behavior. In the context of psychosocial treatments, it is rare to have evidence that focuses on both the development and the amelioration of a clinical problem.

Notes

1. Throughout the book, I use the term *children* to represent children and adolescents, unless the distinction is critical to key findings or critical issues.
2. Occasionally I refer to a clinic in which I work. This is the Yale Child Conduct Clinic, an outpatient treatment service for children and families. Children seen at the clinic are between the ages 2 and 14 and are referred for oppositional, aggressive, and antisocial behavior. Treatments provided at the clinic include variations of cognitive problem-solving skills training and parent management training (see Kazdin, 2003a; http://pantheon.yale.edu/~kazdin/conductclinic.htm).
3. PMT focuses on training parents to change the behaviors of their children and adolescents. One could extend the definition of PMT to encompass interventions in which parents change the behaviors of their parents. Occasionally middle-aged adults are in caretaking roles for their elderly parents and are interested in or responsible for managing the physical and mental health of these parents. Many harsh practices may emerge in these interactions. For example, from 5 to 10% of the elderly may be subjected to some form of abuse (e.g., physical, emotional) (http://www.efmoody .com/miscellaneous/elderlyabuse.html; http://www.elderabusecenter.org/basic/index .html). These adult children could use PMT to develop behaviors in their elderly parents related to mental and physical health (e.g., increasing self-care behaviors, activity and exercise, adherence to medical regimens). PMT has been infrequently applied in these contexts. This book is devoted to the extremely well studied focus on children and adolescents.
4. Many books convey the range of applications (e.g., Austin & Carr, 2000; Cooper, Heron, & Heward, 1987; Kazdin, 2001b). Studies in applied behavior analysis are published in many different scientific journals, but one devoted exclusively to research in this area is called (you'll never guess), the *Journal of Applied Behavior Analysis*.

2

Underlying Principles and Concepts

Chapter Outline

Psychotherapy in general, whether for children, adolescents, or adults, raises a broad question—namely, what experiences can be provided that can treat a clinical problem, reduce impairment, and improve adjustment? From the standpoint of psychological research, the main answer to this question is learning. Learning refers to a systematic way of providing experiences to build new repertoires and override maladaptive ones. Different kinds of learning take place under different conditions, so merely saying "learning" is not very helpful. Three types of learning have been subjected to extensive animal and human research: *respondent conditioning, operant conditioning,* and *observational learning.*[1] Each type of learning has served as a major resource in developing effective treatments for children, adolescents, and adults. In relation to PMT, operant conditioning plays a central role in providing the underpinnings of treatment.

This chapter provides an overview of the key principles of operant conditioning that underlie PMT. The principles refer to general relationships among experiences, the environment, and development of behavior. It is critical to distinguish principles from the *techniques* that derive from them. These techniques or interventions include an enormous range of options. Developing and implementing techniques requires knowing the principles, but the principles alone are not sufficient. As an analogy, think of the aerodynamics of flying an airplane (principles) and actually knowing how to fly an airplane (techniques). This chapter highlights key principles; the next two chapters cover techniques derived from the principles that are used in PMT.

Contingencies: The ABCs of Behavior

The main focus of operant conditioning is the *contingencies of reinforcement,* the relationships between behaviors and the environmental events that influence behavior. Three components are included in a contingency: antecedents (A), behaviors (B), and consequences (C). The notion of a contingency is important not only for understanding behavior but also for developing programs to change behavior. *Antecedents* are stimuli, settings, and contexts that occur before behaviors and influence behaviors. Examples are instructions, gestures, and looks from others. *Behaviors* are the acts themselves, what individuals do or do not do. *Consequences* are events that follow behavior and increase, decrease, or have no impact on what the individual does. Table 2.1 illustrates the three components of a contingency. Even these simple examples from everyday life demonstrate the interdependence of As, Bs, and Cs.

Table 2.1

Three Components of a Contingency and Illustrations From Everyday Life

Antecedent	Behavior	Consequence
Telephone rings	Answering the phone	Voice of person at the other end
Wave (greeting) from a friend	Walking over to the friend	Visiting and chatting
Parent's instruction to a child to clean the room	Picking up toys	Verbal praise and a pat on the back
Warning not to eat spoiled food	Eating the food	Nausea and vomiting

Consider the behavior "answering the phone." Antecedents are obviously critical and clearly control behavior. For example, the ringing of a telephone usually leads to behavior, namely, going over to and picking up (answering) the phone. Not too many people run to answer the phone when there is no ring (antecedent). Consequences are rather important in this example, too. We repeatedly answer ringing telephones because of the consequences that regularly follow our behaviors; almost always there is someone on the other end of the line to speak with us.

Note that ABCs are more complex than one antecedent, one behavior, and one consequence. For example, we may not answer a ringing phone if we don't want to speak with someone we expect to call or if we are too busy to talk. Stated another way, the context or circumstances that form part of the antecedent events may change how we respond—in this case, determine whether we answer or not.

Effective behavior-change programs are based on understanding the influences of antecedents and consequences and how they can be used to promote, develop, and maintain behavior. A misguided and somewhat superficial view of behavioral interventions focuses on consequences alone. Indeed, sometimes merely providing consequences for behavior in a casual way is taken as an application of behavior modification (e.g., "I praise my child when he does what I ask, and he still never listens"). Later in the book, I discuss misapplications and how programs can fail.

Although antecedents, behaviors, and consequences are distinguished here and separated for purposes of presentation, they are quite interrelated. For example, we walk into a room and see an odd facial expression on a friend. That facial expression (antecedent to the next behavior) may prompt a behavior from us (e.g., we say, "What happened?" or "Is everything all right?" or "I didn't do it!"). Many antecedent events such as facial expressions acquire their influence because of their association with certain consequences. We may have learned from frequent pairings of various facial expressions with various consequences (e.g., from our own direct experience or from movies, books, and cartoons). Also, in any given interchange, there are ongoing sequences of antecedents, behaviors, and consequences. However, the sequences always begin with an antecedent.

Antecedents of Behavior

Behavior is influenced greatly by antecedents—what comes before the behavior is performed. Three types of antecedents are distinguished here: setting events, prompts, and discriminative stimuli. They are easily confused.

Setting Events

At the most general level, setting events are antecedent to behavior. They are contextual factors or conditions that influence behavior. They are broad in scope and set the stage for the behaviors and consequences that follow. Setting events include features of the situation, features of the task or demands presented to the individual, conditions within the individual (e.g., exhaustion, hunger, expectations of what will happen), and behaviors of others. Table 2.2 gives a few examples. Consider another example in greater detail. A boy may hear a heated argument or perhaps witness violence between his parents right before school. That morning at school, the child may be a little more irritable, more reactive, and less attentive to schoolwork than usual. His behaviors (e.g., talking to peers, paying attention, completing assignments, provoking arguments) are changed. The changes are not due to consequences or to anything different at school but rather due to events that altered the child, his motivation, and the set with which he approached school. Setting events are, of course, not just for children. Parents who are stressed tend to be more irritable and to respond to their children in argumentative ways that can promote or exacerbate deviant child behavior. Here, stress of the parent is a setting event that changes the likelihood of responding in different ways.

Setting event is useful and easy to remember as a term, in part because it conveys that some event or factor "sets the stage" and influences behavior. External or environmental events (e.g., the actual setting such as home, school, or

Table 2.2
Types of Antecedents and Illustrations

Type of Antecedent	Key Characteristics	Examples
Setting event/ establishing operation	Alters value of the reinforcer and increases likelihood of engaging in behaviors to obtain or avoid consequences	Being deprived of a reinforcer (e.g., food water, attention); exposure to a pleasant or unpleasant interaction; a success or failure experience; seeing a sign on the road or at the beach that says, "hazardous condition"
Prompt	Some event or stimulus that directly guides and facilitates performance; directly connected to the behaviors to be performed	Instructions to guide how to hold, play, or use a musical instrument; modeling (showing) how to do something; guiding physically as a child learns how to form letters during a handwriting lesson
Discriminative Stimuli (S^D)	A stimulus or event indicating that a particular behavior is likely to be reinforced; the stimulus indicates that the reinforcer is available	The ring of a telephone (signaling that someone is likely to be on the other end of the line); the sound of a timer (indicating the food is ready from the oven); an enticing smile from an attractive person (signaling that approach behavior is likely to be reciprocated)

a restaurant; the behavior of others in the setting), as well as internal states and events (e.g., feeling irritable, having had a wonderful or poor night's sleep, being deprived of food, water, or companionship), all qualify as setting events insofar as they can influence subsequent performance. A more precise and specific term is *establishing operation*, which refers to an antecedent variable or factor that temporarily alters the effectiveness of some other event or consequence (Michael, 1993). Motivational states, emotions, and environmental events are establishing operations if they momentarily alter the effectiveness of the consequences that may follow behavior and influence the frequency of some behavior. Two conditions are required for some state or event to qualify as an establishing operation: First, such operations alter the effectiveness of consequences (reinforcing and punishing events) in the environment. Second, such operations influence the frequency of behaviors that can obtain these consequences.

Consider an example. Assume for a moment that food reinforcement is available for a given response of a laboratory animal or human. Let us say the reinforcement is always available and can be obtained whenever a response is performed. Deprivation or satiation of the individual will influence the likelihood of the response. When the individual is deprived, the effectiveness of food as a reinforcer is much greater than it would otherwise be, and behaviors associated with obtaining food become more probable. In other words, deprivation is an establishing operation—that is, an antecedent condition that influences the effectiveness of food as a reinforcer and increases the likelihood that the individual will engage in responses that obtain food.

This example is good in isolating what the establishing operation is, what the reinforcer is, and what the behaviors might be that are increased as a result. In everyday life, the operations may be complex and more difficult to identify. I have used setting events as a broader term to encompass many such influences that serve as establishing operations, even though the criteria for meeting the two conditions are not always met. As an example, how parents interact with their oppositional children appears to be influenced by parent social interaction outside the home (Wahler, 1980); that is, for the parent, social interaction with others serves as an establishing operation for how they interact with their children. When mothers experience positive social contacts outside the home with friends, they show fewer aversive interchanges with their children (e.g., commands, reprimands) and as a result promote less deviant child behavior at home. As assessed on a daily basis, mothers' social interactions seem to provide a setting event that influences subsequent contingencies in the repertoire of the mothers and then of their children. Of course, it is not a brilliant insight to say that how things are going in one part of our lives can influence how things go in another part. Yet, the key insight here is that understanding these relations more systematically enables us to intervene to change behavior.

In everyday life, we can often identify relations between setting events and behavior and use these relations in constructive ways. For example, we can see a parent snap a harsh-sounding command to a child to do something. The child may not comply with the command or may even say "no" in an obstinate fashion. Thus a parent's harsh order sets the stage for noncompliance. This is not a matter of blaming the parent for the child's noncompliance; blame is not relevant. What is relevant is *how* the request was made, perhaps *when* it was made (e.g., in light of the child doing something else such as watching a favorite TV show), and *what* was in the request (e.g., no choices given, demand for immediate compliance rather than a little warning). The command itself is an establishing operation that can affect the motivation of the child and the likelihood of one response rather than another. If the command is embedded in the context of other requests that are likely to be aversive (a bunch of nagging statements), compliance with the request is much less likely than would otherwise be the case (Kazdin, 2001b). Parents often complain that their children are not compliant, which might be perfectly accurate. However, this is discussed as if the characteristic is within the individual, free from other influences. It can be easily shown in PMT that altering the requests increases child compliance. From the discussion of setting events, we can see immediately that understanding and changing behavior is more than merely connecting behaviors with consequences. The initial events, stimuli, and states of the individual influence subsequent behavior and hence have to be considered.

Prompts

Prompts are specific antecedents that directly facilitate performance of behavior. They are distinguished from setting events, which are more contextual, indirect, and broader influences on behavior. Table 2.2 provides some examples of prompts. Other prompts are instructions to engage in the behavior (e.g., "Please wash up before dinner"), cues (e.g., reminders or notes to oneself, lists of things to do), gestures (e.g., come in, leave the room), examples and modeling (e.g., demonstrations to show this is how the behavior, task, or skill is done), and physical guidance (e.g., guiding a person's hands to show how to play a musical instrument or to hit a volleyball). Prompts serve as antecedent events (e.g., instructions, gestures) that help generate or initiate the desired response. They are designed to facilitate the response. When a prompt results in the response, consequences can be provided (e.g., positive reinforcement) to increase the likelihood that the response will recur. Without the prompt, the response might occur infrequently or not at all.

Prompts play a major role in developing a behavior. When an individual does not engage in the behavior, prompts can show the person what to do, how to do it, and when to do it. For example, we might want to provide reinforcing consequences to develop a complex set of behaviors (e.g., driving a car, completing a term paper) or a simple behavior that never occurs (e.g., eating specific foods). If the desired behavior never occurs, it cannot be reinforced. Assisting a person in beginning the response can enable the person to make more rapid approximations to the final response. When a person has partially mastered the task or skill, prompts can help to refine the behavior and add to the complexity. For example, when teaching a complex dance step, the teacher at first may model (prompt) basic movements. As the skill is acquired, the teacher may model subtler little movements of the hands, body, or legs to develop these more specific behaviors.

Several types of prompts can be used alone or in combination. As a simple example, to have a child clean up the room, the parent might give a verbal prompt or instruction (e.g., "Please pick up your toys from the floor and put them in the closet"; many parents are loath to say "please," but think of "please" as a setting event that often changes the likelihood of others' behaviors). A physical prompt might be added by guiding the child to the room (e.g., arm around the child or handholding in a warm fashion), and a visual prompt might be provided by modeling the desired behavior. The parent could pick up one toy and place it in the closet.

While a response is being developed, prompts may be frequently used to facilitate performance of the terminal response. In most cases, the long-term goal is to develop a behavior that is performed without the use of prompts. Although prompts may be required early in training, they can be withdrawn gradually or faded as training progresses. *Fading* refers to the gradual removal of a prompt. If a prompt is removed abruptly early in training, the response may no longer be performed. But if the response is performed consistently with a prompt, the prompt can be progressively reduced and finally omitted. For example, teaching a person how to serve in tennis or how to play the piano may include reminders (prompts) regarding how to hold the racket or how to place one's fingers on the keys. As the person begins to perform these behaviors, the nature of the prompt may change (e.g., from "hold your fingers like this" with the position modeled by the teacher to "fingers" without any other verbal statement or modeling). Also, prompts are provided less frequently. The correct behaviors are reinforced without reminders, and soon these behaviors never or only very rarely need to be prompted.

Removing all prompts is not always necessary. For example, it is important to train individuals to respond in the presence of certain prompts, such as instructions, that exert control over a variety of behaviors in everyday life. Also, prompts have uses other than in training new behaviors. For behaviors that are readily available, prompts can play a very useful role. For example, notes, the sound of a cell phone alarm, and comments to children before they leave home all can serve as reminders and prompt behavior that might not otherwise be completed.

Stimuli often become regularly associated with various consequences. Once these associations occur, the stimuli themselves exert control over behavior. Thus, to understand the influence of the stimuli, antecedents, behaviors, and consequences must be considered together.

In some situations (or in the presence of certain stimuli), a response may be reinforced; in other situations (in the presence of other stimuli), the same response is not reinforced. The concept of differential reinforcement is central to understanding stimulus events and their influence. *Differential reinforcement* refers to reinforcing a response in the presence of one stimulus or situation and not reinforcing the same response in the presence of another stimulus or situation. When a response is consistently reinforced in the presence of a particular stimulus and not reinforced in the presence of another stimulus, each stimulus signals the consequences that are likely to follow.

A stimulus whose presence has been associated with reinforcement is referred to as a *discriminative stimulus* (S^D). A stimulus whose presence has been associated with nonreinforcement is referred to as a *nondiscriminative stimulus* (S^Δ or S delta). The effect of differential reinforcement is that eventually the reinforced response is likely to occur in the presence of the S^D but unlikely to occur in the presence of the S^Δ. When responses are differentially controlled by antecedent stimuli, behavior is said to be under *stimulus control.* When there is stimulus control, the presence of a stimulus increases the likelihood of a response. As mentioned previously, the stimulus does not *cause* response or automatically elicit the response the way reflexes are elicited in classical conditioning. Rather, in operant conditioning, the stimulus (an S^D) increases the probability that a previously reinforced behavior will occur. Another way of stating this is to say that an S^D sets the occasion for behavior—that is, merely increases its future probability. This concept is critically important in changing behavior. In parenting or elsewhere in everyday life, there is a great deal we can do to increase the likelihood that the desired behavior will occur.

Some examples are provided in Table 2.2. When a stranger smiles at us on the street, the likelihood increases that we, too, will smile and say something friendly. Also, if we smile back, the stranger is very likely to say something back to us. Stated a bit more precisely, smiling is a signal (an S^D) that specific behaviors on our part (e.g., acts of friendliness) are likely to be reinforced (e.g., acknowledged, reciprocated). We do not usually initiate friendly statements to others who present us with a grumpy facial expression. Grumpy facial expressions are an S^A; they indicate that reinforcement is not likely to follow. Smiling and grumpy faces of strangers do not *elicit* behavior from us in a reflexive way but rather increase the likelihood of certain behaviors from us.

Instances of stimulus control pervade everyday life. For example, the sound of a doorbell signals that a certain behavior (opening the door) is likely to be reinforced (by seeing someone). Specifically, the sound of the bell frequently has been associated with the presence of visitors at the door (the reinforcer). The ring of the bell (S^D) increases the likelihood that the door will be opened. In the absence of the bell (S^A), the probability of opening the door for a visitor is very low. The ring of a doorbell, telephone, alarm, and kitchen timer all serve as discriminative stimuli (S^D) and signal that certain responses are likely to be reinforced. Hence, the probability of the responses is increased.

Stimulus control is pervasive and governs much of our behavior. For example, the color and smell of foods (such as an orange that has turned green or milk that smells sour) influence the likelihood of our selecting and eating them. Characteristics of the foods are cues for particular consequences (such as flavor or nausea) and exert stimulus control over our eating. In recognition of the importance of stimulus control, natural foods (e.g., fruit) or products (e.g., leather) often have artificial colors and fragrances added to increase the likelihood of their purchase. Often stimulus control is used to decrease the likelihood of behavior. For example, conspicuous signs on a house (e.g., beware of dog, this house is protected by this or that security company) or a car (security alarm system, steering wheel bar) are intended to and no doubt decrease the likelihood of entry and theft. Presumably, they influence behavior even if there is no dog or protection system or the steering wheel bar is a decoy that does not really block theft of the car.

People in everyday life are quite familiar with the concepts of differential reinforcement and the stimulus control that results, although these terms, of course, are not used. For example, children behave differently in the presence of their mothers and fathers, in part because slightly different reinforcement contingencies operate with each parent. Children often know whom to ask (mother or father) in making specific requests because the likelihood of reinforcement (affirmative answer) differs between parents on various issues. Similarly, at home children often behave quite differently from how they behave at school. The different performances may lead to perplexed parents and teachers who argue that the child is not "really" like that. Yet, the child's behavior may vary considerably as a function of different reinforcement contingencies at home and at school.

The notion of stimulus control is exceedingly important in PMT. In many programs, the goal is to alter the relation between behavior and the stimulus conditions in which the behavior occurs. Some behavior problems stem from the failure of certain stimuli to control behavior when such control would be desirable. For example, children who do not follow instructions given by their parents illustrate a lack of stimulus control. The instructions do not exert influence over the children's behavior. Other behavioral problems stem from some stimuli exerting control over undesirable behavior. For example, a child may invariably hit a peer in response to teasing. Different behaviors must be developed in response to such behaviors (cues and actions) of others.

Behaviors

We have considered the antecedents of the ABCs of contingencies. Behavior change is achieved by identifying the behaviors of interest—the behaviors we wish to develop. These are called *target behaviors*. Of course, we do not merely identify behaviors but rather plan how to develop behaviors systematically. Two procedures figure prominently in developing behaviors.

Shaping

The individual may perform target behaviors already, and the goal of the intervention may be to increase performance in some way (e.g., more occasions when the behavior is occurring, more time spent engaging in the behavior, or fostering the behavior in new situations). In these instances, providing antecedents and consequences may be sufficient to increase or extend the behavior. In many other cases, the individual does not have the behavior in his or her repertoire or has the behavior only partially. In these cases, we cannot merely wait for the behavior to occur and provide consequences; the response may never occur. The behavior can be obtained by reinforcing small steps or approximations toward the final response rather than by reinforcing the final response itself.

Shaping refers to the reinforcement of successive approximations of the final response. Responses are reinforced that either resemble the final response or include components of that response. By reinforcing successive approximations, the final response is gradually achieved. Responses increasingly similar to the final goal are reinforced, and they increase; responses dissimilar to the final goal are not reinforced, and they extinguish. For example, when parents are trying to develop use of the words *mommy* or *daddy* in an infant, they usually reinforce any approximation (e.g., *ma* or *da-da*) by smiling, hugging, and praising effusively. At the same time, but usually without thinking about it, they do not attend to (extinguish) sounds that are not close to the words they wish (e.g., *goo, milk*). Over time, the parents reinforce sounds and syllables that come closer to the words *mommy* and *daddy*.

An obvious example of shaping is training animals to perform tricks. If the animal trainer waited until the tricks (e.g., jumping through a burning hoop) were performed to administer a reinforcer, it is unlikely that reinforcement would ever occur. Animals normally do not perform such behavior. By shaping the response, the trainer can readily achieve the terminal goal. First, food (positive reinforcement) might be delivered for running toward the trainer. As that response becomes consistent, the trainer might reinforce running when the trainer is holding a hoop. Other steps closer to the final goal would be reinforced in sequence, including walking through the hoop on the ground, jumping through it when it is partially on fire, and finally jumping through it when the hoop is completely on fire. Eventually, the terminal response is performed with a high frequency, whereas the responses or steps developed along the way will have been extinguished.

Assume that a 13-year-old studies homework for less than 10 minutes a day and only a few days a week. Shaping consists of providing reinforcing consequences (e.g., privileges or points exchangeable for other rewards) for slight increases in this behavior. Note two interrelated and implicit goals or behaviors here: (a) increasing the duration of studying and (b) increasing consistency or the number and proportion of days studied. From a shaping perspective, we would begin by reinforcing small increments above the base rate. Perhaps 15 minutes a day of studying is rewarded each day, and this could be followed with a special bonus if the child works 2 or 3 days in a row. A parent might hear this simple program and ask, "Why reward the behavior at all? The child obviously knows how to study and occasionally does so." We hear this common query routinely at the clinic where I work. The question reflects parental frustration, as well as a key misunderstanding of human behavior.

Knowing how to engage in a behavior is quite different from engaging in the behavior often and consistently. Shaping, along with repeated practice and positive reinforcement, can build frequency and consistency. We can build on the frequency and duration of studying, as in the previous example. As the homework example suggests, shaping begins by reinforcing behaviors that are small increments in relation to what the person may normally do. As the initial approximation is performed consistently (e.g., perhaps 4 or 5 days of homework), the criterion for reinforcement is increased so the response approaches the final goal more closely. In the homework example, it is important to begin with a goal (e.g., perhaps 1½ hours of homework per day for at least 4 of 5 school days). We are not yet discussing the range of available reinforcement programs that might be used to foster the behavior. At this point, the progressive movement of shaping and increases in criteria toward the goal illustrate the point.

Chaining

Shaping usually is thought of as changing a behavior so it goes from one form to another. That is, the behavior may be changed along quantitative dimensions (e.g., studying for 2 minutes) to another form (e.g., studying for 20 minutes) or along qualitative dimensions (e.g., balancing on a beam first with one's hands stretched out to keep one's balance but eventually balancing without the hands out). That is, there is *a* behavior that is developed. In shaping, the final behavior replaces all of the steps along the way, and one does not see early behaviors that have been trained. They have been replaced.

Many behaviors of interest consist of several responses that must be completed in a particular order. A sequence of responses is referred to as a *chain*. Often there is a single or final reinforcer (completion of the task) that follows the completion of the sequence. For example, "getting dressed" is a behavioral chain that includes taking clothes out of a drawer, placing them on a bed, putting on a shirt, and so on for other articles of clothing. Putting on individual articles of clothing also requires a chain of behaviors. Similarly, completing a term paper or writing a book is a sequence of behaviors such as identifying the topic, organizing what will be presented and in what order, obtaining pertinent materials, perhaps reorganizing the material, drafting the paper, and so on. These examples reflect chains of behavior because many individual responses are linked together in a specific order.

Most behaviors in everyday life can be conceived of as chains of behaviors. Developing the sequence of behaviors is a process referred to as *chaining*. Chaining occurs by reinforcing completion of the full sequence of behaviors. That is, rather than just developing one behavior, a sequence of multiple behaviors occurs. Reinforcement is provided for completion of the sequence of behaviors. Consider the sequence of behaviors in putting on a shirt, a dressing skill sometimes taught to children with severe mental retardation who cannot dress themselves. Let us assume for the moment that this is a pullover shirt and that the sequence of individual behaviors is as follows:

1. Taking the shirt from the drawer
2. Spreading it out on the bed

3. Picking up the shirt
4. Putting one arm through the sleeve
5. Putting the other arm through the sleeve
6. Putting one's head through
7. Pulling it down to one's waist

The sequence of behaviors can be developed very much like shaping in the sense that a small requirement for reinforcement is made initially. In this sequence, we might begin with step 1. The child would be assisted (e.g., prompts) to take the shirt from the drawer. Perhaps the verbal prompt "please put on your shirt" would begin this, followed by physical assistance and guidance. Once the first behavior was performed, the reinforcer (e.g., praise, hugs) would be provided. The shirt would go back in the drawer and this behavior would be repeated. After a while, the second behavior would be added, and the child would engage in behaviors 1 and 2 and then receive the reinforcement. This would proceed until the entire sequence is performed. At the end of training, all of the behaviors are performed and still evident, but they are performed in a seamless way. As in shaping, small steps were made toward the goal, and reinforcement was provided for greater performance—in this case, completing more of the steps.[2]

The notion of chains of behaviors is very important because it alerts us to the fact that our interest is not merely in increasing this or that behavior but rather in building sequences of behaviors. For example, to increase a child's completion of homework, the sequence of behaviors may include bringing home an assignment book and the books needed to do the homework, working on the homework, completing the homework, reviewing or showing this work to a parent, and taking it to school the next day or on the due date. In developing this sequence, we must be mindful of the constituent behaviors as well as the sequence of behaviors. At the inception of the reinforcement program, we may reinforce individual acts; eventually, we wish to provide reinforcement at the end of the entire sequence of behaviors.

Consequences of Behavior

We have now considered the antecedents and the behaviors of the ABCs. In the process, we have also mentioned the consequences that follow behavior. However, let us consider consequences more systematically and the different arrangements of consequences and behavior. The most basic feature of consequences is how they relate to behavior. Specifically, for a consequence to alter a particular behavior, it must be dependent or contingent upon the occurrence of that behavior. Stated another way, behavior change occurs when certain consequences are *contingent upon performance.* A consequence is contingent when it is delivered only after the target behavior has been performed and is otherwise not available. When a consequence is not contingent upon behavior, this means that it is delivered independently of or no matter what the person is doing.

Consequences do not magically alter behavior; they must be delivered in specific ways, including in ways contingent on desired performance. When we discuss techniques more concretely, the specifics of how consequences must be delivered will be elaborated. Yet, in highlighting the principles, the notion of contingent delivery is central. The relationship of behavior and consequences is described by the concepts of reinforcement, punishment, and extinction.

Positive Reinforcement

Reinforcement always refers to an increase in the probability or likelihood of a response when that response is immediately followed by consequences. Positive and negative reinforcers are the two kinds of events that can be used to increase the probability of a response (Skinner, 1953). *Positive reinforcers* are stimuli or events presented after a response has been performed that increase the likelihood of the behavior they follow. The word *positive* in this use essentially means that something is presented. *Negative reinforcers* (which also are referred to as *aversive events* or *aversive stimuli*) are events removed after a response has been performed that increase the likelihood of the behavior preceding their removal. *Negative* in this use essentially means that something is removed or withdrawn. Let us consider these in turn.

Positive reinforcement refers to the increase in the likelihood or probability of a response that is followed by a favorable consequence (positive reinforcer). In everyday language, such positive or favorable events are frequently referred to as rewards. However, it is important to distinguish the term *positive reinforcer* from the term *reward.* A positive reinforcer is defined by its effect on behavior. If a consequence follows a behavior and the likelihood of the behavior increases in the future, the consequence is a positive reinforcer. Conversely, any event that does not increase the behavior it follows is not a positive reinforcer. An increase in the frequency or probability of the preceding behavior is the defining characteristic of a positive reinforcer. In contrast, *rewards* are defined as something that is given or received in return for doing something. Rewards such as prizes, sums of money, and vacations are usually highly valued and subjectively pleasing. Rewards do not necessarily increase the probability of the behaviors they follow.

In fact, many rewards or events that a person evaluates favorably when queried may serve as reinforcers. For example, people often say that money is a reward (i.e., they like it), and in fact money, when applied to alter behavior in systematic ways, usually serves as a positive reinforcer. Yet, whether a consequence is a reinforcer cannot be known on the basis of a person's verbal statements alone. A person may be unaware of or not consider as rewards many events that are reinforcers. For example, verbal reprimands (such as "Stop that!") and taking someone out of the room for isolation occasionally have served as positive reinforcers. It is unlikely that anyone would ever refer to these consequences as rewards. The key point is that a reward is not synonymous with a positive reinforcer. Whether an event is a positive reinforcer has to be determined empirically. Does the likelihood of the behavior to which the consequence was applied increase when the consequence immediately follows the behavior? Only if the behavior increases is the consequence a positive reinforcer.

Examples of positive reinforcement in everyday life would seem to be abundant. Strictly speaking, rarely does anyone actually measure whether a favorable event that followed a behavior increases the likelihood of that behavior. Nevertheless, some everyday situations probably exemplify positive reinforcement. Winning money at a slot machine usually increases the frequency of putting money into the machine and pulling the lever or pushing the button. Money is a powerful reinforcer that increases performance of a variety of behaviors. As another example, if a child whines or complains before going to bed and is then allowed to stay up longer, the frequency of whining before bedtime may increase. Letting the child stay up is likely to be a positive reinforcer.

Positive reinforcers include any events or stimuli that, when presented, increase the likelihood of the behavior they follow. There are two categories of positive reinforcers, namely, *unconditioned* or *primary* reinforcers and *conditioned* or *secondary* reinforcers. Unconditioned reinforcers are reinforcing without requiring special learning or training. Food and water are examples. Primary reinforcers may not be reinforcing all of the time. Food will not serve as a reinforcer to someone who has just finished a large meal. When food does serve as a reinforcer, however, its value is automatic (unlearned) and does not depend on a previous association with any other reinforcers.

On the other hand, conditioned reinforcers, such as praise, grades, money, and completion of a goal, acquire their reinforcing value through learning.

Conditioned reinforcers acquire reinforcing properties by being paired with events that are already reinforcing (either primary reinforcers or other conditioned reinforcers). If a neutral stimulus is repeatedly presented before or along with another reinforcing stimulus, the neutral stimulus becomes a reinforcer. For example, praise may not be reinforcing for some individuals. To establish praise as a reinforcer, it can be paired with a consequence that is reinforcing, such as food or money or physical touch. When a behavior is performed, the individual's behavior is praised and reinforced with food. After several pairings of the food with praise, the praise alone can serve as a reinforcer and increase the frequency of other responses.

Some conditioned reinforcers are paired with many different reinforcers. When a conditioned reinforcer is paired or associated with many other reinforcers, it is referred to as a *generalized conditioned reinforcer*. Money is an example. It is a *conditioned* reinforcer because its reinforcing value is acquired through learning. It is a *generalized* reinforcer because a variety of reinforcing events contribute to its value. Additional examples of generalized conditioned reinforcers include attention, approval, and affection from others; for example, attention from someone may be followed by physical contact, praise, smiles, affection, or delivery of tangible rewards (such as food) and other events.

In parent training programs, generalized reinforcers in the form of *tokens* are used frequently. The tokens may be poker chips, coins, tickets, stars, points, or check marks. Tokens serve as generalized reinforcers because, like money, they can be exchanged for many other events that are reinforcing. For example, in an elementary school classroom, tokens may be delivered to students for raising their hands to speak, for completing assignments in class, and for attaining correct answers. The tokens may be exchanged for special in-class activities such as educational games or movies, extra recess, or free time in class at the end of the day, and their potency derives from the reinforcers that back up their value. The events that tokens can purchase are *backup reinforcers*. Generalized conditioned reinforcers, such as money or tokens, are usually more powerful than any single reinforcer because they can purchase many different backup reinforcers.

In identifying positive reinforcers, keep two considerations in mind. First, an event (e.g., praise, candy, or a pat on the back) may be a positive reinforcer for one person but not for another. Although some events have wide generality in serving as reinforcers, such as food or money, others may not (e.g., sour candy). Second, an event may be a reinforcer for one person under some circumstances or at some times but not under other circumstances or at other times. These considerations require careful evaluation of what is reinforcing for a given individual. Because of people's common biological backgrounds, cultural norms, and experiences, some consequences (e.g., praise from parents or peers, money) are likely to be reinforcers for many people. However, there is no guarantee that a particular event will be reinforcing. The critical test is whether the consequence, when presented contingently, increases the likelihood of that behavior in the future.

Negative Reinforcement

Positive reinforcement is a key principle in PMT that is used to generate several techniques and practices in the home, both to develop behaviors (e.g., homework completion, compliance) and to decrease or eliminate behaviors (e.g., fighting, tantrums). The principle or concept of negative reinforcement is important to understand in relation to the contingencies of reinforcement and parent–child interaction. However, negative reinforcement involves aversive events. Techniques that might be generated from the principle generally play little or no role in treatment. Consequently, the principle that is discussed and illustrated here is important background, but it does not usually figure into the techniques described to change parent or child behavior.

Negative reinforcement refers to the increase in the likelihood of a response when an aversive event is removed immediately after the response has been performed. An event is a negative reinforcer only if its removal after a response increases performance of that response (Skinner, 1953). The comments made about the difference between rewards and positive reinforcers hold for negative reinforcers as well. That is, consequences that are subjectively unpleasant or not liked very much may be annoying or otherwise undesirable. They are also likely to be useful as negative reinforcers, but not necessarily. Whether a consequence really serves as a negative reinforcer can be determined only by seeing if the consequence can change behavior. Other qualifications are pertinent, too. An undesirable event may serve as an aversive event for one individual but not for another. Also, an event may be a negative reinforcer for an individual at one time but not at another time. A negative reinforcer, like a positive reinforcer, is defined solely by its effect on behavior.

As with positive reinforcers, there are two types of negative reinforcers, unconditioned (primary) and conditioned (secondary). Intense stimuli, such as shock, loud noise, or very bright light, that impinge on the sensory receptors of an organism serve as unconditioned negative reinforcers. Their aversive properties are not learned. In contrast, conditioned events become aversive by being paired with events that are already aversive. For example, disapproving facial expressions or saying the word *no* can serve as aversive events after they are paired with events that are already aversive.

Once again, *reinforcement (positive or negative) always refers to an increase in behavior.* Negative reinforcement requires an ongoing aversive event or stimulus that can be removed or terminated after a specific response has been performed. The aversive event is "just there" or present in the environment. Once this event is present, then some behavior may stop or end it. That behavior is negatively reinforced.

Positive reinforcement is familiar and more easily remembered than negative reinforcement because many examples of unsystematic reinforcement seem evident in everyday life. For a helpful aid, consider the following. In negative reinforcement, the desired behavior *turns off* an aversive event (e.g., stops a noise, stops pain). The behavior may not directly turn off the event like a switch, but it has that effect. Performing the behavior results in the immediate termination of an aversive event. Think of situations in which escape behavior occurs as instances in which negative reinforcement is operating. Table 2.3 gives some examples to clarify the arrangement of consequences and behavior.

The examples convey the concept that escape from an aversive event or terminating it can negatively reinforce behavior. Avoidance, too, is involved in negative reinforcement, but this is a bit subtler. In avoidance, behavior is per-

Table 2.3
Examples of Negative Reinforcement

Aversive stimulus, condition, situation	Behavior that is performed	Immediate effect is to end the aversive condition	Outcome or effect on behavior
Irritability and mild discomfort (from nicotine depletion)	Smoking a cigarette	Terminates the discomfort	Increases the likelihood of smoking in the future
Loud noise from an alarm clock	Throwing the clock across the room	Noise from the alarm ends	Increase the likelihood of throwing the clock
Nagging parent	Leaving the house or the room	Nagging no longer heard	Increase the likelihood of leaving (escape) in the future
Discomfort from extremely cold weather	Entering a building	Terminates the discomfort	Increase the likelihood of escaping from the cold

formed before the negative event even occurs. Thus, an adolescent may return home from school, only to encounter a nagging parent. Nagging (aversive event) can lead to escape, and escape is negatively reinforced. Cues and learned events that precede negative events often take on aversive properties; that is, they, too, become aversive. Engaging in behavior that terminates these learned aversive events leads to negative reinforcement. Thus, a teenager does not need to hear the nagging parent (aversive event). Escaping from a nagging parent by leaving the room would be an example of negative reinforcement. A parent who nags a lot might well take on aversive properties and be avoided by the teenager. Thoughts about the parent and the sight of the parent can become aversive, and their termination can negatively reinforce behavior. One can avoid the parent altogether or not come home after school, and that, too, is negatively reinforced.

Negative reinforcement requires presentation to the individual of some aversive event, such as shock, noise, or isolation, that can be removed or reduced immediately after he or she responds. Because of the undesirability of using aversive stimuli, negative reinforcement is almost never used in programs designed to alter behavior. Several less objectionable and more positive procedures are readily available. Even so, it is important to understand negative reinforcement and recognize its role in everyday life and in parent–child interactions.

There are many interesting combinations of positive and negative reinforcement in everyday interactions. Consider two examples from parent–child interactions. We begin in a supermarket, where a parent is waiting in line to check out groceries. In the checkout line with the parent is a 5-year-old girl. The child sees candy and asks the parent if she can have some. The parent ignores this or says no. Let us say that the child escalates a little and begins to whine, cry, and tug at the parent's clothing while saying in the most annoying and now loud voice, "I want some candy!" Suppose the parent says, "All right, here's the candy" and hands the child a candy bar from the rack. Where is the positive and negative reinforcement? The child's behavior (whining, tugging at the parent, and repeatedly insisting on candy) was associated with a positive consequence (candy). That is *positive reinforcement* of the *child's* behavior. The parent's behavior (giving the candy to the child) was associated with the immediate termination of an aversive event (whining). That is *negative reinforcement* of the *parent's* behavior.

Such combinations of positive reinforcement are common in everyday situations without the mild drama of a grocery store tantrum. Consider parents sitting in the living room and chatting, when their infant begins to cry loudly from the crib. One of the parents—say, the father—goes into the nursery and picks up the infant. The infant immediately stops crying. At this point, let us say that the infant is unusually bright and amazingly verbal and says, "Yo, Dad, you picked me up after I cried—that is positive reinforcement because my behavior (crying) was followed by a consequence (being picked up, cuddled, patted, and held). Thanks, Dad!" Dad says, "Mildredsina [daughter's name], no need to thank me. The noise from your crying was—well—pretty aversive for us. When I picked you up, the noise ended right away. That is negative reinforcement because *my* behavior (picking you up) terminated the noise." (Of course, at that point, the mother rushes in and correctly notes, "Both of you remember this is not reinforcement unless the likelihood of the behaviors you mentioned increases in the future. Now good night!") This arrangement conveys how both can be operative in a similar situation, but for different people.

In social interaction, the response of one individual is sometimes negatively reinforced because it terminates an aversive behavior initiated by another individual. At the same time, the aversive behavior of the other individual may be positively reinforced. This can be seen in more frightening interactions, such as being mugged or robbed. Positive and negative reinforcement occur when the victims of an aggressive act (such as physical assault) comply with the wishes of the aggressor (e.g., giving up their wallets) in order to terminate an aversive situation. Unfortunately, the victims' act of compliance positively reinforces the aggressor, which increases the aggressor's probability of future aggression.

Punishment

Punishment is the presentation or removal of a stimulus or event following a response, which decreases the likelihood of that response. This definition is quite different from the everyday use of the term. In everyday life, punishment refers to a penalty imposed for performing a particular act. For example, misbehaving children are "taught a lesson" by undergoing pain, sacrifice, or loss of some kind (e.g., slap, harsh reprimand, loss of a privilege). Criminals may receive penalties (fines, probation, incarceration) based on the acts they have committed. Yet punishment in the technical sense is defined solely by the effect on behavior. These examples, while called punishment in ordinary circumstances, might not have any effects on the likelihood of future behavior. In behavior modification, punishment is operative only if the likelihood of the response is reduced. That is, a punishing event is defined by its suppressive effect on the behavior that it follows.

In behavior-change programs, punishment is de-emphasized for many reasons, as mentioned later. When punishment is used, it does not necessarily entail any pain or physical coercion or many of the demeaning, humiliating, and outright nasty consequences provided in everyday life.[3] Indeed, the grabbing, hitting, and shaking that parents or teachers may do with young children in everyday life is not used in PMT.

There are two main types of punishment. In the first type, an aversive consequence is presented after a response. The numerous everyday examples of this type of punishment include being reprimanded or slapped after engaging in some behavior. (These examples convey the sequence of events: behavior followed by a consequence. However, they are unlikely to really influence the likelihood of behavior in the future, given the way they are used, as discussed later in the chapter on punishment.) The second type of punishment is the removal of a positive event after a response. Examples include losing privileges after staying out late, losing money for misbehaving, being isolated from others, and having one's driver's license revoked. In this type of punishment, some event is taken away after a response has been performed.

Punishment and negative reinforcement are often confused, even though they are very different. The key difference is that reinforcement, whether negative or positive, always refers to procedures that increase behavior, whereas punishment refers to procedures that decrease behavior. In negative reinforcement, an aversive event is removed after a response; in punishment, an aversive consequence follows a response. Figure 2.1, which depicts two operations that can occur after a response has been performed, provides a simple way of distinguishing the operations involved in reinforcement and punishment. A stimulus or event can be presented to, or removed from, the child after a response (left side of the figure). The figure also shows two types of events that may be presented or removed, namely, positive and aversive stimuli or events. The four combinations forming the different cells depict the principles of positive reinforcement (A), negative reinforcement (D), and the two types of punishment (B and C).[4]

Extinction

Extinction is an important principle of operant conditioning not represented in Figure 2.1. *Extinction* refers to the cessation of reinforcement of a response that results in a decrease in the likelihood of the behavior in the future. Like the other principles, extinction is defined by the relation of a response to consequences and to a change in the likelihood or probability of behavior in the

Type of event

	Positive event	Aversive event
Presented	Positive reinforcement A	Punishment B
Removed	Punishment C	Negative reinforcement D

Operatoin performed after a response

Figure 2.1 Illustration of the principles of operant conditioning based on whether positive or aversive stimuli or events are presented or removed after a response has been performed. The figure provides a simple way to convey the major principles of operant conditioning, but the simplicity of the figure has a price. In fact, a more technical discussion of the principles would quickly reveal inaccuracies in the figure. For example, the figure implies that a particular event that can negatively reinforce behavior can also be used to suppress (punish) some other response that it follows. Although this is usually true, many exceptions exist.

future. No longer reinforcing a response results in the eventual reduction or elimination of the response. It is important to keep this procedure distinct from punishment. In extinction, a consequence that was previously provided no longer follows the response. An event or stimulus (e.g., money, noise) is neither taken away nor presented. In punishment, some aversive event follows a response (e.g., reprimand), or some positive event (e.g., money) is taken away.

In everyday life, extinction often takes the form of ignoring a behavior that was previously reinforced with attention. A parent may ignore a child when the child whines, which is extinction if the parent had been attending to the behavior (the reinforcer) on prior occasions but no longer does so. A teacher may ignore children who talk without raising their hands, assuming that when children shouted out, they previously were called on. All ignoring is not necessarily extinction. Attention is not always the reinforcer for behavior. Consequently, no longer providing attention may not have impact. For example, a teacher may ignore disruptive student behavior and not see a reduction in that behavior. The reason is that peer attention, rather than teacher attention, is often the reinforcer. Once that is controlled (e.g., by providing students with points contingent on ignoring disruptive behavior), student disruptive behavior can be decreased.

Extinction may contribute to behavioral problems as well as ameliorate them. Often, desirable behavior is accidentally extinguished. For example, parents sometimes ignore their children when the children are playing quietly and provide abundant attention when the children are noisy. Their behavior may extinguish quiet play while positively reinforcing noisy play. Merely reallocating parental attention so that it follows appropriate play is often sufficient to develop appropriate behavior and extinguish inappropriate behavior.

Cessation of attention is not the only example of extinction. For example, putting money into vending machines (a response) will cease if the reinforcer (e.g., cigarettes, food, or drink) is not forthcoming, turning on a radio will cease if the radio no longer provides sound, and attempting to start a car will cease if the car does not start. In each of these examples, the consequences that maintain the behavior are no longer forthcoming. The absence of reinforcing consequences reduces the behavior. Extinction can be used as a technique to reduce or eliminate behavior. First, though, the events that reinforce behavior must be identified so that they can be prevented from occurring after the response. As discussed later, this is difficult to do, and hence extinction is often used with other procedures (e.g., positive reinforcement for the desired behavior) to increase its impact.

Additional Principles and Concepts

Discrimination

A few additional concepts that have direct implications for PMT are important in explaining how behavior develops and is maintained. The first of these is discriminative stimuli, mentioned in the discussion of antecedents that control behavior. Stimuli associated with reinforcement, when present, increase the likelihood of the behavior that has been reinforced. When behavior is performed in the presence of some stimuli (S^D) but not in the presence of others (S^Δ), the individual is said to have made a discrimination, and behavior is said to be under stimulus control. *Discrimination* refers to the fact that the individual responds differently under different stimulus conditions.

Discrimination and stimulus control are almost always operative in behavior-change programs. Programs are conducted in particular settings (e.g., the home) and are administered by particular individuals (e.g., parents). Insofar as certain behaviors are reinforced or punished in the presence of particular individuals or certain environmental cues and not in the presence of other stimuli, the behaviors are under stimulus control. In the presence of cues associated with the behavior-change program, the client will behave in a particular fashion. In the absence of those cues, behavior is likely to change because the contingencies in new situations are altered.

The control that different stimuli exert over behavior explains why behavior often is situation-specific. Individuals may behave one way in a given situation or in the presence of a particular person and behave differently in another situation or in the presence of another person. Because different reinforcement contingencies operate in different circumstances, individuals can discriminate among the stimuli that are likely to be followed by reinforcement.

People make discriminations across a variety of situations for most behaviors. For example, eating habits probably vary, depending upon whether one is at home or in a restaurant. At home people are more likely to place crumpled napkins, books, elbows, and feet on the table when they eat meals; these behaviors are much less likely in a restaurant (with the possible exception of a few of my relatives). Similarly, further discriminations are made, depending on whether one is eating in an elegant place or a fast-food restaurant. Numerous other variations in behavior are evident because of differences in the situations and the contingencies associated with them.

The notion of discrimination is relevant in many ways to PMT. First is the obvious concern that if children make a discrimination in their performance, perhaps they will perform the desired behaviors only when rewards are offered. When rewards are not offered or when the reward program is ended, perhaps the child will make a discrimination and not perform the desired behaviors. This is a common and cogent concern. Special contingency arrangements can be used as part of a program to ensure that any behaviors transfer to new situations, places, and contexts, as desired. In short, discrimination may occur in the program but is not necessarily a problem.

Generalization

The complementary concept to discrimination is generalization. The effect of reinforcement on behavior may either extend beyond the conditions in which training has taken place or extend to behaviors other than those included in the program. That is, rather than a restriction (discrimination) in what is learned and the conditions under which that is performed, there may be broad extension of what has been learned (generalization). The ways in which effects of the program extend beyond the contingency are referred to as *generalization.*

Stimulus Generalization

Stimulus generalization refers to the generalization or transfer of a response to situations other than those in which training takes place. It occurs if a response reinforced in one situation or setting also increases in other settings (even though it is not reinforced in the other settings). Generalization is the opposite of discrimination. When an individual *discriminates* in the performance of a response, this means that the response fails to generalize across situations. Alternatively, when a response *generalizes* across situations, the individual fails to discriminate in his or her performance of that response. Often when a behavior is reinforced in one situation or in the presence of one set of conditions, it may be performed in new situations that are similar, even if reinforcement is not provided in those situations.

Examples of stimulus generalization are common in everyday experience. For example, a child may talk about certain topics in the presence of family because talking about those topics is reinforced (e.g., discussed freely, attended to) among family members. The child may also discuss the same topics in the presence of guests. In that case, the child's behavior (talking about certain topics) has generalized across situations. Parents may be embarrassed when children talk about family secrets or personal topics (e.g., how one's father puts on his toupee or how one's mother looks in the shower). Generalization is also readily apparent when a child responds to a teacher in a fashion as he or she responds to a parent (e.g., in the expression of affection). To the extent that a child sees parents and teachers as similar, the teacher will share the stimulus control exerted by parents. Because the antecedent events (approaches by the adult, expressions of affection) and the consequent events (hugs, kisses) are different for the child in relation to teachers and parents, the child quickly learns a discrimination. Consequently, expressions of affection are more likely in the presence of parents (S^D) than of teachers (S^Δ).

Stimulus generalization represents an exceedingly important issue in parent management training and in behavior-change programs more generally. Invariably, development of a behavior takes place in a restricted setting, such as at home and maybe in the presence of one parent and a sibling. Yet, a goal is to develop the behavior so it carries over to other settings (e.g., at school, at day camp, on the playground). It is desirable that behaviors developed in these settings generalize or transfer to other settings. Sometimes generalization occurs without special procedures. However, there are many procedures to ensure that behaviors transfer from one setting to another, and these are discussed later.

Response Generalization

Another type of generalization involves responses rather than stimulus conditions. *Response generalization* refers to changes in behaviors or responses other than those that have been trained or developed. Response generalization occurs if a specific response is developed through reinforcement or other procedures, and this systematically alters other behaviors that have not been directly trained. Altering one response can inadvertently influence other responses. For example, if a person is praised for smiling, the frequency not only of smiling but also of laughing and talking might increase.

Examples of response generalization are plentiful. According to one report, altering noncompliance (not completing the requests of adults) in four children also decreased such inappropriate behaviors as aggression (pushing, hitting, biting), disruption (whining, crying, screaming), property destruction (pushing, kicking furniture, pounding on or throwing objects), and placement of inedible objects in their mouths (Parrish, Cataldo, Kolko, Neef, & Egel, 1986). The intervention, based primarily on variations of positive reinforcement, effectively increased compliance among these children. Interestingly, when their compliance increased, their aggression, disruption, and other inappropriate behaviors decreased, even though these latter behaviors were not the focus of the intervention.

The notion of response generalization suggests that responses that are not directly focused on but are similar to the target response change in some way. For example, a child praised for studying in class may improve in reading, even though reading may not have been the response to which the reinforcing consequences were directed. Yet, changes and the spread of the benefits of treatment often are not merely a function of the similarity of one behavior (the one reinforced) to another that is not reinforced. The spread of beneficial effects of treatment often is not captured by merely saying the responses are based on how similar they are.

Behaviors are often clustered into classes or packages. All this means is that the behaviors are correlated and covary together. When behavior changes are made in one of the behaviors in a class, other behaviors may change as well. For example, a child's changing compliance at home might well be associated with a reduction in arguing and fighting, even though these behaviors were not the targets. Possibly these other behaviors were inadvertently reinforced because not arguing and not fighting occur when the child is complying. But even without this, sometimes there are concomitant effects. These are loosely referred to as *generalization*, but concomitant effects is a preferable term because there is no implication that similarity of the responses is critical to the changes.

Response generalization is often used to explain changes in responses other than the target response. The concept is based on the view that the effects of an intervention will generalize from one response to other responses that are *similar* in some way. Technically, the term *response generalization* may not be accurate for two reasons. First, responses that are not supposed to be focused on may inadvertently receive reinforcing consequences. Although this may be spoken of as generalization, it may reflect the direct operation of reinforcement and not be generalization at all. When a child is praised for paying attention, he or she may be reading on some of the occasions when reinforcement is delivered. Second, change in one behavior (e.g., studying) often is associated with changes in other behaviors (e.g., socialization, complying with requests) that appear to have no direct relation or resemblance to the target behavior.

In behavior-change programs, the concepts of stimulus and response generalization are ordinarily used to denote that changes occur across various stimulus conditions (situations or settings) or across responses. In fact, however, there is rarely any evidence that the spread of treatment effects across stimulus or response dimensions is actually based on the similarity of the stimuli or responses to those used in training. Technically, therefore, the terms *stimulus* and *response generalization* are often used incorrectly. Even so, the technical difficulties in using these terms do not detract from the importance of the spread of treatment effects across stimulus conditions or behaviors during the course of treatment.

In PMT, prosocial child behaviors are developed in the home but also in other settings as needed (i.e., across a variety of stimulus conditions). Yet, a goal of treatment is to develop behaviors that generalize across new situations that might emerge, whether or not they are included in treatment. Also, we want to change specific behaviors but not just a few concrete behaviors here and there. Broader changes across many response domains are of interest as well.

Summary and Conclusions

The principles outlined in this chapter provide the basis for PMT. They describe basic relations among antecedents, behaviors, and consequences and account for diverse treatment interventions. Settings (situations, contexts), prompts (cues or guides that help initiate the response), and discriminative stimuli (S^D) are key antecedents that influence development of behavior. Behaviors that are altered may include a specific response that is developed or a sequence of multiple responses. Shaping reinforces approximations to attain a terminal behavior that may not be in the individual's repertoire. Chaining is a way of building behavior when several different behaviors are performed according to a sequence or ordered set of actions. Shaping and chaining, as used in PMT, provide reinforcement for steps toward the desired outcome.

Consequences for behavior rely heavily on reinforcement, punishment, and extinction. Reinforcement always refers to an increase in the likelihood of the behavior in the future when consequences are applied contingently for that behavior. Punishment refers to a decrease in the behavior when consequences are applied contingently. Extinction is no longer providing a reinforcer that previously was provided for the response, and it is associated with a decrease in behavior as well.

As discussed in this chapter, discrimination is responding differently across different situations or circumstances. Individuals learn to respond differently to various situations through differential consequences such as reinforcement. Behaviors reinforced in one situation but not in another tend to be performed in the former situation but not in the latter. Generalization is responding similarly across different situations (stimulus generalization) or changing in many behaviors beyond those that are directly focused on in the intervention (response generalization).

Many principles and concepts were introduced in this chapter to provide an overview of the building blocks of PMT. Of course, the effectiveness of PMT depends on the movement from principles to techniques. The next two chapters convey techniques that follow from the principles and concepts.

Notes

1. Discussion of the principles introduces several new terms. To aid the reader, major terms are italicized when they are first introduced. A glossary at the end of the book defines the major terms in this chapter and throughout the text.
2. Chaining is a much more complex topic that includes ways of developing sequences of behavior that begin with the first step and add new steps until all are completed. Chaining can also proceed by beginning with the last step and adding a prior step. Chaining is rarely used in PMT. Shaping is commonly used to develop more of some

behavior along some quantitative dimension (more time in an activity) or more steps or discrete behaviors that form a sequence or chain of responses.

3. Pain and punishment are inextricably bound in language and thought and, indeed, etymological ties. Both words can be traced to the Latin word *poena* ("penalty" and later "pain") (Jewell & Abate, 2001).

4. Occasionally, the terms *positive* and *negative punishment* are used to distinguish whether an event is presented (e.g., reprimand) or withdrawn (e.g., loud noise) after behavior. This is not a common practice in part because juxtaposing the terms *positive* with *punishment* seems like an oxymoron, given the nontechnical use of the word *positive* as something "good." In behavior-change programs, positive and negative refer to presentation or withdrawal, respectively, rather than the subjective value of something.

From Principles to Techniques
Positive Reinforcement

The principles reflect broad relations among antecedents, behaviors, and consequences. It is a huge leap from principles to practice, that is, execution and implementation. The success or failure of PMT depends very much on how well the program is implemented. Occasionally, treatment failures are explained away by vacuous comments that perhaps the treatment was not implemented correctly. The research behind PMT provides a little more guidance. How treatment must be implemented to be effective has been well studied. The purpose of this and the next chapter is to describe and illustrate key techniques and how they can be implemented to change behavior. This chapter focuses exclusively on positive reinforcement, the key principle underlying PMT.

Types of Reinforcers

Overview

Positive reinforcement refers to an increase in the probability or likelihood of a response following the presentation of a positive reinforcer. Whether a particular event is a positive reinforcer is defined by its effects on behavior. If response frequency increases when followed by the event, it is a positive reinforcer. Positive reinforcers are not the same as rewards. Reinforcers are defined by their effects on behavior, whereas rewards are those events that are subjectively valued, liked, and maybe even evoke smiles. Most reinforcers are rewards, and vice versa, but not all. Just because a person likes something (reward) does not mean the event can change behavior. And even if people say they do not like something (e.g., praise from a parent to an adolescent), it still may serve as a reinforcer. The technical term is useful for a therapist to understand so that reinforcers are approached empirically—that is, what is in fact useful for changing behavior. In interactions with parents, we often use the term *reward*, as well as *positive reinforcer*, merely to make the conversation less technical, but the concept of positive reinforcer is made clear to the parent.

Several types of reinforcers can be used. Table 3.1 provides categories of reinforcers that are used in applied settings, such as the home, school, and various institutional settings. The table implies that one selects a particular reinforcer or category of reinforcer as the basis for behavior change. Actually, the various reinforcers are often combined and used together, as described later.

Table 3.1
Types of Reinforcers and Overview of Strengths and Limitations

Type	Strengths	Limitations
Food and consumables (e.g., snacks, gum)	• Immediate • Useful in one-to-one session	• Depends on deprivation and satiation states • Often objectionable to therapists, parents, and teachers • Not feasible in group settings or everyday life on a frequent basis
Social reinforcers (e.g., attention, praise, physical contact)	• Easily administered in group or individual situation • Not as readily subject to deprivation and satiation states in the way that food is	• Usually but not always a reinforcer • Not easily administered on a consistent basis if parent (teacher, staff) is not well trained or monitored
Privileges and activities (e.g., what child does during free time when given a choice, high-probability activities)	• Highly reinforcing • Relatively easy to identify	• Not easily administered immediately • Difficult to parcel out (e.g., going to a movie) for small portions of behavior • Limitations of availability unless present in everyday life (e.g., watching TV, later bedtime, time with friends) • Some of the activities that could serve as a reinforcer may be objected to by therapists, parents, and teachers (e.g., violent video games, time on the Internet)
Tokens (points, chips, stars) backed up by other reinforcers (any of the reinforcers mentioned previously)	• Highly reinforcing • Not usually dependent on deprivation states • Useful for one or multiple individuals	• Requires a medium of exchange (points on a chart) • Requires backup reinforcers (any of those in the previous categories) that can be exchanged for the tokens or points • Requires ultimately eliminating the tokens so behavior is performed without a special program

From Principles to Techniques

Tokens

In most PMT programs, social reinforcers (attention, praise) and token reinforcement (points, chips, marks on a sheet) are commonly used and will be emphasized here. Tokens are conditioned reinforcers such as poker chips, coins, tickets, stars, points, or check marks that are referred to as *generalized conditioned reinforcers* because they can be exchanged for a variety of reinforcing events, *backup reinforcers*. The tokens take on value because of the reinforcers with which they are associated. A reinforcement system based on tokens is a *token economy*. In a token economy, tokens function in the same way that money does in national economies. Tokens are earned and then used to purchase backup reinforcers, such as food and other consumables, activities, and privileges. The basic requirements of a token economy are specification of (a) the behaviors one wants to develop, (b) the number of tokens that can be earned for performance of the behaviors, (c) the backup reinforcers that are available, and (d) the number of tokens the backup reinforcers cost.

Token economies have been used extensively in classrooms (preschool through college), psychiatric hospitals, prisons, detention centers, day-care centers, nursing homes, business and industry, the military, and scores of other settings. Many controlled studies attest to the effectiveness of such programs in changing behavior (Glynn, 1990; Kazdin, 2001b). Token programs can be used for groups and for individuals, which makes them readily adaptable.

In PMT, the focus is usually on a child at home, and that is the emphasis here. In this context, parents are trained to use points, marks on a chart, or stars on a temporary basis to foster behaviors such as completing chores, doing homework, and getting ready on time. Simple programs are an excellent way to manage behavior, to move away from nagging, reprimands, and punishment in general. Usually in such applications, tokens are not "needed"; that is, the behavior could be changed with improved prompts and praise and shaping. Praise as a reinforcer all by itself can be very effective, as demonstrated in scores of studies. There are many benefits of praise, such as ease of administration, its availability in everyday life, and the lack of satiation in comparison with food or other consumables. The use of tokens with praise is even more effective in changing behavior.

Tokens provide a good way to structure and prompt parent behavior so the consequences are applied systematically. Tokens have advantages for both parents and children, as summarized in Table 3.2. First, they are potent reinforcers that can often develop behaviors at a higher level than those developed

Table 3.2
Advantages of Using Tokens as Reinforcers

1. Tokens are potent reinforcers that can be more effective than other reinforcers, such as praise, approval, and feedback.

2. They permit use of a single reinforcer (tokens) that stands for and can be used as a basis for exchanging many other reinforcers, and they provide the benefits of using multiple and diverse reinforcers.

3. They permit use of large reinforcers (special rewards) by parceling them out so they are not earned in an all-or-none fashion. Tokens can be earned toward the purchase of a large or valuable backup reinforcer.

4. They are less subject to satiation than are other reinforcers such as food.

5. They bridge the delay between the target response and backup reinforcement, such as a privilege or special activity that cannot be conveniently given immediately after behavior.

6. They often can be delivered (e.g., marks on a chart, tickets, points) without interrupting the activity or behavior they are reinforcing, as might be the case with activities, privileges, or food rewards.

7. They can be used easily when a program is implemented for more than one person.

8. They can serve as a cue for parents to deliver reinforcers and hence are more likely to be delivered than praise by itself or some other reinforcer that is less tangible.

by other reinforcers such as praise, approval, and feedback. To obtain high levels of performance, it is often useful to begin with a token reinforcement program. After performance is consistently high, behavior can be maintained with praise or activities that occur more naturally in the setting.

Second, tokens permit administering a single reinforcer (tokens) to an individual but still serve as a reinforcer if that individual's preference or interest changes regarding the reinforcer. The child can exchange tokens for different backup reinforcers because tokens are backed up by a variety of reinforcers.

Third, tokens permit parceling out other reinforcers such as privileges and activities that have to be earned in an all-or-none fashion. Tokens can be earned toward the purchase of a large or valuable backup reinforcer or privilege (e.g., going to a theme park or movie, having friends stay overnight). This allows the use of potent reinforcers.

Fourth, with multiple backup reinforcers that can be exchanged for tokens, the tokens are less subject to satiation than are other reinforcers (or any single backup reinforcer). If a person is no longer interested in one or two backup reinforcers, usually many other reinforcers are of value.

Fifth, tokens bridge the delay between the target response and the backup reinforcement. If a reinforcer other than tokens (such as an activity provided at the end of the week or on a weekend) cannot be delivered immediately after the target response has been performed, tokens can be delivered instead and used to purchase a backup reinforcer later.

Sixth, tokens often can be administered without interrupting the target response. Tokens do not require consumption (as do such reinforcers as food) or the performance of behaviors that may interrupt the target response (e.g., participating in a special activity).

Seventh, tokens easily accommodate involving two or more individuals in a common program. For example, in the home, siblings may be included in a point program. Individual differences in the preferences for reinforcers can be accommodated by having a range of backup reinforcers to be exchanged for tokens. Thus a single reinforcer (tokens) can be effective for many people using a common reinforcer and method of delivery.

Eighth, the use of tokens has benefits for parent behavior, leaving aside the benefits of tokens on changing the behavior of children. Delivery of tokens, such as placing marks, points, or stars on a chart, requires discrete acts on the part of the parents that are more likely to be carried out than asking the parent to administer praise. Praise is easily lost—not delivered and not monitored. In contrast, charting tokens requires keeping track. The child is interested in the accumulation of the points, and this, too, prompts parents to administer the program. Also, providing tokens or points a useful cue for the parent to deliver praise.

There are potential disadvantages in employing tokens. First, tokens are not usually provided in everyday life the way they are in a token economy. Yes, money as used in everyday life (wages, bonuses at work, commissions) is the same as token reinforcement in the sense that it can be used for a variety of backup reinforcers, but that is quite different from having a parent temporarily provide points to reduce a child's tantrums or increase completion of homework. Tokens ultimately have to be removed after behavior change has occurred and stabilized.

Second, parents and teachers often object to introducing tokens and delivering them for behavior, in large part because many children (e.g., siblings, classmates) other than the one identified for intervention perform the desired behaviors without such inducements. The objection is understandable, but the key point to convey is that the goal of token reinforcement is to develop the behavior at a high and consistent level. Tokens are a very effective way to accomplish this. The use of tokens can be viewed as a temporary intervention.

Third, and related to the previous concern, is the task of removing the token system after behavioral gains have been made. Children learn that the presence of tokens signals that desirable behavior will be reinforced; the absence of tokens signals that desirable behavior will not be reinforced. Consequently, desirable behavior may decline quickly as soon as token reinforcement is ended. Actually, this is not invariably or, indeed, usually the case; there are many ways of removing the program and maintaining the gains (Kazdin, 2001b).

Although the objections to the use of tokens can be surmounted and argued away, it is important to be sensitive to them. Parents are frustrated when one child engages in some behavior with ease and the other does not. This exacerbates their concern and understandable objections to resorting to a special procedure with one child, especially if that child "knows" how to do the behavior.

Examples of Token Programs in the Home

In parent training, it is best to begin simply because the initial goal is to change parent behavior. This goal includes fostering the use of praise, contingent reinforcement, prompting, shaping, and other techniques. Indeed, even more concretely, the goal is to change how a parent delivers reinforcement to ensure that critical conditions, highlighted later, are included. Consequently, to emphasize token programs here as the critical feature might unwittingly detract from this other focus.

Token programs vary in complexity. At one extreme, tokens can be provided for one or two behaviors, such as cleaning up one's room or starting homework. Marks, stars, smiley face stickers, drawings of balloons, or circles that are filled in (to constitute a token) might be provided if the child picks up clothes from the floor and puts this or that item away. Each day the room would be checked and tokens marked on the chart if the behavior had been performed. Copious praise would accompany delivery of the marks or tokens. One or a few behaviors and one or a few backup reinforcers for which the tokens can be exchanged constitute a relatively simple program. At the other extreme, a program might include several behaviors (e.g., cleaning one's room, watching TV calmly with one's sibling, starting homework, calling when at a friend's house so the parent knows where the child is), each of which has a point value. Multiple backup reinforcers might be available.

Essential Ingredients to Make Programs Effective

In the prior section, I mentioned different types of reinforcers. Yet, the effectiveness of a behavior-change program is more likely to depend on *how* reinforcers are delivered rather than on which reinforcer among the alternatives is selected. Table 3.3 lists key elements that influence the effectiveness of a program. In PMT, a major challenge is training therapists to use praise effectively in the sessions to change specific behaviors in the parents. Training therapists often uses reinforcement to develop behavior. Once the therapists are trained, they work with parents. In training the parents, the therapists use reinforcement and rely very heavily on the factors noted in the table. The challenge for the therapists is training parents to reinforce the behaviors of their children effectively and to apply these same elements of effective delivery in the home.

Ways to Deliver Reinforcers Effectively

Praise, tokens, or some other reinforcer must be delivered in a special way to develop behavior and produce change. In the chaos of many home situations, reinforcers cannot be applied perfectly. Also, all of us are variable in our own functioning and not perfectly consistent. Consequently, each of the critical components is a matter of degree. Even so, one should strive in training parents and therapists to achieve each of these as well as possible.

Contingent Application of Consequence

The most fundamental condition for the effective application is that the reinforcer be *contingent* (or dependent) on behavior. This means that the reinforcer is provided only if the desired response is performed, and otherwise it is not given. To change, develop, or increase a specific behavior, the reinforcer must be given when that behavior occurs. If the reinforcer is provided whether or not the behavior occurs (noncontingently), behavior is not likely to change. For example, a parent may say a child can watch TV after completing homework; that is, TV viewing is contingent on completing homework. As it turns out, the child may not complete the homework but her "show is on," and the parent allows the child to watch the show. Stated another way, TV viewing is not contingent on completion of homework at all, no matter what the parent said. This is not a reinforcement contingency that will change behavior in the desired way.

The contingent application of reinforcers is not necessarily an all-or-none matter. That is, in a sloppy program, the reinforcer may be contingent on some

Table 3.3
Essential Ingredients to Make Programs Effective

Factor	Optimal Application
Contingent application of consequences	The reinforcer is provided when and only when the behavior occurs.
Immediacy of reinforcement	There is little or no delay between the behavior and the reinforcer.
Continuous reinforcement	The behavior is followed by the reinforcer every time or almost every time it occurs during the early stages when behavior is being developed.
Magnitude or amount of the reinforcer	The higher the magnitude (greater amounts) of a reinforcer delivered after the behavior, the more frequent the response will be, unless the reinforcer leads to satiation.
Quality or type of the reinforcer	High-quality reinforcers (e.g., those preferred or those an individual would engage in frequently or as much as possible) are more effective in changing behavior.
Varied and combined reinforcers	Reinforcers combined, especially praise and tokens, can improve effectiveness over either one alone; also vary the reinforcer if possible, such as changing the praise or physical contact (pat, hug) when reinforcing.
Use of prompts	To be reinforced, the behavior must occur. To get the behavior to occur, prompts may be used in the form of modeling the behavior, providing verbal instructions, or actually helping to perform the task so the behavior can be reinforced.
Shaping	Make small demands only in developing behavior. This means reinforcing gradual steps toward the final behavior. Rather than providing 10 tokens for completing 30 minutes of homework, provide 10 for 10 minutes. After 10 minutes is consistent, then this time can be increased.
Practice trials	Ensure that there are many opportunities so the behavior or approximations of the behavior can be reinforced. If many opportunities do not occur, simulated situations can be carried out in the home. Reinforcement is provided for child behavior that the parent wishes to develop, even though this is a simulated or pretend situation.

occasions but not others. This makes a large difference in the extent to which behavior changes. Parents, teachers, and others who wish to implement behavioral programs often state that they have already used reinforcement but with little or no success. Often they are quite correct. However, the reinforcement was usually carried out haphazardly, with slight to large violations of the factors on which effective application depends. The starkest violation is delivering reinforcement contingently on some occasions and noncontingently on other occasions.

Immediacy of Reinforcement

The effectiveness of reinforcement depends on the delay between the behavior and the delivery of reinforcing consequences (food, praise, or points). Responses in close proximity to reinforcement are acquired more quickly and at a higher rate than are responses remote from reinforcement. Thus, to maximize the effect of reinforcement, a reinforcer should be delivered immediately after the desired response. If this is not done, a response different from the target response may be performed during the intervening period. If that happens, the intervening response is immediately reinforced, whereas the target response is reinforced after a delay.

As an example, children are often praised (or punished) for a behavior long after the behavior was performed. If a child straightens up his room, a parent would do well to provide praise immediately. If praise is postponed until the end of the day, it is much too delayed to have a strong impact or perhaps any impact. Moreover, a variety of intervening responses may occur, including, perhaps, messing up the room. Similarly, in classroom settings, children are often told how "good" they are when they are on the verge of becoming restless or disruptive. The teacher may say that the class was well behaved in the morning and that she hopes it will remain that way. Such praise is minimally effective because of the delay after the behavior. The primary task in a reinforcement is to "catch the person" performing the behavior and provide immediate reinforcement.

Immediate reinforcement is especially important when the target response is being developed—that is, early in the behavior-change program. After a response has been performed consistently, the amount of time between the response and reinforcement can be increased without a decrement in performance. For example, in classroom settings, students sometimes receive points or privileges daily while high rates of academic behavior are developing. If a program begins with delayed reinforcement, behavior may not change at all or may change less rapidly than it would if reinforcement were immediate. After the behavior has stabilized, the reinforcers can be delivered every other day or every few days without a deleterious effect on performance. In fact, after a behavior has been well developed, it is desirable to change from immediate to delayed reinforcement so that the behavior is not dependent on immediate consequences. Many consequences in everyday life (accomplishments, wages, grades, and fame) follow long after a series of responses has been completed.

Continuous Reinforcement

When a behavior is being developed, performance is much better if the behavior is reinforced each time it occurs. Administering the reinforcer every time the behavior occurs is referred to as continuous reinforcement. This is distinguished from intermittent reinforcement, which is provided less than every time. Human and animal research are rather clear on the effects of these schedules.[1] When a behavior is being developed, continuous reinforcement is very important. Like other factors mentioned in Table 3.3, departure from this standard is not as serious after the behavior is developed and becomes stable.

In everyday settings such as the home, it is not realistic to ask the parent to reinforce the behavior every time. For example, if the child complies with a request or does not have a tantrum when told "no," it is likely that the parent will not reinforce these responses each and every time. The parent has more to do than hover over one child (among a few children) or to remain in the room with the child every moment. Continuous and intermittent reinforcement are a matter of degree, ranging from 100% to 0; that is, the parent may reinforce the behavior whenever it occurs or most of the time (e.g., 90% of the time) rather than rarely (e.g., 10% of the time). Performance is a direct function of this percent. Thus, in training parents to develop behavior in their children, continuous reinforcement is very important.

There are important and useful differences between continuous and intermittent reinforcement. A behavior developed with continuous reinforcement is performed at a higher rate than a behavior developed with intermittent reinforcement. Thus, while a behavior is developing, a continuous or "generous" schedule of reinforcement should be used. However, once behavior is developed consistently and at a high rate, intermittent reinforcement has the advantage. During extinction, behaviors that were continuously reinforced diminish more rapidly than do behaviors that were reinforced intermittently.

Figure 3.1 plots the general relationship between continuous reinforcement and intermittent reinforcement while the behavior is being developed

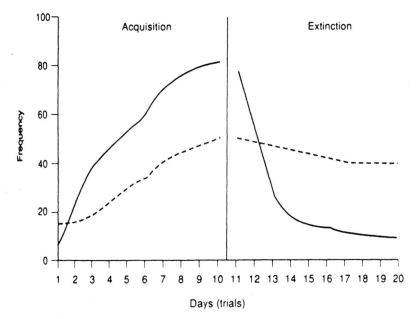

Figure 3.1 Effects of continuous reinforcement (solid line) and intermittent reinforcement (dashed line) when a behavior is being developed (acquisition of the behavior) and when reinforcement is no longer provided for that behavior (extinction). Continuous reinforcement leads to higher levels of performance; intermittent reinforcement leads to behavior that is slower to extinguish. In behavior-change programs, reinforcement can ultimately be eliminated without a loss of behavior. A step towards that is to use continuous reinforcement to establish high and consistent levels of performance and then to use intermittent reinforcement to fade the program.

(acquisition or reinforcement phase) and during extinction (no further reinforcement). As shown in the figure, the advantage of continuous reinforcement is that performance occurs at a high level while behavior is reinforced. The advantage of intermittent reinforcement is that resistance to extinction is greater when reinforcement is discontinued. Both advantages can be obtained by developing behavior with continuous reinforcement until a high rate of behavior has been well established and then, to foster response maintenance, changing the schedule to intermittent reinforcement and making it increasingly intermittent. Even when reinforcement is continued, intermittent reinforcement can maintain behavior very well. Slot machines provide reinforcement on an intermittent schedule. Sometimes putting money into a slot machine (the behavior) is reinforced (with money); many other times, it is not. Behavior is maintained at a high rate.

Magnitude or Amount of the Reinforcer

The amount of reinforcement delivered for a response also influences behavior change. The greater the amount of the reinforcer delivered for a response, the more frequent the response will be. The amount of the reinforcer can usually be specified in such terms as quantity of food, number of points, or amount of money.

Although the magnitude of reinforcement is directly related to performance, there is a limit. A reinforcer loses its effect when it is given in excessive amounts, a phenomenon referred to as *satiation*. Hence, the effect of increasing reinforcement is limited by the point at which the individual becomes satiated. Satiation is especially evident with primary reinforcers such as food, water, and sex—those reinforcers that are appetitive in nature and largely unlearned. In excessive amounts, each of these reinforcers quickly loses its reinforcing properties and may even become aversive. Of course, satiation of reinforcers is temporary. Reinforcers regain their reinforcing value as deprivation increases. Reinforcers such as praise, attention, and tokens, referred to as secondary reinforcers, are much less subject to satiation.

Quality or Type of the Reinforcer

The quality of a reinforcer, unlike the amount of a reinforcer, is not usually specifiable in physical terms. Rather, quality usually is determined by the child's preference. This has been tested by asking individuals which of two or more reinforcers they prefer and then measuring the reinforcer's value on performance (see Green, Reid, Canipe, & Gardner, 1991; Neef, Mace, Shea, & Shade, 1992). In general, reinforcers that are highly preferred lead to greater performance than those that are less preferred.

It is usually not difficult to identify highly preferred activities. Behaviors frequently engaged in indicate highly preferred reinforcers. In addition, a person's stated preference is often quite useful for identifying reinforcers. Yet, whether a preferred event will serve as a reinforcer at all or whether one event will be better than another is not necessarily related to what a person says. The effects of consequences, preferred or otherwise, must be examined directly by observing their impact. Verbal behavior (what people say) is not a substitute for nonverbal behavior (what people do).

The quality of a given reinforcer can vary. For example, praise can range in quality from high to low. Think of intensity of praise as the distinguishing characteristic. Praise that sounds matter of fact or dismissive (e.g., saying "good" in a monotone) would be low in quality and distinguished from praise at the other end of the spectrum, which is delivered with enthusiasm, a positive facial expression, high volume, and physical contact such as touching and hugging (e.g., saying Great!! With all the nonverbal cues that might accompany that). Parents usually must be trained extensively (many practice trials and shaping) to provide high-quality praise.

Not all reinforcers are equal in their effects. In relation to reinforcers discussed previously, token reinforcement is often more effective than praise in altering behavior, and both of these are usually more effective than feedback. However, there is no need to use only one reinforcer. Tokens, which include multiple backup reinforcers, and praise are often combined (and delivered when the behavior occurs) to maximize the quality of the reinforcer.

Varied and Combined Reinforcers

A parent could always provide the same reinforcer (stating "great, you did x or y," the behavior that is being praised), but it is useful to vary the reinforcer. The praise can vary from one occasion to the next in terms of the statements that are provided and the physical touch that accompanies it. This does not mean that all praise must be different. Rather, it means that reinforcer delivery tends to be more effective when the reinforcer is varied. Combining reinforcers (e.g., praise and tokens) is also usually more effective than a single reinforcer provided alone. The increment in effectiveness is not invariably a lot greater, but still it is useful.

One of the advantages of token reinforcement is that the backup reinforcers include diverse reinforcers the individual can purchase with tokens. Thus, inherent in a token economy is varied reinforcement because there are a few backup reinforcers. Still, as points or tokens are provided to the child, it is still better to provide another reinforcer (praise) along with it and to vary how this praise is delivered.

Use of Prompts and Setting Events

The factors mentioned to this point pertain to how the reinforcing consequences are administered. However, PMT and changing child (or parent) behavior are not merely about consequences. Rather, the change is achieved through altering the antecedents (A), behaviors (B), and consequences (C). Programs routinely fail when therapists or parents do not know and use their ABCs.

The effectiveness of reinforcement depends on the individual having the response in his repertoire and in fact being able to readily engage or perform the behavior. Parents often confuse knowing the response or knowing how to do something with actually doing it. Knowing what needs to be done is not the issue. Carrying out the behavior as needed is the critical issue. Antecedents (e.g., setting events, prompts) develop the behavior and consistent perform-ance by helping to initiate the behavior so it can be reinforced. For example, if a parent wants the child to clean up her room, all sorts of prompts might be used, including:

- A verbal statement right before the time the behavior is to be performed
- Walking into the room with the child and standing there
- Modeling the behavior by picking up one item
- Working with the child on the task as each picks up an equal number

These prompts help to develop the behavior. Once the child performs his part, the reinforcer is provided (contingently, immediately, etc.). It is not at all diffi-cult to remove or fade the prompts. A therapist has to emphasize this because parents often see this initial part (prompting) as unnecessary. However, con-sider this in a more complex context. Many parents of oppositional and ag-gressive children do not want their child to have a horrible tantrum when she is told no. Setting events and prompts here can go a long way to develop the behavior. During random times of the day the parent can go to the child (simulations) and say, "I am going to say, 'No, you can't go out.' This will just be practice. If you do not have a tantrum when I say this, you will earn four stars. This will be *really* hard to do, but let's see if you can do it." This en-tire sequence is an antecedent and includes some statement right before a simulated (practice opportunity) and a little challenge ("this is really hard to do"). The part that describes what behavior to do or not do (not to have a tantrum) is the prompt; the challenge is a setting event that further increases the likelihood of engaging in the behavior. These statements will greatly in-crease the likelihood of the desired behavior, which is precisely what ante-cedents do.

Again, fading and eliminating prompts are not so difficult. Getting the behavior to occur is the first task, and antecedents can play a pivotal role. In short, the effectiveness of reinforcement does not depend merely on the con-sequences. One might work on antecedents to ensure that the behavior occurs so that it can be reinforced. Early in developing a behavior, the prompted be-havior is reinforced. Over time, the reinforcer is provided with fewer and fewer prompts.

Shaping

I mentioned prompts as part of the antecedents. A comment about B, the behavior of the ABCs, is pertinent, too. Providing reinforcers for behavior may not be effective if the component behaviors are not developed. For example, teaching someone to drive a car is not just a matter of reinforcing a behavior. One has to develop the sequence of behaviors that constitute "driving." Similarly, in the home, parents often want the complete behavior (1 hour of homework, cleaning one's room completely, engaging in some other behavior 7 days a week). Assuming for a moment that these are appropriate goals, they can be approached gradually. One develops homework, for example, by reinforcing a small period of studying. This can be extended. It is not that difficult to move from 10 minutes a day to longer periods once there is reasonable consistency for the 10 minutes. There is no fixed definition of "reasonable consistency," but 8 of 10 days (weekdays perhaps, excluding weekends) might be a good definition. The parent can continue the reinforcement for 10 minutes per day but provide more points or the same amount for 20 minutes and move up slowly. All homework time would be praised, but increased time would be required to earn the tokens.

Parents intellectually appreciate the maxim "one has to crawl before one walks." However, this understanding does not translate to how they act in relation to children—or at least in relation to children whose behaviors have been enormously frustrating. Parents often believe the child can do the behavior; therefore, there is no need to shape. This is a misunderstanding of how behavior is developed. For example, I *can* do all sorts of things (e.g., exercise, eat correctly, and not emotionally abuse all my relatives). Nevertheless, I do not do these consistently. Reinforcing approximations of the behavior can increase the frequency and consistency of behavior. If someone "knows how" to carry out the behavior, this process is sped up nicely. However, shaping still may be necessary and important.

Practice Trials

Shaping focuses on behavior in the ABC analysis of how to change behavior. Another component pertains to the number of opportunities for the behavior to occur. For reinforcement to be effective, obviously the behavior must occur. Shaping is a way to reinforce approximations of the behavior and to attain the goal. Another facet of behavior pertains to the number of opportunities there are to reinforce the behavior. For example, a common concern among parents is having their children respond to "no" or to a request to do something without having a tantrum. The behavior the parent wishes to reinforce is acting calmly after the parent's request or refusal. However, the tantrums may occur "only" once or twice a day. This once or twice may be enough to challenge the parents' sanity but raises problems for changing behavior. First, there is no easy way to shape acting calmly once on the battlefield of a tantrum. Second, there are too few opportunities to provide reinforcement for appropriate behavior.

The effects of reinforcement depend on the number of behavior-reinforcement occurrences. This is not a new or perhaps even interesting concept because it reflects what we already know from life experience; namely, practice is important. In PMT, increasing the number of opportunities to develop the behavior can be accomplished by *simulating situations* in the home so they occur more frequently, so prosocial behavior can be developed, and so shaping can be used. For example, a program we frequently use in PMT in relation to practice is to develop a point system. The child is told he or she can earn points for being calm when the parent says no or asks the child to do a chore. In one case, a child was told that if he did not shout or throw things when he was told no, he would earn 5 points on his chart. He was told that his mother would practice with him during the day. We asked that she carry this out at least twice a day for the first week.

Setting events were used, that is, antecedents that change the likelihood of certain behaviors and are more general than the highly focused prompts that convey precisely what to do. Tantrums are much less likely if the situation does not involve genuine demands when a child or parent is upset. Using unrealistic simulations of the desired behavior is a fine place to begin in developing behavior. Thus, the parent chose times of the days and occasions in which nothing special was occurring at home, and she and the child were calm. The setting event or context reflects a situation in which no conflict or tantrum is occurring or likely. As the parent thought of it, she went over to the child to begin the simulation. In addition, she provided prompts, quite specific antecedent events to aid performance of the behavior.

Before the program began, the mother explained that there was a new way to earn points and described what this was. On the first occasion of actually carrying out a simulated practice, the mother went to the child and said, "OK, Bill. Now is a chance to earn 5 points. I am going to say that 'you can't go out after school,' but this is really just a practice. If you can stay here and be calm, you can earn 5 points. Remember, we are just pretending. Are you ready to try to earn 5 points?" All of this is said calmly and warmly to the extent possible. Even stating this playfully or in a gamelike fashion is quite good, because as a setting event, this will greatly reduce any chance of a tantrum. Remember, we are shaping some final behavior that will not include any of these antecedents. In any case, the mother says, "Bill, you can't go out after school. You have to stay in the house." (Then the well-trained mother whispers, right away, "OK—this is the hard part—can you stay calm?") Invariably, the child can do this easily with the specific prompts (be calm, do not throw things) and the more general setting events that govern the situation (nonprovocative situation, no real loss of some privilege). When the child is calm, the mother effusively praises the child: "That was great. You were just really calm and did not get mad or throw things. That is worth 5 points on your chart. Great job!"

The simulations can be varied by telling the child beforehand that "on some occasions, I will surprise you and just say, 'no, you can't do this or that.'" The mother then can do one of the simulated practice trials and give a wink or some other cue that this is a practice trial. This would be a way to fade prompts and setting events and make the simulations more like the "real" situations, in which favorable setting events and prompts are not present or provided. In our experience, this more sophisticated level of fading prompts and setting events is not necessary. We have not tested this, in part because the behavior we wish usually emerges without fading in this way.

At some point (e.g., a day or 2), the program can change as follows. First, the parent says, "You can earn 5 points when we practice, *but* you will earn 10 points if you are calm in a 'real' situation, one where we are not practicing." This ensures that the incentives are high for the real situation.

It is possible to avoid simulation and role play sometimes and just give the child points for acting calmly in a real situation. That is, the child may not always have a tantrum in real life, and this calm behavior can be reinforced directly without extra role play and practice. However, simulations and practice of the kind I have highlighted have a purpose I have inadequately emphasized. PMT is equally concerned with developing behaviors in the parents as it is with developing behaviors in the children. Having parents reinforce behavior under simulated conditions in the home and in situations that approximate those where they need to act in specific ways helps develop *their* behaviors. In these simulations, parents practice how to reinforce, what to reinforce, and when to reinforce, all very important aspects of PMT. If the parent is unusually great at giving prompts and praise and the child does not always have an intense tantrum, the parent might forgo simulations or many simulations at home. We err on the side of more practice for the parent and child whenever possible, given the inherent brevity of treatment (once a week for some limited number of weeks or months) and the stability of many untoward parenting practices and disruptive child behaviors.

As this program continued, simulations were reduced and eliminated within about 10 days. The child was not having intense tantrums, and the parents were no longer concerned with them. Points and praise for acting calmly were continued for another week or two, but the program came to a natural end through disuse. This sounds rather simplistic, because we have omitted other reinforcement contingencies that were involved in the program. On the other hand, this is not a very special case; the practice and effects of that practice are rather routine.

Meeting the Requirements

A great deal is known about the use of reinforcers to alter behavior. Now we know many of the circumstances and conditions of administration in which the use of such techniques as positive reinforcement will succeed, produce mediocre effects, or fail. The requirements for administering reinforcement effectively are enormously important.

As I mentioned, parents, teachers, nurses, therapists, and others in applied settings often report that they have tried to use positive reinforcement and that it really does not work. The reports are invariably correct, and the usual culprit is failing to meet basic requirements for effective delivery. That is, reinforcement is too delayed, too intermittent, and even delivered noncontingently. The reason I can note this with some confidence is that the programs, once corrected, often lead to quite different effects on behavior (Kazdin, 1983).

A useful feature of PMT is the guidelines for the therapist on what to check and how to proceed if the behavior-change program is not working or is not working well enough. Among the guidelines are the conditions of administering the program. Checking each of the factors and changing them usually is the first line of attack in rescuing a mediocre or failing program. These factors are analogous to what one does when an electrical appliance is not working. Is the appliance plugged in and turned on? It is amazing (and embarrassing) how often such a question solves the problem. The same holds for making reinforcement delivery effective. Mediocre effects usually can be controverted by changing the schedule (continuous), delay (immediacy), opportunities (number of practice trials), and other facets of reinforcement delivery. More will be said later about repairing ailing programs.

Reinforcement Techniques to Reduce Undesirable Behavior

In many situations, the major goal of the program is to reduce undesirable behavior. Indeed, parents referred to our clinic usually and understandably cast the child's problems as one of excessive, disruptive, and unruly behavior that must be significantly reduced or eliminated. The therapist shares these goals, even if they are not the only goals or even the main goals. What will be widely discrepant from the parents' views is the best way to attain these goals.

Because reinforcement is a technique to increase behavior, people often believe that other techniques are required when the goal is to decrease behavior. Hence, punishment and extinction, discussed in the next chapter, are used because they decrease response frequency directly. However, undesirable target responses can be decreased or eliminated completely by reinforcement (LaVigna & Donnellan, 1986; O'Brien & Repp, 1990). As a rule, reinforcement is the obvious intervention of choice when the goal is to increase or decrease behavior.

Reinforcement is designed to develop positive and prosocial behaviors, and this focus is invariably important. Techniques to eliminate behavior, such as punishment and extinction, even if effective do not necessarily lead to the development of desirable, positive, and prosocial behavior. Reinforcement is required to develop these behaviors. Consequently, reinforcement is central to behavior-change programs.

Overview of Special Reinforcement Schedules

There are several ways of administering reinforcement to reduce or eliminate behavior. These are not exactly intuitive to parents or, indeed, to prospective therapists. I mention the schedules briefly here to provide minimal technical background and then convey more concretely how these are translated to treatment within PMT. Table 3.4 provides the common schedules of reinforcement that can be used to decrease or eliminate behavior. Each of the schedules may be used in PMT, but they are not formally labeled as such or always explained in detail to the parent. For example, we have often decreased children's aggressive behavior by increasing the amount of time during the day between acts of aggression (e.g., providing consequences for an hour in the afternoon with no fighting with a sibling). The time can be extended to larger units (e.g., two consecutive hours or days) with shaping and special incentives. Before the program is over, the aggression is no longer present. Similarly, the goals can be

Table 3.4
Reinforcement Techniques to Reduce Undesirable Behavior

Reinforcement of Other Behavior. Providing reinforcing consequences for all responses except the undesirable behavior of interest (e.g., praising the child any time he is not having a tantrum or screaming).

Reinforcement of Alternative Behavior. Providing reinforcing consequences for a specific response that will compete with or is incompatible with the undesirable response, for example, reinforcing cooperative play of a child with her sibling in an effort to reduce arguing and fighting. Cooperative play is incompatible with and the opposite of arguing and fighting.

Reinforcement of Functionally Equivalent Behavior. Behavior serves one or more functions. In this context, function means the consequences that follow from the behavior. Functionally equivalent behavior refers to using the same consequences to support prosocial, positive behavior rather than deviant behavior. For example, tantrums, interrupting parents, and arguing receive attention from parents. With this schedule, the parents walk away from the child during these behaviors whenever possible but give attention and praise to the child when these behaviors are not going on. This closely resembles the other schedules but emphasizes use of the same reinforcer to support prosocial behavior.

Reinforcement of Low Response Rates. Providing consequences for a reduction in the frequency of behavior over time or in the period of time (e.g., minutes) in which the undesirable behavior does not occur. If a child engages in 10 episodes of some undesirable behavior (e.g., fights, throwing things, not complying), a reinforcement program is provided in which reduction in this number is shaped (gradually reduced). Tokens might be earned for reducing this to 8 per day; as this is performed consistently, the number is reduced. At the end of the program, 0 per day may receive tokens, with a special bonus for 2 or 3 days in a row with 0, and so on.

Reinforcement of Changes in Quality or Characteristics of the Behavior. Providing consequences for changes in intensity or characteristics of the behavior. A child may have very intense tantrums that include throwing things, hitting other people, crying, and screaming. Reinforcement can be provided by shaping less intense behavior, such as keeping the tantrum as is but not hitting other people; the child actually earns points or praise with the usual tantrum but without one of the behaviors. In many different programs, we have had the child hit an object rather than people or hit the air, all steps toward eliminating hitting. The child may receive reinforcement for whispering rather than shouting or screaming. Over time, usually a matter of days, the tantrum or signs of the tantrum beyond acceptable expressions of displeasure can be eliminated.

accomplished by reinforcing the total number of aggressive acts in a given day, if that number falls below some criterion. Over time, the criterion is lowered. This is not very difficult to do in practice. However, we have not usually presented this as reinforcing the behavior of a child when he or she is aggressive, but less aggressive. There are some counterintuitive features that make the presentation to the parents more difficult than changing child behavior.

Presentation to Parents

In presenting to parents the concepts of reinforcement to reduce undesirable behavior, at the clinic where I work, we focused on one superordinate term to encompass the key concept, namely, *reinforcement of positive opposites*. This is not a technical term but a simple, even though not completely accurate, way of characterizing the schedules. Positive opposites refer to reinforcing behaviors "opposite" from those one wishes to suppress.

The notion of positive opposites is designed to help convey two key points. First, part of the treatment is reorienting parents to focus on positive, prosocial behavior. Parents of children with disruptive behavior often have a frustrating history of administering ineffective punishment. Typically, the conduct problems brought to treatment have also served as a basis for escalating the level of punishment in the home. The notion of positive opposites underscores the different orientation of PMT, namely, the focus on developing positive, prosocial behavior. Even when punishment is used in PMT, it is secondary to a program that focuses on positive reinforcement.

Second, the notion of positive opposites gives parents a specific strategy to develop programs to change behaviors of their children. When parents want to change a behavior, it is often to reduce or eliminate it (e.g., tantrums, staying out late). However, even when they want to increase a behavior (e.g., homework completion, interacting nicely with one's sibling), the strategy is invariably the same: Develop contingencies that reinforce positive, prosocial behavior. Essentially, the emphasis on positive opposites gives parents a simple rule and a strategy on how to problem-solve in developing new programs while treatment is in effect and after treatment has terminated.

Examples of programs for reinforcing positive opposites that we have used frequently include praising or providing tokens to children for:

- Saying or expressing anger verbally, rather than throwing things or hitting people when they are told "no"

- Playing cooperatively with a sibling, rather than arguing while watching television
- Going to the teacher or bus driver when provoked or teased, rather than hitting the child who provokes them
- Speaking calmly to a teacher when confronted or accused

Because many of these do not occur frequently and because opportunities to practice are important, sometimes the behaviors are practiced as part of simulations, as mentioned previously. However, simulated practice is quite separate from the notion of reinforcing positive opposites. The challenge to parents is to identify what behavior to increase and what to develop in all those instances in which they began with a behavior they wish to decrease or eliminate.

General Comments

Reinforcement techniques using the schedules discussed previously have reduced or eliminated a wide range of undesirable and maladaptive behaviors in children and adults. The procedures appear to be at least as effective as various punishment procedures in their capacity to decrease undesirable behaviors. Although punishment and extinction, highlighted in the next chapter, can decrease behavior, these procedures do not train people in socially appropriate alternative behaviors. Even if punishment or extinction is used, the effectiveness of the procedures can be greatly enhanced by incorporating reinforcement for appropriate behavior into the program. Also, many ethical concerns and negative client reactions raised by punishment procedures are largely circumvented if the program is based on positive reinforcement. Given these benefits, reinforcement techniques should be used whenever the goal is to increase or decrease behavior.

A challenge in fostering the use of reinforcement pertains to the orientation and focus many individuals (parents, teachers) bring to treatment. Behaviors one wants to eliminate or reduce readily bring punishment to mind. After all, so the thinking goes, if the behavior is to be eliminated, the person ought to see that there are immediate and negative consequences for that behavior. In most instances, this orientation as implemented is doomed to failure or mediocre effects, as discussed in the next chapter. The challenge is to reorient parent thinking and, even more so, parent practices. If we want to suppress behavior, the immediate task is to identify some positive or desirable behavior (alternative, incompatible, functionally equivalent behavior) that can be reinforced. In working with parents and teachers, we often provide many practice opportunities and hypothetical scenarios in which many different deviant behaviors are discussed. The task is to identify two or three different reinforcement programs that might be used to decrease or eliminate an undesired behavior. In PMT, parents are trained to develop hypothetical and real programs to enhance their skills in doing this.

Summary and Conclusions

The most central principle for PMT is positive reinforcement. The principle is simple enough, but implementation is much more complex. There are several types of reinforcers that can be used. Food, social reinforcement, activities and privileges, and tokens are commonly used. Most PMT programs depend heavily on parental use of praise and tokens. Tokens help structure the situation for the parents as well as the child in terms of fostering consistency between behaviors and the consequences provided for them. A token program makes the contingencies explicit, public, and therefore slightly more likely to be carried out by the parent. The parents must deliver tokens (e.g., stars), which prompts them to carry out the program, to praise, and so on. Programs based on praise alone can be very effective. Yet, praise and its delivery are more difficult to monitor and more likely to fall by the wayside when parents carry out programs in the home. The explicitness of a token program and the conspicuous delivery of tokens to the child make token reinforcement preferred.

Providing reinforcing consequences for behavior may range in effectiveness from little or no change to a large change in behavior. Among the factors that determine the effectiveness are those that relate directly to how reinforcement is administered. For reinforcement to be effective, the reinforcer should be contingent on behavior, provided immediately after behavior, and given for every occurrence or almost every occurrence when the behavior is being developed. Also, the high magnitude (amount) and high quality of the reinforcer are important. Combined reinforcers (tokens and praise) and variation of reinforcers can also help. Prompts, shaping, and simulated practice trials that increase opportunities for reinforced practice contribute to behavior change as well. These many factors that influence effectiveness of reinforcement convey the challenges of PMT. Parents are not trained merely to give out tokens or praise but to do so in ways that encompass the dimensions that influence effectiveness.

Positive reinforcement can be used to decrease undesirable behaviors. There are specific schedules that have been studied in laboratory and applied settings to convey the many ways in which behaviors (e.g., fighting, screaming, throwing things, staying out late) in children can be reduced or eliminated. The many ways include reinforcement of other behavior, of alternative behavior, of functionally equivalent behavior, of low response rates, and of changes in quality or characteristics. None of these is usually discussed in PMT. Rather, parents are trained to reinforce positive opposites—prosocial alternatives to the behaviors that parents wish to reduce. Mild punishment is used as part of PMT, as noted in the next chapter. However, in all instances positive reinforcement is the mainstay of a behavior-change program. By focusing on positive opposites, parents are trained to shift their usual focus to developing and reinforcing behavior rather than punishing behavior. Also, parents have a tool they can use to generate new programs as needed, if and when new problems emerge. At the end of PMT, parents ought to be able to develop reinforcement programs, even when the goal is to suppress or eliminate some behavior.

Note

1. The topic of schedules of reinforcement is complex and an area of considerable research. The basic schedules and their effects in everyday life are highlighted elsewhere (Kazdin, 2001b).

From Principles to Techniques
Punishment and Extinction

A lthough positive reinforcement is the main focus of PMT, principles and techniques to decelerate behavior are used as well. I refer to punishment and extinction, the two topics of this chapter. Punishment techniques are often used in the home, and in the case of children with disruptive behavior disorders, they are often misused. The punishment may be harsh, frequent, and inconsistent. Consequently, even if punishment was not emphasized as a behavior-change technique in PMT, the topic must be addressed within treatment. Parents are given new skills to controvert the punishment practices in the home that may actually foster or exacerbate disruptive behavior. In a similar vein, maladaptive behaviors are often unwittingly reinforced in the home by the attention parents provide. This no doubt goes on in all homes and can be ignored without much consequence. In most homes, occasional attention to inappropriate behavior is infrequent, the deviant behavior is not that severe, and there are many other contextual influences (positive parenting practices, good modeling of many behaviors by the parents, and constructive family relations) that are likely to promote positive development. Yet, in the homes of children with disruptive behavior disorders, systematic ignoring of prosocial behavior and attention to deviant behavior are part of broader parenting practices that can foster deviance. An excellent place to intervene is to alter several practices, beginning with direct reinforcement of prosocial behavior and elimination of reinforcement for any deviant behavior. Punishment and extinction can play a critical role in treatment.

Punishment

Parents who bring their children to treatment for disruptive behaviors are often using punishment excessively. At the clinic where I work, clients often use extreme corporal punishment in the home.[1] Punishment alone, even if not especially severe punishment, is not likely to be effective in eliminating or reducing disruptive behavior and may even maintain that behavior (Patterson et al., 1992). For example, if corporal punishment is used to punish child aggression, the punishment itself models aggression and can increase subsequent aggressive child behavior. (We routinely see parents who hit their children to get them to stop hitting or scream at their children across vast stretches of space in stores, parks, and their homes to try to get the children to stop screaming.) Treatment must provide parents with alternatives that have impact and that promote positive child behavior. Reinforcement techniques addressed in the previous chapter are the central focus of the program, and the discussion of punishment in this chapter ought not detract from that. Yet, a significant part of treatment is altering how parents punish.

Types of Aversive Events and Punishment

Punishment refers to a decrease in the probability or likelihood of a response following the presentation or removal of a consequence. This is different from use of the term in everyday life, in which the focus of punishment is retribution, retaliation, inflicting pain, or providing a consequence that is undesired, whether or not it actually changes behavior. Once we focus on suppressing, reducing, or eliminating behavior, we can consider all sorts of events that might be effective, whether or not they are painful, nasty, or aversive. For example, parents routinely spank, slap, or hit a child as part of punishment in the home. Evidence that these acts change behaviors beyond the moment when they are provided is sparse, to say the least (Benjet & Kazdin, 2003). Much gentler punishment (e.g., a few minutes of time out from reinforcement) can be very effective. As part of PMT, parents are trained to de-emphasize punishment and also to use different kinds of punishment from those that may model aggression and have the many deleterious side effects associated with corporal punishment.

Commonly Used Techniques in PMT

All sorts of punishment might be used. In terms of specific techniques, three broad types can be distinguished: (a) punishment by presenting specific consequences (e.g., reprimands), (b) punishment by withdrawing events or consequences (e.g., taking away privileges), and (c) punishment by requiring some activity or effort (e.g., doing a chore). Table 4.1 highlights punishment techniques commonly used in PMT. Again, punishment is de-emphasized, so it is unlikely that all of these will be used or even that on any given day at home any one will be used.

Parents are invariably using some form of punishment in the home. The most common forms are physical punishment, reprimands, or a variation of one of the procedures mentioned in the table. It is quite easy to use one of these procedures in ways that will fail. Thus, parents often say, "I *am* using time out from reinforcement already, and it does not work." We take parents at their word. As discussed shortly, the way punishment is delivered very much dictates the effects it will have.

Table 4.1
Punishment Techniques Used in PMT

Type	Defined	Examples
Time out from reinforcement	Removal of a positive reinforcer for a period of time	Sitting in one's room or a special chair for a few minutes; not being able to watch TV for a few minutes
Response cost	Loss of a positive reinforcer or penalty of some sort	Removal of a point or token after a behavior, part of token program; loss of privilege
Completion of some activity	Some effort-based punishment that the child must perform as restitution	Engaging in an undesired chore, task, or activity (extra chore around the house)

When parents are using corporal punishment, treatment focuses on its complete elimination and on use of other procedures, usually brief time out. Time out is the most commonly used punishment in our PMT program. When parents use reprimands, we focus on changing the content of the reprimands and the style of delivery. Specifically, parents are trained to provide feedback and suggestions for what the child could have done. Reprimands do not play a central role in PMT, but they often play a central role in parenting. Parents tend to lecture their children, shout at them, and pepper statements with sarcasm or annoying rhetorical queries (e.g., "I'm glad you cleaned your room so it does not look like a pig sty anymore" or "Why can't you do your homework like your brother?"). Lectures and shouting do not foster behavior change very well. Also, reprimands can have some undesired side effects if they inadvertently attend to deviant behavior or move to nagging (repeated reprimands) that leads to escape or avoidance behavior (discussed later in the chapter).

The most critical feature is to shift parents away from punishment in general. In a typical case from our program, about midway into treatment, the child has a point program going on in the home and a time out contingency. The child can receive time out for behaviors identified in treatment, based on parental concerns. However, while the child can receive time out for some deviant or maladaptive behavior, the points and praise are being used to reinforce positive opposites. Consequently, in a typical case, the child may receive time out only a couple of times per week. The desired, positive, prosocial behavior is being actively reinforced as part of the program.

Time out from reinforcement may be difficult to do for a variety of reasons. One of them is the child's lack of compliance in going to time out. Actually, before time out is implemented, parents and children practice time out, and the child is praised for this activity. Thus, going to time out can be shaped and reinforced. When time out is actually used (e.g., for fighting), the parent will praise the child for immediately complying and going to time out as instructed. It may seem to be a contradiction for parents to praise a child while he or she is being punished. To change behavior, particularly in the early stages, one wants to reinforce all occurrences. Indeed, compliance with a parental request and compliance during a period of emotional upset (being punished for behavior) are especially important for children with oppositional behavior. Getting the child to go to time out may not be feasible, even with efforts to shape behavior. It might be the case, for example, that trying to implement time out begins a negative and protracted parent–child interaction. In almost all cases, time out is the procedure used in our PMT and raises no special problems.

When there are obstacles to using time out, we shift to response cost (small fines in terms of tokens) as an alternative. With response cost, the parent merely specifies in advance what behaviors will lose tokens, chips, or points. When one of these behaviors occurs, a point is lost (subtracted from the child's earnings). Response cost avoids the extensive parent–child interchanges and does not require the child to do something (e.g., go to a time out place).

Low-rate problem behaviors are actions that by definition occur rarely and are not part of programs to reinforce other behavior, that is, positive opposites. An occasional lie or episode of match play may be critical to provide consequences for but does not occur often enough to include in the usual point program. A punishment is selected just for this so the parent has another option. Some effortful task is usually chosen by the parent, such as a special chore that the child would not otherwise do.

At all times in PMT, punishment is an ancillary technique to augment the more dominant positive reinforcement program. Thus, many options are not provided. We use time out or response cost but not both. We are trying to change the mindset of parents, so they begin with the query, What can be reinforced to obtain the desired behaviors? and emphasize in daily actions shaping and contingent praise. That said, punishment is used as a complement to reinforcement programs and as a replacement for punishment parents may have used prior to beginning PMT. Examples of procedures used in the home are:

- Time out from reinforcement: 5 minutes in which a child sits in a special chair, room, or place in the home contingent on the behavior to be punished (e.g., tantrums, talking back, fighting with a sibling)

- Response cost: loss of one or two (some small number) of points for engaging in any one of the behaviors noted previously
- Consequence for low-rate behavior: a chore involving a special project (cleaning some part of the house, sweeping the garage; rearranging something for the parent) contingent on a behavior that rarely occurs

Absolutely critical is the use of what parents might well regard as very mild versions of these punishments. The goal is to decrease the undesired behavior and not to address some concept of justice where the seeming violation of a code of behavior is penalized in a way commensurate with someone's (in this case, the parent's) conceptualization of what commensurate would be. Justice, punishment equal to the "crime," and related topics are very important but for another book. Changing behavior does not require strong, heavy, or frequent use of punishment.

Factors That Influence the Effectiveness of Punishment

The effectiveness of punishment depends on many characteristics and is a bit more complex than the factors discussed in relation to positive reinforcement. Table 4.2 lists key factors. Most of these have studied from research on the presentation of aversive events rather than the removal of positive events. The first three factors in the table are exactly those discussed in relation to the effectiveness of positive reinforcement. Thus, to be effective, punishing consequences must be contingent, be immediate, and follow the behavior each time or most of the times the behavior occurs. I mention these quickly in passing only because each was discussed in the previous chapter and no new information is needed here to describe their use or importance.

Eliminating Sources of Reinforcement of the Undesired Response

Behaviors parents wish to eliminate may be unwittingly maintained by reinforcement. In everyday life, it is easy to identify deviant or undesirable behaviors that are reinforced. For example, in the classroom, peers probably reinforce inappropriate behaviors (e.g., clowning, teasing). If the teacher punishes disruptive behavior, this punishment would be expected to have little effect if peers continue to provide reinforcement (peer attention, laughter) for those behaviors. That is, the effectiveness of punishment is due in part to the extent to which the behavior to be suppressed is also being reinforced, even if unwit-

Table 4.2

Factors That Influence the Effectiveness of Punishment

Factor	Optimal Application
Contingent application of consequences	The aversive consequence is provided when and only when the behavior occurs.
Immediacy of punishing consequences	There is little or no delay between the behavior and the aversive event.
Continuous punishment	The behavior is followed by the punishing event every time or almost every time it occurs.
Eliminating sources of reinforcement of the undesired response	Making sure that the undesired behavior is not unwittingly associated with positive reinforcement, such as attention from others, submission, or obtaining a particular consequence.
Reinforcement of alternative behavior	Providing positive reinforcement for behavior that is "opposite" of the undesired behavior.

tingly. A reinforcer that may be maintaining an undesired behavior may be difficult to identify. For example, in the home, attention from the parent, even nagging, might be a reinforcer for the deviant behavior. It is surprising how little attention, praise, or comment some children receive on a daily basis and how much of that attention is provided for deviant rather than positive, prosocial behavior.

Reinforcement of Alternative Behavior

Punishment of some undesired behavior is most effective when it is accompanied by reinforcement for performing desirable or prosocial behaviors. This is the point raised in the previous chapter about the various reinforcement schedules and the notion of positive opposites. Aversive events of relatively weak intensity can effectively suppress behavior if reinforcement is also provided for an alternative positive response. Mildly aversive events (e.g., grimaces, statements of disapproval, or saying no) may only temporarily suppress undesired behavior. However, their suppressive effect is greatly enhanced if reinforcement is delivered for positive behaviors. For this reason, most applications of punishment in PMT include reinforcement for desirable behavior.

For example, in PMT brief periods of time out from reinforcement may be used to punish behavior of a child in the home. An example might be a child being sent to his or her room or a special chair in one of the rooms for 5 minutes for initiating a fight with a sibling. This program by itself may produce weak effects and may not work at all. Fighting with a sibling is often reinforced by submission of the sibling, and that alone on an intermittent schedule can help maintain aggressive behavior. Time out will be supplemented by reinforcement for opposite behavior (praise when the siblings play cooperatively). The addition of reinforcement for alternative behavior will greatly increase the effects of the time out procedure.

For at least three reasons, positive reinforcement is advisable whenever punishment is employed. First, reinforcement for alternative behavior increases the efficacy of punishment. Second, reinforcement can develop appropriate behaviors to displace the inappropriate behaviors that are to be eliminated. Third, positive reinforcement combined with punishment may eliminate undesirable side effects that might result from the use of punishment alone. As a general rule, whether the goal is to increase or decrease a particular behavior, reinforcement techniques should constitute the primary basis of the behavior-change program. Any of the various punishment techniques may be a valuable adjunct to reinforcement techniques but perhaps should not be used alone.

Common Parental Beliefs About Factors That Influence Punishment

Many parents have firm beliefs about what influences the effectiveness of punishment, and these beliefs and their associated practices must be addressed in PMT. In most parenting in everyday life, an odd parenting practice here or there, if it is not wildly extreme, is probably benign in the context of many positive influences of family life. Thus a bit too much shouting by one parent or a parent's high expectations, accompanied by criticism when performance criteria inevitably are not met, may have consequences in shaping personality but are diluted by many other influences. In the case of parents of children with disruptive behavioral problems, punishment may take on a much more dominant role in the home. Also, many other influences that can dilute the effects of one or more untoward practices are less likely to be present.

Several myths, questionable beliefs, and unsupported views are quite common among families we see in treatment and indeed common in child rearing more generally. Table 4.3 lists those we have encountered most frequently that usually have to be addressed in some way during treatment. Spe-

Table 4.3
Myths and Questionable Beliefs About Punishment Parents Often Bring to Treatment

1. More of a given punishment (more frequent, longer lasting, greater duration) is better than less.

2. A more intense form of punishment is needed if a less intense form does not work (hitting if shouting does not work).

3. The child ought to be upset (cry or feel bad when punished), and that is in part a mark of how effective the punishment may be.

4. Anything the child dislikes (e.g., doing homework, practice, reading) is fair game and reasonable as a source of punishment.

cifically, parents often come to treatment believing in one or all of these myths or misguided practices, and attempting to persuade parents differently does not help. For example, the therapist could easily draw on decades of research to suggest that punishment, particularly extreme forms of punishment and for extreme forms of child behavior, is not likely to be very effective in changing child behavior. However, parents are unlikely to be guided strongly in their use of punishment by what the research shows. The focus of PMT is concretely substituting new ways for parents to behave and interact with their children. The focus on what parents actually do often leads to changes in how parents think about punishment and what they come to believe. Other therapies might well focus on beliefs at the level of discourse or discussion with the parents. An implicit assumption is that changing beliefs is a necessary precursor to changing what parents do. Beliefs cannot be ignored, but changing beliefs directly, if this could be accomplished, is not likely to be helpful. Behavior changes do not necessarily follow belief changes. PMT focuses on changing parental behavior. The effect often is a change in how parents think about punishment and what they believe, but these are important epiphenomena or consequences and not the goal of PMT per se.

Beliefs About Punishment Intensity

The belief that more punishment or more severe punishment is better is understandable. Our lives run mostly on assumed linear relations so that more is invariably better than less and much more is even better than just a little more. For example, more vegetables in our diet, more exercise, and more vacation time to increase health are examples of wise practices with an empirical base. But these are not linear, and each increment in these practices does not invariably improve health.

In relation to punishment, parents often believe that more intense is likely to be more effective than less intense. Thus, if hitting a little is all right or taking away a privilege for a day is all right, hitting a lot or taking the privilege away for a longer time will be more effective. It is common for a parent to take away a privilege (use of a child's bicycle, roller blades, and computer) for 2 weeks or to cancel access to an event that was given previously (e.g., attendance at a concert that is 1 month away). The parent's view is that such punishment is likely to be more effective than something less consequential. Here the parent is assuming that a punishment that is longer in duration (taking away the privilege for 2 weeks rather than a day or 2) is better. Duration is not likely to make a difference or contribute very much to the effects of punishment. Indeed, many undesirable consequences of such punishment are likely to emerge. To take away a privilege, it is better to do it briefly and to specify positive behaviors that might earn back the privilege. Again, a therapist does not usually reason with parents about such matters; such reasoning is not very persuasive or, if persuasive, is more likely to change parent attitudes than parent behavior. Training parents to punish differently can change practices in the home, and often this translates into belief changes as well.

The assumption (or rather myth) that greater intensity leads to greater effects warrants further comment because it often emerges in the context of corporal punishment. Advocates of "spare the rod and spoil the child" often believe that a "really good" spanking is needed to teach a lesson. In general, however, evidence does not support the view that increased intensity of punishment results in increased suppression of a response, and certainly this is so in the case of spanking (Benjet & Kazdin, 2003; Gershoff, 2002).

Beliefs About What Punishment Ought to Do

In everyday life, punishment of a child serves multiple agendas, such as putatively teaching a child a lesson, conveying how important something is to society or to a parent, eliciting remorse, and providing a penalty somehow equal to the crime or offense. In all of this, having a child cry, show pain, and be very upset may seem or actually be central to the agenda. In contrast, in PMT, punishment that is effective in suppressing behavior need not be upsetting in this way and usually is not. The technical definition of *punishment* is related to the impact of consequences on rate of behavior and likelihood of behavior in the future. Being upset is not a necessary, sufficient, or desirable condition for punishment in this sense. A brief time out period (5 minutes) or loss of a point from a token economy program may be annoying and cause the child to be upset. More often than not, this is not the case. Admittedly, the minimal upset experienced could be due to the infrequent use of punishment in PMT and use in the context of also positively reinforcing prosocial behavior.

In short, being upset on the part of the child may have some purposes that are neglected here. For example, seeing a child upset for violating a rule may in some way reinforce the parent (e.g., submission reinforces aggression, relief of parental anger, relief from doing something in a situation in which we as parents often feel desperate or at wit's end). The comments do not address these important issues. Rather, the key point here is that parental beliefs about making the child upset have no supporting evidence (to my knowledge). In PMT, mild punishment can minimize the child being upset as central to effective punishment and still be part of a program that is quite effective. A goal of PMT is to train parents to interact with their child very differently from their usual way. Every belief and assumption that emerges along the way need not be addressed in depth.

Unsuitable and Unnecessary Punishments

In everyday life, the consequences selected to serve as punishing events often are misguided. The events may include activities that one would like to promote and to increase in children. Consider a familiar set of consequences designed to punish child behavior that parents or teachers may use. Specifically, as a punishing consequence for some action the parent or teacher wishes to suppress, the child may be required to:

- Work or work more on a homework assignment
- Practice more on a musical instrument
- Not go on a family outing
- Write an essay to admit that this or that behavior (e.g., taking or damaging someone else's property at school) violates a Kantian ethical imperative (e.g., "What if everybody did that?")
- Write on the chalkboard multiple times to promise some action (e.g., speaking out in class) will never occur again
- Stay after school or stay in the classroom at recess
- Meet individually with a teacher or principal

As a general rule, it is undesirable and unnecessary to select as punishing consequences those activities, situations, or people that we wish to foster as important, positive, or desirable. We want children to have a positive attitude about reading, spending time with the family, practicing a musical instrument, writing essays, and being in the presence of teachers. True, these often are neutral to negative for a period of a child's life under commonly invoked home and classroom circumstances. However, the long-term goal is to make them positive. Using such activities as punishing consequences increases the likelihood that the activities become aversive and associated with escape, avoidance, and other effects mentioned later. Some activities (e.g., doing chores or extra chores around the house) might be less of a concern as an aversive consequence in a backup plan.

Some activities or privileges might be withdrawn as punishing consequences but still entail indirect benefits that we wish to be careful about. I mentioned previously that privileges can be withdrawn for very brief periods and still be effective. Parents might withdraw a child's privilege to use a bicycle or to go to a movie with friends as part of a punishment contingency. Not using a bicycle is not in the category of using reading as an aversive consequence, because the latter is an activity we wish to foster in a lifelong way and also is related to enjoyment, education, and career activities. At the same time, using a bicycle or going to a movie may include time with peers and positive social interaction, which we wish to foster, too. If loss of these privileges is used as a punishing consequence, the period in which they are withdrawn ought to be brief (one or a few days).

General Comments

In PMT, therapists usually do not spend a great deal of time directly addressing parental beliefs about punishment. For the interest of parents, however, issues might be elaborated beyond providing the rationale for practices to be used in treatment. For example, typically we would not discuss at great length why extensive and excessive corporal punishment ought not to be used and is unwise, although this topic would be definitely mentioned. We would change use of corporal punishment through shaping and reinforcement of parent behavior. Many parents are more receptive to such discussions about the untoward consequences of excessive punishment after their behavior has been changed.

In PMT programs, punishment usually takes the form of withdrawal of positive reinforcers. Parents are trained to develop a reinforcement program (positive opposite of the undesired behavior) and then to use punishment as needed. When a reinforcer is withdrawn for a short period (time out), which does not seem to be an "intense" aversive consequence, response suppression may be dramatic. Occasionally, an increase in the duration of time out, up to several minutes, has led to greater suppression of behavior (e.g., Hobbs, Forehand, & Murray, 1978). Similarly, for response cost (loss of tokens), larger fines have occasionally suppressed behavior more effectively than have smaller fines (Kazdin, 1972). However, these findings do not justify long periods of time out or large fines because far milder consequences are quite effective.

For example, with time out, extremely brief periods, including periods ranging from 15 to 90 seconds, have been very effective in several studies. This is quite different from sending children to their rooms for 30 to 60 minutes, as parents often do, or for 8 or 9 hours, as abusive parents occasionally do. Such harsh punishments are not only unnecessary but also likely to be ineffective for the child and frustrating for the parents. Much milder punishments, included as part of a program that reinforces prosocial or positive behaviors, can accomplish the goals much more effectively.

Considerations in Using Punishment

Punishment is de-emphasized in PMT, but not as the result of philosophical views or ethical objections to punishment per se. To be sure, there are important philosophical and ethical issues involved in punishment, and these are exacerbated when children are involved. However, the strong views on the topic in PMT have an additional source. Punishment has been well studied. Evidence on the effects of punishment serves the basis for the reticence in using punishment.

Characteristic Effects

Immediacy of Effects

The way punishment works is very helpful in informing whether the program ought to be continued or used at all. One characteristic is that the effects should be evident relatively quickly (e.g., a day or 2), if the punishment is going to be effective at all. The immediate effect might not be sufficient to achieve the goal (e.g., elimination of some behavior), but some reduction in the overall rate of response will be evident. If there is no immediate effect, it is unlikely that continuation of the punishment will be effective. Clichés such as the person will eventually "get the message" do not apply here (if anywhere).

The difficulty in using punishment is that there are two types of immediate effects. The first is immediate cessation of the behavior. Thus, screaming or hitting a child usually stops the behavior that was going on at the instant of punishment. This is not the immediacy to which I refer. The second way in which immediacy is used refers to the overall reduction in the problem behavior. If one were to graph the number of occurrences of the behavior per day, punishment would show some reduction in the overall rate on the first day or 2 if punishment is to be effective. If there is not an overall reduction in rate that is evident early in the program, one ought to discontinue the contingency or supplement the contingency with another program (e.g., increased opportunities for reinforcement of the positive opposite).

Punishment when used alone often has little effect or short-lived effects. Immediately, compliance or suppression of behavior is achieved, but no overall effect of the punishment contingency is likely to be evident. Parents often realize this—that is, they cognitively understand and draw this conclusion—but this is not a basis for changing their own behavior.

Adaptation to Punishment

There can be an adaptation to punishment in the sense that it can readily lose its effects over time. If we charted the rate of behavior, we might find that punishment is working on the first few days but that over time the undesirable behavior may return to its original level. Even though the punishment is still in effect, the effects attenuate. There is not always an adaptation in which punishment loses its effects in this way.

The adaptation and loss of effectiveness of a specific punishment contingency can lead parents in a natural way to increases in intensity of punishment (e.g., from screaming, to hitting, to severe hitting and abuse). The adaptation is likely to continue on the part of the child, and the effects are likely to be immediate suppression of behavior but no overall influence on the rate of responding. This can lead to bizarre and harsh practices from everyone's perspective; namely, the parent is punishing often and severely, and there is no evident change in child behavior. Most likely, the immediate reinforcement (negative reinforcement) of punishing a child (i.e., termination of the child's aversive behavior) maintains these parenting practices even though parents often realize that the punishment is not working.

Recovery After Punishment Is Withdrawn

The discussion to this point has focused on the effects while punishment is in effect. If a punishment contingency is stopped, the punished behavior can easily return to its original level. Recovery is likely to occur when punishment has not completely suppressed the response while the contingency was in effect and when reinforcement has not been used to develop an alternative response. The emphasis on developing positive opposite behaviors derives in large part from the importance of substituting positive prosocial behaviors for those behaviors to be suppressed. Indeed, positively reinforcing behavior incompatible with the to-be-suppressed response can redress the concerns noted here about adaptation to punishment and recovery of the undesired behavior.

Punishment Traps for Parents

There are "natural" but rather unfortunate punishment traps for parents. I call them natural only to emphasize that they are inherent in the use of punishment and that they emerge from no ill will or intent. Two salient traps are particularly noteworthy. First, parents' use of punishment is invariably reinforced. This is negative reinforcement, which is defined as termination of an aversive state or situation contingent on some behavior. The aversive state or situation is something the child is doing or not doing (e.g., fighting with a sibling). The parents engage in some behavior (screaming at or hitting the child). The aversive state ends immediately. This is negative reinforcement of parent behavior. That is, the reinforcement (child cessation of the behavior) is immediate, contingent on parent punishment of the child. Punishment is very effective in this instant, that is, in stopping the behavior. The difficulty is that the punishment does not usually influence the child's rate of behavior overall, even though the problem may have ended momentarily. The trap for parents is that this negative reinforcement controls their behavior and is likely to increase their punishment of child deviance in the future. Parents' "realization" of this is not very effective as a way for changing this. The reinforcement operates on their behavior rather directly. So, one trap for parents is the reinforcement that punishment provides, even though the long-term effectiveness of punishment is likely to be weak if evident at all.

Second, punishment often leads to escalation of punishment. Because the child adapts to punishment, the punishing consequence often loses its effectiveness quickly, which can lead parents to increase the intensity of their punishment. In a sense, the child unwittingly shapes parents into more intense punishment. Thus, a reprimand may move up an intensity scale to screaming and then shift into physical punishment. One slap or hit can move to a beating and so on. Indeed, research on spanking indicates that spanking occasionally shades into or is mixed in with physical abuse (e.g., use of objects) (Gershoff, 2002). Among families that spank, occasionally escalation occurs to move this up a degree of severity.

Punishment does not invariably lead to escalation. Sometimes parents simply give up or tune out, and child deviance goes unchecked with no effort to effect changes. At the clinic where I work, this can be evident when parents refer to emergency services or the police for uncontrollable behavior of the child in the home. Parents take the child to the emergency room of a hospital or summon the police for behaviors that hardly warrant this level of intervention (e.g., uncontrollable tantrum but no danger, child not listening to a parent and getting into an argument). Parents sometimes feel desperate and helpless in relation to the management of their children. The immediate, emergency interventions are not likely to change child behavior at home. They do convey how parents can escalate the level of consequences in the face of understandable desperation.

Side Effects

Reticence in using punishment might be easily justified on the basis of characteristic effects noted previously. However, the side effects raise their own concerns. Punishment can have all sorts of side effects, as highlighted in Table 4.4. As a cautionary note, these side effects may occur in very mild doses from sporadic punishment in everyday life but are not likely to become enduring problems. Children who are generally functioning well in families that are functioning well have all sorts of positive influences operating on child behavior and punishment may play a very minor role. In the homes of children with disruptive behavioral problems, punishment is likely to be much more common and the side effects more worrisome.

The professional would like to eschew punishment or use punishment only minimally because of these side effects. Consider just the first two side effects. Essentially, individuals and situations associated frequently with punishment, take on aversive properties very much like the comments noted on stimulus control in chapter 2. Individuals who are punished will try to escape from and avoid the individuals (e.g., parents, teachers) and situations that are associated with aversive stimuli. Some parents and teachers are very frequently as-

Table 4.4
Negative Side Effects That Can Emerge with Punishment

Emotional Reactions. Undesirable emotional reactions such as crying, anger, and outbursts. These concomitant effects are not essential ingredients for punishment to be effective. They are undesirable because they can lead to other effects noted below.

Escape and Avoidance. If a situation is aversive, an individual can terminate the aversive condition by escaping. Successful escape from the situation is negatively reinforced because it terminates an aversive condition. Even if the punishing event is only mildly aversive and too weak to suppress behavior, it may still lead to escape behavior. This is undesirable because usually one wants to keep the child in the situation (home, classroom) where behavior can be promoted.

Aggression. The punished individual will aggress toward the punishing agent. Attacking the agent may remove the source of aversive consequences, the parent.

Modeled Punishment. The punishing agent models (or provides an example of) certain behaviors, namely, the use of aversive control techniques that the punished individual may learn. If a parent uses physical punishment with a child, especially harsh punishment, the likelihood that the child will engage in physically aggressive behaviors increases.

Perpetuation of Punishment. Use of punishment (by the parent) is usually reinforced in the person who administers it. Punishment usually results in rapid (though temporary) reduction of the target response. This means that punishment is likely to be perpetuated, used often, and used more. That use increases the likelihood of the side effects noted above.

sociated with aversive antecedents (commands, nagging) and consequences (reprimands). Even weak and ineffective consequences that will not change the behavior that is to be punished can lead to escape and avoidance. As a general rule, we do not want children to escape or avoid parents and teachers or to consider them aversive, which would decrease children's time in their presence and diminish their influence on child behavior.

Side effects other than escape and avoidance are no less troublesome. It has been known for some time that the more children are hit by their parents, the more these children hit others (e.g., fighting peers) outside the home. Ironically, corporal punishment of children, at least among children with disruptive behavioral problems, is often used as a consequence for the child's fighting. The irony is that hitting children is likely to increase child aggression. More generally, what parents do in the home models behavior that influences what their children do. Fighting is merely one bad example of what can happen on account of corporal punishment by the parents.

Source of Controversy

Punishment raises special ethical, legal, humanistic, and value issues because of the aversive nature of the interventions. Questions are raised about whether punishment techniques ought to be used in principle, apart from their effects; whether they are necessary to use, given alternative procedures; and, if they are to be used, at what point, when, and with what procedures (see Repp & Singh, 1990). These controversial issues rarely emerge in PMT because punishment is mild, part of a positive reinforcement program, and infrequently used. The relatively mild punishments (e.g., 5 or 10 minutes of time out) stand in sharp contrast with those punishments evident in everyday life.

Parents who bring their aggressive children to treatment rarely object to punishment procedures used in PMT. Indeed, when they do object, invariably it is in the direction of wanting to use more punishment or more severe punishment than what is incorporated into PMT. Before coming to treatment, parents may have come to adopt a punishment mindset. Controlling their children's conduct problems has been difficult, and in the parents' efforts to restrain deviance, punishment has increased; deviant behavior is "caught," criticized, and heavily punished whenever evident. This is understandable and eventually is altered with treatment. However, this punishment mindset is evident as families come to treatment. As a single mother at our clinic noted when we were developing a token program for her child, quite early in treatment, "This is fine, but I can't wait until we get to the punishment part!"

An important source of controversy pertains to whether punishment is needed at all to achieve behavior change. Severe behavioral problems such as self-injurious behavior (e.g., head banging) and aggression can be eliminated without relying on aversive procedures (Pelios, Morren, Tesch, & Axelrod, 1999; Sturmey, 1996). Such research has had important implications for treating children and adults, especially in institutional settings, where individual rights, consent, and the least restrictive and invasive procedures are central concerns (Kazdin, 2001b). Aversive procedures are not necessarily needed at all, and when they might be beneficial, very mild procedures can be used as an adjunct to a reinforcement program.

In PMT, the concerns are slightly different, and the question is not what can be accomplished without any punishment. Parents who bring their children to treatment for aggressive and antisocial behavior are already using punishment in the home. Indeed, these practices may be contributing directly to the child's problems (Reid et al., 2002). A central task of PMT is to redirect the parents to focus on positive reinforcement as a way of developing prosocial behavior and to use milder but more effective punishment (e.g., brief time out with positive reinforcement for incompatible behavior). Punishment usually is an important focus because it is already used in the home and parents often ought to reduce their reliance on it.

Guidelines: When and How to Use Punishment

Punishment is a procedure to be used cautiously for many reasons, including its checkered effects on performance, the potential side effects, and the ethical issues (see Kazdin, 2001b). Many of these issues are skirted in PMT because punishment plays a secondary role and the types of punishment used are quite mild, such as loss of a point or a brief time out. As a general rule, punishment can be used as part of a larger program based on positive reinforcement. It might well be that positive reinforcement alone alters the behavior that needs to be reduced or eliminated. Even if this is not the case, positive reinforcement ought to be emphasized. Brief and mild punishment can be very effective when added to a strong reinforcement program.

Even though reinforcement techniques present viable alternatives to punishment, in certain situations punishment will be useful, required, and possibly even essential. First and perhaps most obviously, punishment is a viable alternative when the inappropriate behavior is physically dangerous to oneself or others and some immediate intervention is required to suppress responses before the relatively delayed effects of reinforcement and extinction might operate. In the home, sometimes an intervention is needed to stop the behavior immediately, and whether the effects are enduring or produce a side effect or two takes on a lower priority. This rationale is never a justification for harsh or abusive practices. Removing the person from the situation (time out) will serve the purpose.

Second, punishment is useful when reinforcement of a behavior incompatible with the disruptive behavior cannot be administered easily. For example, if a hyperactive student is literally out of his or her seat all of the time, it may be impossible or unfeasible to reinforce in-seat behavior. Punishment (e.g., response cost along with shaping) may be helpful in initially obtaining the desired response. Eventually, punishment can be faded or perhaps eliminated completely, with increased reliance on shaping with positive reinforcement.

Third, punishment is useful in temporarily suppressing a behavior while another behavior is reinforced. This may be the most common application of punishment in the home. Mild forms of punishment (e.g., mild reprimands, brief time-out durations, and small penalties or costs) usually are sufficient to suppress behavior as long as reinforcement for alternate responses is provided. Indeed, we have known for some time that very mild punishment can enhance the effectiveness of reinforcement (e.g., Bierman, Miller, & Stabb, 1987; Pfiffner & O'Leary, 1987). Mild punishment procedures that might not be effective on their own can become effective as part of a program involving reinforcement for positive, prosocial behavior.

Fourth, punishment is a required focus of PMT because of what parents are doing in the home to discipline or punish the behavior of their child. Often more severe and less effective punishment techniques are being used (e.g., corporal punishment, locking the child in a room, withdrawal of activities for extended periods). Punishment techniques are included in PMT to develop more effective and less aversive ways of disciplining children. Thus, at the clinic where I work, we routinely "replace" corporal punishment with time out from reinforcement or "replace" excessive isolation that the parents call time out (e.g., 1 or more full days locked in the child's room) with a brief time out period (5 minutes without being locked up). Harsh parent punishment practices can exacerbate child deviance. Consequently, punishment is a theme in treatment, even though the procedures to change the child do not rely very heavily on punishment practices. Indeed, in most programs, the net amount of punishment (number of times some aversive consequence is delivered to the child) is greatly reduced with PMT.

It should be clear that the best use of punishment in PMT is as an ancillary technique to accompany positive reinforcement. Usually, punishment will suppress undesirable responses but not train desirable behaviors. Reinforcement is essential to develop appropriate behaviors to replace the suppressed behaviors.

Extinction

Extinction refers to withholding reinforcement from a previously reinforced response. A response undergoing extinction eventually decreases in frequency, ideally until it is eliminated. In PMT, extinction is relied on as an ancillary technique. The primary reason for addressing extinction at all is that parents (teachers, peers) in everyday life often attend to deviant behavior, and their attention may serve as a reinforcer for the behavior. Consequently, parents are alerted to extinction, and they practice not attending to deviant behavior to be sure that it is not unwittingly reinforced.

In many parent–child interactions, the parent may say that the child is "only doing the behavior for attention." This phrasing suggests that there is something rational, conscious, and volitional about the child's actions. In this sense, the phrase is misleading. It is rare that such volitional control would be evident or that the child could invoke this in a conscious or calculated fashion. On the other hand, many behaviors in fact *are* maintained by attention. The phrase is accurate in noting that feature but inaccurate by putting the source of responsibility in the child. If attention is in fact maintaining the behavior, the responsibility falls to those in contact with the child rather than to the child. Cessation of the attention is likely to lead to extinction.

Use in PMT

Extinction by itself is not a very potent behavior-change technique in real-world settings, in part because of the difficulty in identifying the reinforcer maintaining the behavior and controlling its delivery. In fact, several reinforcers (e.g., attention from others, submission of a victim, getting the consequence one wishes) may maintain a behavior. Difficulties in extinguishing behavior and the characteristics of the extinction process, discussed later in the chapter, are the reasons extinction is used in conjunction with positive reinforcement. As with punishment, positive reinforcement is provided for behavior that is opposite the one the parent wishes to decrease or eliminate.

In PMT, parents are trained in a session referred to as attending and ignoring. This session amounts to training in attention, praise, and positive comments for prosocial behavior and in no longer providing attention for deviant behavior (e.g., tantrums). It may not be intuitive to note that a parent arguing with a child during a tantrum could actually be serving as a reinforcer. This seems counterintuitive if one confuses reward (something subjectively liked) with a reinforcer (a consequence that can increase the likelihood of a behavior it follows). Parents in PMT are trained to ignore annoying behavior whenever possible and to attend to positive behavior. Specifically, parents turn away or walk away from deviant behavior and as soon as possible attend to and praise prosocial behavior, compliance, or a positive opposite.

Mentioned in the previous chapter was reinforcement of functionally equivalent behavior. This amounts to identifying a reinforcer and making sure it follows appropriate rather than inappropriate behavior. While PMT increases the parent's use of contingent attention and praise, much of treatment redeploys attention so that it is shifted to prosocial behavior from deviant behavior.

Table 4.5
Factors That Influence the Effectiveness of Extinction

Factor	Optimal Application
Previous schedule of reinforcement	The extent to which the behavior one wants to eliminate has been reinforced in the past influences the effects of extinction. It is more difficult to reduce a behavior previously maintained by intermittent reinforcement.
Identifying the source(s) of reinforcement of the undesired response	Hypothesizing what the reinforcer might be so the connection between the behavior and that reinforcer can be ended. If the behavior is performed in the presence of one individual or in one setting rather than another, this might help to identify who or what might be providing the reinforcing consequences.
Eliminating sources of reinforcement of the undesired response	Making sure that the undesired behavior is not unwittingly associated with positive reinforcement, such as attention from others, submission, or obtaining a particular consequence. It is possible that eliminating one source of reinforcement (parent attention) will still leave another source of reinforcement maintaining behavior (e.g., submission of a sibling)
Reinforcement of alternative behavior	Providing positive reinforcement for behavior that is the "opposite" of the undesired behavior. If the behavior to be extinguished was associated with a particular reinforcer (e.g., attention), redeploy the attention so it occurs after a positive behavior (reinforcement of functionally equivalent behavior).

Factors That Influence the Effectiveness of Extinction

To this point, I have mentioned that ignoring behavior leads to its reduction and elimination. I lied. As with reinforcement, the effectiveness of extinction depends on many characteristics. Extinction can be a challenge because identifying and controlling delivery of the reinforcer are often difficult. Table 4.5 lists key factors on which the effective execution of extinction depends. I will comment only briefly on these because they are quite similar to the factors highlighted earlier in relation to delivering punishment.

The main issue in the effective use of extinction is identifying the reinforcer for behavior and then ensuring that this reinforcer is no longer provided.

In principle, this can be quite complex. Consider just three of the complexities. First, the behavior may be reinforced intermittently so that the reinforcer is not present most of the time and cannot be easily identified. For example, the attention provided to a tantrum or yielding to a child so he gets something he is whining about may only occur intermittently. On some occasions, one would not see any consequence provided. Reinforcement on some occasions but not others is intermittent reinforcement and can maintain behavior.

Second, some behaviors (e.g., head banging) are reinforcing by themselves; that is, the stimulation can serve as a reinforcer so that reinforcers provided by other people are not very much involved. Other behaviors generate their own rewarding consequences. For example, hitting a peer, taking a toy away, or intimidating someone is reinforced immediately by the reaction of the victim. Those reinforcers are very difficult to control.

Third, because behaviors can be maintained by more than one reinforcer, control of one may have little or no effect. For example, in a classroom setting, disruptive behavior can be inadvertently reinforced by teacher and peer attention. Removing teacher attention can have no impact because the peer attention alone is sufficient. One cannot assume that merely ceasing attention to a behavior is sufficient to decrease the frequency of the behavior.

In practice, and specifically in PMT, extinction is much easier than these complexities suggest. An assumption is made that parent attention is probably reinforcing behavior. Having parents provide copious attention for prosocial behavior and for positive opposites will be fine. The backbone of the behavior-change program is a reinforcement program, and so merely ensuring that key deviant or disruptive behaviors are not attended to usually is not sufficient to effect significant change.

Considerations in Using Extinction

Characteristic Effects

Gradual Reduction in Behavior

Although extinction effectively decreases and often eliminates behavior, the process of extinction is usually gradual. Unlike punishment, extinction typically does not result in an immediate response reduction. (Remember, if punishment is going to work at all, some signs of immediate change are likely, even though these may not be dramatic or of practical significance.) Rather, during extinction, several unreinforced responses may occur before behavior begins to decline. When the undesirable behaviors are dangerous or severely disruptive, the delayed effects of extinction can be deleterious to the individual or to others. Because the process is so gradual, there is also the prospect that the behavior will be accidentally reinforced, which would slow extinction greatly because of the intermittency of the reinforcement. For example, ignoring bedtime tantrums can readily decrease and eliminate the tantrums. Yet, accidental attention (reinforcement) if the parent attended to the tantrum (went in the room, visited, allowed the child to get up "just this one time") as the tantrums are decreasing in intensity and duration could delay the process.

Extinction Burst

At the beginning of extinction, the frequency of a response may become greater than it was while the response was being reinforced. *Extinction burst* refers to an increase in responding at the beginning of the extinction period. Thus, the bedtime tantrum, from the previous example, might get much worse for a day or two before it begins to taper off and cease. The increase is temporary but can be a problem if the behavior is severe or difficult for others to tolerate. Thus, during a burst of responses, there is a greater likelihood that others will provide reinforcement for the behavior. For example, a young child may have tantrums when going to bed. Understandably, the parents may attend to the child, try to calm the child, and even allow the child to stay up a little longer in an effort to end the tantrum. Assume that the parents now begin an extinction program and no longer provide attention and other reinforcers to the child. If a child's tantrum becomes worse (extinction burst) when parents systematically ignore the behavior, this is a "good" sign in the sense that extinction is probably working. Even so, it is understandable if the parents give in to the child and provide attention and comfort. Parents may not be able to tolerate the more severe tantrum and not wish their child to be so upset. On the other hand, when they provide attention, they increase the probability of intense tantrums because attention is provided when the behavior is worse than usual. To the parents, of course, extinction may appear to be failing because the behavior has become worse. However, the effects of extinction are merely beginning.

It is likely that reinforcement during a burst of responses is a basis for undesirable behaviors often seen in children, such as protracted whining and excessive demands for attention. Parents, teachers, and others who may be involved in the extinction program ought to be forewarned of the possibility of a burst of responses so that they do not overreact to a temporary increase in behavior. An initial burst of responses does not always occur. However, when it does occur, the possibility of reinforcement (e.g., parent attention) adds to the risk in relying on extinction in the absence of other procedures.

Spontaneous Recovery

After extinction has progressed and behavior is declining systematically, the undesired response may temporarily reappear, even though it has not been reinforced. The temporary recurrence of a nonreinforced response during extinction is referred to as *spontaneous recovery*. When a response recovers during extinction, its strength is ordinarily less than it was prior to extinction. For example, if a child's tantrums are ignored, the frequency of tantrums will probably decrease over time, possibly after an initial burst of responses. However, a tantrum may occur after extinction has progressed for some time. Such a tantrum is likely to be of a lower intensity than that of the tantrums during baseline. As with extinction burst, a major concern with spontaneous recovery is that the response will be accidentally reinforced. Spontaneous recovery occurs after several responses have not been reinforced. If reinforcement is provided, it follows a long series of nonreinforced responses. This is tantamount to a highly intermittent reinforcement schedule, which may further increase resistance to extinction. If extinction continues and no accidental reinforcement occurs, the frequency and intensity of the spontaneously recovered response decrease. It is important to realize that the spontaneous recurrence of a response during extinction does not necessarily reflect the ineffectiveness of the procedure. Such recurrences often characterize the extinction process.

Side Effects

Another characteristic of extinction is that the cessation of reinforcement may result in "emotional responses," such as agitation, frustration, feelings of failure, rage, and aggression (Lerman, Iwata, & Wallace, 1999). Apparently, the transition from positive reinforcement to extinction is aversive and may lead to side effects similar to those evident with punishment. There is no need to elaborate these here because of the prior comments, but it is useful to convey side effects of extinction in everyday life. For example, instances of emotional reactions in response to extinction abound in everyday experience. After individuals place money into a malfunctioning vending machine (reinforcement such as a can of soda is no longer delivered), statements of anger, swearing, and aggressive attacks on the machine might be evident. In the context of athletic performance, instances of emotional reactions can be seen as side effects of extinction. Individuals who have experienced repeated reinforcement of certain responses may view the cessation of such reinforcement as a failure. When an athlete performs poorly, for example, he or she may swear, express feelings of failure, and throw something (e.g., tennis racquet, hockey stick) to the ground in disgust. The notion of a "poor loser" signifies a person who engages in emotional behavior when his or her responses are not reinforced in a contest—that is, when he or she loses.

Side effects and other characteristics of extinction are not invariably present. Indeed, there is little research to help identify when the various characteristics (e.g., burst, recovery) are or are not likely to occur. However, guidance can be provided on the use of extinction. Providing positive reinforcement for opposite or incompatible behavior to the behavior undergoing extinction can alter all of the characteristics. The reduction of behavior may be sped up, and the burst, recovery, and side effects are less likely.

Guidelines: When and How to Use Extinction

Extinction is quite useful in PMT when parents report or it is clear from observations of parent behavior that attention is likely to follow some undesired behavior in the home. In PMT, one usually begins with a reinforcement program early in treatment to ensure that positive, prosocial behaviors are developed in the child. As part of this, parents learn how to praise better over time. The therapist shapes parent behavior to address all the factors that influence the effectiveness of reinforcement delivery, as discussed in the previous chapter. In this context, parents learn to ignore inappropriate behavior to which they may have previously attended. This is accomplished without the therapist or parent being very certain that attention was in fact actually involved in maintaining the behavior.

If a behavior does not respond to the reinforcement program (e.g., tokens, praise) supplemented as needed with mild punishment (e.g., time out, response cost), then a therapist might well look into what might be reinforcing the behavior and ought to be better controlled. These issues rarely emerge in PMT with conduct disorder, at least in the experience of our clinic. The task is to get parents to attend to positive prosocial behavior and to ignore, whenever possible, the child's undesirable behavior. When this is done carefully and reasonably well, the effects can be rather dramatic.

Summary and Conclusions

In PMT, parents are trained in how to apply punishment and extinction. It is important to underscore that the treatment begins with and emphasizes positive reinforcement. Punishment often is a critical focus in the context of treating disruptive behavior disorders because parents may be using harsh or abusive corporal punishment and/or punishing excessively. These practices can be altered with PMT.

As used in PMT, punishment consists of relatively mild procedures that are added to complement a reinforcement program. Brief time out periods, loss of tokens, removal of a privilege, and completion of some chore are commonly used. Mild punishment given periodically can enhance the effects of a reinforcement program. It would be rare that punishment would be the core feature of a program. Punishment contingencies by themselves without reinforcement are not likely to be very effective or effective for very long, in light of the characteristics of behaviors undergoing a punishment contingency without reinforcement, as noted previously. Also, the prospect of untoward side effects of punishment was discussed.

Extinction in the context of PMT consists of training parents in how to ignore behaviors that they may unwittingly reinforce by merely providing attention or comment. Like punishment, extinction is rarely used as a stand-alone procedure to alter some child behavior. There is good reason for this in light of key characteristics of extinction (e.g., very gradual change in behavior) and factors related to its effective application (e.g., difficulties in controlling delivery of the reinforcer). Extinction is introduced in a session that focuses on attending and ignoring. Parents are challenged in role play situations to ignore those behaviors of their child to which they have attended. Training emphasizes delivery of praise and attention for positive opposites.

The complexities of punishment and extinction I have highlighted are diminished in significance from the standpoint of treatment by the general guideline; namely, mild punishment and extinction are quite fine as adjuncts to a positive reinforcement program. In PMT, a positive reinforcement program in the home is initiated early in treatment and serves as the superstructure onto which other contingencies can be built.

Note

1. Corporal punishment is hitting a child, and it is distinguishable from physical abuse. Spanking a child for misbehavior would be the usual example of corporal punishment. Abuse usually is defined as more extreme instances of corporal punishment in which objects other than the hand (e.g., belts, paddles) are used and there may be marks (e.g., bruises, burns) or physical injury. The definitions of corporal punishment and physical abuse are not fixed in principle or in practice. For example, parents who spank may occasionally introduce into their punishment procedures that are physically abusive (Gershoff, 2002). In the homes of children with conduct disorder, punishment often is excessive. Harsh punishment (e.g., extreme loss of privilege) and corporal punishment may be provided often.

Characteristics of Treatment

The previous two chapters reflect movement from the more abstract (principles) to the concrete (intervention techniques). This chapter continues in this direction by focusing on what is done in treatment and how treatment is implemented. The treatment manual at the end of the book conveys actual dialogue, statements, and materials used in the sessions.

Treatment Foci and Goals

The primary goals of treatment are to change the referral problems and adaptive functioning of the child and to change parent behavior and parent–child interaction. The priority of these goals and how they are achieved vary over the course of treatment. Also, the goals may not act in concert, so that a given point in time, the priority of one of these is clearly emphasized over the other. For example, the child's referral problems may include screaming, hitting, and throwing objects (e.g., scissors, dishes, books) at parents, siblings, or teachers, running away, and firesetting. Treatment will focus on these problems—and relatively soon into the treatment process. Yet these referral problems are not likely to be the initial focus in the first session or two of PMT. If the child or others in the child's life are in danger because of the child's aggressive behavior, then hospitalization may be required. In our own work, we have had young children who showed several severe presenting problems, such as attempting suicide, trying to drown or suffocate a younger sibling, and stabbing a sibling on multiple occasions. In such cases, of course, urgent attention is needed (evaluation, emergency visit, inpatient treatment), and outpatient treatment, whether or not PMT, may not be the place to begin. In our early work, we have begun PMT as a treatment while the child was an inpatient in a psychiatric hospital. Currently, we carry out treatment on an outpatient basis. The applications in this chapter and the manual at the end of the book are based primarily on our outpatient work.

The initial goal is to develop the parents' skills and the child's responsiveness to the parents' skills. To ensure that the programs are effective, changing the child's presenting symptoms is briefly postponed to initiate a modest (small-scale) reinforcement program in the home that develops the parents' skills and begins to restructure parent–child interaction. The initial behavior of the child addressed in the program may be minding (listening and complying with requests). Usually this behavior is somewhat problematic but not as flagrant, dangerous, or volatile as other problems to be addressed later, such as fighting or stealing.

Behaviors that evoke intense reactions from parents and children are probably not the place to begin, because the program will not be executed very well and the parents may not be able to implement even the small steps that we are trying to shape in the parent's behavior. In starting slowly and with basics, PMT bears a resemblance to training someone to play a musical instrument or fly an airplane. In the early stage of training, very basic skills are mastered, and these build to develop the repertoire. Teachers do not begin by asking students to play an intricate musical score or to take off and land in a storm. The skills ultimately required for these actions need to be developed first under easy and maybe even artificial conditions. Fortunately, the analogy breaks down because PMT does not require the years of practice that mastery of a musical instrument or piloting an airplane may require.

Parent skill development and changes in child behavior proceed in a gradual and cumulative way. For example, parents' delivery of praise is critical in PMT. How parents should deliver this praise is easily conveyed through instructions, but extensive practice is usually required to ensure that several conditions are met, as noted in chapter 3 on how to deliver reinforcers effectively. Even parents' behaviors that the therapist might wish to end as soon as they are discovered (e.g., harsh parenting practices) may require gradual approximation.

Structure of Treatment

Treatment Sessions

Content of the Sessions

Treatment is conducted primarily with parents, who directly implement several procedures at home. In our program, we provide PMT individually to families rather than in a larger group format. We have used the group format with parents who are not experiencing clinically significant problems (e.g., child-rearing classes, prevention). In our clinical work, child impairment and parent and family dysfunction usually require intense focus on the individual family; group treatment becomes more diluted.

The treatment sessions, usually provided weekly, cover operant conditioning principles and the procedures that can be derived from them. In our program, the core treatment is 12 to 16 weekly sessions, with each session lasting between 45 and 60 minutes. (The number of sessions we have used has varied across projects as we have combined some themes into one session and ex-

Table 5.1
Parent Management Training Sessions: Overview of the Core Sessions

A. Pretreatment Introduction and Orientation. This session is an orientation to the clinic and the treatment program. It provides an overview of the program, outlines the demands placed on the parents, and solicits information from the parents about the scope and nature of the child's problem and the context in which the child functions.

1. Defining, Observing, and Recording Behavior. This session trains parents to pinpoint, define, and observe behavior. The parents and therapist define specific problems that can be observed and develop a specific plan to begin observations.

2. Positive Reinforcement: Point Incentive Chart and Praise. This session focuses on learning the concept of positive reinforcement, factors that contribute to its effective application, and rehearsal of applications in relation to the child. Specific programs are outlined whereby praise and points are to be provided when behaviors are observed during the week. An incentive (token or point) chart is devised, and the parent's delivery of praise is developed through the therapist's modeling, prompting, feedback, and praise.

3. Time Out from Reinforcement. Parents learn about time out and its effective application. Delivery of time out is extensively role-played and practiced. The use of time out is planned for the next week for specific behaviors.

4. Attending and Planned Ignoring. In this session, parents learn about attending and ignoring and choose undesirable behavior that they will ignore and a positive opposite behavior to which they will attend. These procedures are practiced within the session. Attention and praise for positive behavior are key components of this session and are practiced.

5. Shaping and School Program. Parents are trained to develop behaviors by reinforcement of successive approximations and to use prompts and fading of prompts to develop terminal behaviors. Also, in this session plans are made to implement a home-based reinforcement program to develop school-related behaviors. These behaviors include individual targets in academic domains, classroom deportment, and other tasks (e.g., homework completion). Prior to the session, the therapist identifies domains of functioning, specific goals, and concrete opportunities to implement procedures at school. The specific behaviors are incorporated into the home-based reinforcement program. After this session, the school-based program continues to be developed and monitored over the course of treatment, with changes in foci as needed in discussion with the teachers and parents.

panded other themes so they form their own session or extend to two sessions.) Table 5.1 presents the core treatment sessions and their foci.

I refer to the sessions as core treatment sessions for two reasons. First, most variations of PMT include these themes and procedures in varying degrees. Second, in relation to our program, these sessions may be supplemented

6. Review and Problem Solving. Observations of the previous week and application of the reinforcement program are reviewed. Details about the administration of praise, points, and backup reinforcers are discussed and enacted so the therapist can identify how to improve parent performance. Changes are made in the program as needed. The parent practices designing programs for a set of hypothetical problems. The purpose is to develop skills that extend beyond implementing programs devised with the therapist.

7. Family Meeting. At this meeting, the child and parent(s) are bought into the session. The programs are discussed, along with any problems. Revisions are made as needed to correct misunderstandings or to alter facets that may not be implemented in a way that is likely to be effective. The programs are practiced (role-played) to see how they are implemented and to make refinements.

8. Low-Rate Behaviors. Parents are trained how to deal with low-rate behaviors such as firesetting, stealing, or truancy. Specific punishment contingencies (usually using chores as consequences) are planned so they can be presented to the child, as needed for low-rate behaviors.

9. Reprimands. Parents are taught effective ways of using reprimands. Because parents routinely reprimand children, they learn how to reprimand and how to combine reprimands for undesirable behavior with positive reinforcement for prosocial behavior.

10. and 11. Compromising. The child and parent meet together to negotiate new behavioral programs and to place these in contractual form. In the first of these sessions, negotiating and contracting are introduced, and parent and child practice negotiation. In the second of these sessions, the child and parent practice with each other on a problem or issue in the home and develop a contract that will be used as part of the program. Over the course of the sessions, the therapist shapes negotiating skills in the parent and child, reinforces compromise, and provides less and less guidance (e.g., prompts) as more difficult situations are presented.

12. Skill Review, Practice, and Termination. Material from other sessions is reviewed in theory and practice. Special emphasis is given to role playing application of individual principles as they are enacted with the therapist. Parents practice designing new programs, revising ailing programs, and responding to a complex array of situations in which principles and practices discussed in prior sessions are reviewed.

Note: The details of treatment sessions are provided in the manual at the end of this book.

with additional or optional sessions. Optional sessions are interspersed as needed to address a theme or to vary a procedure that was covered in a previous session. For example, if a reinforcement program implemented early in treatment is not working very well or if a parent's applications of prompting and praising are poor, an additional session is added to work on these areas before we move on to the next theme. Prompting and delivery of contingent praise are so critical to the program that it is not wise to proceed until the parent achieves some minimal level of performance. The skills can be worked on in an optional session that emphasizes role play, modeling by the therapist, and repeated practice of the behaviors. Further progress may be shaped through the regular sessions, but some "remedial" work may be needed. An optional session also may be added to complete the session that was given short shrift. Often this situation emerges when a parent arrives late and receives less than the usual training in the session because the treatment session cannot spill into the next patient's appointment or because the parent has to leave at a fixed time and cannot stay later. In our program, these optional or extra sessions are added in fewer than 10% of the cases, so the sessions and core treatment noted in Table 5.1 represent our treatment program.

Reinforcement as the Core Intervention

Positive reinforcement is the core focus of treatment and is emphasized in three ways. First, treatment underscores the importance of conceptualizing problem behaviors in terms of positive reinforcement. Invariably, parents come to treatment with the idea of suppressing, eliminating, or reducing problem behavior. Punishment (spanking, hitting, taking away privileges) comes to mind. The treatment emphasizes that parents ought to think in terms of positive opposites; that is, for any behavior they wish to eliminate, the task is to identify the positive behavior the parents would like in its stead. This is taught didactically but more critically is practiced with all sorts of hypothetical and real examples. For example, the parents are asked what to do if they want their child to stop screaming, slamming the door, or throwing breakable objects. The answers involve reinforcing talking quietly, closing the door gently, and handling objects with care or not throwing objects. Technically, these schedules would be referred to as reinforcing other behavior or incompatible behavior, but positive opposite is a useful term to encompass these; what the term loses in precision, it gains in ease of communication. Positive opposite is not merely an abstract way of discussing the goal and focus of the program. From the second session on, parents have programs in the home to develop positive prosocial behaviors that are opposites or the prosocial counterparts of behaviors they wish to suppress or eliminate completely.

Second, positive reinforcement pervades treatment by emphasizing parental use of praise in the home. Training parents to praise is more complex than it sounds in that parents are often hesitant to praise a behavior or to use reinforcers in general, because they feel the behavior ought not require any intervention. "After all, my child knows how to clean up his room, but he just refuses to do it" is a typical parental comment. (I say this with the authority that being a parent accords. I have used the equivalent statement as a parent scores of times.) This phrasing expresses well the parental frustration of seeing behavior come and disappear or be performed with great inconsistency. However, a key issue is whether the child performs in the way parents want from the standpoint of treatment or child-rearing goals. Positive reinforcement can increase the level of performance (change the mean) and reduce the inconsistency (variability) in performance.

Apart from parental hesitancy to praise, typically parents do not praise very well when they do praise. A vacuous, unenthusiastic statement of "good" is not likely to change child behavior. Recall from chapter 3 that several conditions must be met to make reinforcement effective (e.g., contingent application, immediate, rich schedule). Training parents to praise is a key part of treatment. Parents are trained to provide praise that is enthusiastic, that mentions specifically what the great behaviors were, and that usually includes nonverbal behavior (touching, high fives). The parent's skills in praising are shaped very carefully during PMT by repeated practice with the therapist and occasionally with the child.

Third, reinforcement plays a central role in the development of a point or token reinforcement program in the home. A token program provides the parent with a structured way of implementing the reinforcement contingencies. The tokens may include stars, marks, points, coins, and other materials, based on the age of the child, ease of delivery for the parent, and other practical issues. The tokens, paired with praise, are contingent on specific child behaviors. The many advantages of using tokens as reinforcers were presented previously (chapter 3). Among them is the prompting function tokens serve for the parent to reinforce consistently. That is, delivering something tangible (points, check marks) increases the likelihood of delivery and is more reliable than praise alone. Tokens facilitate tracking reinforcement exchanges between parent and child (earning and spending the tokens). Marks on a chart (e.g., on a refrigerator or in the child's room) mean that the exchanges are documented, if for no other reason than that the child is involved and interested in the documentation of the accumulating tokens.

The token reinforcement programs reflect an effort to shape both children's (e.g., prosocial behaviors) and parents' behavior (e.g., child-rearing practices). Over the course of treatment, child behaviors included in the token reinforcement may become increasingly complex (e.g., more provocative behaviors, more stringent demands). Also, more complex token programs may be implemented (e.g., bonuses for special behaviors in difficult situations, consequence sharing among siblings) as parent skills allow. At the beginning of each treatment session, the therapist reviews precisely what occurred in the previous week or since the previous phone contact and in many cases reenacts what the parent actually did in relation to the child.

The token program may also focus on child performance at school. Teachers are contacted to discuss individual problem areas, including deportment, grades, and homework completion. A home-based reinforcement system is devised in which child performance at school is monitored, with consequences provided at home by the parents. Teachers may also implement programs in the classroom, but this is not central to the treatment program. The school program is monitored through phone contact with the school, as well as in discussions in the treatment sessions with the parent.

Structure of the Sessions

The general format of the individual sessions is to convey content, to teach specific skills, and to develop use of the skill in the home in relation to child behavior. The sessions are likely to include one or more of the following features, which characterize treatment after a reinforcement program is implemented in the home (session 2 on Table 5.1).

- A review of the previous week and how the behavior-change program is working at home
- Presentation of a principle or theme and how it translates concretely into what to do at home (or school, other setting)
- Practice and role playing with the therapist and/or the child if the child is in the session
- Addition of some assignment or changes in the program that will be implemented for the next week

The review means beginning the sessions with a discussion of what happened during the previous week. Typically, parents bring in a chart to discuss the point program, and the therapist can see what was done during the week, whether the child earned points, whether and how often consequences were delivered, and related matters. The therapist is searching for what the parent has done well in relation to the skills taught and the program implementation. In addition, the therapist is looking for any problems that emerged, including programs that are not working or not working well, but also for behaviors the parents did well.

Whether or not there are "problems," we ask the parent to demonstrate one or two interactions during the week that happened with the child. For example, if the parent says the child cleaned up her room as asked or did not have a horrible tantrum when he was told no, the therapist responds that this is great and then asks the parent to show what he or she did. The therapist may play the role of the child as the parent reenacts what happened. This provides an opportunity to see what the parent is doing and to develop the parent's skills through shaping and positive reinforcement. For example, typically the therapist is working to increase the enthusiasm of the parent's praise and the specificity of the comments associated with the praise ("great, you did [this or that]" to the child) and to add some facet to improve the reinforcement (e.g., touching, hugging, going over to the child).

If the program in the home is not working well or clearly the parent's delivery or administration of the program is seriously wanting, the entire session may continue with this review part: role play, repeated practice, and reinforcement to develop the parent's skills. In most cases, the first 15 minutes of treatment serves as a review, and the therapist can move on. The parents are encouraged to discuss problems and departures from the program rather than just convey that all is well. The general tenor of the review part of the session is to work on the program together so that it fits within the family situation (is feasible) and is leading to behavior change (is effective).

The next part of the session is didactic. The therapist presents the principle and the procedure. The focus is on concrete examples as applied to parent–child interactions in the home. The comments and examples convey procedures (attending versus ignoring, praising) that focus on fairly universal parent–child issues (a child not listening to or defying the parent) as well as on the behaviors for which the child was referred. Conveying information (to a parent or child) is not one of the stronger interventions for changing what people actually do. Consequently, the session moves next and relatively quickly to procedures directly designed to change parent behavior.

The therapist provides examples of situations, and the parent and the therapist get up from their chairs and engage in role-play. In the initial situation, the therapist plays the role of the parent and models what is to be done, while the parent plays the role of the child. Some of the situations are hypothetical, especially early in treatment, to facilitate developing parent behaviors in relatively simple and nonprovocative situations. The situations evolve to realistic and difficult situations over the course of treatment. For this segment of the session, the parent and therapist usually take turns delivering praise in the parent role. When it is the parent's turn to play the parent, the therapist serves in the role of the child but switches back and forth within each scene or vignette from enacting the part of a child to the role of a therapist. The therapist uses prompts while the parent is carrying out the parent role. For example, in a whisper, the therapist may say, "OK, walk over to me and tell me what you would like me to do [parent does that] and the therapist says good." When that entire role play is completed, the therapist gives effusive praise and mentions specifically all that the parent did well. If the parent behavior is not very good or consistent, the therapist does not delay prompts and praise until the role play is completed. The therapist interrupts with praise to ensure the immediacy of the reinforcer for component behaviors.

Invariably, parent performance could be better. Consequently, after praising effusively what was done well, the therapist is likely to say, "OK, let's do that again, and this time add even *more* enthusiasm to your voice, and then come over and pat me as part of the praise." Parent and therapist repeat the role-play situation, and the parent is apt to be slightly more effusive. A situation is practiced twice or occasionally three times. Because multiple situations are presented in this part of the practice, there is no need to focus on just one situation. The therapist wants the parent to practice and become better but does not want to belabor one single situation and unwittingly convey that treatment will not move forward until the parent gets the point. Parent behaviors can be shaped over the course of different situations and, indeed, over the course of treatment.

In this part of the session, the therapist is very actively using prompts, shaping, feedback, and praise. Style of delivery here is critical and difficult to manualize. For example, it is important for the therapist to convey that the parent's performance could be better but not be condescending or give the message that this was just not right. In shaping, one does not suggest that performance was inadequate if it approximates the end goal. Instead, one reinforces steps along the way and does so without reservation. We have some frequently used phrases in correcting parents such as "That [specify exactly what this means] was great. To move from a B+ to an A, maybe add a little more enthusiasm. For example, you could say, '[therapist delivers the praise exactly how he or she would like it to sound].'" The therapist would not usually say, "That was good but you forgot to . . ." or just "that was good." These statements are mixed, punitive, or vacuous and do not specify and effusively praise what was done correctly or fairly well (to shape improvements). Also, the word *but* detracts greatly from any positive comments. The guideline is to praise all that is good in what was observed; model and prompt the additional behaviors that are needed, with the therapist momentarily acting as the parent; and then reenact the situation one more time. It is easy to see progress within sessions as this practice continues. A friendly, easy, and occasionally playful style from the therapist can move the parent forward (shaping). The parent usually can see the progress.

The session ends with a discussion of concrete plans to implement the procedure in the home for the next week. The parent has an assignment of adding some new procedure to the behavior-change program or crafting a change to improve the effectiveness of an existing program. The therapist and parent work this out in very concrete detail. It may include additions to a point chart and use of time-out procedures. The therapist and the parent work out what will be done and when and how the program is introduced to the child, if needed. The therapist models how to implement the procedures and what to do if they do not go smoothly. Again, there is a brief didactic part, but the focus is on actually enacting the desired parent behaviors.

Outside the Treatment Sessions

There is still a mindset in much of therapy training that treatment is conducted primarily if not exclusively in the sessions. PMT is rather clear on this point. Most of the treatment is conducted outside the session and carried out by parents or guardians. Thus, a common query about PMT is "How can you expect to change this [e.g., oppositional, conduct] disorder in 1 hour a week when the child lives in a difficult environment for the remaining hours?" The answer is that we cannot expect that result, but also that this is not the expectation of PMT. In the sessions, parents learn skills, endlessly practice how to apply them, and receive reinforced practice opportunities. These skills are then implemented outside the session and in the home.

Treatment continues outside the sessions in two ways. First, the therapist usually telephones the parent during the week and is available to the parent to address problems in relation to the program. The behavior-change program may be refined or even redesigned during these contacts. For example, if time out from reinforcement is being used, the procedure (e.g., 5 minutes of sitting in a relatively isolated place) may be invoked a few to several times a day. This is not how this procedure is supposed to be used. Punishment occupies a small place in behavior-change programs, and frequent use of the procedure suggests that the program is not working and ought to be altered. In this case, among the alternatives would be increasing the frequency of reinforcement of opposite behavior. The child might be asked to simulate (practice under artificial conditions) with the parent to engage in the prosocial behavior and then receive praise and points for behaviors incompatible with those that led to time out from reinforcement. In any case, the telephone contacts between the treatment sessions allow the therapist and the parent to address problems and refine the program as needed, rather than wait for the next treatment session to review what was not working very well during the previous several days.

Second, treatment outside the sessions is mainly the parent's provision of consequences for the child's behavior in the situations in which the behavior is problematic. Parents use antecedents, behaviors, and consequences, shaping, practice, simulations, and so on in the home. Consequently, the behaviors are developed directly in those situations in which the child is functioning. Child behavior-change programs are implemented at home but also in other settings in which change may be needed. Day-care centers and schools are the primary other places in which programs are implemented, and I shall say more about that later. Parents also extend programs to other settings: athletic fields, grocery stores, restaurants, riding in the car on errands, camp, the homes of various relatives, and any other settings in which they interact with the child.

Assessment and Evaluation of Progress

Much of what transpires in PMT pertains to or is used to assess and evaluate progress so the therapist can make changes as needed. Four ways to evaluate progress during treatment include:

1. Review of the programs at the beginning of each treatment session;
2. Role play to see what the parent actually can do in the session and does do at home;
3. Phone call contacts during the week to see how the program is working;
4. The contact sessions in which parent and child are seen together and reenact interactions from the home.

For example, during the time between treatment sessions, phone calls to the parents and occasionally to the teacher provide feedback about the progress of treatment. The teacher may report that the child has not changed at all or that the child has made an important change but the main problem requires some other focus. The feedback is used concretely to alter the behavior-change programs. Similarly, assessment of parent behavior is also informally conducted in those sessions in which the child and parent are seen together. As the parent and child reenact scenes or situations from home, the therapist sees what the parent does or can do, provides social reinforcement for behaviors, shapes better performance, and continues to practice. During these contact sessions, the therapist chats with the child about the program to see when and if points are provided, whether there has been any exchange of points for backup reinforcers, and whether one or both parents are involved in administering the program.

The different ways in which child and parent progress is evaluated are critical to treatment. PMT can be considered a treatment that includes constant mid-course corrections, based on changes in the parents and the children. This means that treatment is individualized, based on the rate of progress or lack thereof and the specific ways in which parent and child behavior are shaped to achieve the goals. The assessment used to obtain the information is integrated into treatment. Although this assessment is informal, the focus is on concrete actions rather than on global impressions about "how treatment is going."

The PMT therapist is searching for ways to shape parent or child behavior to new levels throughout treatment. Sometimes this effort involves correcting programs that are not working well. Other times it means improving programs that are working well. If behavior change is not going very well, there are scores of options for the therapist, as I discuss later. Improving a mediocre or ineffective behavior-change program during PMT is not a difficult part of treatment. The difficult part is obtaining the information the therapist needs to decide what facets of the program ought to be altered. Discussing with the parent what happened in the previous week, reviewing the point chart, role play with the parent and child, and phone calls between the sessions are designed to help the therapist make these decisions.

The treatment and informal assessment is a collaborative effort that is parallel to a coach or music teacher providing information, practice opportunities, and feedback to a student (in this case, a parent). Thus, the therapist does not view the failure of a specific program or procedure to change child behavior as the fault of the parent. Also, a parent's failure to carry out a procedure that was agreed on in the session is not viewed as "resistance" or catastrophic. What the parents *do* in the home, not what the parents say they can do, have done, or will do, is the beginning point of shaping parent behavior. Because the therapist is not in the home, a parent's verbal report must be relied on to some extent. At the same time, the assessment options, including reenactments of parent–child interactions in the sessions involving parents and child and reports from both of them, provide information that is concrete and focused.

Assessment and evaluation of progress are central to the treatment process itself and, in my view, account for some of the success of treatment. The ability to judge how treatment is progressing permits the therapist to identify mediocre effects or failure and to make changes in the program. Also, as the program begins to succeed, new behaviors of the child are incorporated into treatment, and the parent's repertoire of behavior-change techniques is expanded.

Participants and Their Roles

Minimally, PMT involves a therapist and a parent. In our program, the child is seen in some of the sessions and joins the parent and the therapist to review the program. Beyond the minimal configuration, several people may be involved. The therapist serves as the person responsible for the training. He or she functions as a coach and trainer who leads the treatment sessions. The parent or guardian is the person to be trained. Generally, we like two parents to come to treatment, but this is infrequent.

Some research has addressed the matter of whether treatment is more effective if both parents are involved. Treatment with just one parent works well. If both parents are involved, treatment outcome is not necessarily improved (e.g., Adesso & Lipson, 1981; Firestone, Kelly, & Fike, 1980). Interestingly, evidence suggests that a year after treatment, maintenance of child gains is greater among families that included both the father and mother (Bagner & Eyberg, 2003; Webster-Stratton, 1985). The reason for this is not known. The benefits may have little to do with father participation in treatment. Children in two-parent families and/or with fathers who are involved in treatment may differ in so many other ways from children in single-parent families. For example, the severity and chronicity of psychopathology in the child or parent, the socioeconomic status and economic resources of the family, and the IQ of the child, all of which also relate to maintenance of therapeutic change, might explain or account for the effects associated with father participation. These and related influences have not been ruled out or controlled (e.g., statistically) in research. In short, a host of characteristics are likely to be related to single parenthood or to single-parent participation in treatment. Many of these characteristics are known to influence treatment outcome, as discussed in the next chapter. Even so, PMT can be quite effective with one parent participating in treatment, whether from a single- or two-parent family.

Teachers or day-care workers may be involved in the program if there are problems or behaviors to be developed at school or day-care centers. During the course of treatment, the therapist calls the teacher to discuss the child's behavior. As needed, a behavior-change program is developed in which the teacher provides information to the parent daily or at least regularly. The parent provides reinforcing consequences (praise, points) at home based on child's performance at school, an arrangement often referred to as a *home-based rein-*

forcement program. This type of program takes the onus off the teacher for any special arrangements for one child in a large classroom; that is, the teacher does not have to implement a program for the entire class or monitor a reward program to deliver and exchange tokens. The school program is woven into the existing token reinforcement program that the parent already has in the home (e.g., use of backup rewards). The therapist works more closely with and has greater access to the parent than the teacher and can better help the parent fine-tune the program. The therapist is available to consult with both teacher and parents to shape child behavior (e.g., completion of homework more regularly, improved deportment). Teachers are not always available but usually are quite cooperative if a home-based program of the type mentioned here is provided. In some cases, teachers are interested in developing a praise or token program to support changes in the child. This is very helpful, of course, but not essential.

Others who may be involved in treatment represent a rather large category. A criterion for including a person in the treatment sessions is whether he or she has regular contact with the child during the day and, of course, is available for the sessions. Stepparents, divorced parents who share custody, live-in boyfriends or girlfriends, partners and significant others, grandparents who live in the home or who are responsible for child care for a few hours or more per day on a regular basis, and others who have several hours of contact with the child may be incorporated into treatment.

It is critical to be clear about inclusion of others. First, there are two ways to be included in the program. One way is to come into the sessions and participate fully. The second way is to participate in the setting (e.g., at home). The parent who does attend treatment can involve other people in the home who do not or cannot attend the sessions. Sometimes others who cannot attend treatment want to be involved; other times they do not. In our program, we take the view that involvement of those responsible for child care is desirable. This is based on findings that generalization and maintenance of behavior change are improved if the program includes varied conditions of administration (people who administer the program, settings in which the program is administered) (Kazdin, 2001b).

Participation is a matter of degree, so that those persons who do not or cannot attend treatment are involved in some way in almost all instances. Often they can be involved by engaging in minor tasks in the child's program (e.g., administering occasional praise, participating in an activity that serves as a backup reinforcer for a point program). Also, the parent who attends treatment may actually shape increased involvement of others in the home by developing a few behaviors such as helping out with the program, placing points on the point chart, or administering prompts and praise. Participation of all or indeed most people responsible for the care of the child is not essential. It would be a mistake to assume that PMT requires the family to come into the session and therefore is not very feasible or effective where this is not achieved. In most of our treatment, the sessions include one parent without others directly in the session. Others in the home who cannot or do not want to attend the sessions can be involved in the program in the home in varying degrees.

The child is last but not least among participants and warrants more extended comment. PMT programs vary on the extent to which children attend the sessions. In some programs, the child may not be seen very much and come to some of the sessions so the therapist can observe and develop parent–child interaction. In other programs, the child may come to all or most sessions where parent-child interactions are developed directly. In our program, the child is brought into the PMT sessions in selected sessions over the course of treatment to ensure that the child understands the program and that the program is implemented as reported by the parent and also to negotiate behavioral contracts between parent and child. The review of the program focuses on concrete examples of what was done, by and to whom, and with what consequences. An effort is made to identify how parent and child behavior can be improved (shaping), to practice and provide feedback to the parent, and to refine or alter programs as needed. Modeling, rehearsal, and role play are used here as well. It is helpful to develop a parent's delivery of praise, points, prompts, and time out in relation to the child, even if only through role play.

In relation to participation in treatment, PMT is often seen by parents as novel at best or discrepant with their expectations at worst. As an illustration, parents often view the locus of the problem as within the child, and hence only the child should be seen in the treatment sessions. At our clinic, we have heard endlessly, "He [the child] has the problem; why do I need to come to treatment?" It is very easy to respond to this question and its variants with a rational, cogent, and indeed evidence-based answer. Yet, that type of answer partially misses the point. Parents expect treatment to be of a particular model, and merely providing statements about that can inform and increase understanding (intellectual) but may not necessarily have an impact on their expectations (beliefs, attributions) about how treatment really ought to proceed. Also, if parents are the primary focus of treatment, this may seem to imply that the parent is the source of the problem. This, too, can be dismissed intellectually by pointing out that the ways to change child behavior may have little or no relation to the origins of the problem. Thus, we may not know why the child steals at school, gets into horrible fights, and does not comply with requests at home. However, we can change these behaviors by altering parent–child interaction. I shall say more about parent expectations later and only mention the matter here to convey that the focus of treatment and who serves as the primary behavior-change agent (parent rather than therapist) are critical issues and often seen by parents (and therapists) as novel characteristics of PMT.

Individualization of Treatment

By having themes or core topics for each session (Table 5.1), it might be easy to misrepresent PMT as fixed, formulaic, and standardized. I prefer to use the words *systematic* and *programmatic* to emphasize that there are specific tasks the therapist wishes to accomplish: developing parent–child interaction and promoting prosocial child behaviors. The notion that treatment is fixed or standardized is inaccurate because it ignores the extent to which treatment is individualized. Treatment is individualized along several dimensions, including:

- Who participates in treatment (parent plus others)
- Target behaviors focused on in the child
- Settings encompassed by or emphasized in the behavior-change programs (in the car, in restaurants, at home, at school, in other settings in various combinations)
- Token program (chart, time and place of token delivery, backup reinforcers, schedule of delivery, special bonus opportunities)
- Range of techniques that are used (e.g., variations of time out, response cost, simulated practice, group contingencies with siblings)
- Details of family life in the home

These dimensions lead to rather large differences in programs from one family to the next. Thus, two families may have a token reinforcement program. However, what behaviors are reinforced, with what amount of tokens, during what time of the day, and with what backup reinforcers may have little resemblance from one family to the next. For example, in the case of one of our families (two parents, two boys), all four ate dinner together each evening. Among the contingencies in the home was one in which not swearing for a certain amount of time during dinner (first a few minutes and then shaped to encompass the entire meal) was followed with a dessert for the family. The dessert was not provided unless the criterion was met for the child who swore. Obviously, there are special details here (e.g., eating dinner together, interest in dessert, a target behavior present during mealtime) that are quite individual to this family.

There is a more salient feature of PMT that attests to the extent to which it is and can be individualized. As I mentioned in chapter 1, the themes (principles and techniques) highlighted in Table 5.1 have been used in many different contexts and with many populations. Sample applications include developing academic behavior among students (preschool through college), developing behaviors among children and adults with developmental disabilities or mental retardation, and improving adherence to medical regimens. We would not count these extensions as PMT because they may not involve parents at all. Indeed, it is much more meaningful to count PMT as an extension of these other applications because they derive from the same principles and techniques (contingent praise, token reinforcement, time out from reinforcement). These techniques have been applied across the entire developmental spectrum, from infants through geriatric patients; in diverse institutional, educational, community, and business settings; and for clinically important problems, as well as the mundane actions of everyday life (see Kazdin, 2001b). I mention these applications here to demonstrate that the techniques are adaptable to quite diverse situations and contexts. Consequently, individualization of the techniques to parents and families is in keeping with this broad adaptability of treatment.

Variations of PMT

This book presents a version of PMT that our group has used with children (ages 2–14) referred to treatment primarily for oppositional and conduct disorder. Many other variations have manuals or books to guide professionals and parents (see Table 5.2). These variations have developed from approximately four decades in which PMT evolved. The many variations stem in part from nuances of individual programs but, more important, from the youths and families who serve as the focus of the intervention. For example, PMT with children 2 to 4 years of age referred for oppositional behaviors differs from PMT with youths age 12 to 16 referred for criminal behavior, given the scope of impairment, activities out of the home, and influences (e.g., peers, school) that are integrated into treatment. Variations of PMT reflect the order in which treatment themes are presented, different emphases of various techniques (e.g., in the use of praise, points, time out, the extent of role play, whether and how often children are in the sessions), and duration of treatment.

Typically, PMT is used as a stand-alone intervention, that is, as the main and sole treatment. We, and many others, have used PMT in that way, and the treatment has been shown to be effective in a number of studies. PMT also has been combined with other treatments that are distinct interventions that can be used alone (e.g., anger management training, family therapy) or with components of other treatments (e.g., medication, relationship therapy) that are woven into the delivery of PMT. Consider a few variations.

Incredible Years Training Series

The Incredible Years Training Series has focused on children 2 to 8 years of age (Webster-Stratton & Reid, 2003) who are referred for oppositional and conduct problems. The program is called a series because separate complementary training curricula or modules have been developed for parents, teachers, and children. The program is a video-based intervention that is presented, overseen, and discussed by a therapist or trainer. This program is one of the more intricate variations of PMT because of the options available. This is also one of the better evaluated PMT programs, although each program highlighted in this chapter is well studied.

The initial module is videotapes that are provided to a family, usually in a group of 8 to 12 parents. The tapes include many situations (250 vignettes or scenes) in which parenting skills are modeled. Key skills (administering praise, prompts, ignoring, time) are covered. This initial treatment component includes 26 hours of tapes, completed in 13 or 14 weekly sessions, each of 2 hours.

After this initial training in basic skills is completed, a second module expands on the treatment and addresses conflict management and communication. Specifically, 14 additional videotaped sessions (with 60 vignettes) show situations in which parents are taught to manage anger and reduce their own self-blaming talk, to cope with conflict in their lives (e.g., at work and in the family), and to increase social support and self-care (e.g., seeking support from others). The initial and supplementary training sessions are covered in a text that parents use as part of the program (Webster-Stratton, 1992).

A third module focuses on the child's school functioning. It includes 4 to 6 additional sessions that focus on collaboration with teachers and address children's academic readiness and school behaviors. The components focus on helping parents make children feel confident about their own ideas and ability to read; foster reading, writing, and storytelling; developing homework routines; setting limits on activities that may compete with homework (e.g., television, computer games); participating in the child's homework, and contacting teachers to develop joint plans to address school difficulties (e.g., aggression, inattentiveness).

Table 5.2
Parent Management Training Resources (Selective List)

Treatment Manuals and Guides for Conducting Therapy

Barkley, R. A. (1997). *Defiant children: A clinician's manual for parent training* (2nd ed.). New York: Guilford.

Cavell, T. A. (2000). *Working with aggressive children: A practitioner's guide.* Washington, DC: American Psychological Association.

Forehand, R., & McMahon, R. J. (1981). *Helping the noncompliant child: A clinician's guide to parent training.* New York: Guilford.

Forgatch, M., & Patterson, G. (1989). *Parents and adolescents living together—Part 2: Family problem solving.* Eugene, OR: Castalia.

Hembree-Kirigin, T. L., & McNeil, C. B. (1995). *Parent-child interaction therapy.* New York: Plenum.

Patterson, G. R., & Forgatch, M. (1987). *Parents and adolescents living together—Part 1: The basics.* Eugene, OR: Castalia.

Sanders, M. R., & Dadds, M. R. (1993). *Behavioral family intervention.* Needham Heights, MA: Allyn & Bacon.

Sanders, M. R., Markie-Dadds, C., & Turner, K. M. T. (1998). *Practitioner's manual for enhanced triple P.* Brisbane, Australia: Families International Publishing.

Sanders, M. R., Markie-Dadds, C., & Turner, K. M. T. (2000). *Practitioner's manual for standard triple P.* Brisbane, Australia: Families International Publishing.

Webster-Stratton, C. (2000). *How to promote social and academic competence in young children.* London: Sage.

Webster-Stratton, C., & Herbert, M. (1994). *Troubled families—problem children: Working with parents: A collaborative process.* Chichester, England: Wiley.

Booklets, Pamphlets, and Other Materials for Parents

Barkley, R. A., & Benton, C. M. (1998). *Your defiant child: Eight steps to better behavior.* New York: Guilford.

Christophersen, E. R. (1988) *Little people: Guidelines for common sense child rearing* (3rd ed.). Kansas City, MO: Westport.

Christophersen, E. R., & Mortweet, S. L. (2003). *Parenting that works: Building skills that last a lifetime.* Washington, DC: American Psychological Association.

Dishion, T. J., & Patterson, S. G. (1996). *Preventive parenting with love, encouragement, and limits: The preschool years.* Eugene, OR: Castalia.

Forehand, R., & Long, N. (2002). *Parenting the strong-willed child* (2nd ed.). Chicago: McGraw-Hill.

Markie-Dadds, C., Sanders, M. R., & Turner, K. M. T. (1999). *Every parent's self-help workbook.* Brisbane, Australia: Families International Publishing.

Patterson, G. R. (1976). *Living with children: New methods for parents and teachers* (revised). Champaign, IL: Research Press.

Robinson, P. W. (1983). *Answers: A parents' guidebook for solving problems.* Canby, OR: Lion House Press.

Shiller, V. M. (2003). *Rewards for kids! Ready-to-use charts and activities for positive parenting.* Washington, DC: American Psychological Association.

Webster-Stratton, C. (1992). *The incredible years: A trouble-shooting guide for parents of children ages 3–8 years.* Toronto: Umbrella Press.

Videotapes and CD-ROMs to Use in or to Deliver PMT

For videotapes see http://www.incredibleyears.com (for access to Webster-Stratton videos)

For CD-ROMs, see http://www.parentingwisely.com.

Additional Resources on the Web/Internet

http://www.mhs.com/onlineCat/product.asp?productID=PARTAPE
http://www.strengtheningfamilies.org/html/programs_1999/03_IY_PTCTS.html

There are hundreds of PMT statements, comments, and materials on the Web, and they are not screened by any formal agency for their effectiveness or evidence base, as far as I can tell. I would provide the usual proviso—the Web may be useful for familiarizing one with the facets of the topic. However, look to a source with known credibility. The listing of references in this table is not an endorsement or an effort to include all materials that encompass procedures used in PMT. They are included here because most have been part of or emanated from a research program on PMT and include principles and procedures of operant conditioning as applied to parenting.

A fourth module is a 4-day teacher-training program (32 hours) that helps teachers develop effective classroom management training strategies. In addition to effective behavior-change practices, the teacher training program focuses on developing problem-solving skills in the child, decreasing classroom aggression, fostering peer prosocial behavior, and communicating and collaborating with parents to develop programs that change children's school behaviors. The contents and curriculum for this program are available in a separate book used for the course (Webster-Stratton, 2000).

Finally, the child training program focuses on the child's social and play skills (e.g., taking turns, helping others), use of problem-solving and self-control strategies, awareness of the feelings and views of others, reduced aggressive and other antisocial behaviors, and increased positive attributions, self-esteem, and self-confidence. This is a 22-week program that includes nine videotapes (more than 100 vignettes) that teach children problem-solving skills and social skills. This program can be provided in small groups (six children) for 2 hours and is administered concurrently with the basic parenting module, mentioned previously.

Each of the treatment modules emphasizes videotape modeling, role play, practice, and feedback from the therapist or other group members. A wide variety of real-life situations are portrayed in role play. Group members see how the interaction ought to be completed and then discuss how the interaction might have been handled even more effectively. Thus, in addition to the learning opportunities, parents, teachers, and children also learn how to analyze social situations and gain confidence in their own ideas.

The video-based parenting program has been carefully evaluated in many randomized controlled trials in which no treatment and other forms of treatment have been compared (see Webster-Stratton & Reid, 2003). The bulk of the studies have focused on the basic parenting program and its effects. Evidence supports the effects of each of the programs in the series. Multisite studies and replications in clinical settings by the principal investigator add considerably to an impressive set of studies. The scale of applications, too, has been impressive. For example, in one report, the interventions were extended to 34 Head Start programs. Also, the emphasis of the research has been on children in need of treatment but also extended to high-risk samples and prevention. The evidence for PMT more generally, including research from this program, is highlighted in the next chapter. Suffice it to say here that this program has been as well evaluated as can be expected of an intervention.

Noteworthy in this treatment program is the inclusion of interventions that move well beyond the application of operant conditioning principles. The focus on parent and child problem solving, anger management skills, interpersonal communication between parent and child and between parent and teacher, discussion of vignettes in groups, and efforts to bolster self-confidence and self-esteem expand this treatment program beyond the usual PMT. The extent that each of these ingredients contributes incrementally or at all to the treatment outcomes is not fully known. For example, does attention to self-esteem have an impact on child functioning and any other beneficial effects in relation to the same intervention without this focus? Are there some children for whom the minimal version of PMT is no less effective than the full package? Questions like these are easy to raise but difficult and sometimes impractical to investigate. All the variants and permutations could not be compared in light of resources available to support such research and the difficulty in showing empirically what might be small differences among treatments.

The use of videotaped materials is an excellent feature of this program. First, standardizing the tapes ensures that critical situations and skills are covered. The tapes may optimize the likelihood that treatment will be provided as intended, with few lapses on the part of the therapist. Second and related, the tapes allow the therapist to provide stimuli material (vignettes) across many situations and circumstances. Thus, parents (children, teachers) can see proso-cial behaviors under many different circumstances in the home, at school, and in other settings. Generalization of learned behaviors is enhanced when the training includes a wide range of situations and settings (Kazdin, 2001b). Third, dissemination of treatment is greatly facilitated by the use of tapes. Therapist training can be difficult, and PMT and its variations require exacting skills. Using videotapes as a guide is no substitute for training, yet the tapes provide much of the treatment content, including the modeling of the desired behaviors. Many of the behaviors that therapists ordinarily would be trained to model are provided on the tapes. This increases the likelihood that the programs can be adopted in various clinical services. Indeed, for clinics that have begun to adopt evidence-based treatments, this series is often one of the first to be put into place. Finally, the videotaped materials are supplemented by books and materials that also facilitate dissemination of treatment.

A point on dissemination is worth mentioning in passing. In discussing treatments with clinical staff and clinical directors, I often learn that this or that treatment is being used. However, when I see the treatment in action or discuss specifics about the content, it is clear that the treatment is very diluted, bears little resemblance to the version for which there is evidence, and is identical to that original version in name only; that is, on the face of it, many techniques *are* very widely disseminated. Yet, much is lost in the translation of many treatments as they are adopted from a conference, a workshop, or an encounter with a treatment manual. The use of videotapes does not guarantee perfect treatment integrity, but it greatly increases the standardization of treatment across settings. Establishing an evidence-based treatment through a set of empirical studies is difficult enough. Ensuring that the treatment can be extended to new settings and is carried out as intended can be even more challenging.

Parent–Child Interaction Therapy for Oppositional Children

Parent–Child Interaction Therapy (PCIT), another well-studied variation of PMT, focuses primarily on families of oppositional children between the ages of 3 and 6 (Brinkmeyer & Eyberg, 2003; Herschell, Calzada, Eyberg, & McNeil, 2002b). The goals of treatment are to improve the parent–child attachment relationship and to develop parenting skills. The focus on attachment in addition to the more usual PMT skills is based on findings that poor parent–child attachment is related to severity of disruptive child behavior.

The treatment is individually provided to the family. Parents and children are seen in the sessions. Coaching of the parent takes place in a playroom and in the context of the parent playing with the child. The room is equipped with a one-way mirror and a "bug in the ear" system that allows the therapist to be in another room and to coach the parent. If this room system is not available, the therapist merely remains in the room and coaches in a low voice while next to the parent.

The sessions include teaching the specific parenting skill via the therapist's explanation and modeling. The parent then practices the skill (e.g., prompting, praising) with the child in the session. The therapist provides prompts, reinforcement, feedback, and corrective statements to shape parent behavior while the parent is working with the child (e.g., comments such as "nice praise," "good direct command," "great at staying calm," "the child quieted down when you ignored the whining"). For some of the sessions, there is a 5-minute observation at the beginning, during which the therapist observes parent–child interaction (e.g., observing through the one-way mirror or while next to the parent). These observations serve as the basis for determining what skills the parent has mastered and what behaviors are important to target for the parent in the session for that day.

Two parts of treatment can be distinguished: In child-directed interaction, which is similar to play therapy, parents restructure play interaction designed to foster attachment and improved relations. Parent-directed interaction uses behavior management skills. The child-directed interaction teaches parents specific communication skills that are represented by the acronym PRIDE.

P = praising the child's behavior
R = reflecting the child's statements
I = imitating the child's play
D = describing the child's play
E = using enthusiasm

The parent-directed interaction uses common PMT skills such as positive reinforcement, clear prompts, and time out from reinforcement. Behavior-change programs based on these skills are implemented at home, and progress is evaluated in each session.

The program has several novel features. First, PCIT focuses on the parent–child relationship and communication. PMT usually addresses communication skills by virtue of decreasing nagging and reprimands and of increasing clear prompts and praise. However, PCIT does this much more explicitly and fosters better reflective listening on the part of the parent as well.

Second, treatment and evaluation are intertwined. At the beginning of the treatment session, parent–child interaction is observed. The observations are used as the basis for deciding which skills of the parent to concentrate on during that session. In addition, before each session parents provide information about disruptive behaviors at home that is graphed to provide information to the parent as well.

Finally, treatment is performance based rather than limited by duration or number of sessions. Treatment continues until the parents express confidence in their ability to manage child behavior and say they are ready to end treatment. Mean length of treatment is 13 sessions (range 8–27) in a recent report (see Brinkmeyer & Eyberg, 2003).

PCIT has been evaluated in several controlled trials that contrast the intervention with various control procedures (e.g., waiting list) and other interventions (Brinkmeyer & Eyberg, 2003). Treatment has been effective, and intervention effects have been maintained up to 2 years later. Longer follow-up (up to 6 years) has shown maintenance of the treatment gains but without comparison data for children without treatment or children who received some other treatment. Improvements in treatment extend to untreated siblings, to parent characteristics (e.g., reductions in anxiety and pessimism), and to family functioning (e.g., reduced marital discord).

Positive Parenting Program (Triple P)

Another variation of PMT is the Triple P-Positive Parenting Program (Sanders, Markie-Dadds, & Turner, 2003). The program is aimed at both preventing and treating behavioral, emotional, and developmental problems. There are different levels or tiers of the program to provide a continuum of increasing intensity or strength of treatment for parents of children and adolescents from birth to age 16. At the initial level (Level 1) is a community-based and universal intervention applicable to parents interested in parenting and promoting child development (e.g., well child care). Consultation, use of media (e.g., radio commercials, press releases, series of programs on TV), and self-directed training are involved. At the other extreme (Level 5) are interventions for children referred clinically, in which intensive parent training, partner support, and stress coping skills address family dysfunction. Intermediate levels are more abbreviated, self-directed or in groups, and treatment may use fewer sessions than the higher levels.

The different levels have notable advantages, including the ability to target children with varying levels of severity of dysfunction, to focus on children in different developmental periods (infants, toddlers, preschoolers, school-age children, and teenagers), and to provide the clinician with a series of options to determine the scope and type of intervention likely to be needed. In the context of clinical work, higher levels of the program permit the clinician to provide intensive individualized treatment and add other modules (e.g., focus on mood problem or marital conflict as needed). For the more intensive clinical foci, coping skills and stress management may be included in the treatment.

The program began more than two decades ago and has continued to develop. Several randomized trials have evaluated the different versions of the program (see Sanders et al., 2003, for a review). The program has been effective for children with varying levels of severity of disruptive behaviors and conduct problems and from families varying in degree of dysfunction (e.g., presence of marital discord, clinical depression) (e.g., Dadds, Schwartz, & Sanders, 1987; Sanders, Markie-Dadds, Tully, & Bor, 2000; Sanders & McFarland, 2000). Benefits of the program are reflected in improved child behavior (e.g., parent ratings and direct observations), greater parenting competence, and reduced depression in parents who are treated. Follow-up to a year has shown maintenance of the changes.

Comparisons of variations of the program have yielded interesting findings beyond demonstrations of efficacy. For example, in one demonstration self-directed versus therapist-assisted programs were provided to parents of preschoolers at risk for conduct problems (Sanders, Markie-Dadds, Tully, & Bor, 2000). Variations of treatment, compared with a waiting list control, showed reliable changes that were maintained up to a year after treatment. Although therapist-assisted and self-directed programs were equally effective, parents who received assistance from a therapist were more satisfied with their roles as parents. Another demonstration evaluated a 10-week self-directed program (e.g., Connell, Sanders, & Markie-Dadds, 1997). The program was completed at home by parents of oppositional children ages 2 to 5. The families were living in rural areas; the program was supplemented by phone calls to help parents apply self-help materials. Compared with a waiting list control condition, children in the self-help condition improved significantly, and the effects were maintained up to 6 months later. A self-directed program is very important to develop because many families cannot otherwise receive services (e.g., in rural areas) or are at high risk for dropping out of treatment once they begin.

The research program for the Triple P interventions continues to be quite active. Follow-up shows maintenance of the gains in improved child behavior, parenting skills, and parent functioning (e.g., adjustment, parental depression). Even without further work, some two dozen controlled studies provide a strong body of research in support of the program (Sanders et al., 2003). Among the unique features in the design of the program are the different levels of treatment that can be used with children and families with different levels of severity of dysfunction. This feature is important because child and adolescent therapy in general has had no empirically based guidelines for providing services at different levels of intensity and cost. Who receives how much treatment and how it is delivered (e.g., self-help, group, individual) are rarely studied. This intervention provides a portfolio of parenting training variations that are effective for quite different populations of children and families and for both treatment and prevention. Materials available for use include workbooks, self-help guides, and videos that convey treatment (e.g., Markie-Dadds, Sanders, & Turner, 1999; Sanders, Markie-Dadds, & Turner, 1998, 2000).

Problem-Solving Skills Training and PMT for Oppositional, Aggressive, and Antisocial Children

Occasionally, PMT is combined with other interventions. In some cases, the interventions added to PMT might be components that would not stand alone as a separate treatment. Programs highlighted previously (PCIT, Triple-P) include components (e.g., improved communication training, stress management) that complement PMT. Some of the components might not be a stand-alone treatment that would be very feasible or effective in treating oppositional and conduct problems. In other applications, PMT is combined with treatments that could stand alone as reasonable interventions for the problems.

We have evaluated the addition of problem-solving skills training (PSST) in combination with PMT. In separate studies, we have evaluated PSST and PMT alone and in combination (Kazdin, 2003a). We began looking at PSST because in inpatient and, to a lesser degree, outpatient treatment work, sometimes there is no parent available. The parent could not or would not participate in treatment (e.g., because of mental illness, serving a prison term, mental retardation, or simple unwillingness) or engaged in practices (e.g., current drug abuse) or occupations (e.g., prostitution) that interfered with participation. For such cases, providing intensive treatment of the child with little or no parent intervention has been important. Therefore, we have worked on PSST as a stand-alone treatment. At other times, there may be parents who can participate actively in PMT. Some children referred to us are very young, and PSST is not feasible. In these cases, too, PMT is a viable treatment. Finally, when the stars are positioned just right, both PSST and PMT can be used with the family. Another reason for exploring the combination of the two treatments is the fact that the conceptual models of the treatments are compatible and complementary. PSST focuses on processes internal to the child that can be deployed to address diverse interpersonal situations. PMT focuses on interpersonal changes to develop new repertoires in diverse situations. We felt that integrating these two treatments would optimize therapeutic change.

PSST focuses on the cognitive processes of the child—the child's perceptions, attributions, and beliefs. Individuals who engage in conduct-disordered behaviors, particularly aggression, show distortions and deficiencies in various cognitive processes. These distortions and deficiencies are not merely reflections of intellectual functioning. Examples include generating alternative solutions to interpersonal problems (e.g., different ways of handling social situations), identifying the means to obtain particular ends (e.g., making friends), understanding the consequences of one's actions (e.g., what could happen after a particular behavior), making attributions to others of the motivation of their actions, perceiving how others feel and having expectations of the effects of one's own actions (Lochman, Whidby, & FitzGerald, 2000; Shure, 1997; Spivack & Shure, 1982). Deficits and distortions among these processes relate to disruptive behavior, as reflected in teacher ratings, peer evaluations, and direct assessment of overt behavior.

PSST develops interpersonal cognitive problem-solving skills and includes several characteristics. First, the emphasis is on how children approach situations—that is, the thought processes in which the child engages to guide responses to interpersonal situations. The children are taught to engage in a step-by-step approach to solve interpersonal problems. They make statements to themselves that direct attention to certain aspects of the problem or to tasks that lead to effective solutions. Second, the behaviors (solutions to the interpersonal problems) that are selected are important as well. Prosocial behaviors are fostered through modeling and direct reinforcement as part of the problem-solving process. Third, treatment utilizes structured tasks involving games, academic activities, and stories. Over the course of treatment, the cognitive problem-solving skills are increasingly applied to real-life situations. Fourth, therapists play an active role in treatment. They model the cognitive processes by making verbal self-statements, apply the sequence of statements to particular problems, provide cues to prompt use of the skills, and deliver feedback and praise to develop correct use of the skills. Finally, treatment combines several different procedures, including modeling and practice, role play, reinforcement, and mild punishment (loss of points or tokens), to develop an increasingly complex response repertoire for the child.

In our program, PSST consists of weekly therapy sessions with the child, with each session usually lasting 30 to 50 minutes. The core treatment (12–20 sessions) may be supplemented with optional sessions, if the child requires additional assistance in grasping the problem-solving steps (early in treatment) or their application in everyday situations (later in treatment). (In separate projects, we have varied the duration of treatment.) Central to treatment is developing the use of *problem-solving steps* designed to break down interpersonal situations into units that permit identification and use of prosocial responses. The steps and what they intend to accomplish are given in Table 5.3. The steps serve as verbal prompts the children deliver to themselves to engage in thoughts and actions that guide behavior. Each self-prompt or self-statement represents one step in solving a problem. Over the course of treatment, the steps are applied to a wide range of situations in the sessions and also to everyday life (see Kazdin, 2003a, for further details). Critical to treatment is use of the problem-solving approach outside the treatment setting. In vivo practice, referred to as *supersolvers*, provides systematically programmed assignments designed to extend the child's use and application of problem-solving skills to everyday situations. The parents, as available, are trained to help the child use the problem-solving steps. Parents are brought into sessions over the course of treatment to learn the problem-solving steps and to practice joint supersolver assignments with the child at home.

Our results have indicated that PSST and PMT alone and in combination lead to therapeutic change in children referred for aggressive and antisocial behavior. The combined treatment (PSST + PMT) is more effective than either treatment alone, a finding replicated by others (Webster-Stratton, 1996). Occasionally, the fact that a combined treatment is more effective is an obvious argument for its use. However, greater therapeutic change is only one consideration in combining treatments. Other considerations are whether the increased effectiveness of the combined treatment makes a genuine difference over the outcomes achieved with the individual components of treatment, whether the added cost of the combined treatment (treatment time, loss of cases) is worth the benefits, and whether some individuals can be identified who would profit as well from individual components as from the combined treatment. Data are not available to address these issues in relation to PMT and other interventions with which it might be combined.

Medication and PMT for Attention-Deficit/Hyperactivity Disorder

The treatment of attention-deficit/hyperactivity disorder (ADHD) might be an area where PMT would have considerable success, given its strong outcome evidence for oppositional defiant disorder and conduct disorder, which are also part the constellation of disruptive or externalizing behavior disorders

Table 5.3
Problem-Solving Steps and Self-Statements

Self-Statement Steps to Solve a Problem	Purpose of the Step
1. What am I suppose to do?	This step requires that the child identify and define the problem.
2. I have to look at all my possibilities.	This step asks the child to delineate or specify alternative solutions to the problem.
3. I'd better concentrate and focus in.	This step instructs the child to concentrate and evaluate the solutions (s)he has generated.
4. I need to make a choice.	During the fourth step (s)he chooses the answer which (s)he thinks is correct.
5. I did a good job (or) Oh, I made a mistake.	This final step to verify whether the solution was the best among those available, whether the problem-solving process was correctly followed, or whether a mistake or less than desirable solution was selected and the process should begin anew.

Note. The steps are taught through modeling; the therapist and child alternate turns in using and applying the steps, and each helps each other. Prompting, shaping, practice, and effusive praise develop the child's mastery of the steps usually by the end of the first treatment session. As the child learns the steps, the therapist modeling and prompting are faded and omitted or used to help only as needed. The steps evolve over the course of treatment in multiple ways. Among the most significant changes, they are abbreviated and combined. Also, the steps move from overt (made aloud) to covert (silent, internal) statements. By the end of treatment, use of the steps cannot be visibly seen; their overt features have been faded completely.

and often comorbid with ADHD. However, oppositional defiant disorder, conduct disorder, and ADHD differ in relation to the treatment literature. As is well known, the standard treatment for ADHD has been stimulant medication, and the effects of such medication on core symptoms of oppositional defiant disorder and conduct disorder are not so well established.

In relation to ADHD, the weight of the evidence consistently points to medication as the treatment of choice (Barkley, 1998). Indeed, a review of more than 180 placebo-controlled trials attested to the effects of medication in altering core symptoms of ADHD (Greenhill & Ford, 2002). In this review, approximately 70% of patients were considered to have responded well to stimulants, in contrast to 13% who responded as well to placebo. Medication has its own controversies, such as whether it is overprescribed and provided to children who are active and bothersome rather than seriously impaired. Actually, some evidence suggests that medication may be overprescribed (i.e., provided to children who may not need it and who do not meet criteria for a diagnosis) and also underprescribed (i.e., not provided to most of the children who meet criteria for ADHD) (see Angold, Erkanli, Egger, & Costello, 2000; Jensen et al., 1999). Moreover, the evidence indicates that effects of treatment last only as long as children continue on the medication (Greenhill & Ford, 2002; Weiss & Hechtman, 1993). In most of the research studies, treatment is continued for 3 months or less. All that said, medication continues to be the treatment of choice for ADHD.

Hyperactive children often represent behavior management problems at home and at school. This is related in part to the fact that ADHD and conduct disorder are often comorbid. Behavioral management problems, whether or not they can be connected to a specific diagnosis, are candidates for PMT. The effects of PMT on ADHD have been demonstrated in several studies (Hinshaw, Klein, & Abikoff, 2002). Yet, the improvements with PMT tend to be weaker than those attained with stimulant medication. Parent and teacher ratings, rather than more objective behavioral indices, are more likely to show the effects.

PMT has often been used in combination with medication (Hinshaw et al., 2002). The largest scale test of this combination has been a multisite study (NIMH Multimodal Treatment Study of Children with Attention Deficit Hyperactivity Disorder [MTA Study]). Seven sites and 579 children (ages 7–9) were included in a 14-month regimen of treatment (MTA Cooperative Group, 1999a, 1999b; Swanson et al., 2002). The groups included in the study were (a) medication management; (b) behavioral treatment involving parents, school, and child programs; (c) medication and behavioral treatment combined; and (d) treatment as usual in the community. "Treatment as usual in the community" was mostly medication (for 2/3 of the children) but without the careful management and titration of medication of the medication management condition. Among the key findings, both the medication and the combined treatment groups showed greater improvement than those in the behavioral treatment only or treatment as usual groups. On core symptoms of ADHD, medication and combined treatments were no different. Some superiority of the combined treatment was evident in relation to non-ADHD symptoms and prosocial functioning (e.g., internalizing symptoms, prosocial skills at school, parent–child relations), but these effects were not strong. Many other facets of the MTA study are of interest but well beyond the scope of this chapter.

The MTA study represents the most extensive study of PMT combined with medication for ADHD. In light of the MTA results, it is not clear that PMT is worth the effort across the board as an addition to stimulant medication. It is often the case clinically that parents are unwilling to try medication for their ADHD child or the child has behavioral problems that are not addressed or abated with medication. In such cases, PMT might well be useful. Also, perhaps PMT is advisable as an adjunct to medication in some cases but not others. However, the routine combination of PMT with medication would be difficult to support from the research on the incremental effects of PMT. At this point, there is no firm basis for deciding for whom PMT might be appropriate (see Owens et al., 2003). There are seemingly obvious guidelines. If parenting practices of ADHD children are harsh and if child management is a problem at home, perhaps PMT ought to be combined with medication. Harsh parenting practices can contribute directly to deviant behavior (e.g., increase aggression), and hence the obvious guidelines might be reasonable. At the same time, judgment as to who profits from treatment has not been well tested by randomly assigning individuals with ADHD to receive PMT or not, based on pretreatment classification of whether they "need" or do not "need" that intervention.

Multidimensional Treatment Foster Care

The multidimensional treatment foster care program was developed originally to treat youth with severe and chronic delinquent behavior and from that was extended to work with children and adolescents referred from mental health, child welfare service, or juvenile justice systems (Chamberlain & Smith, 2003). The intervention with delinquents focuses on providing treatment in a community-based, family-style setting. Multiple interventions are provided, including PMT, family and individual therapy, and medication as needed.

Youths referred for their delinquent behaviors are placed in foster homes (one child per home) and provided with intensive support and intervention. The core of the foster home program is PMT, as described in previous applications. PMT is provided to the foster parents who will care for the child and to the biological parents who will be responsible for aftercare, following foster placement. Foster care is a placement before return to the home and substitutes for what might have been institutionalization. The foster placement provides a community-based environment and one closer in many other characteristics (e.g., family style) to the home than inpatient services would provide. When the child is placed in the foster home, training of the biological parents begins as well. The placement lasts 6 to 9 months.

The foster parents are trained to implement behavior-change programs, including a point system to address several behaviors in the home (e.g., attending school, following directions). In addition, other treatments may be provided, including case manager supervision of foster parents, individual therapy, and family therapy). The case managers have supervision over approximately 10 youths and families at any one time, stay in close contact with the families (e.g., weekly foster parent meetings, daily phone contact), and are available to the foster families 24 hours per day. Case managers also oversee contacts with the school and help run a home-based reinforcement program.

In most cases (85%), youths return to their biological family or relatives (others remain in long-term foster care placement). The family has been trained in PMT and hence the same procedures used in the foster care setting. Youths make home visits in which parents practice using these techniques. As parents become more skilled in PMT techniques, the visits are gradually extended (e.g., from day to overnight or weekend visits). A family therapist provides supervision and has weekly sessions with the family during this period.

Individual therapy for the child focuses on problem-solving skills, anger management, social skills, and academic or occupational plans. The behaviors focused on in therapy are also included in the reinforcement program in the home. Also, intensive individual therapy (one or two sessions per week, 2–6 hours total) focuses on role play, modeling, and practice of prosocial behavior in diverse situations. For those youths on medication, a consulting psychiatrist is available. Many of the youths have multiple psychiatric diagnoses and are taking multiple medications at the time of placement.

Well-controlled treatment trials have attested to the effects of this program. During the intervention, fewer youths run away from their placement or drop out of the program than those assigned to traditional community placements (e.g., group care facilities) (Chamberlain & Smith, 2003). Also, after the intervention, those who receive this special program show lower criminal referral and arrest rates and lower rates of self-reported offenses than those in traditional placements.

Other Variations

There are multifaceted treatments in which PMT is one of several interventions provided to the child and family. The foster care program noted previously is one of many excellent examples. Consider two other examples briefly to convey the breadth of the literature. Another prominent example is multisystemic therapy (Henggeler, Schoenwald, Borduin, Rowland, & Cunningham,

---

1998). Its primary focus of treatment has been with delinquent adolescents, including seriously disturbed repeat offenders. Multisystemic therapy focuses on systems in which behavior is embedded and on altering these systems in concrete ways that can influence behavior. Treatment draws on several different techniques, including PMT, problem solving skills therapy, marital therapy, and other techniques as needed. Several domains may be addressed in treatment, such as parent unemployment, parent stress, marital conflict, and child-discipline practices, because they reflect broader system issues and affect how the adolescent is functioning. Treatment has been effective in multiple randomized controlled clinical trials with very seriously disturbed adjudicated delinquent youths and their families, including chronic juvenile offenders, juvenile sexual offenders, youths with substance use and abuse, and maltreating (abusing, neglectful) families (see Burns, Schoenwald, Burchard, Faw, & Santos, 2000; Henggeler et al., 1998, for reviews).

Another example is the use of PMT as part of treatment for children with autism under 4 years of age (Lovaas & Smith, 2003). The program reflects an intensive, comprehensive effort (e.g., for most children 40 hours/week of one-to-one intervention for 2 or more years). Behavioral procedures are used to develop behaviors in a wide range of personal, language, and social skill domains. Many different service providers (student therapists, senior therapists, case supervisors, and program directors) are directly involved in treatment. They differ in the extent to which they have direct contact with children and families and decision-making responsibilities in relation to the family. I mention the different people involved to convey that parents are only part of the treatment. PMT consists of having parents work alongside an experienced therapist for several hours per week. The parent takes turns with the trainer in discrete trials that focus on training a particular skill (e.g., identifying objects, using language). At home, the parents use reinforcement procedures to encourage the use of communication skills or self-help skills in everyday life.

Evidence, including replication of the original work in research and clinical application (Lovaas & Smith, 2003), has supported the effectiveness of treatment. For example, in the original study of this treatment (Lovaas, 1987), 47% of the children were eventually placed in normal first-grade classes and improved markedly on standardized intelligence tests. These gains were not evident in control children who were not involved in the training program. Follow-up was conducted for both treatment and control groups years later (McEachin, Smith, & Lovaas, 1993). At the time of follow-up, intervention youths had been out of treatment for a mean of 5 years (range 0 to 12 years); control subjects had been out of treatment for a mean of 3 years (range 0 to 9 years). More youths in the intervention group remained in a regular class placement, mean IQ scores were higher, and adaptive behavior scores were superior to the control group.

General Comments

As the variations mentioned in this chapter suggest, PMT is often combined with other treatments. Before adding PMT routinely to other treatments, a few conditions might be reasonable to consider, if not require. First, the other treatment ought to have some evidence on its behalf that it produces therapeutic change or improves some facet of treatment (e.g., increasing family involvement, decreasing attrition). In clinical work, occasionally an effective treatment such as PMT is seized and added to a treatment that is not very effective or has no evidence or, worse, has been studied but without evidence that it produces change. Second, at some point it must be shown that there is an increment of benefit when PMT is added to some other treatment or, even more, when some other treatment is added to PMT. Adding treatments bears a cost in terms of patient, therapist, and clinic time and the monetary consequences with which these are associated. Consequently, before adding PMT to another treatment (or vice versa), one would want evidence that PMT adds incrementally in some important ways to the other treatment. There is little evidence available to address this matter except that PMT as an addition to medication for ADHD has been evaluated relatively well.

In some areas where PMT might be argued for as a treatment of choice, adding PMT to some other treatment raises a slightly different question. For example, for oppositional children, a therapist might add PMT to some other regimen. Yet, PMT has been shown in many studies to alter the behaviors of oppositional children. It would be important to see if some other regimen adds incrementally to the effects of PMT before any combination is advocated. Occasionally in clinical work, combined (eclectic) treatments are used with the view that more or additional treatment cannot hurt. Combined treatments are not always better than the constituent treatments provided alone. Indeed, sometimes the combination is worse than either of the constituent treatments (see Kazdin, 1996a).

The purpose of this chapter was to illustrate the characteristics of PMT and its variations. Some of the variations are a function of different clinic samples to which the intervention is applied and the other treatments that may be included as part of a broader package. When referring to the evidence that supports the effectiveness of PMT, as discussed in the next chapter, I focus primarily on PMT as a stand-alone treatment. Extensive evidence is available for some treatments in which PMT is a part. Multisystemic therapy is one example. This evidence is not cited as support of PMT because many other components are involved and the role of each has not been tested.

Summary and Conclusions

PMT focuses on altering the clinical problems for which the child was referred and parent–child interaction in the home. Although these foci are obviously related, they are worth distinguishing. At any given point, one of these may take priority over the other in the therapist's focus or emphasis within the sessions. The content of PMT sessions draws on the principles and intervention techniques discussed in the previous two chapters. Certainly, the core intervention of PMT is positive reinforcement. Invariably, parents, teachers, and therapists wish to eliminate or markedly reduce some behaviors as part of treatment. Reinforcement programs are central to these goals and play a critical role in how behavior change is achieved, whether in the parent or in the child.

The structure of treatment was discussed to show how individual treatment sessions are organized. Typically, a session begins by reviewing the program in the home and what transpired during the previous week; presentation of a new principle and theme and the concrete procedures that follow from them; extensive practice, modeling, and role play between the therapist and the parent; and some assignment to implement in the home for the next week. Outside the treatment session, the behavior-change programs are carried out at home, at school, and in the other settings and contexts of everyday life, as needed. Shaping is used to gradually develop parent behavior as well as child behavior.

Although PMT includes the parent or guardian for the child, other adults who play a role in supervising or caring for the child are welcome in treatment. Live-in significant others and relatives may attend sessions and go through the training. Teachers are integrated into the program usually by providing information to the therapist and feedback regarding child performance. The child, too, attends some sessions. The child conveys how the program is implemented (usually through role play) and participates with the parent in reenacting situations that occur at home.

This chapter has emphasized the PMT program we have been using with oppositional, aggressive, and antisocial children and their families. Other variations of PMT used alone or in combination with several other interventions were highlighted as well. Mention was made in passing about evidence for PMT and its variations. It is important to consider the strengths and the limitations of the evidence more systematically, and that is the goal of the next chapter.

6

Evidence
Key Findings, Strengths, and Limitations

PMT is among the best established of the evidence-based treatments for children and adolescents. This is a rather strong claim. This chapter provides an overview of the evidence in support of this claim and complements the prior chapter, which sampled key programs of parent training research. In the process of describing the programs, I highlighted supportive research as well. In this chapter, I consider additional research, along with the conclusions that are warranted from the body of literature more generally. This research includes the expected lines of work, such as randomized controlled clinical trials that examine the outcome effects and studies of factors that influence therapeutic change or responsiveness of children to treatment. There are additional lines of work about PMT, about how treatment may operate, and about procedures that rely on the techniques used in PMT. This chapter highlights key findings, as well as the strengths and limitations of the evidence.

Overview of Current Evidence

Treatment Outcome Studies

Direct Tests of PMT

The strongest body of evidence in support of PMT in terms of sheer volume and quality of research is in the treatment of oppositional, aggressive, antisocial, and delinquent child behavior. PMT has been evaluated in many randomized controlled outcome trials and single-case experimental designs with youths varying in age from 2 to 17 years old. Two notable features of the evidence are worth mentioning. First, several programs of research have developed and elaborated PMT and its effects.[1] Systematic progress can be seen in the types of questions addressed (e.g., from simple treatment/no-treatment studies, to mediation and moderation). Also, research continues to emerge from these programs. Many others have contributed to the literature as well, but several lines of programmatic studies are unique among treatment techniques for children and adolescents. Second, many reviews of the PMT literature are available. The reviews began in the 1970s and 1980s and continue today.[2] Indeed, there are more reviews of this treatment than there are outcome studies for many other evidence-based treatments. Considering the focus on oppositional, aggressive, antisocial, and delinquent behavior, several conclusions are warranted from the studies to date:

- PMT has led to marked improvements in child behavior as reflected on parent and teacher reports of deviant behavior, direct observation of behavior at home and at school, and institutional records (e.g., school truancy, police contacts, arrest rates, institutionalization). These effects have emerged in controlled studies comparing PMT with no treatment, wait-list controls, and routine care (or treatment as usual) provided in the settings or communities in which the studies were completed.
- The magnitude of change has placed conduct problem behaviors and the behaviors of clinically referred samples to within nonclinical levels of functioning at home and at school, based on normative data from non-referred peers (e.g., same age, sex). Return to normative levels of functioning on standardized measures has been the most common way to operationalize "clinically significant" change, as a supplement to the more familiar statistically significant change.
- Treatment gains have been maintained in several studies for 1 to 2 years after treatment. Longer follow-up (e.g., up to 14 years) has been reported but without appropriate controls to permit attribution of the effects to PMT (Long, Forehand, Wierson, & Morgan, 1994).
- Therapeutic changes extend beyond the specific areas (e.g., symptoms) targeted in treatment. These improvements include behaviors of the child other than those directly focused on in treatment and behaviors of the child's siblings in the home. In addition, maternal psychopathology, particularly depression, and stress decrease, and family interactions and relations improve with PMT.

Overall, outcome evidence in controlled trials replicated in different centers has shown that PMT leads to therapeutic change. When individuals learn of a therapy with strong evidence in its behalf, the usual claim is, "Yes, but this is not the answer for everyone in need of treatment and will not work with everyone." This claim is certainly true, but it is also true of virtually all treatments (e.g., antibiotics, antidepressants, chemotherapy). Even so, noting the strong evidence in behalf of PMT is not sufficient. It is critical to understand for whom treatment is particularly effective and what can be added or altered in treatment to augment therapeutic change.

Extensions and Other Applications

I mentioned earlier in the book (chapter 1) that one of the novel features in support of PMT are two rather large bodies of research that do not focus on parents or psychotherapy. I have given short shrift to each of these because they are vast areas well beyond the scope of the book, but I mention both again because they are quite relevant to the outcome evidence in support of PMT. First, basic research (experimental analysis of behavior) that consists of animal and, to a lesser extent, human studies of operant conditioning provides the underpinnings of the core procedures of PMT.

Much of what is trained in PMT has a foundation that is quite strong in relation to reinforcement, punishment, extinction, stimulus control, and related concepts. For example, praising child behavior (positive reinforcement) relies on a simple application of procedures that have been studied in detail. Parameters that the therapist uses to guide training in delivering reinforcement (e.g., contingent, immediate, and continuous delivery of reinforcement) are based on an extensive literature. PMT does not draw on the complexity of the laboratory research that includes basic research to address a broad range of questions (e.g., using math models, multiple schedules of varying contingencies provided simultaneously or concurrently, neurological underpinnings of operant learning). Having an experimental foundation that is closely connected to PMT procedures not only informs treatment but also provides a basis for understanding processes involved in developing and eliminating behavior.

Second, applied research (applied behavior analysis), in which procedures used in PMT are applied in other contexts, is huge.[3] PMT is a derivative of a broader treatment approach in which the principles and techniques of operant conditioning are applied. PMT uses the principles and techniques in the context of changing family interaction and promoting prosocial behaviors of the child. Reinforcement programs have been used as interventions in education (preschool through college), for special populations (e.g., medical and psychiatric patients to reduce pain, improve recovery, increase adaptive skills), and in athletics, business, and industry (e.g., to improve performance, reduce accidents). In the late 1970s, these applications were already vast (e.g., Kazdin, 1977). The applications have increased (Austin & Carr, 2000; Cooper et al., 1987; Kazdin, 2001b). I hasten to add that these "applications" are not mere extensions. Empirical evaluations and demonstrations of reinforcement techniques in these other contexts constitute their own literatures.

I mention these applications in passing because PMT has a very interesting set of sibling literatures. We know from these literatures that the techniques of PMT can be effective in many other contexts, as attested in controlled studies. Thus, the techniques have rather broad empirical support in relation to producing changes in human functioning. One would be hard-pressed to identify other forms of therapy that draw fairly directly from basic research and where the techniques used in therapy have been effective in many other areas of application.

Factors That Contribute to Treatment Outcome

The effects of treatment are influenced by other factors that are referred to as moderators. A *moderator* is any characteristic, variable, or factor that influences the effect of treatment. Treatment is differentially effective or can vary in outcome systematically as a function of some other variable such as characteristics of the child (e.g., age, sex), parents and family (e.g., parent history of antisocial behavior, marital discord), and treatment (e.g., how many sessions). Identifying moderators goes beyond treatment trials that compare PMT with another treatment or control condition. The primary focus of research on moderators is who responds to treatment or under what conditions is treatment optimally effective.

Child, Parent, and Family Characteristics

Considerable attention has been devoted to identifying factors that influence treatment outcome and can be used to identify who responds particularly well or poorly to treatment. Child, parent, and family characteristics have received the greatest attention. Research has asked what factors predict, contribute to, or moderate treatment outcome. Table 6.1 lists those factors studied most frequently in the context of children with oppositional, aggressive, and antisocial behavior. Many of these factors are interrelated, and in most studies only a few are included at a time. Occasionally, several are included, and the results suggest that each may predict responsiveness to treatment. That is, it does not seem to be the case that one of the variables (e.g., severity of child dysfunction or family socioeconomic disadvantage) is a proxy for and explained by other variables with which it is correlated.

The factors listed in the table have a broad influence on treatment process and outcome for children with oppositional, aggressive, and antisocial behavior. Specifically, they predict (a) who remains in treatment, (b) the magnitude of change among those who complete treatment, and (c) the extent to which changes are maintained at follow-up (e.g., Dadds & McHugh, 1992; Dumas & Wahler, 1983; Kazdin, 1995a; Ruma, Burke, & Thompson, 1996; Webster-Stratton & Hammond, 1990; Webster-Stratton, Reid, & Hammond, 2001). Although

Table 6.1

**Factors That Influence Responsiveness to Treatment Among
Oppositional and Conduct Problem Children and Families**

Diminished responsiveness to treatment is associated with . . .

Child Factors

Greater severity and duration of the disorder
Comorbidity (presence of two or more psychiatric disorders)
Poor reading achievement
School dysfunction (social and academic)

Parent and Family Factors

Parent psychopathology (current and past)
Parent stress (life events and perceived stress)
Poor family relations (e.g., marital conflict, few shared family activities)
Adverse child-rearing practices (e.g., harsh punishment, poor monitoring and supervision)

Contextual (Socioeconomic) Factors

Lower family income and/or receipt of public assistance
Lower socio-occupational-educational status
Poor living accommodations (e.g., run-down neighborhood, inadequate living space)

these factors are obviously important to treatment, the precise role that each factor plays in treatment and how it exerts its influence are not clear.

For example, socioeconomic disadvantage influences treatment outcome; greater disadvantage is associated with less therapeutic change. This outcome could be because parents with greater socioeconomic disadvantage do not attend treatment as reliably as others, do not profit from the didactic portions of treatment because they have less education, are more likely to be single parents, use harsher punishment practices in the home and hence have more to change (unlearn) in treatment, do not monitor the whereabouts of their children so their children have more time with deviant peers, and so on. Each of these characteristics is associated with socioeconomic disadvantage and may contribute to treatment outcome but still does not explain precisely or fully how or why socioeconomic disadvantage exerts its influence.

Similarly, parental stress plays a role in treatment outcome. Greater parental stress at the beginning of treatment is associated with less therapeutic change of the child at the end of treatment. Parental stress might be related to the severity of the child's problems or to any of the factors just noted in relation to socioeconomic status. How stress influences treatment outcome is not yet clear. From both clinical and research standpoints, it is important to clarify the interpretation of the factors. If we better understood why a particular factor led to poor responsiveness to treatment, we might be in a better position to mitigate the influence of that factor.

To say that various factors influence treatment outcome does not mean that families who show several of the factors will not respond to treatment. Risk factors and predictors of responsiveness to treatment are based on data from groups of individuals. Any given family at high risk for not responding (i.e., with several of the risk factors present) may respond well to treatment, and of course another family without these factors may respond poorly. Risk refers to the probability of responding in varying degrees as a function of the characteristics. The accumulation of more of the factors places the family at greater risk of responding poorly to treatment but does not doom or guarantee a specific level of responsiveness.

Research has not turned to the important questions of who invariably will not respond or who ought to receive some other treatment from the outset in light of this information. PMT may still be the treatment of choice for families of children with conduct problems, even if several predictors of poor responsiveness are present. It may be most prudent to begin with PMT for the treatment of a child with oppositional, aggressive, and antisocial behavior and to move to another treatment if needed. To my knowledge there is no evidence available at this time that another treatment for such families is a viable or more viable alternative. The factors that predict attenuated responsiveness to PMT may exert a similar influence on every other treatment.

The information on the factors that contribute to outcome has not been translated into practices that may be clinically helpful for matching patients with treatments. Many clinicians may feel strongly about their ability to make a decision about whether a particular family is a good candidate for PMT based on the factors noted here. Although clinical judgment is often all one has, the data on clinical judgment teach humility (Dawes, 1994). Judgment about who ought to receive what variant of treatment or individually tailoring treatment to the case does not have a strong base in available evidence. A better guideline is as follows: If PMT can be applied (i.e., there is an available parent or guardian in the home), the treatment is probably the treatment of choice as an initial line of attack for oppositional and aggressive child behavior. If PMT is not feasible, objected to by the patients, or weak in the effects it produces in that family, of course, that would be strong grounds for shifting treatment.

Characteristics of treatment also contribute to outcome. Providing parents with in-depth knowledge of social learning principles, rather than just teaching them the techniques, improves outcomes. Also, including mild punishment (e.g., brief time out from reinforcement) along with reinforcement programs in the home enhances treatment effects. These components are now standard in most PMT programs.

Processes within treatment have also been studied to identify who responds to treatment. Measures of parent resistance (e.g., parents saying, "I can't," "I won't") correlate with parent discipline practices at home; changes in resistance during therapy predict changes in parent behavior. Moreover, specific therapist ploys during the sessions (e.g., reframing, confronting) can overcome or contribute to resistance (Patterson & Chamberlain, 1994). This line of work advances our understanding of PMT greatly by relating in-session interactions of the therapist and parent to child functioning and treatment outcome.

We might expect many other facets of treatment to influence outcome, such as the amount of treatment (e.g., duration, number of sessions) and whether there are "booster" (extra) sessions over a period of time after the initial treatment is completed. These factors have not been well studied in ways that would permit strong conclusions for a given clinical population or age group.

General Comments

Overall, several factors have been identified that influence the extent to which children improve with PMT. Research has not addressed whether these factors would influence the effectiveness of any treatment applied to children with conduct problems. For example, a child and family referred to treatment might show all untoward characteristics that place them at risk for not responding to PMT. Should another treatment be applied, or are the characteristics that influence responsiveness to PMT likely to influence responsiveness to some alternative technique? Clearly, if PMT is applied and there is no therapeutic change, then one would want to select another treatment, as I have mentioned. However, when would one want to select another treatment in advance of applying PMT, based on the likelihood of a child not responding? The research evidence has not been very helpful on these questions. A child and family at risk for not responding to PMT may be equally or even less likely to respond to another treatment, particularly one without evidence in its behalf.

The PMT literature and more generally the child, adolescent, and adult therapy literatures have not been very useful in deciding what treatments to give to what families based on characteristics that might moderate outcome. Therapists often speak of this or that family being a good or not so good candidate for a given type of treatment. Such claims can be made on the basis of understanding factors that contribute to outcome. However, the use of this information to provide some alternative, less well-studied treatment goes way beyond the data and may even not be in the interests of the family.

Why Treatment Leads to Change

In child, adolescent, and adult psychotherapy, there has been a great deal of discussion of why treatment works. Lamentably, almost no research has focused on the mechanisms of action or the causes of therapeutic change. A randomized controlled trial can show *that* treatment caused the change (i.e., when treatment surpasses the effects of a no-treatment control group). However, the basis for the change—that is, why treatment led to change or to greater change than another treatment or control condition—is quite another matter. The "why" refers to mechanisms of action or *mediators* of change.

For example, in adult therapy, one of the most studied and supported treatments is cognitive therapy for depression (Hollon & Beck, 2004). By all counts, this treatment is evidence based and then some in light of the range of trials. But why does cognitive therapy work—through what mechanisms? In fact, little can be stated as to why treatment works. It is not obvious, clear, or established that changes in cognitions are the basis for therapeutic change (Burns & Spangler, 2001; Ilardi & Craighead, 1994; Whisman, 1993, 1999). Indeed, suitable studies are rarely done. Some studies have demonstrated that changes in cognitions during treatment predict symptom change (e.g., DeRubeis et al., 1990; Kwon & Oei, 2003). Yet, it has not been clear in such studies whether (a) changes in cognition preceded symptom change, (b) symptom change preceded changes in cognitions, or (c) both changed at the same time and as a function of some other mechanism. There are very special assessment and design requirements to establish the time line for identifying what caused therapeutic change, and these are rarely included in treatment research (Kazdin, in press; Kazdin & Nock, 2003). I mention this topic here because of the importance of understanding why treatment works. Among the many reasons is that treatment effects are likely to be optimal when we know what the critical ingredients and processes are, how to vary them, and by how much.

That PMT can lead to change has been well established. Why change occurs has been studied but not very thoroughly. I highlight two broad areas that may shed light on how and why treatment leads to change and a third area to raise other questions that require critical thought and empirical research.

Contingencies of Reinforcement

I have mentioned previously that PMT treatment techniques are derived primarily from an area of learning referred to as operant conditioning. The principles of reinforcement, punishment, use of antecedents, and many technical features of how performance changes as a function of environmental changes have been very extensively studied in both animal and human learning. Thus the basis of the procedures—that is, how they influence acquisition, maintenance, and elimination of various behaviors—is fairly well worked out.

If one asks why the principles and their derivative techniques lead to change, one level of answer is based on learning. By providing specific experiences during the treatment and by systematically using antecedents and consequences, the parent and the child learn and perform new behaviors. Many animal laboratory and human tests have shown that very special relations are needed among antecedents, behaviors, and consequences for change to occur. For example, PMT uses techniques that are intended to change behaviors of the parent during the course of treatment. Positive reinforcement (praise from the therapist) is used to change concrete parent behaviors during the treatment sessions. Behavior of the parent is likely to change if reinforcing consequences provided by the therapist are contingent and immediate and meet other characteristics discussed in the chapter on reinforcement. The same point, of course, could be made in relation to the parent's use of positive reinforcement to change child behavior at home. That is, several conditions must be met or closely approximated in how the parent delivers antecedents and consequences, if child behavior is to change. Indeed, it is easy to demonstrate in laboratory research or applied settings how praise can be delivered and yet be quite ineffective. We know from endless demonstrations that there is no magic in delivery of reinforcers such as praise and tokens; several specific characteristics of delivery make an enormous difference. Knowing the factors that are required for developing the behaviors of interest and how behaviors are acquired and maintained provides one account of how the treatment procedures work.

In general, research on operant conditioning provides the underpinnings of PMT and how procedures can be used to change behavior. Operant learning does not account for all learning by any means. Basic research has identified the conditions under which the techniques do and do not work. The detailed description of these conditions, at one level of analysis, describes how the techniques operate and work. There is another sense in which basic research on operant conditioning does not explain precisely how learning comes about. We may know the conditions and how they relate to acquisition and performance in a descriptive way, but this is not quite an explanation. What does repeated reinforced practice do to the individual that develops new repertoires? Research has focused on the neurological underpinnings of learning through operant conditioning. More specifically, reinforcement experiences alter quite specific molecular and cellular processes of the brain (e.g., Brembs, Lorenzetti, Reyes, Baxter, & Byrne, 2002; Nakajima, Liu, & Lau, 1993). Moreover, blocking these processes at the neurological level impedes operant learning. Thus, the key requirements for operant learning at the level of procedures and brain processes are beginning to be elaborated. There is progress at multiple levels in advancing the bases of operant learning in general and how contingencies of reinforcement produce change.

It is a leap to suggest that PMT changes contingencies of reinforcement in the home and the neurological processes of participants in that interaction. In some sense, there must be neurological changes that underlie the effects of practice and learning. Yet, the precise changes and how they translate to behavior represent a gap in neurological research aside from PMT.

Inept Child-Rearing Practices

In the context of oppositional and aggressive behavior among children, the reasons for PMT's effectiveness have been studied. Several parenting practices are known to foster child deviance, particularly child aggression. These practices include attending to and reinforcing deviant child behavior, using commands excessively, using harsh punishment, failing to attend to appropriate child behavior, engaging in coercive parent–child interchanges, and failing to monitor children (e.g., their whereabouts). Decades of work on parent–child interaction in the home have elegantly demonstrated the sequence of changes during the interactions and how these escalate to aggression (Patterson, 1982; Patterson et al., 1992; Reid et al., 2002). This research has established that child-rearing practices can directly foster and increase aggressive child behavior. The next steps were also completed, namely, to show that altering these practices can reduce aggressive behavior and conduct problems. The results from several studies supported the role of child-rearing practices as critical to treatment (Dishion & Andrews, 1995; Dishion et al., 1992; Forgatch, 1991; Forgatch & De-

Garmo, 1999; Martinez & Forgatch, 2001). These are powerful demonstrations in the sense that parenting practices have been shown to be causally related to aggressive behavior in children. This does not mean that parenting practices are the only cause or the cause for all children with aggressive behavior, but it does establish parenting practices as causally involved in aggressive behavior rather than merely a correlate or antecedent (risk factor) (Kraemer et al., 1997).

PMT changes parenting practices, and these practices clearly improve child behavior. Indeed, changes in parenting practices during treatment continue to predict antisocial behavior years later (Schrepferman & Snyder, 2002). Overall, the findings on parenting practices during PMT advance our understanding of why and how changes occur. At the same time, there is not the clarity of surgical isolation of one influence (e.g., use of reinforcement) that is a single, necessary, and sufficient condition for changing child behavior. Many changes occur in PMT (e.g., discipline practices, parent supervision, and monitoring of the child), and any of these can influence outcome (Forgatch, 1991).

Parenting practices and changes in these practices provide a fine-grained account of what may happen in the home of aggressive children when there are coercive parent–child interchanges. As an interpretation of PMT, inept parenting practices do not have the advantage of parsimony in explaining how PMT achieves its changes. As I noted previously, the techniques used in PMT enjoy widespread application to many areas where inept parenting and coercion are not relevant. Indeed, the techniques can greatly improve child behavior in homes where parent–child interactions are not particularly problematic. Changing the contingencies of reinforcement and developing new learning experiences provide a reasonable and parsimonious interpretation for the factors that lead to change in PMT. No doubt changing inept parenting helps as well. There is no need to lobby for a single reason that explains why PMT works.

Other Influences That May Be Responsible for Change

PMT leads to changes in parent and child behavior. In the case of families of children with disruptive behavior, other changes occur as well. For example, parental stress in the home and parent symptoms (e.g., depression and symptoms across a range of dysfunctions) decrease, and family relations improve over the course of PMT in the treatment of conduct disorder and oppositional defiant disorder. Conceivably, the broad changes are the consequences of improving child behavior in the home. On the other hand, the broad changes raise a question about the basis of therapeutic change in the child. Perhaps broader influences are operating in treatment beyond merely changing rein-forcement practices, and these influences are responsible for the broad range of changes. For example, perhaps improved communication between parent and child and decreases in parental feelings of stress, helplessness, or despera-tion as a function of participating in treatment are critical factors of treatment.

These other influences are unlikely to be the key factors responsible for changes in the child. Implementation of reinforcement contingencies (e.g., contingent versus noncontingent reinforcement) has been shown in many studies to account for changes, whether programs are implemented by parents, teachers, or others. At this same time, the comments convey the broader point. Many aspects of the parent, child, and family interactions change during PMT. These changes have not been carefully assessed to chart the progression and time lines of these changes. It is possible that changes in the child, parent, and family are influenced by several facets of parenting and family life, including but beyond the contingencies of reinforcement, or that the benefits of treat-ment depend on both specific changes in the contingencies in the home and the broader contextual changes in which these are embedded. There is no rea-son to suppose that there is only one source of influence leading to change.

General Comments

Virtually all forms of psychotherapy have a theoretical explanation about how therapeutic changes are achieved and a set of procedures that follow from the theory that reflect what is done to and with the patient to bring these changes about. Many years ago, an eminent therapy researcher (Frank, 1961; see also Frank & Frank, 1991) proposed that therapies work because they have a *myth* (story line, explanation to the patient of how the problem emerged) and *ritual* (set of procedures that one must enact to get better). Embedded in this is the provocative view that the specific myth and ritual may not be essential to mo-bilize hope in the patient and to improve symptoms. That is, what is required is a persuasive myth and ritual—and whether it is based on psychoanalysis, learning theory, self theory, or some family-based theory may not be very im-portant. The case for this view can be made in many contexts. For example, treatments are often compared with other treatments or to attention-placebo conditions (i.e., nonveridical therapies). Improvements in therapy are related to expectancies that are mobilized by the treatment or control condition. When treatments surpass control conditions in their effects, one rival inter-pretation is that the conditions varied in the expectations for improvement they mobilized; that is, their myths and rituals were not equally persuasive. This is a larger topic to be sure (Baskin, Tierney, Minami, & Wampold, 2003; Frank & Frank, 1991; Kazdin, 2003b).

PMT goes a bit further than presenting a good story and a set of procedures to families. Research shows rather specifically what facets of treatment are essential for change. Altering the contingencies of reinforcement in the home clearly makes a difference. Many other influences may be operative as well, but much is known about the procedures, that they work, and what is needed to optimize their effects. Even so, we would like to know many other influences that may be operative in PMT and to chart the progression of changes.

Clinicians in need of effective interventions may worry little about identifying precisely why and how PMT achieves change. At the same time, a better understanding of the processes of change and the underlying mechanisms could further improve the treatment. There might be influences to harness that would make treatment more effective or effective with individuals who might otherwise respond minimally.

Supplementing Treatment to Improve Outcome

Adding Components and Separate Treatments

Supplementing treatment with some other component or intervention might enhance the strength of PMT. Perhaps for children and families who show many factors that predict attenuated response to treatment, these other components will be particularly well advised. For children referred for aggressive and antisocial behavior, many of the factors that influence therapeutic change, as noted previously, are present to some degree (Maughan, 2001; Stoff, Breiling, & Maser, 1997). Child behavior is embedded in a context with multiple factors, and these factors influence adherence and attendance to treatment, in addition to therapeutic change. Understandably, efforts have been made to supplement PMT with other interventions to enhance participation in treatment, as well as test whether addressing specific factors in the parents and family can augment therapeutic change.

As an illustration, many families with conduct problem children experience stress. Stress is directly related to the untoward child-rearing practices that PMT attempts to alter. Parents with high levels of stress are more likely to attend to (and unwittingly reinforce and foster) deviant child behavior, to sustain aversive interchanges with their children, and to counterattack in response to their children's aggression (e.g., Patterson, 1988). PMT can improve child behavior. It is reasonable to ask if addressing parent stress would enhance treatment. If parent stress were decreased, perhaps parenting and use of the parenting skills would be enhanced, and that would lead to greater changes of the child. This formulation of the question is rather simplistic because there are many kinds of stressors (e.g., daily hassles, major life events) and sources of stress (e.g., from one's job, spouse, health, living conditions), as well as resources to buffer them (e.g., personal competences, social support, religion).

"Simplistic" is not a bad place to begin. Consequently, in one of our studies, we focused on helping parents manage stress. All families received PMT; some (randomly determined) received supplemental sessions interspersed with PMT. During these sessions, the parent or guardian of the child received problem-solving skills training and assignments to engage in activities to reduce stress (e.g., more time with friends or spouse, activities, work). (Only one parent received this, even in two-parent families. Pilot work with two parents revealed that little could be accomplished because the sessions were difficult to keep from turning into marital therapy, venting, and blaming among the parents.) Those with the added treatment component showed greater therapeutic changes than those who received PMT without this added component (Kazdin & Whitley, 2003). There are many other such efforts to supplement PMT by addressing parent and family issues, focusing specifically on marital discord, and providing social support and problem-solving skills to the parents. The effects have been evident on improved parent attendance and retention in treatment, as well as on therapeutic changes of the children (e.g., Dadds & McHugh, 1992; Dadds et al., 1987; Pfiffner, Jouriles, Brown, Etscheidt, & Kelly, 1990; Prinz & Miller, 1994; Sanders, Markie-Dadds, et al., 2000; Webster-Stratton, 1994).

PMT focuses on the parent and parent–child interaction. An immediate question is whether focusing more directly on the child with an additional intervention can enhance the treatment effects. A few studies have provided cognitive problem-solving skills training to the child as an additional treatment. Problem-solving skills training focuses on how the child approaches interpersonal situations, the cognitive steps the child traverses before responding, and then the actual responses. Variants are effective as a treatment in their own right for conduct problem children (Durlak, Fuhrman, & Lampman, 1991; Kazdin, 2002). Supplementing PMT with problem-solving skills for the child enhances the effects of treatment (Kazdin, 2003a; Webster-Stratton, 1996).

Cautions

The research highlighted here suggests interventions that can be used to augment the effects of PMT. All this is to the good, but the information is difficult to use as a basis for clinical work. How and when to provide supplementary and complementary interventions are difficult to know. For example, it may seem reasonable to say that when there is evidence of family stress or marital discord, these ought to be focused on as part of treatment. Perhaps so. However, PMT has effected change in studies without these foci and in cases where these are salient issues among the families. Similarly, PMT alone has been effective, even though a few studies suggest it is more effective when supplemented by a cognitively based problem-solving skills intervention for the child. Here too, when to provide this supplementary treatment is not at all clear.

Perhaps the greatest single caution about supplementing treatment derives from the faulty logic often leading to treatment decisions. Quite commonly, if there is a factor that predicts poor responsiveness to treatment or is correlated (concurrently) with a problem, an assumption is made that focusing on that factor is important or essential as part of treatment. A factor (variable, characteristic) that is a correlate or a precursor of a clinical problem is not necessarily a useful target or focus of treatment (Kraemer et al., 1997). Not all predictors (risk factors) are causally involved in a problem, and modifying those that can be altered may not necessarily improve therapeutic change.

In clinical work and in research to a lesser extent, there is interest in adding components to treatment to address many, most, or all facets of the problems that emerge in assessing children and families. Throw-in-the-kitchen-sink approaches, as well as using all the treatments that work and that one personally likes (sometimes referred to as eclectic therapy), have a price.[4] Combinations do not always work and are not always better than the individual components provided separately (Kazdin, 1996a).

Several conditions limit our ability to pile on treatments in clinical work. First, supplementary treatments may add more sessions to treatment. Loss of patients through attrition has been known for some time to bear a direct relation to the duration of treatment (Phillips, 1985). Adding more treatment is likely to increase attrition, if this is accomplished by longer (e.g., more weeks of) treatment. If one tries to squeeze a second (supplementary) treatment into the same treatment duration as a single intervention, then either the supplementary treatment or the original treatment is likely to be diluted, that is, given in a smaller dose or for fewer sessions than if provided as a stand-alone treatment. Dilution of two treatments could be much less effective than a full or more complete dose of the primary intervention by itself.

Second, combined treatments, even when desirable, raise issues about cost and reimbursement. If combined treatments add costs to treatment, any added costs will raise issues. Combined treatments would need strong evidence to mobilize the support of third-party payers to cover additional cost. There are excellent examples of multiple and combined treatments that provide a critical increment in treatment effectiveness (e.g., treatment of HIV). The case is not so clear with the various combinations available and in use for treatment of child psychopathology.

Third, as a final caveat, the status of supplementary interventions warrants comment. PMT and its effects have been replicated extensively. Supplementary interventions that are added to focus on parent and family issues are less well studied. There is no standard supplementary intervention that has been evaluated sufficiently to argue strongly for its use as an essential or desirable component. Also, supplements to PMT are not widely available in manual form so that others could use them in clinical work.

A general clinical guideline is that if some parent or family issue or problem is interfering with delivery of, or adherence to, treatment, then perhaps it ought to be focused on as part of PMT. For example, untreated or uncontrolled clinical depression in the parent or guardian, marital discord, and domestic violence may be so blatant as to require intervention in addition or prior to PMT. This is not a very fine or empirically derived guideline to help clinicians in practice. In many other cases, it is not so obvious that a domain needs to be addressed, even though it might be desirable to do so for several reasons. For example, marital discord or divorce often present in families of children clinically referred for antisocial behavior may or may not have to be addressed to effect change. There are degrees and types of discord, variations in supports for parents and children (e.g., from relatives) that may influence treatment. Insufficient empirical information is available on these issues to guide clinical work.

Limitations of PMT

The limitations of PMT can be discussed in relation to other treatments available for children and adolescents and in relation to what we wish to know about treatment in general, independent of its standing in relation to other treatments. The former considers the standing of PMT in relation to other treatments (relative status of PMT). The latter considers the extent to which PMT achieves the goals we would want of a treatment (absolute status of PMT as a treatment). These different perspectives are important to bear in mind because they can lead to conflicting conclusions and misstatements. For example, the evidence in behalf of PMT could be far and above many other treatments (relative standing) but still not take us to where we would like (absolute standing) because it does not eliminate the clinical problem for everyone or have the degree of impact we would like, even among those children who do change. Consider the limitations raised by both relative and absolute perspectives.

Treatment Outcome Effects

Basic questions can be raised about therapeutic changes that result from PMT, including the magnitude and scope of the changes and the number (proportion) of children who respond. This discussion considers changes among children with oppositional, aggressive, or antisocial behavior where the PMT evidence is the strongest. Needless to say, the benefits of PMT in randomized controlled trials establish that treatment is better than no treatment based on statistical differences and changes. The differences are examined from direct comparisons of treatment and no-treatment (or some other treatment) conditions; improvements are evaluated (within subjects) by changes from pretreatment to posttreatment. An issue in treatment evaluation in general is to discern whether statistically significant differences or changes from pretreatment to posttreatment translate to an effect or change that is useful or relevant to individual children and their families.

In treatment evaluation, *clinical significance* has been introduced to examine whether the impact of treatment makes a difference in everyday functioning and includes many ways of examining the data that go well beyond statistical significance (see Kazdin, 2003b; Kendall, 1999). That is, are the children and families who receive PMT better in palpable ways? The most frequently used method of assessing clinical significance has been whether the symptoms of individuals who receive treatment fall within normative levels (of nonclinic samples) after they complete treatment. In several studies of PMT, children referred for aggressive and antisocial behavior are well outside the normative range before treatment but fall within normative levels after treatment, that is, PMT can produce clinically significant changes.

There are still some ambiguities associated with measures of clinical significance (Kazdin, 1999). In most cases, the measures used to operationalize clinical significance have not been tested to see if they reflect differences in the clients that make a difference. For example, if a child shows a reduction in symptoms on a parent- or teacher-report scale and that reduction places the child into a normative range, is the child functioning as well as a child from a community sample who achieves the same score? How do the changes on the scale (questionnaire, inventory) translate to how the child is performing in everyday life? Parent ratings of child behavior, the most common outcome measure in child treatment research, are greatly influenced by parent factors (parent depression, stress), which can also change with child treatment. Whether the child has changed enough to make an important (clinically significant) change may or may not be evident in the score on parent ratings. Sometimes the measures that depend less or not at all on parent ratings (e.g., school grades, truancy, detention) and dramatic change on a given measure (e.g., elimination of fights at home or at school) attest to the impact of treatment on the child's functioning and allow more to be said than that the changes are "statistically significant."

A critical outcome question is the proportion of children who improve, improve significantly, or respond to PMT. After all, PMT might be more effective than other treatments and produce statistically significant results without helping many individuals. Clinicians and researchers would like a clear answer to the question of how many improve. Several obstacles conspire against providing a defensible or at least firm answer to what proportion of children respond to treatment. Among the obstacles are the enormously diverse samples and age ranges included in the studies, the difficulty in deciding when a child has "improved," and the varied answers one would get if the criterion for that decision came from parent or teacher report or direct observation. Also, patients drop out of treatment, and those who drop out are often more severely disturbed than those who remain in treatment (Kazdin, Mazurick, & Siegel, 1994). Thus, we ought not take very seriously any statistic or summary number or expect a summary statistic to extend widely across diverse samples.

The difficulties in interpreting summary measures are nicely illustrated by work at the clinic in which I am involved. We have found that approximately 79% of clinically referred youth who complete treatment have made a change that parents see as important—we might even say clinically significant (Kazdin & Wassell, 1998). This percentage suggests a rather significant impact on the clinical problem for most children referred to treatment. However, using this same index, we have found that 34% of families that drop out "prematurely" make such changes as well. This is very difficult to interpret because dropouts include families that are success stories and leave early as a result and also families who probably do not profit at all. The summary statistics hide the complexity and information about who responds and why.

The statistics about treatment effects often gloss over what the measure is and the limited domain the measure may address. Child psychotherapy outcome research in general focuses almost exclusively on symptom reduction, and PMT has not been immune from this. From the standpoint of both short- and long-term child adjustment, many other outcome domains are likely to be relevant, including impairment in everyday life, participation in activities, academic functioning, and peer relations, to mention a few. These domains are likely to be impaired among conduct-problem youths and also influence long-term prognosis. Symptom improvement is important but by itself omits critical information about functioning in domains that may be just as critical.

Maintenance of Therapeutic Changes

In relation to durability, the poor prognosis for conduct problems raises the question of the extent to which treatment will make a long-term difference. Children referred for antisocial behavior are at risk for dysfunction in adolescence (e.g., substance abuse, criminal activity) and adulthood (e.g., criminal behavior, antisocial personality disorder in males, depression in females) (see Kazdin, 1995b). PMT results have been sustained for 1–2 years beyond treatment in several studies. Studies with longer follow-up for oppositional and aggressive children suggest that the effects of treatment are maintained several years later (Brinkmeyer & Eyberg, 2003; Long et al., 1994). Longer term follow-up studies have evaluated how treated individuals are doing and in the examples cited do not continue to evaluate control group participants. Consequently, one cannot tell whether the benefits of treatment exceed changes that would occur over time as a function of development and other life experiences. One might regard the data as "promising." Strictly speaking, conclusions about the impact of PMT must be tempered until long-term follow-up data are available.

I mentioned the relative and absolute perspectives one might take in evaluating PMT. Comments on the magnitude, scope, and durability of treatment results convey this nicely. The follow-up data are a case in point. Most treatments for children have not been studied empirically; among the treatments that have been studied, most have not reported follow-up data. For the minority of studies in which follow-up data are obtained, the duration tends to be 6–12 months (Kazdin, 2000b). In this context and relative to other treatments, PMT looks sparkling and refreshing. Yet, we need to know whether there are durable effects of treatment. PMT is deficient, and in this respect the weaker status of many other treatments is not relevant or helpful.

Applicability Among Clinical Problems

For the treatment of oppositional and conduct problems, PMT has excellent support and might well be viewed as the treatment of choice or place to begin in selecting an intervention. In this context in particular, PMT is the best studied and established treatment for oppositional, aggressive, and antisocial behavior (see reviews cited earlier in the chapter). For other clinical problems, the treatment is much less well established. The clinical problem "closest" to conduct disorder is ADHD. I say *closest* in the sense that the overlap of the two disorders clinically emerges because of their high rate of comorbidity. Also, ADHD, along with conduct disorder and oppositional defiant disorder, is part of externalizing behavior or disruptive behavioral problems that act outward on the environment.

The impact of PMT on ADHD is mixed at best. PMT can reduce conduct problems among ADHD youths and ADHD symptoms among youths identified with behavioral problems (e.g., Anastopoulos & Farley, 2003; Strayhorn & Weidman, 1991). Yet, PMT is not usually viewed as a sufficient treatment for ADHD. Stimulant medication is still regarded as the treatment of choice in relation to the core symptoms (e.g., impulsivity, inattention). The previous chapter highlighted the MTA Study (Multimodal Treatment Study of Children with Attention-Deficit/Hyperactivity Disorder). This was the largest and most comprehensive investigation on the effects of medication combined with PMT. Medication with or without the addition of PMT was about equally effective on the core symptoms of ADHD. On other outcomes or indices of treatment effects (e.g., functional impairment, consumer satisfaction), medication and PMT combined surpassed medication alone (MTA Cooperative Group, 1999a, 1999b; Swanson et al., 2002). In addition, in the combined PMT plus medication group, lower doses of medication were needed to achieve similar outcomes than in the medication alone group. Thus, PMT had beneficial effects when added to medication depending on the outcomes. Whether the increment of effects warrants routine use and is worth the added cost is a judgment call.

Children with ADHD often show oppositional, aggressive, and antisocial behaviors as part of the clinical picture, whether or not they officially meet criteria for the diagnoses (e.g., oppositional defiant disorder or conduct disorder). PMT is quite likely to be effective in relation to these behaviors and hence is regarded as a suitable adjunct for ADHD symptoms. On the other hand, some children may show primarily or exclusively the core symptoms related to attention and impulsivity, and hence oppositional, aggressive, and antisocial behavior may not be present. This is not a very sophisticated guideline for whether PMT is a suitable supplement for medication. However, the treatment decision can be made sequentially; that is, if medication effects do not improve outcomes that PMT augments in the MTA study or still leave considerable oppositional and aggressive behavior, PMT would be a reasonable addition.

In relation to other clinical problems, PMT outcome research is rather sketchy. As an illustration, there is no standard evidenced-based treatment for children with autism. PMT has been part of a more comprehensive program in which the contingencies are altered throughout the everyday life of the child, at home and in outpatient treatment. Others (e.g., teachers, special trainers to work with the child during the day) also are used as part of a more intensive effort. Although contingency management in which PMT plays a central role has been identified as the best available treatment (e.g., Smith, 1999), it is not established as an effective treatment by any means.

In relation to other problems, PMT is not usually used for internalizing problems such as depression, anxiety, and social withdrawal. Reinforced practice is one of the procedures used for anxiety, and this entails use of one of the principles on which PMT relies. However, treatments for internalizing problems among children, particularly in contemporary research, focus primarily on cognitively based interventions and are beyond the scope of this book (see Kazdin & Weisz, 2003).

Neglected Areas of Research

Although many areas of research can be identified in which much further information is needed, three lacunae stand out. First, there is a paucity of studies that focus on adolescents with conduct problems (Woolfenden, Williams, & Peat, 2002). There are interesting applications with adolescents, such as training teenage mothers in rearing their children (Coren, Barlow, & Stewart-Brown, 2003). However, this is different from youths referred clinically for their disruptive behavioral problems as the focus of treatment. Most PMT studies focus on youths 3–10 years of age. Within this age range, parent delivery of praise, attention, and privileges may be especially useful and have a significant impact on child behavior. As the child enters adolescence, peers take on a salient role in general and in the promotion and maintenance of antisocial behavior (Elliott, Huizinga, & Menard, 1988; Newcomb & Bentler, 1988). The child may be out of the home more and less amenable to those easily mobilized influences (praise, tokens) that are central to PMT. Controlled studies have shown PMT to reduce offense rates among delinquent adolescents, as well as school behavioral problems and substance use among adolescents at risk for serious conduct problems (Bank, Marlowe, Reid, Patterson, & Weinrott, 1991; Dishion & Andrews, 1995; Farrington & Welsh, 2003). Thus, PMT has been effective with adolescents.

Some authors have suggested that adolescents may respond less well to PMT than do children (Dishion & Patterson, 1992). Direct comparisons to make this claim firmly have not been completed, at least to my knowledge. Such comparisons would include studies in which both adolescents and children were in the same study, were similar in presenting problems (e.g., relatively similar in severity), and were evaluated with at least roughly equivalent outcome measures. In the absence of firm data, assume for a moment that adolescents do respond less well to treatment. The effect might be accounted for by severity of symptoms (Ruma et al., 1996). Adolescents referred for treatment tend to be more severely and chronically impaired than preadolescents. Indeed, once severity is controlled, age does not invariably influence outcome. Yet, in light of limited applications with adolescents, the strength of conclusions about the efficacy of PMT applies mainly to preadolescent youths.

A second area that has been neglected within PMT is consideration of ethnic and cultural issues (Forehand & Kotchick, 1996). Variation in parenting practices and family values among ethnic groups may influence receptivity to changes in parent–child interaction patterns. The use of corporal punishment, the role of extended family members in raising children, and parents' expectations for the child's self-control and obedience could readily influence the effectiveness and indeed applicability of PMT. These factors often vary as a function of socioeconomic status as well as ethnicity. Diverse ethnic groups and the full range of socioeconomic status have been encompassed by studies of PMT. However, the effects of ethnic, cultural, and socioeconomic status on disseminability, treatment implementation, and clinical outcomes of PMT remain to be investigated.

The comments on diversity of samples are not a call for research that shows PMT can be applied to diverse ethnic and cultural groups; there are hundreds of such groups worldwide, and a mere extension would be uninspired (see Kazdin, 2003b). However, cultural groups and variations within a group might have beliefs or practices that influence the applicability or outcomes of PMT. Efforts to elaborate these beliefs and practices and their relation to outcome could have important clinical implications. One task of research is to identify individuals who are well suited (i.e., respond well) to various treatments. Better triage (i.e., directing people to treatments from which they are likely to profit) is critically important for the individual patient and for service delivery more generally.

A third area in need of research pertains to the amount of treatment that is helpful or enough for a given family. This is a broad issue in child therapy research and not unique to PMT. In research, fairly fixed doses of treatment are provided (e.g., 8–12 sessions), with flexibility to address clinical issues. In clinical work, the duration is likely to be very flexible. Treatment may end for reasons other than a fixed regimen, such as dropping out, end of insurance payments for the sessions, and improvements in the child. The number of sessions required or essential for PMT to be effective and the criteria for ending treatment are neglected areas. The number of sessions may not be critical if the parents meet specific objectives or child behavior has improved. However, we do not know how much improvement is sufficient to serve as a basis for ending treatment or when additional sessions do not make an incremental difference in outcome.

The issue has emerged at the clinic in which I am involved. Families drop out of treatment. Although the rates are lower than the 40% to 60% that apparently characterize child, adolescent, and adult therapy, they are notable. Dropping out of treatment before the researcher or clinician believes treatment is completed is often called *premature termination* of treatment. Experience at the clinic has led us to question whether the notion of "premature termination" is presumptuous. We have seen remarkable improvements in several families who dropped out, and indeed, improvements in the child seem to be a critical influence to dropping out. Approximately one-third of early dropouts show quite significant improvements (Kazdin & Wassell, 1998), as I noted previously. What ought to be the criteria for enough treatment? Are the criteria how the children are functioning, how much they have changed, and how stable the changes have been (e.g., consistent for a few weeks or months)? These are broader questions. As clinicians, we often believe that we can "individually tailor" treatment to patients and determine when to end treatment at the right time. However, there is no good empirical basis for deciding when enough is enough and when changes are likely to be stable and maintained.

Extensions of PMT to Parenting in Nonclinic Populations

The applicability and benefits of PMT may extend well beyond the context of treating clinical problems. Child rearing in everyday life presents enormous challenges under normal circumstances, given the parent's responsibility for taking care of children, guiding their present and future, and developing scores of behaviors in the context of home, school, and community. Understandably, parents may rely on or resort to parenting practices to which they were exposed in their own upbringing. Usually, this turns out to be fine, even if not optimally effective. Yet, even in "normal" child rearing, parents often resort to punishment or harsh punishment, excessive commands, and ineffective nagging. These procedures tend to be frustrating to parents, as well as weak or ineffective in their impact. Moreover, some of the practices can have deleterious consequences.

Rare or very occasional spanking has not been shown to have positive or negative effects. The research is simply not clear on the impact of this level of spanking. Yet, frequent spanking can contribute to behavioral problems (e.g., aggressive and antisocial behavior) and even have untoward long-term physical consequences. A dramatic example emerged in the findings of the World Health Organization report, which noted that frequent spankings and harsh punishment in general are associated with many untoward consequences in adulthood including morbidity and mortality from major illnesses (e.g., heart disease, cancer, lung disease) (Krug, Dahlberg, Mercy, Zwi, & Lozano, 2002). This is a dramatic finding and at first blush perplexing—how can spanking predict or lead to early death from serious illnesses? The interpretation of this is that frequent corporal punishment increases risk behaviors directly related to health including smoking, overeating, and sedentary lifestyle that increase the likelihood of these diseases.

PMT is a useful adjunct to "normal" parenting. Judicious use of prompting, attending, ignoring, shaping, and very mild punishment is the cornerstone of PMT. Use of these could go rather far in easing child rearing for both parents and children. Each new generation of parents complains about the lack of training in basic parenting skills. A brief course of PMT might be a useful part of a larger package that teaches new parents how to care for the social, emotional, and other needs of the child.

Summary and Conclusions

Many controlled outcome studies attest to the effectiveness of PMT, particularly for treating children with oppositional, aggressive, and antisocial behavior. In terms of evidence-based treatment, PMT would rank among those whose effects have been the best replicated. Beyond outcome studies, research has evaluated several child, parent, family, and treatment factors that influence outcome.

The effects of PMT are achieved by altering the contingencies of reinforcement in the home, specifically in relation to parenting practices and parent–child interaction. Although the basis of the effects of PMT—that is, why it works—has been studied, there are many influences that have yet to be studied. In the process of changing specific parenting practices (e.g., promotion of prosocial behavior, discipline), many broad influences may change as well (e.g., level of parent stress, family relationships), and the role of such factors in PMT and therapeutic change is not well studied.

In the case of oppositional and aggressive children, children, parents, and families often evince untoward characteristics other than the referral symptoms (e.g., broad deficits of the child, high stress and marital discord in the parents). Occasionally, treatments have been added to PMT to address these in an effort to improve treatment effects. Two examples include problem-solving skills training for the child and support or stress management for the parent. Some of these supplements improve outcomes, but supplements to PMT are less well studied and replicated. When and when not to add a supplementary treatment is not well worked out. What may seem like obvious guidelines (e.g., treatment cannot succeed without treating marital discord, maternal depression, child anxiety) are not clear at all. In clinical work, one tries to manage the issues that emerge in treatment to ensure that some effort is made to address each of the problems.

PMT has limitations. The magnitude and durability of change are two issues not yet resolved. Precisely what the impact is on the everyday functioning of children and families is not studied very often, an issue that applies to child and adolescent therapy research in general. One would like to see more studies with measures of everyday functioning (school achievement, participation in activities, reduced expulsions or contacts with the courts). Change on such measures already has been shown, but the literature is weaker on real-world indices of treatment impact.

The durability of change is an issue as well. Long-term follow-up is rare in light of the many difficulties of following treated samples and separating the impact of treatment from so many other influences that transpire over the course of follow-up. Unlike large-scale longitudinal studies, sample sizes of treatment studies tend to be small. The "normal" or expected attrition of some portion of the sample in long-term follow-up makes it difficult to test whether the changes are evident (e.g., statistical power).

An important feature of PMT is that it has applicability well beyond a specific clinical problem. For example, child rearing in the homes of community samples can be and has been improved with PMT. The principles and techniques on which PMT is based have been applied to individuals of all ages (e.g., infants, toddlers, college students, geriatric patients) and in diverse settings (e.g., the home, school, the military, business and industry). Evidence from applications in these other contexts provides further, even if indirect, support for the procedures used in PMT.

Notes

1. I mentioned in chapter 1 that several programs of research have developed PMT and reported multiple outcome studies. Major research programs on PMT for oppositional, aggressive, and antisocial behavior include Sheila Eyberg (University of Florida), Rex Forehand, (University of Georgia), Gerald Patterson (Oregon Social Learning Research Center), Carolyn Webster-Stratton (University of Washington), and Matthew Sanders (University of Queensland). Other programs have focused on PMT for hyperactivity, including the programs by Russell Barkley (University of Massachusetts) and Arthur Anastopoulos (University of North Carolina). The programs of research by these investigators have been reviewed in many articles and books (e.g., Hibbs & Jensen, in press; Kazdin & Weisz, 2003; Mash & Barkley, 1998).
2. Here is a sample of some of the many literature reviews: Barlow, Parsons, & Stewart-Brown, 2002a, 2002b; Brestan & Eyberg, 1998; Coren et al., 2003; Farmer, Compton, Burns, & Robertson, 2002; Farrington & Welsh, 2003; Kazdin, 1997; Serketich & Dumas, 1996; Woolfenden et al., 2002. The reviews are not entirely redundant; they address slightly different samples (e.g., delinquent vs. oppositional and conduct problems; age ranges) and use somewhat different selection criteria for identifying studies. Largely excluded from the reviews are single-case experimental designs that demonstrate the effects of treatment on one or more families.
3. Basic and applied research in operant conditioning are published in many journals, but two journals devoted exclusively to these areas are the *Journal of the Experimental Analysis of Behavior* and the *Journal of Applied Behavior Analysis*, respectively.
4. It is often stated that eclectic therapy is individually tailored to the needs of the patient. I have been unable to find evidence that we know how to do this effectively and that efforts to individually tailor treatment surpass the outcomes obtained by simply providing the best available treatment. A supercynical view, to which of course I do not subscribe, is that eclectic therapy *is* individually tailored. However, it is individually tailored to the needs of the therapist.

7

Critical Issues in Applying and Implementing Treatment

Providing treatment to children and their families has its own obstacles that are not specific to PMT. These include identifying when to intervene (e.g., when a problem warrants referral to treatment rather than reflects a developmental perturbation that may pass), the little or no motivation that children may have to come to treatment, deciding the appropriate focus of treatment (e.g., child, parent, family, and in what combinations), and retaining cases in treatment (see Kazdin, 2000b; Remschmidt, 2001). These are not specific to any one form of treatment, such as PMT, hence the reader is referred to other sources. There are special obstacles and issues that can emerge in relation to applying and implementing PMT in particular, and these serve as the focus of this chapter. I have organized these into three categories to facilitate their presentation: parent and therapist issues that may emerge at the outset of treatment and limited treatment effects as the program is applied. The issues are intertwined, of course, but meaningful distinctions and emphases permit their delineation.

Parent Issues

The parents play an obviously central role in PMT, and any issues they bring to treatment or obstacles that emerge in relation to their implementation of treatment are pivotal. In applying PMT, several parent-related issues can readily emerge.

Parent Expectations of Therapy

The Conceptual Model of PMT

Many characteristics of PMT often are discrepant with what parents coming to treatment expect from child therapy. As abstract as this may appear, the conceptual model of PMT, taken for granted or as a given by the therapist, may clash with parent expectations. By model, I refer to the overall approach and focus of treatment. The model for PMT, stated simply, is that providing new learning experiences can alter parent and child behavior, and these changes can achieve the goals of treatment. The focus of treatment is on what parents and children *do*, as distinct from how they feel or how they perceive their plight. Actions rather than the child's emotional life, insight, and understanding are the focus.

Many parents want to know *why* their child is angry, *why* their child hits them, *why* the child "can't get along," and *why* the child is not like a more angelic brother or sister. This is not mere intellectual curiosity that is easily satisfied with information or cast aside with a cryptic answer ("Good question, we do not know") or indeed even a detailed, honest answer. As a therapist, we can experience the deeply felt and emotionally moving frustration of parents as they ask these questions. I raise the conceptual issue as critical to application and implementation because many parents do not find the conceptual model very satisfactory.

In PMT, therapists typically spend little time discussing how the child developed the problem or what the problem means in some psychological sense. PMT is quite concerned with the causes of the clinical problem. Indeed, the successes of treatment have emerged from understanding many of the determinants of behavior. But these are the current determinants or what can be done right now to change behavior, and they are not quite the same as the parents' concerns. Parents are concerned usually with the cause of the onset of the problem, and even effective treatment does not necessarily satisfy this.

Of course, for many of the problems brought to treatment, we can say a lot about risk and protective factors associated with the onset of disorders. We can even go further in some cases. For example, we can say that physical punishment and inept parenting can lead directly to aggressive behavior (e.g., Patterson et al., 1992). Yet, there are many paths to a given disorder, so a single cause or set of causes is unlikely to be the culprit for all cases. Moreover, based on current knowledge, we cannot really say why this child before us now has the problem.

PMT provides a conceptual model about what to do in treatment, and that emphasis is on behavior of the child. One would think this is really what the doctor ordered because almost all complaints of parents coming to treatment for their children focus on behavior, especially externalizing behavior. However, many parents are not satisfied with the seeming focus on behavior, given the seeming neglect of emotions and thought processes of the children. I say *seeming* because therapy usually cannot be so surgical as to merely carve out change in one domain (behavior) without influencing other domains (affect, cognition). Even so, the rationale for PMT does not focus on what many parents expect from treatment. This expectation may come from years of stereotypic portrayals of psychoanalysis and client-centered therapy and adults on couches talking about their pasts. Perhaps in time, with applications of evidence-based treatments, and with increased use of technology in treatment (e.g., computers, DVDs), expectations and stereotypes of treatment will change. Alternatively, therapists using PMT may want to address the concerns that parents often bring regarding the emotional life of the children. Parent concerns by definition are important, and addressing the etiology of the child's problems in a broader way may be a spoonful of sugar that makes the medicine go down. (I recognize that for other therapists "relating" to the parents is considered to be the medicine.)

Parents often have in mind an automobile repair model of treatment. That is, treatment amounts to bringing the child to the clinic, having him or her "fixed," waiting in the reception area while the repairs are made, and then driving home with the child better (and maybe with a 90-day warranty). Parents usually believe that the responsibility for improvement falls with the therapist and that treatment will be primarily conducted at the clinic. These expectations may fit, in varying degrees, to other forms of therapy (e.g., play therapy). Yet, in PMT much of the responsibility for improvement falls to the parents, who implement behavior-change programs at home.

To underscore this role, we begin at our clinic by telling the parent that the primary role of the therapist resembles that of a coach. The therapist guides, trains, and practices many of the skills and provides the conditions to optimize the impact of training, is responsive to all issues that emerge, and so on, but most of the treatment takes place at home. Therefore, parents have to do some work at home, take responsibility for "running" behavior-change programs, work with the therapist to craft programs that are at once feasible and effective, and deal with the school and/or teachers, as needed. Needless to say, these demands can be modified to meet the abilities of individual parents. Also, therapists invariably shape parent behavior to develop what the parent does and can be trained to do within the confines of a limited treatment period. Yet, the broader point is the one to make here; namely, the model of treatment has direct implications for the demands made of the parent, and these demands often depart from what the parents expect of child and adolescent psychotherapy.

Concrete Procedures Used in Treatment

The model of treatment and the concerns the model raises may be reflected in more specific aspects of the procedures used in treatment. Two such aspects are mentioned here to convey the point. First, positive reinforcement plays a central role in changing the behavior of the child. In conjunction with the therapist, parents develop "reward" programs such as simple token or point charts to develop child behavior. The use of rewards for compliance, not fighting with a sibling, and related behaviors can raise multiple concerns.

- "Isn't this just bribery of the child?"
- "My child *knows* how to do the behavior and is just being oppositional."
- "My *other* child does this without any special rewards."
- "At best, this reinforcement program will just get the behavior while the program is in effect."
- "Will I have to reward the child for the rest of his [or her] life to get this behavior?"

Each of these concerns can be readily addressed. Briefly, no, it is not bribery; yes, but knowing and doing consistently are not very related in human behavior; it *is* frustrating that a sibling performs the desired behaviors without any special program, but the question before us is what we can do now to improve the other child's level of performance and functioning. And no, the reinforcement program is quite temporary and will end during the course of treatment while the behavior is maintained.

Answering these questions does not necessarily resolve the overarching issue, that key procedures of PMT may be at odds with parents' beliefs of what ought to be done in treatment or in parent interaction more generally. There is, of course, another side to this. Many parents have experienced years of "talk" therapy for their oppositional and aggressive child and have seen little palpable improvement. They often come to our clinic eager to try something that might have an effect on the daily problems of fighting, school, and functioning in everyday life.

A quite different facet of treatment can also reflect concrete concerns of parents during treatment. Treatment includes a great deal of reinforced practice for the parent. Some of this is in role play with the therapist. The therapist and parent(s) act the roles of the child and parent in diverse scenarios. In other sessions, the child is brought into treatment, and there is additional practice in which the therapist, parent, and child enact what happens at home or practice some new skill for the parent or child.

Parents may be concerned and uncomfortable with role playing. Parents are asked to get up out of their seats and start pretending. The therapist then models, reinforces with praise, and shapes various behaviors in the parent. The style for doing this in an effective way is not easily conveyed in a treatment manual. The tone must be like a very supportive, evenhanded, and noncondescending teacher, coach, or instructor. Our group has found that if the therapist explains why practice is important and then asks in a matter-of-fact way, parents routinely get up and role play. This issue rarely emerges as a problem in treatment.

In role plays, parents' praise is often flat, mechanical, and without the non-verbal cues (smiles, touching) that can help. Chapter 3 mentioned the conditions required for effective delivery of positive reinforcement. All of this has to be squeezed into the repertoire of the parent, which can emerge as an issue. The task of the therapist is to make interactions that could be awkward, natural and comfortable. In almost all instances, we have found that role playing and reinforcement for parent behavior work well. Indeed, many parents enjoy this facet of treatment, as reflected in their own smiles, spontaneity, and verbal statements.

Beliefs About Child-Rearing Practices

A curse—or, on a more positive note, a challenge—of PMT principles and techniques is that virtually all parents coming to treatment have strong views of discipline practices, what works and what does not, and how children ought to be treated. These views are based on parents' experiences (e.g., raising at least one child and often many children), memories of their own past and an interest in continuing or discontinuing some practice to which they were exposed, religious beliefs ("spare the rod, spoil the child"), moral views not necessarily tied to a religion (what is or is not right), cultural and ethnic views, and no doubt other influences. PMT may conflict with deeply held beliefs about child-rearing practices and values about what constitutes good and appropriate parenting.

The parents' views about child rearing and their actual practices in use on a daily basis can be counterproductive and exacerbate the problems treatment will focus on (e.g., frequent corporal punishment of aggressive children). Other practices merely make the parent ineffective in child–parent interactions (e.g., frequent commands and nagging). PMT may have to undo existing practices, as well as develop new practices. A challenge for treatment is developing new parent–child interaction patterns and doing so in ways that are in keeping with parents' views, their dignity, and their freedom to choose how to rear the children.

As an example of the challenge, one father at the clinic I have mentioned said, "I am going to keep beating my child until he learns not to get into fights. My father beat me and it worked with me; it will work for him [my child] too." This is a common view we encounter at the clinic, and it illustrates the point. The irrationality and veracity of the statements are irrelevant (but interesting). The boy was referred to the clinic because of endless fighting at school; as to whether being beaten worked with the father—not very plausible. He physically abused the boy, beat his wife regularly (but never touched a young daughter), and had been in jail for 3 months for beating up a neighbor and brandishing a gun somewhere during this episode. The father has deeply held beliefs about child rearing and practices that accompany these beliefs.

Having stated the challenge, I hasten to add that this obstacle can be surmounted. In PMT, we do not try to persuade parents to believe differently or challenge their views. Some brief comments convey arguments against a child-rearing practice that is counterproductive, but we emphasize shaping what the parents actually do in the home. For example, the abusive father beat his boy at least once a day, with only rare exceptions. We trained the parents to use time out from reinforcement. The mother agreed to try the procedure, and parents and therapists practiced using it in the session. Yet, practice in the session, however intensive, would seem unlikely to change the daily corporal punishment from the father. Also, asking the father to understand, mend his ways, and have new insights, in my opinion, represents a naive view of how human behavior changes.

We began implementing time out by having the father choose a day when he would not beat the child—the easiest day when this might be completed. (We asked the father to choose only a half-day, but he said he could do a whole day.) With phone prompts (a reminder) to the father and praise (in response to his statement of what he did in relation to the program), this strategy proved to be immediately successful and was extended to more days. Despite an occasional relapse on a day we selected, there was progressive movement. By the end of treatment, there was no physical abuse on any of the days. When punishment was provided, it was 5 minutes of time out. The father was brimming with new insights and changed attitudes, and he was proselytizing the deficiencies of beating one's children. (We have encountered these reactions scores of times: insight, attitude change, and proselytizing that *follow* behavior change. Indeed, many of our parents have end up being "proselytutes." They advocate quite extremely about how inept and abusive parenting is and how parents ought to behave differently.)

In general, one can alter many specific practices in the home. The procedures central to PMT (e.g., praise, shaping, prompting) can readily change parent behavior. As one does this, many parents come to alter their deeply held beliefs. However, the point of intervention to change the child as well as the parent is in what the parents do. Changing deeply held beliefs, on the assumption we know how to do this, might not translate into actions that would improve child behavior.

Parent Adherence

With treatment, whether medical or psychological, ensuring that the patient or client adheres to the treatment regimen is obviously important. I mention the issue here to reiterate that PMT may make more demands on the parent than other forms of treatment. Parents are asked to implement token reinforcement and praise programs with their children, to administer time out in special ways, to walk away from their children rather than to engage in arguing, and so on. Occasionally, parents may be asked to simulate (i.e., practice) difficult situations in the home to help the child respond to hearing no or to not having his or her way. In short, there are many demands, and adherence to them can be an issue.

I cannot identify any other treatment that at once provides an intervention and includes a plan and set of strategies to promote adherence. Specifically, in PMT, tasks are introduced and trained gradually in the parent(s) (as evident in the manual later in the book). Based on the parent's execution of these tasks, the program continues, and new or varied tasks are introduced. If performance falters, if parent adherence is poor, or if the parent complains, the tasks can be reduced. A goal is to have the parent execute the contingencies really well, even if at first this applies to only one or two child behaviors. The full-blown program includes contingent praise, a point chart, planned ignoring, time out from reinforcement, prompts, special punishment for low-rate behavior, and more. This sounds terribly complex, in part because of how I wrote the last sentence. I could also say, in a different context, driving a car includes pressing a pedal (on some cars), starting the ignition, placing the car in gear, looking around and signaling, pressing the gas slightly, and moving into the appropriate lane (and oh, I forgot, if you have not done so already, release the emergency break). These driving behaviors are fairly seamless and include many steps. In PMT, the program is introduced quite gradually and all the time with attention to what is going on in the home and how the parent and child are doing.

Often in therapy, clients do not adhere to demands that are placed on them. Traditionally, the responsibility for a client's failure to carry out what is asked is placed on the client. Actually, it is placed *in* the client by referring to abilities and personality characteristics. Therapist phrases that reflect this view are "this is beyond the client's ability" and the "client is resisting." In fact, any given client may not have a particular ability or may be resisting. Yet, PMT and the approach it reflects place primary responsibility for parent adherence on the therapist. The therapist is interested in moving the parents toward improved performance on a gradual basis. If some tasks are not working or take a little time to acquire, the time is taken with an optional treatment session here or there. This does not mean that every parent can learn everything and perform wonderfully well. It does mean that there are systematic ways of teaching and training parents that are inherent in treatment. The teaching can be individualized in terms of the rate of learning and how much of the learning is provided. Although adherence problems emerge, the therapist's use of ABCs provides many options to address the matter.

Attrition

Dropping out of therapy is a pervasive issue and concern in clinical practice and research. As a general rule, clients' premature termination is a function of the duration of treatment, a relation that has been demonstrated with varied patient samples, treatments, and clinical settings (Phillips, 1985). In general, the longer the treatment, the higher the percentage of clients who drop out. Most clients who drop out do so early in treatment, and then additional losses trickle off over the course of time. As usually defined, *dropping out* refers to terminating treatment prematurely and against the advice of the clinician. In child, adolescent, and adult psychotherapy, 40% to 60% of cases drop out of treatment, a rather high percentage (Kazdin, 1996b; Wierzbicki & Pekarik, 1993).

Although I could find no evidence that shows attrition to be greater with PMT than with some other treatment, comment is warranted nonetheless. Whether parents can and will engage in the procedures required of them in PMT or just give up and drop out of treatment is a concern that therapists sometimes voice. It is true that PMT makes greater demands on the parent and family than some more traditional (talk therapy) forms of treatment. One might expect that greater demands would lead to greater attrition, a topic that deserves investigation. Our own research on the matter has shown that the *perception* that treatment is demanding is associated with dropping out of treatment. Parents who receive the same treatment vary in their likelihood of dropping out based on how demanding they perceive the intervention to be (Kazdin, Holland, & Crowley, 1997; Kazdin, Holland, Crowley, & Breton, 1997). Characteristics of the parents at the beginning of treatment (e.g., parent psychopathology, poor quality of life) predict how demanding they will perceive treatment to be (Kazdin & Wassell, 2000a). Thus, one can identify at the outset families likely to experience obstacles during treatment. The extent to which different treatments vary in how they are perceived and whether these perceptions influence dropping out or therapeutic change remain to be studied. The perception of treatment is worth underscoring, however. It may be difficult to make treatment less demanding, but people's perception of how demanding treatment is may be malleable.

Several features of PMT may compensate for the greater demands this form of treatment places on the family. First, as a rule, parents evaluate PMT quite positively and thus do not see the intervention as onerous (Kazdin, Siegel, & Bass, 1992). Second, parents often see palpable gains in their children during treatment. The concrete changes that occur, usually fairly early in treatment, provide some incentive and proof that their efforts are worthwhile. Third, gains in the child appear to spread to other facets of parent and family life. Parent stress and depression decrease, and perceived quality of life improves with treatment (Kazdin & Wassell, 2000b). I mention attrition in relation to PMT but again note that there is no clear evidence either way that this form of treatment is associated with more or less premature termination of treatment.

General Comments

The parent issues I have mentioned do not invariably arise in treatment. Some of the issues may vary systematically as a function of the child population treated. For example, PMT applications have focused primarily on children with externalizing problems. If the children are referred clinically for conduct disorder and are severe cases, many of the parent-related issues are more likely to emerge than if the children are referred for oppositional disorder. This has not been studied as such, but I make the comment for the following reasons: Children referred for conduct disorder are more likely to come from families with harsh child-rearing practices, high levels of stress, parent psychopathology (e.g., current depression), socioeconomic disadvantage, and other such factors. These are not necessarily present, of course, but they are more likely to be present. These factors place families at risk for some of the issues I have raised (poor adherence to the procedures, dropping out of treatment). Also, families who engage in harsh child-rearing practices are more likely than not to have beliefs that are discrepant with the procedures that form the basis of PMT.

Many applications of PMT focus on children with disruptive behavior that is not at the level that might be referred clinically. Parent issues may be less likely to arise in this context than with clinically referred children whose disruptive behavior is much more extreme. Also, PMT is applied to many other populations (e.g., children with pervasive developmental disorders, mental retardation) in addition to children with externalizing behavior problems. The issues that emerge in these other applications have not been as well studied.

Professional Issues

A few issues pertain to the mental health professionals who administer PMT or are considering adding this treatment to their repertoire. Some of the professional issues relate to expectations and beliefs about treatment and are similar to those issues discussed in relation to the parents.

Characteristics of Treatment

Conceptual Clash

I mentioned that the conceptual model of PMT may conflict with parent expectations of what treatment ought to be. This issue can be of even greater significance for professionals in clinical practice. Indeed, several facets of PMT may generate in many mental health professionals the equivalent of conceptual "sticker shock." Many of us were trained in some variation of psychodynamic, relationship-based psychotherapy in which talk, play, the therapeutic alliance, and intrapsychic processes serve a central role. The conceptual model of PMT may seem to be wanting, simplistic, and indeed outright misguided when compared with the conceptual orientations on which we may have imprinted. PMT appears to ignore or minimize emotions, cognitions, and nuances of relationships that may play a role in the development and amelioration of the clinical problems, such as externalizing behavior, to which treatment is applied.

It is not quite accurate to state that PMT ignores anything that is not behavior. Rather, PMT embraces a broader conceptual position, namely, that one of the best ways to alter psychological and interpersonal domains is by having individuals (children) behave differently. For example, to change cognition, affect, or psychodynamic processes, it is not clear or empirically evident that talk, insight, and the therapeutic relationship is a way or the best way to accomplish this. Underlying processes may as well or better be altered by engaging the person in action. Learning by doing rather than by understanding is a reasonable way to characterize PMT sessions, even though, of course, "doing" is enhanced by understanding what to do, why to do it, and how it is to be done.[1]

Although PMT focuses on changes in a child's concrete behaviors, broader changes in other spheres are altered. PMT affects parent expectations, despair, conflict, family relationships and dynamics, and attitudes (see Thompson, Ruma, Schuchmann, & Burke, 1996; Webster-Stratton & Spitzer, 1996). Indeed, parent depression and stress also decrease with treatment, which alone can be expected to have a cascade of effects in the home and in relation to child functioning (Kazdin & Wassell, 2000b). As is probably true of most psychological treatments, the changes that occur with PMT are likely to extend beyond the target focus. Thus, focusing on cognitions in the case of depression is associated with changes in affect, cognition, and behavior. This argument might suggest that one can intervene in any domain and achieve broad therapeutic changes. The difficulty with this proposal stems from the fact that most treatments in use have not demonstrated that a change occurs in any domain.

Notwithstanding the possible breadth of changes, the direct and almost exclusive focus on the parents' and children's concrete behaviors is alien to many of the approaches that dominate clinical training. It is possible and perhaps likely that the conceptual model of PMT is discrepant with many of the other models to which most therapists in clinical practice were exposed in their training. The focus of PMT will be unfamiliar to most clinicians and researchers working with children. This unfamiliarity will probably limit adoption of PMT in clinical work. Among those who try the treatment, implementation may be limited as well. How well and how carefully professionals execute treatment is a function of the extent to which they view the intervention as reasonable and otherwise acceptable (Allinder & Oats, 1997).

The Therapeutic Relationship

The therapeutic relationship plays a central role in conceptualizations of traditional psychotherapy, whether the treatment is for children, adolescents, or adults. Facets of the therapeutic relationship such as alliance and bonding are studied in the context of psychodynamically oriented, experiential, and client-centered therapies. Not only is the therapeutic relationship thought to be important but also it is often viewed as pivotal to therapeutic change. The change may be considered to occur because of the relationship (mediator or mechanisms through which change occurs) or to be something on which change depends (moderator of change).[2]

In traditional therapy, the therapeutic relationship is conceived as a mechanism of change, that is, what makes treatment effective—sort of the "medicine." In PMT, the therapeutic relationship is more likely to be seen as something very helpful in delivering the treatment itself—sort of the spoonful of sugar that makes the medicine go down. In PMT, the relationship is important, and, indeed, all else depends on having the therapist and parent work together constructively. The relationship with the therapist can be thought of as an important setting event insofar as it increases the likelihood of specific interactions during the session and of parent adherence to treatment at home. Consequently, one would want a good relationship between the therapist and the client, but this is a somewhat different thrust from the role of the relationship in traditional therapy.

The interpersonal interaction within PMT sessions is unique, and this certainly is relationship related. Therapists and parents work together. Much of the "work together" consists of practice and role-play, rather than alliance, bonding, and transference types of processes. In PMT, the therapist–parent interaction ought to be constructive, pleasant, engaging, and motivational for the parent. This is more complex from the standpoint of the therapist than it may appear.

As an example, the therapist provides feedback to the parent for something that was just practiced in the session, such as pretending to praise a child for a particular behavior. Delivery of this feedback requires special skills so the therapist is constructive, nonthreatening, and nonoffensive. Moreover, in keeping with shaping, it is likely that the parent will need to repractice that skill again as the therapist provides further guidance (contingent praise for what *was* done and then modeling and instructions) to move the parent to improved behavior. One could call this the use of antecedents and consequences to shape behavior, but the style in which this is accomplished is critically important. The importance of this facet of the relationship can be more readily conveyed in the context of the style of a teacher, coach, and dance instructor. Although teachers may overlap in the methods they use, their style is very important in conveying the material, mobilizing motivation on the part of the student or athlete, and so on. In PMT, the style of interacting with the parent no doubt is an alliance of sorts, when one moves to a higher level of abstraction from concrete interactions to the relationship these have fostered between the therapist and the parent. Some minimal level of alliance is essential to ensure that the teaching of the parent is accomplished in a constructive way and, of course, that the parent remains in treatment. Even so, the alliance as I have discussed it here is discrepant with relationship issues as they are conceived in many other forms of therapy. I mention this as professional issue in applying PMT because the role of the relationship in PMT may not match the expectations and training of many clinicians.

The application of PMT is greatly limited by the paucity of training opportunities in child psychiatry, clinical psychology, social work, and nursing. Continuing education programs and conference workshops can certainly familiarize professionals with the intervention, but they cannot be expected to provide the necessary background and application skills. PMT requires mastery of social learning principles and multiple procedures that derive from them, as highlighted in earlier chapters. The principles are straightforward, but the range of applications that follow from them and the requisite therapist skills in shaping parent behavior require more than passing familiarity. As an illustration, the concept of positive reinforcement is quite easy to convey. The concept and underpinnings at the level of basic experimental research include all sorts of complexities and nuances about how, why, and when reinforcement leads to change and the mathematical relations about how consequences influence behavior. PMT does not draw on the complexities of the experimental research. For PMT, the simple version is fine for effective programming.

Moving from the principle to technique is quite another challenge. Assume a parent wishes to eliminate a tantrum—what should be the program in the home that parents could use to achieve the desired changes? The question entails devising an effective and feasible program and making sure the parent can and does carry it out. Assume for a moment that the program is in place but is not working very well. The therapist must devise a new plan that may include improved procedures (more immediate antecedents or consequences), changes in shaping to reduce response requirements of the parents or child, or the addition of novel procedures (as addressed later in the chapter). PMT is not necessarily more complex than another treatment. At the same time, unlike many other therapies, there are guidelines that are based on research and parameters of administration required for behavior change (e.g., immediate and contingent consequences). Departures from the parameters make the program less effective or ineffective. Consequently, there is much to learn and to follow.

Most training programs for mental health professionals who are to be involved in child and adolescent therapy are not yet likely to "cover" training in PMT. Indeed, one wonders what proportion of programs even mention the treatment. Several resources are available to facilitate use of PMT. The treatment manual in the second part of this book conveys the treatment on a session-by-session basis and with materials the therapist can use with the parents. I have mentioned and enumerated other manuals and videotape materials as well (see chapter 5). In short, although formal training opportunities are few, resources are available to familiarize oneself with the treatment and how it is applied.

Repairing Weak and Limited Intervention Effects

Perhaps the most salient issue in any treatment pertains to the impact of the program. Although PMT is effective, the program may produce weak effects. Some children may not respond, and others may respond but only minimally. The comments that follow pertain to strategies to improve the effects of a program. Two broad strategies are adopted to enhance the impact of a program: evaluation of basic aspects of implementation and the addition of ancillary procedures that can augment the effects of a program that is implemented well but otherwise not working as well as one would like.

Diagnosing and Tinkering with the ABCs

When a program is not working or not working sufficiently well, there are a number of components of the program that should be checked. Checking these is equivalent to seeing if an electrical appliance is plugged in and turned on when the appliance is not functioning. Clearly, these checks are not always the problem, but often they are. Analogously, in most cases of weak or ineffective programs, the problem stems from how the program is implemented. For example, features that maximize the effectiveness of a program, such as delivery of reinforcers contingent on behavior, immediately after behavior, and on as continuous a schedule as possible, are not always easy to implement or to implement consistently. Consequently, ensuring that these features are in place or approximated much better than they have been may be all that is needed to improve a program. Similarly, punishment programs based on time out or reprimands may not work very well initially but can usually be improved by checking on how the reinforcement program for desirable (incompatible, alternative) behavior also is conducted.

In my experience, as a first step, it is helpful to ask basic questions of any program that is not working well and to redress the inadequacies that the answers reveal. Table 7.1 illustrates key questions and some of the solutions. The

Table 7.1
Initial Steps in Diagnosing and Repairing Weak Intervention Effects

Question	First Line of Attack Answer(s)
For the reinforcement program, are the consequences contingent, immediate, continuous (all or most responses are reinforced), and adequate (preferred or valued consequences that are not otherwise available)?	Check each of these by asking the parent about the program with verbal, open-ended essay questions (rather than true-false questions) so the parent describes what happens. Also, role playing the delivery of reinforcement is likely to convey the quality of praise and style of delivery. One wants enthusiastic praise and a statement of the specific behaviors that earned praise/points.
Could other reinforcers be brought to bear to support prosocial behavior (other parent, sibling, or peer attention)?	Quality and magnitude of a reinforcer are part of the previous question but warrant mention here. Multiple incentives (backup reinforcers for a token program) ought to be available and used. Adding or ensuring there are highly preferred reinforcers may help the program. More often than not, increasing the attention from others (e.g., both parents, other relatives) contingent on performance will help.
Are there multiple opportunities to earn the reinforcers?	It may be that there are too few opportunities for the behavior to occur and then to be followed by reinforcing consequences. If so, opportunities for occurrences of the behavior must be increased. These opportunities can be simulated with practice in the home (e.g., "Pretend I said you could not watch TV, and if you do not break things and hit me, you can earn a point—OK, let's try this now, OK?" In general, the program requires multiple trials (opportunities) of the behavior, followed by reinforcement.
Are there antecedents that promote and increase the likelihood of the desired performance or are stronger antecedents needed to prime the behavior?	Prompts can take many forms and can vary in how subtle or blatant they are. If the behavior does not occur or occur at the level one wishes, prompts in the form of detailed instructions immediately before the behavior are more likely to get the behavior. Even stronger prompts can be added to these, helping, guiding, or modeling some of the behavior (i.e., doing part of it). Prompted behavior is then heavily reinforced. Gradually removing the prompts is not such a difficult task, so what-

Question	First Line of Attack Answer(s)
	ever can be done to increase behavior is helpful. Subtler antecedents would be setting events. Are activities immediately before the desired behavior ones that might promote that behavior better? For example, behaviors right before going to bed or doing homework ought to make a good transition to these activities.
Are the demands for performance too stringent? Would reduced demands initially (better shaping) make a difference?	Invariably, programs demand too much behavior because the people designing or implementing the intervention know what the child can do. The task is to develop behavior consistently, and a little behavior performed consistently is usually better than a lot once in a while. Reduce demands to earn the reinforcer—perhaps less of a behavior is needed on a given day or fewer days of the behavior are needed. As behavior at this low level becomes consistent, the reinforcement contingency can be altered so that added incentives are provided for a higher level of performance.
Are there reinforcers (e.g., parent, sibling, peer attention) that unwittingly maintain or contribute to the deviant behavior?	Contingencies that compete with the program might be examined. Some reinforcers follow deviant behavior, such as submission of a victim (e.g., sibling) after an aggressive act or attention from peers or siblings for some other behavior. Also, one parent may prompt and reinforce a behavior (e.g., hitting others) that the program is designed to redress.
Can another contingency be added to improve program effects?	Among the alternatives, can a special incentive (bonus) be added if behavior improves in some way (e.g., some criterion is met 2 days in a row, some level of performance is achieved in 3 of 5 days during the week)? Also, tokens or points are spent, but could they also be accumulated on a chart. When the child has earned so many points, some larger reward is provided. Thus, the child can earn and spend points daily but still see a record of how many points have been earned to date. When that number reaches some larger total, the additional bonus (e.g., special outing) is provided.

table considers varied aspects of the contingencies (ABCs) and what to look for. Let us consider a few of these in greater detail than the table provides to convey their interrelations better.

Antecedents

If the program is not working or not working well, manipulation and better use of antecedents often makes a large difference in performance (as discussed in chapter 2). Specifically, increasing the use of prompts and/or varying the nature of prompts can rescue a failing program. Prompts can be verbal statements, gestures, guided assistance, modeling, or other interventions to help the individual initiate the response. For example, a child may not clean up his or her room, even though a reinforcement program has been put into place. Prompts to initiate the behavior might include helping the child clean the room, picking up one or two items to model the desired behavior, gently reminding the child, or keeping the child company while he or she cleans. Prompts help the individual begin or complete the response and are especially useful at the beginning of a program or in moving behavior to higher levels (more behavior, more consistent behavior, or behavior that meets a higher criterion). Eventually, the prompts can be faded and eliminated. Although I am emphasizing antecedents in this discussion, prompts, followed by the behavior, followed by reinforcement is the sequence we are trying to achieve in the behavior-change program. Antecedents are intertwined with contingent consequences.

Consider an example where a mother wishes a young child not to have a tantrum and pout every time the mother says no or does not give in to a request (e.g., the child asks, "May I stay up late tonight, have some candy, have a friend over, have a cell phone, have a car?"). The mother learns that praising the child for not having a tantrum is one intervention likely to work. The difficulty is that the child may have a tantrum every time, and therefore non-tantrum behavior cannot be reinforced. The desired behavior does not occur whenever the mother says no to a request.

There are many options, but the use of prompts can usually help. A way to do that would be for the mother to go to the child and say, "In one minute, I am going to say 'no' to you. This is just pretend, but I am going to say, 'No, you cannot stay up late tonight.' If you say back to me, 'Why not?' in a calm way and without crying or hitting something, you can earn a token." This is an antecedent event that sets the stage for the desired behavior. Now, the mother says to the child, "No, you cannot . . ." and right before she says that or right before the child has a tantrum, she whispers to the child, "Remember, if you talk calmly, you can get a token." If the tokens are tangible items (e.g., a penny, a ticket), the mother may even hold up a token for the child to see to signal that the reinforcer can be earned. The token displayed before the behavior serves as an S^D and increases the likelihood of the behavior. With this heavy use of antecedent events, the child is very likely not to have a tantrum and will earn the token plus praise. The program would be repeated; the child would have many opportunities.

In the clinic where I work, we recommend a few (e.g., two to five) such prompted trials per day for a few to several days, but there is no research to support any particular number. The general rule is the more practice opportunities and trials in which behavior can occur and be reinforced, the better. To return to our hypothetical child, there will be unprompted occasions when the child does not have a tantrum or has a low-magnitude tantrum (a little whining). These can be reinforced, and perfect behavior that is unprompted, of course, would be quite heavily reinforced (e.g., maybe two or three tokens and enthusiastic praise). In this example, prompts were used to virtually ensure that the desired behavior is performed. Also added were simulated trials or opportunities for the child to engage in the behavior. Once the behavior is established, the prompts can be readily faded and eliminated.

Parents, teachers, and others often mention that they *do* prompt behavior in everyday life and that the prompts do not "work." Ineffective use of prompts is fairly common. Familiar examples include nagging children to clean up their rooms, complete their homework, do chores, not stay out late, and so on. Prompts of this kind are likely to be ineffective in part because they are not associated with consequences (reinforcing) when the desired behavior occurs. Moreover, the aversiveness of repeated prompts for the child (constant reminders, sometimes sarcastic tone) probably leads to other undesirable behaviors (side effects of aversive procedures) such as escape or avoidance, as reflected in not listening, "tuning out," leaving the situation, or staying away from the person who provides the prompts. Ineffective prompts are also a source of frustration for the parents. Expressions of frustration are evident in such statements, as, "I told him a thousand times and it is like talking to a wall" and "She knows what to do, but doesn't do it." These expressions and the frustration they reflect derive in part from the fact that instructions, reminders, and explanations by themselves are not likely to work or to lead to sustained performance. Frustration also stems from continued beliefs that telling people what to do by itself is sufficient to change behavior. Sometimes it is; invariably, it is more effective to combine instructions and other antecedents and consequences to develop the behavior

Prompts can be effective in initiating and occasionally in sustaining behavior. Prompts appear to be more effective when: (1) they are delivered immediately before the opportunity to engage in the desired behavior, (2) they specify the precise behaviors that are to be performed, (3) they are provided in a nondemanding and polite fashion, and (4) the prompted behaviors are followed by immediate reinforcement. If the behavior is performed but not quite at the desired level, prompts to guide to the next level with contingent consequences often work very well. Shaping (reinforcing approximations of the behaviors) and prompts to guide better approximations are key.

If behavior is not changing or is not being performed consistently, one of the first lines of attack is to examine the use of antecedents that can increase the likelihood of the behavior. In an earlier chapter, setting events and prompts were noted as antecedents. Setting events consist of more contextual influences on behavior that set the stage (e.g., having a child engage in calming behaviors before going to sleep to help set the stage for going to bed calmly, saying "please" before a request to change the likelihood that the person will comply). Setting events are less well studied. Prompts were discussed here because much is known about their use and influence and because they directly initiate, mold, and develop the behavior of interest. It is important to ensure that the prompts are provided and that they meet the conditions noted previously. Prompts can usually be altered, expanded upon, or provided more consistently to help initiate behavior. At the same time, it is critical to bear in mind their limitations. Prompts are designed to initiate performance. Whether performance is sustained and behavior improves depends on the consequences that follow.

Behaviors

Shaping

One of the initial areas to examine in enhancing the impact of the program is the behavior required for reinforcement. Typically, "too much behavior" or too stringent demands for behavior change are placed on the child (or parent) at the beginning of a program. Thus, a problem in shaping behavior is often the reason that a program is not working well. Parents invariably ask for too much of the behavior before providing the consequences. There usually is no good reason (in relation to the goals of the program) to begin with stringent demands or to be stingy in delivering the reinforcers (praise, tokens). The goal is to get the behavior and to move progressively forward. This goal is accomplished by ensuring that the initial criteria are met and the consequences are provided, as implied by the first question in Table 7.1. For example, at the beginning of the program, we may not want homework for 1 hour, or bedtime at the new time of 2 hours earlier than before, or all the toys picked up every day, and so on. Shaping suggests that some slight improvement will be reinforced and that after this level of performance is reasonably consistent, the criteria will be extended a bit. It is not necessarily the case that demanding large leaps in performance and making stringent demands speed up the goal.

A common statement from parents is "I know she can clean her room [set the table, do homework, pick up her clothes] because she does it once in a while." That a person *can* do this large sequence of behavior is only one component of performance. The question for a behavior-change program (and for life in general) is whether the person does the behavior and does so consistently. In PMT programs, if the behaviors are not performed very well or not performed consistently, shaping the behavior and then shaping consistency (reinforcing engaging in the behavior on multiple occasions, perhaps consecutively or an increased proportion of occasions) is usually the way to intervene to improve the program.

For example, in a nonclinical context, one father wanted his 12-year-child to practice a musical instrument (trumpet) between weekly lessons. The goal was to have the child practice 45 minutes to 1 hour per day. Currently practice was 10 minutes at most, with little of this time actually spent playing the instrument. The parent began a reinforcement program. He told the child that he could play a new computer game for up to an hour if the child practiced for 45 minutes that day. Before the first day of the program, the parent and child bought a computer game of the child's choice so they had it in the house. The next day the program began.

This program might be effective, but it has a few weaknesses that could readily lead to failure. Among the salient weaknesses, too much behavior is being asked (a leap from 10 to 45 minutes on the first day), a single reinforcer is used (interest in the computer game may wane quickly and not be present on any one day), and consistent performance (e.g., two medium-to-good days of practice in a row) is not reinforced at all. The parent did this on his own and asked for assistance because the program was not working.

The first place to begin is with shaping. The contingency would be better if set at 15 minutes for earning a reinforcer. After, say, 5 days of this, whether consecutive days or not, the parent might add to the program in the following way: 15 minutes still earns *x*, but 30 minutes earns more time or some additional reinforcer. Any week in which there are 2 days over 15 minutes or over 30 minutes of practice, depending on how the child progresses, might earn some other reinforcer. This latter reinforcer might be delayed a bit (given at the end of the week), just to make the program manageable to the parent. One can see the advantage of using points or tokens: The points allow for back-up reinforcers that have different values so that some can be earned immediately (are inexpensive) and others are delayed (and are expensive). Eventually, the final behavior could probably be obtained but only after gradually shaping the behavior and reinforcing on several occasions the desired behavior at small durations.

In this particular program, the changes developed the behavior, and the practice time of 45 minutes was met 6 days a week. Eventually, the child could have 1 day off in any week when he had practiced for 6 days in a row. Human behavior is often unpredictable, however. The child did not always elect this option and continued to practice on the days when practice was not required.

Although I have emphasized shaping in this case, I have not mentioned that we also added more praise and attention. The parent praised completion of practice that met the criterion for reinforcement. Also, in any day when the practice criterion was met, both parents discussed the practice, the music, and the child's wonderful progress at the dinner table that evening. (No comments were made at dinner if the criterion had not been met.) It would be great to end the story by noting that the program was very effective and that the child has become a famous musician. Well, at least the program was effective. The contingencies were discontinued, and music practice stayed at the desired level up to a year later when last checked.

Simulations and Practice

Critical to changing behavior in PMT are opportunities for the behavior to occur that are reinforced. It may be that the behavior of greatest interest (responding to frustrations or "no" or teasing by fighting and tantrums) does not occur in a way that allows careful delivery of consequences and shaping. Practice trials are key, whether training parents or the child. If the behavior does not occur frequently enough to shape its quality and develop its frequency, simulated practice situations in everyday life are fine.

In the discussion of prompting, I mentioned the use of prompts and simulated situations in the case of developing nontantrum behavior in a child. A child may respond poorly on each occasion in which the opportunity occurs (e.g., tantrums, fighting). More practice trials are needed in which the positive opposite behavior can be developed. We encourage the use of pretend situations in the home, as I described previously.

A few practice trials a day, as feasibility allows, are used. The parent approaches the child, presents setting events to set the context (by saying, "OK, as we discussed, you have an opportunity to earn a point—this is a pretend situation") and presents more specific prompts (". . . and if you can act without a tantrum or just say 'all right' without throwing things or hitting me"). The parent continues, "Here goes—let's try it. OK, you cannot go out with your friends today" (parent says out loud) and then whispers, "Boy, this is tough. You are doing *great* so far!" Invariably, the child engages in the positive prosocial behavior in these practice situations. These behaviors are copiously praised. These simulations have a direct bearing on other situations that are genuine. In such situations, the likelihood of the prosocial response is greatly increased and can be praised.

Do simulations help? Yes, greatly. Indeed, highly skilled professionals (surgeons, airline pilots), fortunately for us, engage in simulations of the desired behaviors frequently. As a general rule, reinforced practice of the desired behavior is key to the success of behavior-change programs. If the behavior does not occur enough to allow reinforced practice or the form in which the behavior occurs (e.g., tantrum reactions) do not allow one to craft changes through shaping, simulated practice is extremely helpful. To improve the effects of a weak program, one can ask if there are many opportunities for reinforced practice. If a few opportunities are not available per day, we add pretend (role play, practice) situations in the home.

Response Priming

Shaping is not the only way to focus on behavior and to improve the effects of a program. In many instances, the child can readily perform the desired behavior and perhaps has often done so on recent occasions. In such instances, extensive shaping may not be required. The response merely has to be primed in some way. By primed, I refer to initiated in some way so that it is likely to be completed. Once completed, the response can be reinforced. There is a technique that serves this purpose, and, not surprisingly, it is called response priming.

Response priming refers to any procedure that initiates early steps in a sequence of responses. Response priming requires the client to engage in the initial components of the sequence. Engaging in responses that are early in a sequence increases the probability of performing the final behaviors in the sequence. As noted earlier, any act can be broken down into a sequence or chain of responses. A difficulty with initiating a sequence of responses is that the final reinforcement (at the end of the chain) is remote. For example, a frequent difficulty with completing a term paper, writing a book, or doing a chore is merely beginning the task. Once the task is begun, the prospect of reinforcement is less remote, and the sequence of the requisite behaviors is more likely to be performed.[3] To prime these responses, provide reinforcement for merely beginning the work or for getting the materials together and sitting down to do the work.

Response priming has been used to initiate responses that otherwise have an exceedingly low frequency. For example, in one program, the goal was to increase initiation of social interaction among preschool children (ages $2\frac{1}{2}$ to 5) with autism (Zanolli, Daggett, & Adams, 1996). Priming consisted of prompting children to engage in social behaviors such as looking at peers, smiling, and talking to others in a period prior to activities in which their social interaction was to be changed. These periods of priming social behavior led to increases in spontaneous initiations with peers in activity periods when the behaviors were not prompted. That is, initiating the behavior led to continuation and extension to other people and time periods when social behaviors were unprompted.

Another example comes from the clinic at where I work. Once in a while, a child will not want to come to the clinic for a treatment session and instead argue with a parent about coming to the session. Given the population we treat (conduct disorder), severe tantrums are common in the home. What are we to do? The parent may phone us out of desperation, and, of course, we do not always have the answer. But response priming is a useful guide.

In this case, we convey to the child (via the parent) that he or she does not have to have a session. The child just has to come to the clinic—he can sit in the waiting room (and perhaps play with toys). A therapist trained in traditional therapy might throw a tantrum just hearing about this part of what we have done. Traditional stereotypic interpretations of the child's behavior and concerns about "feeding into the child's problem," "undermining the parent's authority," and "allowing the child to manipulate the parent" make this strategy countertherapeutic. (As attractive as these interpretations might be, I might add that none of them has any support that I could find. This is critical— unsupported interpretations that thwart use of a strategy that may help the problem at best is a questionable clinical practice and at worst perhaps borders on the unethical.)

The rationale for response priming is as follows. The probability of having a treatment session is zero if the child stays at home. "Having a treatment session" can be seen as a chain of responses, and moving the child to an early part of the chain greatly increases the likelihood of completing the rest of the chain. Priming does not force the behavior or guarantee its performance. Rather, it merely increases the likelihood that the sequence of behaviors and the behavior at the end of the chain (having a session) is increased. The question in response priming is always what behaviors early in the sequence one might be able to obtain. In this case, as I mentioned, coming to the clinic is one behavior we have selected.

Invariably, the child comes to the clinic, having been given a guarantee that he or she does not have to do anything else. Once the child comes to the clinic, the therapist goes out to the waiting room and asks, "Wanna come in for a session?" This is a one-question effort with no pleas, attempts at inducement, and so on. The child may even be reminded that we promised she or he would not have to come into the session. (The problem-solving skills training sessions are enjoyable, include abundant albeit contingent praise, and can end in concrete rewards, so these facets are not minor features.) The child is very likely to come into the session. Once in the session, performance of the child and the tenor of the session usually are no different from any other session the child has had.

One child said he would come to the clinic only if he could stay in the car. (We worried that he knew about response priming because coming inside the clinic is a closer link in a chain leading to "having a session." In chaining, the probability of the behavior is higher the closer one is to the final behavior in the chain. Staying in the car is more removed from having a session than is being in the clinic waiting room.) His mother entered her PMT session while the child was in the car. The therapist went out to the car and asked if he wanted to have a brief session, to which he assented. As a rule, response priming has been very effective in this context. We have not researched the procedure, although others have (see Kazdin, 2001b). The instances are too infrequent in our work to subject them to controlled trials.

Priming procedures achieve their effects by making the initial responses easier or more likely. They make them easier in circumstances in which someone brings the person to the early steps. For example, getting one to exercise may be primed by bringing the person along to a gym. Being at the gym, with all of the cues, makes exercising more likely. The cues of the situation are setting events as well, and hence response priming also takes advantage of the use of stimulus control. In programs in which the target responses are performed infrequently even though they are in the repertoire of the clients, a priming procedure can be used. Even if the responses are not in the child's repertoire of responses, the priming procedure can initiate early response components and facilitate shaping.

Consequences

Basic Parameters of Delivery

Usually the first place one looks to improve weak programs is in the consequences and their administration. As already mentioned, the effects of reinforcement depend on several parameters (contingency, immediacy, continuous reinforcement) that need to be in place. Each one ought to be looked at in turn. The program may be well designed, but a basic requirement may not be carried out. In one program, for example, the child came home from school and was required to begin schoolwork and do a chore or two. We were concerned with immediacy of reinforcement as the child engaged in these because the parent (single parent living with one 12-year-old child) could not be there to reinforce and could not reinforce immediately. The child agreed to call the mother right before and after starting homework. This allowed for her prompts and praise to be immediate. Tangible consequences (point earnings) could be provided on her return. Immediacy of reinforcement may not be feasible, but some approximations might be achieved.

Similarly, continuous reinforcement for the behavior refers to reinforcing the target behavior every time it occurs. This may not be feasible, but one wants to ensure that this is approximated as much as possible. We find that parents (and teachers) often let behaviors that they wish to develop linger without consequences. Practice with the parent in the PMT sessions is devoted primarily to ensuring that the delivery of reinforcement is optimal, or at least optimal in relation to any constraints in the situation due to scheduling or individual life circumstances. How reinforcement and punishment are to be delivered were discussed in chapter 2. I mention the delivery issues to underscore that these tend to be the main culprit when programs are not working very well.

Reinforcement for Consistency

In the usual case, reinforcement is provided for a particular behavior. The child performs the behavior (e.g., completion of homework or calm response to a provocative event) and is praised or receives a point. All instances or as many instances as possible are reinforced. Apart from individual responses, parents want and life often demands some consistency. Consistency in this context refers to consecutive occasions when the desired behavior is performed.

The mediocre effects of a program may reflect that performance is fine a few times but is not very consistent. If this is the case, reinforcement ought to be provided for consistent performance. This is a bit subtle because it is easy to do this carelessly. Consider an example of a child having homework 5 nights a week. Assume that we would like the child to work on homework for 1 hour per night for 5 nights a week (e.g., Monday through Thursday, Sunday). Let us say we shape this behavior with a point program that begins with 20 minutes and works up to an hour. The child meets the criterion 2 or 3 times a week.

One way to increase this is to reinforce for consecutive nights or something like that. An example would be to continue to provide reinforcement for any night in which 1 hour is achieved. This contingency ought to continue at least for a while. However, an added incentive is provided. This can be done in many ways, depending on what the child actually does. One possibility would be that whenever the child meets the criterion 3 days in a row, an extra bonus or separate privilege is earned. Another possibility would be that any week in which all 5 nights were obtained leads to a special privilege. (This latter possibility may be too stringent; unless the child is achieving 4 nights a week regularly, it would not be good to demand perfection for the extra incentive. Shaping applies here as well.)

In short, an extra contingency can be added to reinforce any behavior that occurs twice (or more) in a row or when a specific proportion of days meets some criterion. In this way, consistency is reinforced, and one reduces the variability of performance over time. In most programs, a separate program to reinforce consistency is not needed. The initial incentive for each occasion is sufficient.

As I mentioned, when reinforcing consistent behavior, it is important to continue to reinforce the individual performance occasions. That is, it is usually unwise to begin by conveying to the child that only several behaviors in a row will receive the reinforcement. One wants to continue to reinforce the individual performances so they do not extinguish. For example, if four homework occasions were required to earn the reinforcer and no other reinforcer was provided, then each night when homework was completed, no reward would be provided. At least when beginning to move to larger units of performance (e.g., several days), some reinforcer ought to be provided for the individual days of performance. Praise alone might be sufficient for the individual days and eventually just points or more potent reinforcers for the large blocks of the desired behaviors.

Assuming that the delivery of reinforcers is fine, there are other issues related to the consequences that can improve intervention effects. In reinforcement programs, it is very important that the clients utilize the available reinforcers if they include privileges, activities, or tokens and their backup reinforcers. The rationale is that use of the backup reinforcers will increase the likelihood or ensure that the children engage in the target behaviors required to earn them.

There are exceptions in reinforcement programs (and in life) where earning the reinforcer (e.g., tokens, money) is highly reinforcing, even though the individual does not exchange them for backup reinforcers. Earning and accumulating points (as money) can serve as its own reward and can still sustain performing the behaviors that earn the reinforcers. Thus, the child may engage in the desired behaviors to earn the points but not utilize the backup reinforcers (i.e., spend any of the points or tokens). As a general rule, one wants the child to utilize the available reinforcers to increase the likelihood of continued earning and spending. Reinforcer sampling is one procedure to facilitate this.

The utilization of a reinforcer can be viewed as a sequence of responses. If the initial responses in the sequence can be primed, the likelihood of completing the sequence is increased. To initiate the sequence, a client can engage in the initial part of, or briefly sample, the reinforcing event. *Reinforcer sampling* refers to procedures that provide a brief or small sample of the reinforcing events in order to promote greater utilization of them. As a way of remembering this, think of reinforcer sampling as a free sample of some product such as a small bar of soap or tube of toothpaste that companies often provide to introduce a new product and to encourage people to buy the product.

Reinforcer sampling is related to response priming, discussed previously. In both cases, there is an attempt to encourage the individual to engage in some behavior. Reinforcer sampling is a special case of response priming. The responses primed are those involving the use of a potentially reinforcing event. For example, a child who is not utilizing the backup reinforcers can be given a brief sample. If a reinforcer is playing at the computer, watching TV, or staying up late, the child can be given a few minutes of this noncontingently (e.g., 10 minutes of one of these) and then asked if he or she wants to buy (with points or tokens) this reinforcer. When the sample is provided, the likelihood is much greater that the individual will purchase the reinforcer.

In PMT, reinforcer sampling is not usually needed. Once reinforcers have been identified, most children draw on them freely and engage in the behaviors to earn them. Ensuring that a number of reinforcers are available rather than just one or two usually is sufficient for the program. Nevertheless, reinforcer sampling is useful to know and to use. In any situation in which it is possible to provide a small sample of a reinforcer, the sampling procedure is likely to enhance performance. Provide only a small sample of the event so as to avoid satiation. Sampling a large portion of the event, such as food or an activity, may amount to noncontingent reinforcement and thus not increase the behaviors that are required to earn the reinforcer. Occasionally, the effect of a reinforcement program may be relatively weak, in part because the "reinforcers" provide little incentive to engage in the target behaviors. If the activity that is designed to serve as a reinforcer can be made more "valuable" to the child, the likelihood of the child's engaging in the target behaviors to earn that activity is increased. Evidence suggests that the benefits of reinforcer sampling are maintained after the sampling procedure is terminated (Kazdin, 2001b).

Special Contingency Arrangements

The prior strategies consist of tinkering with the ABCs to improve program effects. In most of those strategies, relatively minor changes are made in the behavior-change program to improve treatment. Other strategies can also be added to the program to augment intervention effects. Several of these strategies are highlighted here.

Contingency Contracts

Many programs are imposed on children and adolescents without their input. There are obvious reasons for this. Typically, children are not in a position to determine goals and the means through which they can be attained. For example, in child rearing, all sorts of behaviors might serve as goals for children (e.g., toothbrushing, eating nutritious meals, bathing, completing homework, taking tuba lessons) without children having any interest in the short- or long-term benefits. Yet, in many instances, including some of these child-rearing examples, the input of the children can be solicited, and the effectiveness of the program may improve as a result.

A common way in which the children and adolescents are directly involved in a behavior-change program is though a *contingency contract*. This is a written agreement between individuals who wish behavior to change (parents, teachers) and clients whose behavior is to be changed (children, students). An actual contract is signed by both parties to indicate that they agree to the terms.

The contingency contract specifies the relationship between behaviors and their consequences. Specifically, the contract specifies the reinforcers desired by the child and the behavior desired by the parent who wishes behavior change. This is translated into explicit and precise terms that denote precisely what behavior (how much behavior, when, how often) will earn what consequences (how much, when delivered). The contracts can be quite simple, brief, and oriented to the age of the child or adolescent.

Ideally, contingency contracts include several elements, as listed in Table 7.2. First, they detail what each party expects to gain. For example, parents may want a child to complete his or her work or attend school regularly. The child may want free time with friends, extra allowance, and other reinforcers. Second, the stipulated behaviors of the child are readily observable. If parents cannot determine whether a responsibility has been met, they cannot grant a privilege. Thus, some behaviors may not be readily incorporated into a contingency contract. For example, parents often cannot easily monitor whether an adolescent visits certain friends, so it would not be advisable to include a stipulation regarding such visits in the contract. Third, contingency contracts provide sanctions for a failure to meet their terms. The consequences for not meeting the contract terms are systematic and planned in advance (agreed to by all parties), not arbitrary and after the fact. Fourth, contracts often include a bonus clause that reinforces consistent compliance with their terms. Bonuses (extra privilege, activity, or extension of curfew limit) can be used to reinforce consistent performance over an extended period. For someone whose behavior was recently developed, bonuses for consistent performance may be especially important. Reinforcement for longer sequences of performance (e.g., performance for 2 consecutive days or 4 of 5 days) helps to fade or gradually remove the program and to make behavior less dependent on immediate consequences. Fifth, contingency contracts provide a means of monitoring the rate of positive reinforcement given and received. The records inform each party when reinforcement is to occur and provide constant feedback. Moreover, the records may cue individuals to make favorable comments about desirable behavior when the backup reinforcer is about to be earned. Sixth, contracts provide a means of renegotiating the contract conditions. As the program is implemented, it may become obvious that it is unfair or not working. Each party ought to have the opportunity to initiate a conversation to renegotiate. Also, if the program is working well, as in any behavior-change program, the contract ought to be terminated or moved to the next step, such as more delayed reinforcement, reinforcement for consistency of the behavior over time, or larger segments of behavior.

Table 7.2
Key Elements of Contingency Contracts

1. State what each party expects to gain.

2. Specify the behaviors of the child so they are readily observable.

3. Specify any sanctions for a failure to meet the terms (e.g., loss of points for the child, extra backup reinforcers if the person who administers the consequences forgets to do so or engages in behaviors such as nagging that specifically are not allowed).

4. Include a bonus clause that reinforces consistent compliance with their terms.

5. Monitor execution of the contract including the rate of positive reinforcement given and received.

6. Specify the means (when, how initiated) for renegotiating the contract conditions.

Many elements of a contingency contract are merely elements of good behavior-change programs. The extra features of contracting are that these elements are written down and the child plays a clear role in their development and negotiation. Contingency contracts do not have to be elaborate or complex. Table 7.3 is an example of a simple contract that was used to increase completion of homework of a 9-year-old fourth-grader named Ann (Miller & Kelley, 1994). Ann usually completed her work quickly but was inaccurate. She showed other classroom problems as well, including inattention, hyperactivity, impulsivity, and other conduct problems. In this study, four separate families (parent–child dyads) were included; in each case, the focus was on homework. Before the program began, the parent, teacher, and child were interviewed to clarify the problem for each child. During the program, time spent working on homework, accuracy of homework completion, and working on homework were observed in the home.

The parent presented the contract and discussed it with the child. The discussion identified what materials would be needed, how and when homework was to be completed, and the reinforcers that could be earned. Goals were set with the parent and child to decide what was reasonable (e.g., how many problems to complete within a given time period). Each week the parent and child renegotiated the contract to specify the goals for that week, the rewards to be used, and sanctions for not completing key terms, such as bringing home the necessary materials. The effect of the program was evaluated experimentally in single-case experimental designs that showed that the program led to change and that the contract specifically contributed to these effects.[4] Ann improved in the accuracy of her homework assignments from a mean of 64% during baseline to 88% during the first contracting phase. By the end of the evaluation

---

Table 7.3
Sample Contingency Contract

The following materials need to be brought home every day: <u>homework pad, workbooks, text books, pencils.</u>
If Ann remembers to bring home all of these materials, then she may choose one of the following rewards: <u>gumballs, 10¢.</u>
However, if Ann forgets to bring home some of her homework materials, then she <u>does not get a snack before bed.</u>
Ann may choose one of the following rewards if she meets 90% to 100% of her goals: <u>late bedtime (by 20 minutes), 2 stickers</u> or one of these if she meets 75% to 89% of her goals: <u>soda, 1 sticker.</u>
If Ann meets <u>80%</u> or more of her goals on at least <u>3</u> days this week, she may choose one of the following BONUS rewards: <u>renting a videotape, having a friend from school over to play.</u>

_____   _____
Child's signature   Parent's signature

Reprinted with permission from Miller, D. L., & Kelley, M. L. (1994). The use of goal-setting and contingency contracting for improving children's homework performance. *Journal of Applied Behavior, 27,* 79.

program, she averaged 92% accuracy. The effects were similar for the other children, who also improved.

Contingency contracts are mentioned here in the context of PMT. However, contingency contracts have been studied in many other contexts and used successfully to alter a variety of problems, such as overeating, alcohol and drug abuse, cigarette smoking, problem behaviors of delinquents, academic and disruptive behavior of elementary school children, and studying in college students. Procedures for developing contingency contracts that can be applied to a wide range of problems have been nicely described elsewhere (Hall & Hall, 1998).

Contingency contracts have several advantages. First, children's performance may be better if they are allowed to have some input into designing or implementing a program. Participation in the design and development of the program is likely to make the program more acceptable to them and foster greater compliance. Second, contingency contracts are usually flexible in that participants can renegotiate their terms. The reinforcers delivered for particular responses can be adjusted, response requirements can be increased, and so on. Third, the contract makes the contingencies explicit. Specification of the contingencies provides the rules or instructions for the child on how to behave and defines the consequences that will follow behavior. Although explicit instructions alone may not produce durable changes in performance, they often increase the effectiveness of reinforcement. Fourth, contingency contracts make explicit the requirements for delivering positive consequences and increase the likelihood that reinforcement for the desired behaviors will actually be provided. Putting the contingencies in writing makes it easier to monitor whether they are carried out in the desired fashion. Also, in families where child rearing tends to be authoritarian and perhaps extreme, introducing contracts and the idea of negotiation may have additional benefits in improved family communication.

Contracts, whether they are used in legal matters or in behavior-change programs, are not flawless. Making things explicit does not always resolve ambiguities. However, writing programs down into contract form helps to minimize misunderstandings. For the child, the written statement can limit fiat imposed by a parent who might be frustrated and invoke some contingency that is a direct violation of the agreement in place at the time. For the parent, the written statement can give something concrete and external to show when the child says, "I never agreed to that."

Contingency contracts have been used frequently. However, extensive research has not been completed to guide many of the specific details that would make contracts maximally effective or acceptable to children or others who participate in behavior-change programs. Even so, the use of contracts to structure reinforcement programs, to make the requirements explicit to all parties, and to encourage negotiation among the parties is to be strongly encouraged. Finally and related, there is not a firm body of evidence to show that programs guided by contingency contracts are more effective than similar contingencies that are imposed without a contract. The benefits of contracting may or may not be evident in behavior change but rather in the acceptability and palatability of the program to the persons involved. Consequently, contracts can be a useful adjunct to make the program more acceptable.

For very young children or children with serious impairment (e.g., severe mental retardation), use of a contingency contract may not be feasible because of the negotiation and discussion that underlie development of a contract. Even so, the broader point of a contract—namely, involving the child in the program and some decisions about the program—might be useful, even if these facets are not central to the contingencies. For example, young children can be involved in selecting the reinforcers and participate in marking their charts where points are recorded and other aspects of the program. This is not a "contract" but may capture some of the benefits of involving children in the program in ways that make the program seem less imposed on them.

Group Contingencies

In a behavior-change program, typically the children earn reinforcers for themselves, and this works extremely well. A group contingency can augment the effects of an intervention. The term *group contingency* is used because the applications have extended to many settings such as the classroom, athletic team, college dormitory, and business firm, where some common or similar behaviors of several individuals within the group are the focus (Kazdin, 2001b). In the home, however, the group refers to all children or the family as a whole.

Group contingencies refers to programs in which the criterion for reinforcement is based on the performance of the group as a whole. The group must perform in a particular way for the reinforcing consequences to be delivered. Whether the individual child receives the reinforcer depends not only on his or her behavior but also on the behavior of others in the group. In the home, reinforcers are provided if both (or all) children meet some performance criterion in relation to a particular target behavior. For example, if all children did some behavior (room cleaning, some other chore), all would receive the consequence (e.g., a star on a chart). These stars could be exchanged for reinforcers.

A group contingency such as this example raises the concern that the performance of one might interfere with the reinforcement of another child. For example, if two or three siblings performed the behavior but the other did not, none of the children would earn the reinforcer. Ideally, both individual and group contingencies would be provided so that each individual would receive the reinforcer (individualized contingency) when earned, but if all of the children completed the behavior, a special reinforcer or bonus would be provided (group contingency). This dual arrangement captures the benefits of the group influence without penalizing individuals just because a sibling did not complete the behavior.

I mention siblings as the "group" focus, but there is no need to restrict the focus in this way. In one PMT program at our clinic, we used a group contingency for the entire family. Swearing was a major problem for the three young boys all day in the home. There would be no way to convey the scope of the problem (frequency and severity of the language) without providing an audiotape here, so I ask the reader to "trust me." When we see such a level of swearing, we immediately look to very strong influences that might be operating. We did not have to look far in this situation. The mother and father swore horribly all of the time and routinely in everyday conversation. This did not influence the parents' views of the children's swearing. Along with the treatment focus on aggressive and antisocial behavior, the parents were deeply concerned with the child's swearing (i.e., the child referred for treatment). (I am just the messenger here, so please do not ask me to defend the inconsistency between the parents' behaviors and what they demanded of their children. However, such inconsistencies are common between what we want and expect of others and what we ourselves do.) This child's swearing, as noted by the parent, was followed by fighting at home and at school, and we were asked to get control of this situation.

In such circumstances, of course, it is tempting to reason with the parents and point out that their swearing is a large part of the problem. There is no reason to avoid mentioning the dilemma, but reasoning with parents is usually not an effective intervention in such circumstances. Of the program devised to change the child's behavior in the home, I mention only the swearing program here. It seemed that a reinforcement contingency to reduce swearing based solely on the child's behavior would be naive as well as ineffective. However, we briefly tried it anyway as one of a few behaviors in the child's point chart program. Swearing was just another behavior on the chart. The swearing did not change, so we quickly moved to a group contingency involving the entire family.

Merely to see if we could achieve any change, we began with a brief period when the family was together and elected dinnertime. At dinner, when all family members were present, the parents agreed to a contingency in which dessert was earned contingent on group behavior. The family bought ice cream and various toppings that family members could use to make sundaes of their own. Early in the program, we began with a small criterion. If the family could begin dinner and continue at the table without any swearing (we specified the words and what constitutes the beginning of dinner), they would all receive dessert at the end if they wanted. If the criterion was not met, no dessert would be earned. This is a group contingency because earning the reinforcer (dessert) depended on the behavior of the group (all persons, no swearing). Among the benefits, a group criterion can foster mutual help (e.g., antecedents and consequences from each other) to increase the likelihood of the desired behaviors. In this program, we increased the time of nonswearing required to earn dessert once control was demonstrated with the brief time. Swearing decreased considerably but was not eliminated.

Group contingencies can be used for a variety of reasons, such as simplifying a program when several individuals are involved or delivering reinforcers that seem inherently group based (e.g., recess for students in class, a family outing). I mention them here because they can increase the effectiveness of a program. If a program is working but not well, the addition of a group contingency can increase the effectiveness of the contingencies.

General Comments

I have mentioned some options for special contingency arrangements that can be used to augment a program that may not be working well or as well as we would like. There are many other procedures and techniques (see Kazdin, 2001b; Sturmey, 1996). For example, *functional analysis* is a way of identifying factors that currently maintain behavior. It is a systematic way to assess the connections between antecedents, behaviors, and consequences and then use this information to develop effective interventions to change behavior. The assessment identifies contexts, antecedents, and consequences that are associated with a specific behavior and hypotheses of what facets of this can be changed that would alter behavior. Functional analysis has been used effectively in the context of changing many behaviors in applied settings (e.g., institutions, classrooms). The most dramatic applications have been directed toward eliminating self-injurious behavior (see Kazdin, 2001b; Pelios et al., 1999). By identifying key factors that influence behavior, self-injury has been eliminated without use of punishment techniques. PMT rarely relies on this procedure to alter parent and child behavior in the home. When an aspect of PMT is not working, our usual approach is to alter specific contingencies in the home and to check to be sure that the programs are delivered as intended, as already discussed. Usually, tinkering with the antecedents, behaviors, and consequences I highlighted earlier is sufficient.

In everyday life, the challenge is getting the parent to administer reinforcement as close to optimally as possible. Adherence and execution of the basic techniques are much more important for therapeutic change than adding something novel or ancillary to the behavior-change program. The extensive practice in the treatment session is geared toward enabling the parents to deliver positive reinforcement and to cease behaviors (nagging, screaming, harsh punishment) that can contribute to the problems we are trying to treat.

Summary and Conclusions

The principles and techniques that form the basis of PMT are detailed in several treatment manuals. Less well documented and discussed are the manifold issues that influence how, whether, and the extent to which the intervention can be applied. This chapter has addressed several issues that can emerge in PMT and influence treatment delivery and outcome. Among parent issues discussed are the conceptual model of PMT and how it might be discrepant with parent views of the causes of deviant behavior and the nature of therapy, specific concerns with some of the procedures used in treatment (e.g., use of rewards for behaviors they would like to occur without any artificial intervention), and parent beliefs about specific child-rearing practices and how children ought to be treated and disciplined.

Parent adherence to treatment was also discussed. Because so much of the treatment is carried out by the parent in the home, parent execution of the intervention is critically important. Dropping out of therapy is a pervasive problem in psychotherapy, and there is no reason to expect that PMT is any different in this regard. The issue was mentioned because it is so pervasive and because strategies have been devised to address the matter.

Professional issues also are pertinent to the use and application of PMT. The conceptual model of PMT, by focusing on parent and child behavior, may clash with the still dominant intrapsychic models in which many mental health professionals were trained. This is an issue because the compatibility of the model of PMT with the models to which therapists subscribe may contribute to adoption, use, and implementation of PMT. To illustrate this point more concretely the therapeutic relationship and its role in more traditional forms of treatment and PMT were contrasted.

Perhaps the key professional issue is the limited training opportunities for mental health professionals. There are many resources in the form of books, tapes, and manuals. The tapes might be usable with minimal training. However, the simplicity of many of the core concepts of PMT (reinforce positive behavior) belies the complexity of effective application. Consequently, more than an academic experience is likely to be needed to learn how to apply treatment effectively.

With any treatment, some individuals may not respond well or, indeed, may not respond at all. This chapter also discussed what to do when the effects of a behavior-change program are weak or nonexistent. In the usual situation, tinkering with antecedents, behaviors, and consequences (ABCs) in straightforward ways can improve program effects. It is essential to examine how the current contingencies are being implemented and to ensure that basic requirements for effective administration are optimal. For example, the consequences may be delayed too long after the behavior is performed or administered intermittently or inconsistently. A small change in these or in other characteristics on which effective programs depend, as identified in an earlier chapter, often improves performance.

If there is not a stark deficiency in how the program is administered, several strategies can be used to enhance program effects. Major options discussed were response priming, reinforcing consistency in performance, reinforcer sampling, contingency contracts, and group contingencies. These options are often used in developing behavior-change programs, but they can also be added when the initial efforts to change behavior have not been effective.

Notes

1. The view that changing overt behavior is an effective means to alter intrapsychic and interpersonal processes is not unique to behavioral approaches. The psychoanalyst A. Herzberg (1945) maintained that the best way to alter intrapsychic processes was to change behaviors in everyday situations. He required patients to perform a graduated series of tasks outside the therapy sessions related to their clinical problems (e.g., anxiety, depression, sexual dysfunction, and many others). This requirement is very much like the contemporary exposure-based therapies that are so effective in treating anxiety disorders.
2. The role of the therapeutic relationship in adult psychotherapy has been studied extensively (Norcross, 2002; Orlinsky, Rønnestad, & Willutzki, 2004). Research has shown repeatedly that a good relationship, alliance, or bond between the therapist and patient predicts a better treatment outcome. This has led some to conclude that the relationship leads to, causes, or accounts for therapeutic change. In most studies, the timeline has not established that a good relationship precedes therapeutic change. Indeed some evidence suggests that early improvements in treatment lead to a good therapeutic relationship (Kazdin, in press).
3. The effectiveness of response priming is based on chaining, as discussed in chapter 2. In a chain of responses, each behavior further along in the chain is closer to the final behavior and the reinforcing consequence that follows once the chain is com-

pleted. Each response in the chain serves to reinforce the previous response and provides an S^D for subsequent responses. Thus, once the chain of responses begins, it is more likely to be completed. Response priming attempts to begin the early responses in the chain to start the sequence.

4. Single-case experimental designs are true experiments that can lead to causal inferences as that term is used in science. The designs, well beyond the scope of this book, utilize multiple observations over time (rather than pre and post testing) and use subjects as their own controls (see Kazdin, 2003b). In this demonstration, contracting was shown to exert influence in a multiple-baseline design across children.

8

Parent Management Training in Perspective

Chapter Outline

This chapter considers key findings, the strengths and limitations of PMT, and what can and cannot be concluded in light of the evidence. The limitations are discussed in relation to research on PMT as well as to child and adolescent therapy research more generally. This distinction is useful for purposes of presentation because PMT is one of the more studied interventions. Consequently, many limitations that pertain to PMT are likely to apply to many other forms of child and adolescent therapy as well.

Key Findings

Effects of PMT

PMT has been shown to lead to therapeutic changes among children and adolescents in scores of studies. Randomized controlled clinical trials, regarded as the strongest basis for drawing conclusions about interventions, provide the basis for this claim. Such trials have been conducted in the context of treatment and prevention.

In current discussions of treatment, the distinction is made between evidence-based and non-evidence-based treatments. I have complained elsewhere that this is a gross distinction that glosses over so much information about the status of a treatment (Kazdin, 2000b). For example, there are some treatments that are well studied and shown not to work, and a few that have been studied and shown to make children worse. These are merely counted as "non-evidence-based treatments." An analogous problem is evident with PMT. Merely noting that PMT is evidence-based underplays the evidence. The evidence for PMT greatly surpasses the criteria commonly used to make this designation of evidence-based treatment because of the number of studies and independent replications of outcome effects.

Outcome Effects

The effects of treatment have been evident in a wide range of symptoms and measures of adjustment of children and adolescents. Most studies focus on symptoms and functioning at home and at school and include parent and teacher reports and direct observations of behavior at home, at the clinic, or at school. In a few studies, measures of parent and family functioning (e.g., psychopathology, depression, and family relations) have been included and also reflect improvements.

The magnitude of effects is invariably an issue in treatment research. How much change is enough to make a difference? One can immediately discern the complexity of the issue by merely adding a "to whom?" to the question. Children, parents, and teachers may differ considerably on how they evaluate a given change. In the evaluation of psychotherapy, measures of clinical significance have been devised to address just this question (see Kazdin, 2003b; Kendall, 1999). Measures pertain to the magnitude of change, whether the changes move individuals to within a normative range on measures of symptoms, whether individuals still meet diagnostic criteria for the disorder, and others.

Several studies of PMT have shown that the changes are clinically significant. The most commonly used measure has shown that at the end of treatment, performance (usually mean level) falls within the range of a normative (community) sample of children who have not been referred for treatment and who have not been identified for the dysfunction or deviance. This does not settle the question of whether the change makes a genuine difference in the life of a specific child and family. Measures of clinical significance have not been carefully validated; whether they reflect palpable changes is not obvious (Kazdin, 2001a). Even so, efforts to operationalize "important changes" in therapy are laudable. PMT has shown that the improvements extend beyond mere statistically significant changes and also that parents view the changes as important.

Samples

Most applications of PMT have been with young children (<10 years old) who are referred for oppositional, aggressive, and, to a lesser extent, antisocial behavior. Adolescents, too, have been the focus of PMT but much less often, and conclusions about the effectiveness of treatment with teenagers are more tentative. In terms of diagnosis, the most common focus is children who are characterized by oppositional defiant, and conduct disorder, although studies often omit information about diagnoses. If they did include diagnoses, that, too, would not necessarily clarify the results because PMT has been studied for decades and across many changes in diagnostic systems, the disorders they delineate, and the criteria for a given disorder.

PMT has also been applied to children with mental retardation, learning disabilities, and pervasive developmental disorder. In these areas, PMT has had an impact on functioning, but the notion of what an effective treatment would be raises interesting questions. For example, PMT and the principles on which it is based are considered the most promising psychosocial treatment for children with autism (see Rogers, 1998; Smith, 1999). Researchers, clinicians, and families would not regard the treatment as achieving the level of amelioration we would want in all domains of dysfunction that pervasive developmental disorders can reflect.

Similarly, the effects of PMT have been evident for the treatment of children with attention-deficit/hyperactivity disorder. Although behavior improves, the effects of treatment on core symptoms are relatively weak. Medication is still regarded as the best treatment for the core symptoms. PMT can add to the effectiveness of treatment.

The focus of this book has been on treatment. PMT has been applied in the context of prevention, which I have mentioned only in passing. Several prevention studies are available. For example, two programs have conducted large-scale randomized controlled trials with hundreds of high risk youth (e.g., Head Start Children, children of divorce) and have shown similar positive outcomes as those mentioned in the context of treatment (e.g., Martinez & Forgatch, 2001; Reid, Webster-Stratton, & Baydar, 2004). Overall, PMT has a broad literature that establishes the evidence base in different contexts.

Underpinnings of Treatment

Those of us involved in the treatment of clinical dysfunction usually are elated when there is evidence for the effectiveness of a treatment, even if the basis of the effects is not well understood. PMT has a little more to offer because of the principles on which treatment draws and the conceptual work on disruptive behaviors. That is, the conceptual and empirical underpinnings of treatment are unique among treatments.

First, the principles on which PMT is based derive from operant conditioning within the psychology of learning. The principles have been well studied in animal laboratory and human research beginning in the 1930s and continuing to the present. The principles focus on how to change, develop, and maintain behavior rather than on a particular form of therapy. PMT draws on techniques derived from these principles and the supportive research. Research on reinforcement, punishment, extinction, and other principles is much more technical than what PMT utilizes. Even so, the principles and their techniques are directly translated to change parent and child behavior. Moreover, the techniques derived from these principles have been applied widely with many different populations (e.g., psychiatric patients, special education students, nursing home residents), in many different settings (e.g., schools, college dormitories, business and industry, communities), and across all age groups (infants through the elderly). This means that the support for PMT derives from its own empirical literature as well as from experimental research on the underlying principles and applications to many other areas of human functioning.

Second, many applications of PMT focus on oppositional and aggressive child behavior. Outside the context of treatment, parent–child interaction patterns have been carefully studied and shown to contribute directly to child aggressive behavior. Inept discipline practices and coercive interchanges, as highlighted previously, are among the key areas shown to contribute directly to child aggressive behavior, when analyzed on a moment-to-moment basis (Patterson et al., 1992). Moreover, intervention studies using PMT have shown that changing these interaction patterns leads to reductions in child aggression. Demonstrations of problems in parent–child interaction and that changing these interactions leads to improved child behavior are powerful. There is no other example to my knowledge in which a form of psychotherapy for children, adolescents, or adults has demonstrated a basic process implicated in clinical dysfunction, moved to intervention research, *and* shown that changing specific processes derived from that research leads to therapeutic change.

Of course, for many problems to which PMT has been applied, inept discipline practices are not necessarily involved. Here one draws on the psychology of learning as the basis for explaining how the effects are obtained. Reinforcement, punishment, and other principles effect change in behavior. These principles, when implemented optimally, can lead to change even when there is no "problem" with what the parents are doing already. Child rearing is usually a lovingly based, well-intended, less than systematic application of efforts to teach, educate, and socialize children. Helping parents be more systematic could ease small burdens in everyday interactions regarding the usual child actions and skills that parents try to develop.

General Comments

PMT focuses on changing parent behavior in concrete ways. These changes are used to produce change in the child who has been referred for treatment. PMT is conducted primarily in the home, at school, and in other settings in which the child is functioning. Because parents are conducting the intervention techniques, it might be that the effects extend to other children in the home beyond the child identified and referred for treatment. Siblings of children referred to treatment are themselves at greater risk for clinical dysfunction than a community sample of children in families with no clinical referrals. To the extent that treatment effects spread to siblings is a benefit. This has yet to be carefully studied, although improvements in siblings have been documented.

A few studies suggest that PMT improves parent functioning as well, as reflected in reduced parent depression and perceived stress and in improvements in family relations. It is not clear that these effects are unique to PMT. It might well be that any treatment that improves a child's functioning in the home has beneficial effects because of the dynamic and reciprocal nature of child dysfunction in the context of the family. The scope of impact of child therapy on parent and family functioning has not been well studied, but it is important to mention the broad benefits evident on some occasions in which it has been studied.

Myths and Red Herrings

There are genuine limitations of PMT, and these warrant attention. Prior to considering these, there are a few myths and red herrings to note as well.[1] They are worth mentioning because they are at once "fun," superficial, and broad, but also partially cogent concerns of child and adolescent therapy.

PMT Does Not Work with Everyone

This is a claim one can readily evoke in noting that PMT is an evidence-based treatment. The claim may then be made that the treatment does not work with everyone. This is certainly a true claim but a red herring. The concern is fairly true of most interventions, whether chemotherapy, bypass surgery, or psychotherapy.

It would be useful to catalogue the percentage of individuals for whom PMT is effective. The difficulties include coming up with a satisfactory and agreed-on measure. Therapy has many indices (e.g., symptoms, impairment, positive adaptive functioning) and the perspectives of different individuals (children, parents, teachers, clinicians), and quite different verdicts can result from which of these is consulted. All that aside, PMT, like polio vaccines, antidepressant medications, and ideal child rearing, does not work with everyone. This is not a unique, specific objection to PMT.

The Focus on Behavior Ignores Affect and Cognition

PMT emphasizes what the parents and child do in their interactions and how the child behaves in the settings in which functioning has been impaired. In this sense, the treatment definitely focuses on behavior. However, a statement that the treatment ignores affect and cognition would be difficult to defend. To my knowledge, the mental health professions do not have an intervention at this point and in the context of therapy that can be surgically applied to address behavior all by itself, that is, without influencing affect and cognition. PMT research has shown that when child behavior improves much more is altered, including family relations, quality of life of the family, parent views of their children, and depression (affects, cognitions, and behaviors) of the parent. These certainly encompass affect, cognitions (perceptions, attributions, beliefs), and behaviors. The impact is more poignant at the clinical level with individual families.

For example, one of the mothers at the clinic where I work called to tell us that we taught her to love her child again. Another mother told us we changed her child from being a horrible person to being a wonderful person. Of course, we did not do any of these in a very important sense. However, in each case, treatment did alter parent and child behavior and, in the process, broad statements of affect and attribution. There is nothing surprising here. We know that effects in one area can have a cascade of effects; change depression with medication, for example, and a person sees the world differently, well beyond the lifting of symptoms of depression. Also, it is no surprise to report that changing how an individual behaves (child) or how an individual behaves toward others (e.g., parent) is likely to alter perceptions. In short, it a bit mythical to suggest that PMT can change behavior without also having broader effects.

Treatment Ignores the Roots of the Problem

PMT has been applied most extensively to oppositional, aggressive, and antisocial behavior. Scientific models of these disorders emphasize the multiple paths and many risk factors likely to be involved. There is no clear causal path, although we know of a genetic component, a child-rearing component, and piles of other factors that place individuals at risk. Probably there are multiple "roots" of the problem. Perhaps if we knew them, we would not ignore them. Perhaps we might.

It is important to distinguish how a problem came about (theory of onset), how the problem is maintained (theory of maintenance), and how to change the problem (theory of change). Often knowing the cause conveys rather precisely what the intervention will be (e.g., cure for rabies, bacterial infection), so that theories of etiology and change are quite related. For many problems, change is achieved by focusing on what can be done with little or no information about etiology. Chemotherapy to cure cancer is an example where an effective treatment is not based on a clear understanding of etiology. When chemotherapy works, it is not because it addressed the original cause of the problem. The many ways that conduct problems come about are important to know and might have great implications for prevention and treatment. In the meantime, change can be achieved by understanding how to change behavior—in advance of knowing the roots of the problem.

In some cases, even if we could know about the root of the problem, it may be unclear how to effect change. For example, individuals who were sexually or physically abused as children might have some significant adjustment problem later. Let us say that the problems could be traced to this original root. The challenge for therapy is deciding what can be done right now to controvert something that happened long ago. How to change the affect, cognition, and behavior of individuals is the challenge.

The Child Will Become Dependent on Incentives, Rewards, and Praise

A concern is that children who participate in PMT will perform the desired behaviors only as long as the reinforcers (praise, points) are given. Once the rewards stop, will the behaviors stop as well? Indeed, extinction refers to no longer providing a reinforcer for a previously reinforced behavior that leads to a reduction in responding.

The concern is reasonable. There are three responses. First, follow-up data, already mentioned, indicate that gains in treatment are maintained at least up to 2 years after treatment. Second, most programs in PMT fade from point to praise programs, and then the programs are discontinued after the behavior is consistent and no longer a problem. Parents may reinvoke a program later as needed, but by the end of treatment, many of the programs are no longer in place and behavior continues. Third, and perhaps most relevant, there are specific procedures one can use to ensure that behaviors are maintained. Many of these involve fading (reducing, withdrawing) the program gradually (see Kazdin, 2001b).

As a general rule, children do not become dependent on rewards or perform behaviors only because the rewards are provided, any more than most adults do not depend on moment-to-moment incentives to continue to do what they do (e.g., work, hobbies). If programs are begun and quickly ended (e.g., a few days), dependence on the incentives seems to be more likely than if the program is in place for a while (e.g., weeks). Duration of a program seems to be related to maintenance after the program is terminated, but this is not well studied. Therapists do not have to implement a behavior-change program and hope for maintenance. There are procedures to develop and maintain behaviors, and these latter procedures can be used as needed.

The Child Will Show the Behavior Only in Those Situations in Which Incentives Are Given

This concern, related to the prior one, suggests that the conditions of the program may limit the circumstances in which that behavior is performed. Two comments may address this. First and most obviously, many behaviors that are brought to treatment *are* problems in restricted situations. Examples include paying attention in class, playing cooperatively with siblings, complying with parent requests, and behaviors related to eating, sleeping, and self-care. For many of these, the problem itself is restricted to a particular situation, so one only wants change in that situation.

Second, often children have a particular problem that does extend to more than one situation. For example, the child may receive reinforcers for engaging in the behavior at home but not at school or at the homes of relatives, where the behaviors may also be significant problems. Will the improvements be evident only at home, where the incentives are provided? Prior comments about discrimination and stimulus control suggest restricted performance in precisely this way.

If one wants the behavior to occur in more than one situation, it is important to extend the program to the other setting (Horner, Dunlap, & Koegel, 1988). It does not seem to be the case that the program (e.g., point chart) has to encompass all situations, just at least a few situations. For example, a parent might extend the program to home and to school or to home and out in the community. If this is accomplished, behavior is likely to generalize to new situations that have not been included in the program. In short, one can build generality of the behavior if and as needed (see Kazdin, 2001b).

General Comments

The myths and red herrings include genuine concerns. What makes them interesting, mythical, and herringlike is that they reflect points that are not particularly special or unique to PMT. For example, even the seemingly specific issues about whether the child will perform the behaviors without incentives or in situations when no incentives are provided reflect a concern in all therapy. Specifically, will anything that transpires in treatment (e.g., play therapy, relationship therapy, graduated exposure) transfer beyond that setting? For example, will family therapy generalize beyond the treatment session or to behaviors beyond the home? This would be a huge conceptual stretch (explaining how improving family communication will improve school work) and empirical stretch (what evidence is there for such "transfer" of the benefits of treatment?). Therapies of all sorts have not grappled with issues of maintenance and transfer.

Challenges and Limitations

There are many challenges and limitations that restrict the conclusions we can draw. Challenges draw attention to the glass-half-full side of the issues; limitations draw attention to the glass-half-empty side. Clearly, more needs to be known, and some of what needs to be known is basic information rather than subtle nuances about treatment (Cavell, 2001; Forehand & Kotchick, 2002; Herschell et al., 2002a). Consider central issues and questions briefly.

Durability of Treatment Effects

A perennial obstacle for evaluation of treatment for children, adolescents, and adults is the durability of treatment. It is not so much that the effects of treatment are shown to be transient. Rather, assessment of follow-up in treatment studies is not common. Follow-up, when evaluated, usually runs from 6 months to a year after treatment has ended. Consequently, there is very little follow-up information beyond a few years in studies of child and adolescent therapy.

In relation to PMT, follow-up has been studied but up to relatively brief durations. The effects of PMT have been evident up to 1 to 2 years after treatment in several studies. Longer follow-up durations have been reported (e.g., Hood & Eyberg, 2003; Long et al., 1994). In these studies, treatment effects are maintained. However, without a control group, one cannot strictly attribute the current functioning of children to PMT, as opposed to maturation or the impact of other influences. It is definitely fair to say that the long-term effects of PMT are not established. Again, the short-term effects of treatment are not established for most child therapies.

Moderators

As noted previously, moderators are characteristics that influence the effects of treatment. The question is for whom does PMT work or work especially well, for whom is it ill advised or not likely to be effective, and under what conditions will treatment be effective? We have some ideas with regard to the "for whom." In the context of treating oppositional, aggressive, and antisocial children, we know that several child, parent, and family factors influence the effectiveness of treatment. As mentioned previously (chapter 6), child severity of symptoms, presence of comorbid disorders, parent psychopathology and stress, marital conflict, and socioeconomic disadvantage attenuate the effects of treatment. Yet, these findings are not very helpful for several reasons.

First, these influences are not likely to be specific to PMT, or at least this has not been shown. Each of the influences reflects what might be expected; namely, greater adversity and disadvantage are pertinent to treatment outcome. Second, the bases for these influences or how these influences operate are not known. For example, these same moderators affect adhering to treatment, attending treatment sessions, and dropping out early. If we knew why the moderators influenced outcome, we might do something different in treatment or investigate methods to improve adherence and attendance. Third, to say that these factors attenuate treatment does not mean that PMT is ineffective or not the treatment of choice. Treatment can produce therapeutic change among families with several untoward influences (e.g., socioeconomic disadvantage, parent depression, and so on) and often does.

Fourth, it is difficult to translate the research on moderators into useful decision-making tools for clinical work. We know about some influences on outcome, but we do not know what to do with them in relation to treatment decisions. For example, perhaps a family with multiple factors that predict poor outcome would profit from a combined treatment or some non-PMT treatment. For any patient coming to treatment, it is not obvious how to act on the findings. For oppositional and conduct problems, PMT is still probably the treatment of choice, and a departure from this based on clinical judgment or research on moderators will be quite speculative and not necessarily any more helpful. We need research on moderators but also research that helps us use our knowledge in an informed way.

Are there individuals to whom treatment cannot be easily applied? That is, merely getting families to carry out the procedures may be difficult or impossible for parents with some characteristics or under some living conditions. Indeed, in our clinic, we developed a non-parenting-based treatment for severely disturbed children who do not have a parent who is willing or able to participate in treatment (Kazdin, Esveldt-Dawson, French, & Unis, 1987). (Parents may suffer severe mental illness or lose the custody of their child, or the child moves from home to home without a consistent guardian.) Obviously, the absence of a parent or other responsible adult figure may preclude use of PMT. Among those with a parent or guardian, we do not know if there is a specific group for whom PMT has very little chance of working. In clinical work, we often provide platitudes such as treatment does not work for everyone. Research has some obligation to add substance to this to find out who does not respond to treatment, why, and what to do about it.

Cultural, Ethnic, and Related Issues

Cultural and ethnic influences are potential moderators (characteristics) that influence the effectiveness of treatment and are worth mentioning separately. The extent to which PMT extends to different cultural, ethnic, and religious groups and geographic boundaries warrants comment (Forehand & Kotchick, 1996). In the United States, discussions about the generality of treatment usually pertain to underrepresented groups. If one ethnic group is studied, will the results extend to another group? Applications have indicated that PMT is effective with diverse ethnic groups, including European American, African American, Hispanic American, and multiethnic groups (e.g., Gross et al., 2003).

It is always possible to ask whether a treatment is applicable to one group versus another or whether it can be generalized to a group not yet included in the research. It is easy to formulate the question in an uninspired fashion, namely, by just identifying a group not yet included in the research and then asking if the results would apply. All groups, even two groups of the same ethnicity and age, are necessarily different in some respects, and hence merely raising the question by itself is not optimally useful. More is needed when raising the question of generality to suggest *why* one would expect groups to respond differently. Different ethnicity, age, sex, socioeconomic status, and other variables might limit applicability, but why and how? For example, ethnicity is seized as a main and likely moderator of treatment; it might well be. However, ethnicity is often confounded with other variables, such as socioeconomic disadvantage and levels of stress that contribute to PMT outcomes (e.g., Capage, Bennett, & McNeil, 2001; Kazdin, Stolar, & Marciano, 1995). It is not clear if or the extent to which membership in an ethnic group independently contributes to the outcomes, once these other factors are controlled.

Are there cultural, ethnic, and perhaps religious characteristics of families that might limit the applicability of PMT? For example, PMT programs are carried out in the United States primarily by mothers who are usually with the child for more time during the day than are the fathers. In addition, treatment is often provided to single-parent families headed by the mother. In cultures with more paternalistic or male-dominant families or where several extended family members are involved in parenting, would the treatment be feasible or effective?

In the context of families of antisocial children, punishment is one of the villains and part of inept parenting as I have mentioned previously. Corporal punishment has been shown to be associated with aggressive behavior and this too has been mentioned previously. Does corporal punishment have the same meaning, impact, and outcome as a function of culture and ethnicity? Much work would be needed to answer this and to show that culture and ethnicity, rather than some other variable with which these might be associated, are central moderators. Some work has already been completed. For example, greater amounts of physical discipline in young children (age 5) are associated with *higher* levels of aggressive and antisocial behavior years later for European American children but with *lower* levels of aggressive and antisocial behavior for African American children (Lansford, Deater-Deckard, Dodge, Bates, & Pettit, 2004). This may or may not be pertinent to the outcome effects of PMT for these different groups. However, the findings sensitize us to fundamental differences in processes leading to antisocial behavior. PMT relies heavily on the use of "rewards" in terms of tokens or points and praise—effusive praise in particular. It is readily conceivable that parents from various cultures would not want to be involved in delivering rewards of any kind to children for engaging in behaviors. Also, shaping child behavior may seem like coddling the child. Core techniques of PMT may clash with central views of a culture regarding the role of children and parents in the home and the legitimate ways of influencing child behavior. What changes, if any, are needed to apply PMT to various cultures? Are there some groups for whom the treatment is simply out of the question? PMT embraces assumptions (e.g., it is all right to induce behavior with incentives, to negotiate with children in contingency contracts, and to have children play some role in their own management) that might conflict with deeply held cultural beliefs. The question is whether PMT might be adaptable or in some cases clearly out of the question in any form.

Disseminability of Treatment

A question for any treatment is the extent to which it can be disseminated. *Disseminability* refers to the ease with which treatment may be extended to others who provide treatment (therapists) and to those who seek treatment (children, adolescents, and their families). The ease of dissemination can refer to a variety of characteristics of treatment, including the complexity of the procedures, type and amount of training needed to implement the procedures, likelihood of adherence to the treatment among those who implement or receive the procedures (therapists, patients), and the degree to which a departure from the prescribed procedures leads to a loss in effectiveness. Also, disseminability encompasses the efficiency of treatment, as reflected in how many persons in need can be served. For example, a familiar and long-standing distinction in treatment is delivery via individual or group therapy. If administration in a group versus individually were equally effective, group treatment might be preferred because of its efficiency in terms of number of clients per therapist and treatment session. Even better would be a treatment that can be delivered through a medium (e.g., television, videotapes, and Internet) that can reach very large numbers of clients. Therapy by Internet (referred to as *interapy*) is likely to increase in use and already has evidence in its behalf in controlled trials for both children and adults (e.g., Lange et al., 2003; Ritterband et al., 2003).

Disseminability is not a criterion to be advanced or advocated in its own right. Rather, a presumption here is made that the treatment is one that warrants dissemination in light of evidence in its behalf. This seemingly obvious point warrants mention, nonetheless, because the media often disseminate widely various procedures or equipment to help our minds and bodies but with no evidence that the interventions are effective. It is not fair to criticize the media alone. In our training as clinicians, we learn many treatments that have no evidence on their behalf, and these are "disseminated" to us for use with the public.

PMT has excellent outcome evidence, but can the treatment be disseminated widely and retain its effects? Studies have shown that abbreviated versions of treatment and treatments that rely less on face-to-face contact and more on aids (e.g., videotapes) can be effective and extend treatment (e.g., Nixon, Sweeney, Erickson, & Touyz, 2003; Sutton, 1992). Efforts to disseminate PMT are quite promising. One line of work has developed self-administered PMT on a CD-ROM (Gordon & Stanar, 2003). The program is designed for low-income families with delinquent children or children at risk for becoming delinquent or substance abusers. Various parenting skills are presented by computer in an interactive fashion, for example, praise, feedback, and further information by computer, based on parent performance with the program. Vignettes presented by video cover various situations (e.g., getting a child to do homework) and ask the parent to select various strategies. Feedback conveys the consequences of actions selected by parents. Parents learn effective and ineffective strategies. Quizzes and examples throughout are designed to develop mastery of several skills, such as administering praise. Several controlled-outcome studies using the CD-ROM indicate that intervention effects can be attained in this way. In keeping with therapist-administered treatment, the effects of PMT are evident in reductions in child behavior problems, maternal depression, and improved family functioning. Clearly, a self-administered program for use with low-income families could have a remarkable impact on the disseminability of PMT.

Another example mentioned previously antedated the CD-ROM program and focused on the development of videotapes (Webster-Stratton, 1996; Webster-Stratton & Reid, 2003). The tapes present the material to groups of parents, and a therapist facilitates the discussion. This program, too, has been evaluated empirically; the tapes, when used as noted here, effect change, as highlighted in chapter 5.

Both of these examples are important efforts to disseminate treatment. A difficulty of any treatment is training therapists. These aids permit therapists and families to have greater access to treatments than might otherwise be the case. In the CD-ROM version, the program can be self-administered individually or used in a group format.

Beyond the issue of PMT, much more information is needed on the assessment and evaluation of disseminability of treatment. There is no single measure or index to evaluate whether treatment is disseminable, although cost and acceptability, discussed next, are no doubt pertinent. The lack of empirical attention to the factors that influence disseminability and to developing some objective indices of disseminability reflects a limitation of therapy research. Two treatments that may have evidence may differ in such dimensions as disseminability or cost, and this information is very important to know.

Costs of Treatment

The monetary *costs* of providing treatment and delivering services are relevant for evaluating treatment. Obviously, a less costly treatment is preferred to a costlier treatment, given evidence that both are effective. There are different ways of evaluating cost (see Cummings, O'Donohue, & Ferguson, 2002; Yates, 1995). For example, cost-effectiveness analysis examines the costs of treatment relative to a particular outcome. The outcome must be quantifiable (e.g., reduction in symptoms, increase in family harmony). Cost-effectiveness can be used to evaluate two different treatments or variations of a given treatment.

For example, one study compared two variations of PMT for parents of kindergarten children with behavior problems (Cunningham, Bremner, & Boyle, 1995). One variation was individual treatment provided at a clinical service; the other was group-based treatment conducted in the community (at community centers or schools). Both treatments were better than a wait-list control condition. On several measures, the community-based treatment was more effective. Even if the treatments were equally effective, the monetary costs (e.g., start-up costs, travel time of families, costs of the therapist-trainer in providing treatment) of individual treatment were approximately six times greater per family than the group treatment. Clearly, this is a significant criterion for evaluating the different ways of administering treatment.

Within psychotherapy research, costs of treatment are rarely evaluated. Estimating cost is not entirely straightforward because of the range of costs that can be included. Also, those who do therapy research are rarely trained to evaluate costs. Even so, efforts to describe the costs of different treatments represent a worthwhile addition to intervention research. In fact, decisions about what treatments to use at the level of individual services (e.g., clinics and hospitals) and public policy are driven heavily by costs and related disseminability data. For those involved in clinical service delivery and health care, it is clear that cost is often much more of a concern than whether there is evidence in behalf of the treatment that is used.

Acceptability of Treatment

Acceptability of treatment refers to the extent to which those who participate in treatment (e.g., children, adolescents, families, but perhaps mental health professionals as well) view the treatment as reasonable, justified, fair, and palatable. Among treatments that are equally effective, those viewed as more acceptable are more likely to be sought, adhered to, and executed correctly (e.g., Reimers, Wacker, Cooper, & DeRaad, 1992). Acceptability draws attention to the procedures and how user-friendly and reasonable they may seem.

As I mentioned in the context of disseminability, acceptability is to be considered along with effectiveness rather than by itself. It is quite possible to develop procedures that are acceptable and widely disseminated, even if they have little or no impact. For example, fad diets, alternative medical treatments, and cosmetics often are quite acceptable and widely used, even if they make no difference in altering weight, disease, or wrinkles, respectively. Consequently, it is important to consider acceptability as a complementary criterion to effectiveness.

Different treatments for a given problem may not be equally acceptable to prospective clients. For example, various forms of psychotherapy and medication are viable options for the treatment of depression. For many patients, medication may be less acceptable because there are often side effects in reduced sexual activity, interest, and functioning. On the other hand, for many patients, psychotherapy may be less acceptable because of the notion of "therapy" and what that might mean to them personally or to significant others with whom they live. Clearly, there are personal and perhaps cultural differences on the acceptability of medical versus "psychological" treatments. The dimension of acceptability is relevant to evaluating treatment and one that rarely is included in treatment trials.

The challenge for child and adolescent therapy is that treatments need to be acceptable to the child or adolescent as well as to the parent, for the obvious reason that retaining the child in treatment may depend on evaluations of acceptability. Evaluations of acceptability may depend heavily on how the treatment procedures conform to what participants expect from treatment. If talk or play is the medium of treatment but the family is expecting some other intervention, or vice versa, treatment may be less acceptable than it would otherwise be.

Although it is meaningful to speak of the acceptability of different treatments (e.g., talk therapy, PMT), perhaps even more important is consideration of acceptability of different versions of the same treatment. Once an effective treatment is identified, perhaps there are ways to make the treatment and its delivery either more acceptable or acceptable to a wider range of clients. The use of abbreviated and self-help versions of PMT, already mentioned, would be examples. It may be that such treatments make slightly fewer demands on the families (e.g., fewer sessions, do not require coming to treatment at a clinic) and afford greater autonomy (e.g., administration at home with little or no help from a therapist). Such features may well make treatment more available to many more parents than would otherwise be the case but also more acceptable as a treatment. This discussion implies that acceptability is a property that adheres in the treatment, when in fact it has to do just as much with the perception of the family about treatment.

Information on the acceptability of treatment can greatly supplement data on effectiveness. Moreover, acceptability may be an important dependent variable for developing effective treatments. It will be useful to understand what can be done in the delivery of treatments to make them more acceptable (e.g., Foxx, Bremer, Schutz, Valdez, & Johndrow, 1996).

Closing Comments

PMT is an evidence-based treatment for children and adolescents. The treatment and the principles on which it is based have been widely applied to many clinical problems and samples. PMT has been used most frequently with children with oppositional, aggressive, and antisocial behavior, and this focus has been emphasized in this book.

In relation to the multitude of treatments available for children and adolescents, involving both psychotherapies and medications, a few characteristics make PMT especially interesting. First, there is a strong evidence base for the treatment. I have noted that probably no other form of psychotherapy treatment has been as well studied as has PMT in relation to children and adolescents. Second, PMT has been used for prevention among youth at risk for clinical dysfunction. Third, PMT has been applied in clinics in the traditional model of outpatient service delivery. However, the intervention has been extended to groups of parents in school and other community settings. This raises the prospect that it might be disseminable on a larger scale than individual outpatient therapy provided at a clinic.

There may be utility in extending PMT more broadly, not necessarily as a "treatment" or "preventive" intervention. On a good day, parenting and child rearing are challenging. Small doses of the principles and practices that comprise PMT may make child rearing a little easier for both parents and children. Encouraging children to complete homework, to bathe, to eat healthful foods, to use eating utensils during meals, and to let us know where they are at all or most times *are* eventful in normal child rearing. These usually do not rise to the level of requiring clinical attention but still are challenging to parents. Brief versions of PMT might be useful as part of school curricula or programs to prepare individuals about to become parents.

There are many unknowns and areas where the evidence in behalf of PMT is inadequate. Thus, PMT is not a panacea for child problems. The long-term effects of treatment, the impact of treatment on everyday lives of children and parents, the individuals for whom treatment is very or not at all effective, and other questions I have raised previously are quite important. Relative to other therapies, PMT fares well on research to address these issues. PMT is clearly a treatment of choice for oppositional, aggressive, and antisocial behavior among children. However, significant gaps in knowledge remain, even after decades of studying this treatment. At the same time, so much has been learned that children, adolescents, and parents could benefit enormously from the evidence currently available.

Note

1. A *red herring* refers to a distracter, misleading clue, or matter that diverts attention. The term derives from the fact that herring, when smoked and cured, changes color to reddish brown (similar to smoked salmon or lox). In training hounds to hunt foxes, red herrings were used to lay down trails of scents for dogs to follow. After dogs were trained, the herrings were sometimes dragged across a scent of a trail of a real fox to test the ability of the hounds to ignore false clues. This etymology is difficult to verify completely; however, there is agreement that the use of *red herrings* to mean "false clue" began in the late 1800s.

Parent Management Training **MANUAL**

Over many years, several therapists and staff contributed to the development and ongoing revisions of this manual, as acknowledged in the preface. I am pleased to acknowledge in particular the contributions of Elif Attaroglu, Erin Carrubba, Karen Esveldt-Dawson, Lisa Holland, Bernadette Lezca, Molly McDonald, and Elaine Weissberg.

Contents

Introduction to the Manual

The manual focuses on Parent Management Training (PMT), an intervention designed to alter parent–child interactions in the home. The goal of the intervention is to alter specific child-rearing practices and to increase the prosocial functioning of the child at home, at school, and in the community. A number of PMT manuals are available commercially. This manual has been designed specifically for families with children referred clinically for oppositional, aggressive, and antisocial behavior (ages 2–14). This version has been used with children 7–14 and their families. We have a version for younger children (up to age 6) that has slight modifications. The children who receive the treatment are referred to an outpatient clinical service (Yale Child Conduct Clinic) because of their oppositional, aggressive, and antisocial behavior. The clinic is affiliated with Child Psychiatry services at the Child Study Center (Yale University School of Medicine) and the Department of Psychology at the university.

Use of the Manual

The goal of treatment is to develop specific response repertoires in both parents and their children. Several content areas of social learning principles are covered in this manual. This is a manual to detail the procedures administered to parents. In developing complex repertoires of parent behavior, therapists actively utilize the principles this manual discusses. In particular, administration of this intervention and development of parent behaviors depend heavily on effusive and frequent social reinforcement by the therapist. The timing of this reinforcement and its modulation for purposes of shaping parent behavior are trained quite explicitly among therapists. The manual conveys the procedures that comprise PMT but may not adequately convey the training of therapists and the style in which the material is delivered. In this overview, I will mention each of these areas because they materially affect the ability to change parent and child behavior.

Session Format and Materials

Most of the sessions are similar in format. After an initial behavior-change program is implemented in the home, the next treatment session begins with a review of the program, how it is working, and any problems or obstacles in delivery or execution on the part of the parent. The therapist problem-solves with the parent, makes repairs in programs that may have gone awry, and has the parent practice delivering consequences to the therapist in various role play situations. Once the program has been reviewed, the session moves forward to a new theme and set of skills that will be added to the program at home. Typically, treatment does not move forward to a skill if the prior skill still needs a great deal of work or if a program that was implemented is failing and producing unanticipated untoward effects or could simply be improved in light of new information.

The treatment is delivered on a weekly basis. If something is not working or working well or indeed if it is working very well, changes in the program are made during the week. Between the sessions, the therapist calls the home to check on what is happening or to provide prompts and praise for what was completed by the parent. Calls during the week mean that a program that has gone awry does not need to continue until the parent comes to a session.

The manual includes 13 sessions, an overview and orientation session and 12 sessions devoted specifically to PMT. Over the years, we have varied the number of sessions as a way of tinkering with the best way to present the skills. The current 12-session version may be supplemented with additional or optional sessions. Optional sessions are interspersed as needed to address a theme or to vary a procedure that was covered in a previous session. For example, if a reinforcement program implemented early in treatment is not working very well or if a parent's applications of prompting and praising are poor, an additional session would be added to work on these before moving on to the next theme. Prompting and delivery of contingent praise are pivotal skills, and some minimal level of competence is essential. An optional session is likely to be interspersed to give the parent the opportunity for more role play, modeling by the therapist, and practice of the behaviors. More often than not, an optional session may be added to complete the session that was given short shrift. Often this situation emerges when a parent arrives late and receives less than the usual training in the session because the treatment session cannot spill into the next patient's appointment or the parent has to leave at a fixed time and cannot stay later.

In our program, these optional or extra sessions are added in only a small proportion of the cases, so the 12 core sessions represent our treatment program. In those cases in which an optional session is provided, there is usually just one session, and it is provided because the therapist could not complete all of a session (e.g., not complete all of the role-play situations) because the parent arrived late or review of the program required extensive discussion.

Most of the sessions include handouts and various charts. These are usually didactic devices and outlines the therapist discusses during the treatment. All of this material is in the manual. The parent keeps a binder, and handouts are added over the course of the session to convey the key points. The charts include point charts used by the parent for the child's behavior-change program. Parents record points delivered on a daily basis. Not all parents do this, but most can do this. This information is important as one source of deciding how well the program is going at home.

Therapist Training

Characteristics to Train

In the training of therapists and the conceptualization of PMT more generally, it is useful to identify three interrelated facets of treatment. First, therapists are trained in *principles and techniques of operant conditioning*, much of the content of the first part of the book. Understanding what setting events and prompts do, how they work, and the myriad types of prompts that can be used to foster parent behavior is essential. Therapists are trained to understand the techniques and to use them to shape parent behavior.

Second, therapists learn the many details of the *procedures of the manual*. The manual codifies many practical aspects of treatment, including the materials used in the sessions, the dialogue used by the therapist on a session-by-session basis, and the situations that serve as the basis of practicing and training the parent in the sessions.

Third, there is a *style of delivering the treatment* that is pivotal to treatment but difficult to codify in the manual. A few key characteristics capture the style of treatment and the nature of the sessions. Therapists are trained to be constructive and to identify what needs to be changed and developed in the parent. The challenge is developing behavior and having palpable impact. Conceiving many problems that families present begins with an approach of what needs to be developed constructively. For example, parental physical abuse of a child can be altered, but the focus of the therapist is on positive opposites and shaping rather than lecturing about the abuse.

Therapists use the ABCs very methodologically, as discussed in earlier chapters in the book. For example, the therapists use effusive praise, feedback, and frequent prompts. The manual may say, "The therapist should praise the parent for this or that." However, the delivery of that praise is worked on extensively in training so that the therapist does not miss parent behavior that should have been praised and so that the therapist's praise reflects effusive comments.

Emphasis on the sessions is on practice, role play, and executing what the therapist is trying to teach. There is a temptation only to explain to the parent some nuance or even gross aspect of a skill the therapist wishes to develop. Once the parent and therapist nod in shared understanding, this is only part of the treatment. Therapists require the parent to practice the skills. Explanation and refinement through verbal feedback from the therapist are not substitutes for practicing the behavior so the therapist can shape performance and so the parent has repeated practice trials. Therapists are invariably saying, "Let's practice this" or "show me how you do that." Each practice opportunity is a training opportunity, and therapists are constantly shaping and reinforcing behavior.

Therapist Background and Experience

The therapists who have administered this treatment have had a graduate degree (a master's in psychology, social work, counseling, or education; two therapists in special internship program arrangements had doctorates) and experience (at least 1 to 3 years) in treatment with children and/or families. We require training and/or experience in child and family mental health because the families of children with conduct problems often present a complex set of disorders and sources of family dysfunction. The children alone usually have multiple psychiatric disorders at the time of admission to the clinic. (Approximately 70% of the cases meet criteria for two or more psychiatric disorders, based on the criteria of the *Diagnostic and Statistical Manual of Mental Disorders.*)

Training Procedures

Administration of this manual is learned in a period of approximately 6 months and occasionally longer. The training begins with didactic work (readings, informal discussion, with examples of applications) of the principles of operant conditioning (e.g., positive reinforcement, punishment, and extinction) and many of the techniques that derive from them, material highlighted in the first part of this book. It is critical for therapists to be facile with the principles and the techniques outside the context of the manual. PMT adapts behavior-change programs to the individual circumstances of the family, so it is important for the therapists to know critical aspects of the procedures and manifold options for implementing them.

After review and discussion of the principles and procedures, training with this manual begins. The goals are to teach the specific procedures and the style of presenting the material. Learning the manual begins with viewing videotapes of therapy. We have a library of tapes with different therapists administering the sessions. The therapist in training views these repeatedly. Then the therapist begins to practice administering the treatment one session at a time until each session is mastered. This is accomplished by the therapist pretending to be a parent and receiving the session, as delivered live by a trained therapist. Then the therapist in training delivers the session to another therapist who pretends to be a parent. Throughout these experiences, the session is stopped to provide feedback and answer questions of the therapist in training. Receipt of the session and practice of the session are conducted for each session.

After the first few sessions are mastered (e.g., up to Session 3), the therapist in training is assigned a clinic case of a family whose child is referred for oppositional, aggressive, or antisocial behavior (all families are clinically referred). The therapist continues to learn additional sessions of the manual until the entire manual is mastered. However, emphasis is placed on the sessions the therapist is currently delivering to the family. Typically, three cases are assigned in close proximity so the therapist has the opportunity to deliver a session (e.g., Session 1), receive feedback, deliver the same session again to a different family, and so on with a third family.

All sessions are videotaped, so review of the tapes with the therapist is readily available. For a therapist in training, experienced therapists sometimes watch the session live from a remote video and give immediate feedback for the session. Sessions are videotaped for all therapists, not just a therapist in training. A select number of sessions are reviewed in a group meeting weekly, and segments of individual sessions of all the therapists are shown and discussed. Consequently, "training" is ongoing at the clinic, even after the treatment has been mastered.

We have developed a method to train therapists to know and administer this manual. However, we have not tested alternative methods of teaching or the dose and duration of training therapists. The time period and number of cases we have used to develop skills are somewhat arbitrary. It may be possible for others to circumvent or reduce the period of training and achieve the goals with different experiences. Even so, reading and applying the manual alone are likely to be insufficient to carry out the treatment and to develop the skills for treating families of children with severe antisocial behavior.

Style of the Manual

The manual is written in a colloquial style because much of the material provides the actual statements and narrative for the therapist. Material in quotes usually refers to what the therapist says to the parent. The language has been adopted to make the material comfortable and natural for therapist and parent. The informalities are reflected in heavy use of contractions (*It's, won't*) and lapses in grammar (e.g., invariably use of will instead of shall), and many uses that are now technically correct or allowable (e.g., a *child* might lose *their* [rather than his or hers] tokens), and infinitives that are as sadly split as many of the families we see. Again, these are intended to make the conversation between the therapist and parent natural.

In a few cases, we have slightly sacrificed technical accuracy in the service of easy presentation. For example, we use the terms *reinforcer* and *reward* interchangeably for many of the sessions. Rewards and reinforcers are different, and the differences have implications. The manual conveys the distinction to the parents but still reverts to reward merely to avoid jargon. Of course, mixing the terms is a no-no in applied behavior analysis for reasons highlighted in chapter 3 in the first part of the book. As another example, we occasionally encourage the parent to praise or reinforce *the child* when the child engages in this or that behavior. Here, too, this is not quite right. One reinforces *behavior*, not people. In short, for presentation we have made some sacrifices in purity of the language.

Careless language can reflect careless thought. More often than not, we teach concepts that are quite accurate without burdening the parent with terminology. For example, there are several reinforcement schedules to reduce and eliminate undesirable behaviors, as discussed earlier in this book. We do not use the technical terms in presenting these schedules to the parents, but we do present the core concepts and utilize procedures to change behavior. Also, aficionados of applied behavior analysis will note that we do not use some of the esoteric terms (e.g., to occasion a response, establishing operations, and stimulus control). To be sure, therapists learn the concepts, terms, and their technicalities. For the families, the manual tries to be rigorous in concepts and techniques but user-friendly in the manner of delivery. The reader will be able to judge the successes and failures in accomplishing these goals.

Words on Terminology

To facilitate preparation of the manual and to avoid many awkward passages, we have adopted some conventions of language. Throughout the manual, we usually refer to the child as "he." It is relevant to note we are treating children identified because of their antisocial behavior. Most of our cases and, of course, most children with these behaviors referred to treatment generally are boys. Because the child is referred to often in this manual, the constant reference to *he/she* or *himself/herself* was awkward. To facilitate communication and flow, we adopted the masculine pronoun with no intent to indicate a sex bias.

The parents are referred to often in the manual as well. In the majority of cases, our treatment sessions are with the mother or mother figure. When the mother and father or multiple relatives are included, it is still generally true that the mother is the person who spends most of the time with the child and hence has the major responsibility for implementing behavior-change programs. Consequently, for purposes of convenience, we have typically referred to the parent as *she* rather than to construct more cumbersome language.

Pretreatment Introduction and Orientation

Prior to beginning treatment with any of the families at the Child Conduct Clinic, we provide a Pretreatment Introduction and Orientation Session. The purposes of this session are to learn about the child and family, to familiarize the parent(s) with our approach to treatment, and to explain important aspects of clinic operations. The session also enables the parent to meet the therapist(s), and to ask questions. The following material is not central to PMT specifically but is an introduction to treatment, the clinic, and assessments. (In some of our projects, we have evaluated problem-solving skills training alone and combined with PMT. Projects with these other interventions are noted in the Reference section of the book.)

Explanation of Treatment and Information Gathering

This meeting is designed to introduce the parents to the treatment and the clinic. This session helps to obtain clinical information about the family that will be helpful in understanding the problem and ultimately in developing programs for the child. Questions related to the treatment and clinic procedures are encouraged so the parents leave the session with a clear idea about treatment, the clinic, and any other related issues of concern.

Objectives

- To provide the therapist and parent(s) an opportunity to get acquainted.
- To provide the parent(s) with an opportunity to discuss problems and stressors openly.
- To introduce the parent to treatment and clinic procedures.

Equipment/Materials

To the Reader: In subsequent sessions, materials listed in this section are part of PMT procedures and administration of the session. The materials (e.g., handouts and charts) are included in each of the session. The materials for this session are not part of PMT per se and are not included. The materials consist of consent forms to permit evaluation of treatment, forms to evaluate fees (sliding scale) for the treatment, and a packet of measures used to evaluate treatment. The measures have been described in publications about our treatment program and are cited in the Reference section of the book.

Welcome and Introductions

Welcome the parents and make them feel comfortable. Say something positive about their efforts (i.e., getting to the session on time, scheduling the appointment, cooperating with intake procedures, recognizing problems and seeking treatment, etc). Personal introductions should be made at this time.

"Welcome!! It's great that you are early (on time). . . . Did you have any trouble finding us?"

"There are three things I would like to cover with you today. I would like to gather more information from you regarding (child's name), then I would like to tell you more about our program and what we do here in treatment, then to discuss some of the materials we would like you to review and complete."

Family Issues and Concerns

(Note to the therapist: Please use the Introduction Form to gather the information below.)

Parents will begin with problem behaviors. Probe for specifics. Use basic interviewing skills, paraphrasing what they are saying, and periodically summarizing the major points covered. Be empathic by aligning yourself with the parents' feelings and perspective and reflect back their feelings. The questions of the introductory session have several purposes (i.e., getting to know the parent, sharing information, etc.). Empathize with the parents, understand their concerns and goals, and convey that support is available at the clinic. To this end, the therapist should spend a certain amount of time dwelling on the concerns of the primary care-taking parent.

Stems for statements that can be asked for all topics (below) are:

1. It must be rough (tough, difficult, frustrating, stressful) . . .
2. I can understand . . .
3. I'll bet you . . .
4. You must have felt . . .

5. I can tell you really feel . . .
6. It sounds/seems as though you . . .

Try to get as complete a picture as possible of the home and school situation. The questions on the Introduction Form (end of this session) are suggestions only; they were designed to assist and guide the discussions. Remember we want to know the problems and issues in each domain, although assets and strengths (e.g., family support) are queried as well. Ask open-ended questions and take a supportive, understanding role. Again, the questions are provided only as guidelines. All areas need not be covered, although at least two questions from each topic are recommended.

Always begin with, "Just to give me a picture of who is living at the house: there's you, your child, and. . . ." This is to find out about significant others, siblings, grandparents, other family members, and so on. If possible, construct an informal genogram. Proceed with the questions and the Introduction Form at the end of the Session. (The therapist now uses this form as a basis for the semistructured interview.)

Summary of Parents' Description of Problem

Well, it looks as though you have given me a very clear description of the types of problems going on with (child's name). Let me tell you about our program so you have a better idea of how we can help.

PMT Comments

"We will be working together in Parent Management Training over the next several months. Including today, there are approximately 11–15 sessions, which last for one hour each week." (*To the Reader:* The number of sessions and the time period would seem to conflict with the manual of 12 weekly sessions after this session. However, we allow for optional sessions and allow for the fact that treatment is not likely to be weekly due to weather [e.g., snow], schedule conflicts [e.g., school, camp events for the child], and cancelled sessions on the part of the family.)

"During these sessions you will be learning skills and techniques to help you manage (child's name) differently at home. Many of these skills may be familiar in some ways; however, we will ask you to do them in very specific ways to make them quite effective. At times you may disagree with what we are asking you to do. If this happens, please let us know. We will work closely together to make sure the programs fit with your personal circumstances. We want to try the programs in the home to help your child. By trying out the programs, you will have a chance to actually see if it works or not, and you will also have questions that we can address."

"In order to make changes in your child that are long-lasting, you will need to practice and apply parenting skills at home on a daily basis. I will also need for you to keep records of (child's name)'s behavior and spend time presenting, discussing, and reviewing programs with him. This may sound like a lot. It is, but most parents find the program quite helpful. In addition, I will be calling you once a week to help you along and to answer your questions. And, of course, you can call me anytime at the clinic. Do you have any questions?"

"Now let me explain to you why we focus treatment on the parents. "Until recently, the primary types of treatment for children with problems were either individual counseling with parents or individual counseling with the child about his or her feelings and emotions. However, research has shown a more effective way to treat children's problems is to teach parents new ways of understanding why their child behaves the way he or she does and new ways of handling their child's problems. The focus of this treatment is to teach parents special skills for changing their child's behavior; this is an effective way to help children act more appropriately. Another advantage is you can apply the skills you learn to future child behavior problems and with your other children. One thing important to understand is that *you* will be treating your child. You will learn to be, in effect, a therapist for your family. You will learn to anticipate problems and apply the skills independent of input from a therapist."

"One thing that distinguishes this program from others is the relationship between the parent and the therapist. In the beginning, I will teach and demonstrate the various techniques. Later, however, I will assume the role of coach to work with you and give suggestions. By the end of our program, you will be working successfully on your own. Learning how to use these new techniques is similar to learning how to play a musical instrument or perform gymnastics. A lot of time is spent practicing and working with the procedures at home. Then, as you use the skills, you will master them and will be able to manage your son/daughter more effectively."

"This treatment does require much time and effort on your part. Problem behaviors are not "cured" over a brief period of time and should not be confused with medical problems in terms of a "cure." For example, if a patient has diagnosed appendicitis, an appendectomy is performed. After the operation and recovery, the problem is usually cured. With behavioral problems we do not speak in terms of a "cure," rather we speak in terms of using specific behavioral interventions to modify or improve a behavioral problem. You can improve child functioning at home and at school.

Assessments

"Because this is a special clinic for children like (child's name), there are some things we would like to mention. First, the treatment is one of the most promising treatments available for children with aggression and related problem behaviors. This is a difficult problem to treat and we have been developing and studying these treatments now for over 20 years."

"Second, to see how our treatments are working and how (child's name) is doing, we need your help. To understand (child's name)'s behavior and how he is doing in many different areas of his life, we need to get a lot of specific information from you and your child. We will need you to complete a fairly large packet of forms that are especially relevant to this clinic. These forms do not need to be completed today. You will have the next two weeks to finish them. This information is absolutely vital for evaluating your child now and after treatment. In fact, as part of our treatment program we need the assessments completed right before and right after treatment is finished."

"We will *also* want to do assessments periodically throughout the program *and* following completion of the program. These assessments during our program are significant to what we do as well. We truly want to know if your child is improving and whether you are satisfied with the changes you are seeing. Now, as I mentioned earlier we do compare your child's behavior from before the program started to after the program, but we also evaluate throughout the program so we can make any changes. Next week you will be meeting with me to go over four additional forms, which are in an interview format. That is why they are not included in your packet. Your part should take about an hour. Your child's part may take a little longer."

Attendance

"There is one last point related to our program and that is attendance. Because of the nature of the program, regular attendance is extremely important. The reason for bringing this up now is to emphasize that missed sessions and sporadic attendance only make the program fail. Because it is important to us and I'm sure to you that this program is helpful, we must ask that you attend appointments each week. Situations occasionally arise like illness or emergencies that prevent you from coming. Please call and we will try to reschedule or accommodate you in any way possible. Also, we need you to be on time for appointments. This ensures that you will get the necessary time and attention and avoids unnecessary pressure for us. If you think you are going to be late please call and, depending on our schedule, we will either reschedule the appointment or have you come in. Thanks very much."

Summary

The therapist should summarize any of the parent's concerns and should provide reassurance; give a few examples of how the treatment(s) will help change the child's behavior. This is done by tying behavior problems into the treatment approach. "You have given me a lot of information regarding (child's name) behavior. I think that we can really help if you are able to come in and try the programs that we set up each week."

"Families often have crises and we will respond as needed. However it is important to stay focused and move forward if we are going to be most helpful and effective. As treatment progresses we will address one problem at a time. We may not have time to work on all problems, but we will work on and improve key problems. We will prepare you for dealing with other problems with your child later on."

Materials

To the Reader: At this point various consent procedures are explained and presented to the parent including Privacy Practices, Research Authorization Form, Health Insurance Portability and Accountability Act (HIPAA), and consents to tape the session for training purposes and to obtain information from the schools. The therapist also reviews the fee structure of the clinic, a topic that will have been addressed at the initial call when the family contacted the clinic.

Wrap-Up

Answer any questions. Thank/praise the family for coming. Make statements about looking forward to getting started if appropriate and reinforce commitment to treatment. "Many parents are not willing to make a commitment and you should be commended for being willing to work with your child in the ways we have discussed."

Defining, Observing, and Recording Behavior

Objectives

The purpose of this first session is to teach parents how to define, observe, and record behavior. The concept of positive opposites is also introduced.

Equipment and Materials

Handouts
- Behaviors and Nonbehaviors
- Problem Behaviors and Positive Opposites
- Prompting: Getting Behaviors to Happen
- Helpful Hints for Observing
- Behaviors That Can and Cannot Be Recorded
- Rewards List

Observation Chart

    Weekly Assignment Sheet (first page of each week's handouts, marked with a large checkmark)

    Folder with information about the clinic, which can hold all the handouts over the course of treatment

Therapist Introduction

"Welcome and thank you for coming. It's nice to see you again. Do you have any questions about the treatment or anything we talked about at our last meeting? How are the questionnaires? Last week I said that in our meetings I would teach you new skills which will help you manage your child's behavior and help his behavior in school and at home. Today, we will be discussing some new skills such as defining, prompting, and observing behaviors. Let's begin by discussing what a behavior is."

What Is a Behavior?

"A behavior is an action like waving my hand [wave hand] or clapping my hands [clap hands]. These are examples of my behavior because they can be seen or heard. Thoughts, feelings, and attitudes are not behaviors because you can't see or hear them. Tell me whether you think the following are behaviors." Show Chart I.

Chart I: Behaviors and Nonbehaviors

Running

Crying

Swearing

Fighting with Other Children

Having a Bad Attitude

Feeling Bad

"If you think the word or phrase describes a behavior, say yes; if it is not a behavior, say no. Remember, it is a behavior only if it can be seen or heard. Let's begin with running."

Read each word on the handout, pausing after each to ensure correct responses. If the parent identifies a nonbehavior as a behavior, the therapist should say, "What do you see or hear that makes _____ a behavior?" If the parent can list concrete examples (e.g., "When my boy has a bad attitude, he pouts, stomps his feet, and yells"), say, "OK, that's good because these can be seen or heard," but help the parent understand that although having a bad attitude may be accompanied by a behavior or behaviors, feeling bad or having a bad attitude is not a behavior because it cannot be seen or heard.

Defining Behavior

"Before using any of the techniques you will learn throughout this program, you want to start with clearly defining the problem and the positive behavior you would like to increase. Let's practice. Let's say you have decided to observe the smiling behavior of someone you know. Remember, when you define a behavior, do so in terms of what you can see or hear. Can you define smiling for me?" (Pause and praise effort.) "What else would define smiling?" Their suggestions might include:

Corner of mouth upturned
Twinkle in the eye
Teeth showing
Eye contact

"I think that definition is good because it doesn't leave much room for confusion or for guessing what we mean. Let's try another behavior. How about nail biting?"

"What we have just done, then, is identified and defined a few simple behaviors. Now we need to define more serious behaviors. It is important to get a clear picture of what a given problem behavior is, as well as how often it is occurring. Here's an example: not minding. Can you define *not minding* for me?"

Their suggestions might include:

Doesn't do what is asked after the first time
Disobeys a request
Talks back when given a request
Ignores request or doesn't comply within a certain period of time

"Does our definition sound *clear* to you? The best test of a good definition of a behavior is what we call the 'stranger test.' From our definition, could a stranger tell you whether 'minding' was happening? Do you think so?" [If the answer is no, ask the parent to explain and modify the definition. Praise the effort.] "There, that seems like a good definition."

Positive Opposite Behaviors

"Whenever you want to change behavior, focus on the positive opposite. The positive opposite is the key to increasing positive behavior, and every problem behavior has a positive opposite. It is the behavior you want your child to be doing instead of the negative behavior. To change any behavior, it is crucial to increase the positive opposite rather than punish the negative behavior. So if your child is fighting, to say 'stop fighting' or 'don't fight' tells your child what not to do, and your child can then decide to do another problem behavior instead. Your child is more likely to do the positive behavior if given the positive opposite than if punished." Show Chart II, giving more examples if necessary.

Chart II: Problem Behaviors and Positive Opposites	
Problem Behavior	*Positive Opposite*
Not minding	Minding
Yelling or throwing tantrum when told "no"	Calmly accepting being told "no"

| Teasing | Talking nicely |
| Fighting | Playing cooperatively |

Ask the parent to give the positive opposite of slamming a door. "So, if your child is slamming doors, how would you use the positive opposite to tell your child what to do?" Use further examples if the parent has difficulty with the concept.

Defining Positive Opposites

"Now that we know what a positive opposite is, let's define the positive opposite of *not minding*. Can you define *minding?*" Their suggestions might include:

Does what is asked after the first time.

Does the request calmly.

If the request has a time limit ("Wash your hands before coming to the table"), it should be done within that time limit.

Repeat this process until the parent can be very specific by giving either a good definition or concrete examples.

Prompting: Getting Behavior to Happen

"Just as positive opposites make a positive behavior more likely, so do prompts. A prompt is a cue or direction we give to get someone to do a behavior. When you are prompting, it's important to remember to give a good specific definition of the behavior you want. You just did a great job of defining *smiling*, *minding*, and *not minding*. There are some additional things you want to remember." Show Chart III.

Chart III: Prompting—Getting Behaviors to Happen

Be specific. Tell your child specifically what you want.

Poor	Better
"Pick up your toys."	"Please pick up your trucks and put them in the toy box."
"Be good." "Don't fool around."	"When you're on the school bus, remember to keep your hands to yourself and stay in your seat."

Be calm. Keep a positive or neutral tone in your voice when you give a prompt. (You can add the word *please* to set a nice tone.)

Poor	Better
"Put your dish in the sink!"	"Please put your dish in the sink when you are done."

Be close. Go up to your child when you talk and make eye contact.

Poor	Better
"Suzy, go tell your brother to hurry up with his shoes."	"Johnny, please put your shoes on in the next minute or so, so I can help you with your coat."

Give the prompt as close as possible to when you want the behavior to happen.

Poor	Better
Asking your child to put on his shoes 2 hours before you leave.	Reminding your child right before you leave to put on his shoes.

Avoid asking a question as a prompt. You'll get an answer to your question and no behavior.

Poor	Better
"How many times do I have to tell you?"	"Johnny, please turn off the TV."
"Is it a good idea to play so rough with your toys?"	"Roll the car more slowly on the ground or it will break."

Prompt for a behavior no more than twice. Three prompts for the same behavior is nagging. If your child is not doing the behavior you are asking for, then let it go or do it yourself for now. (We will work on having your child follow directions the first time he is asked in future sessions.) If the problem can be broken down into smaller parts, prompt for each part. For example, instead of asking your child to clean his room, you could ask for the bed to be made and the toys put away.

Consequences Influence Behavior

"You are probably thinking that your child still isn't going to do the behavior, even if you give your child these great prompts. Here's some background on what we have learned about why people behave the way they do. A great deal has been learned about why children behave or misbehave. We've found that both positive behavior and problem behavior are influenced by how others respond to the behavior. Another way to say this is that behavior is influenced by the consequences that immediately follow the behavior. How others respond influences how *often* a behavior occurs.

"During our meetings, we will talk about how to increase desired behaviors and decrease problem behaviors and show you ways to encourage your child in that direction. We will use a skill called *positive reinforcement* to increase desired behaviors. We will also learn specific punishment techniques that can be used to decrease undesirable behaviors.

"Today we will focus on what positive reinforcement is and how to use it. During our sessions, we will develop reinforcement programs for you to use at home with your child. Next week we will work on setting up what we call a point incentive program."

Reinforcers and Reinforcement

"Positive reinforcement is the most powerful and useful method of changing or developing behaviors. Reinforcement is the procedure of increasing the desired behavior by following it with a reward or reinforcer. One way to give reinforcement is to praise a person for doing a behavior. For example, let's say you see your child cleaning the room. You could say, 'This is terrific! You are doing such a good job of cleaning your room!' When you reinforce your child for cleaning his room, then he is more likely to clean his room again. However, if you forget to reinforce the behavior, then the behavior is less likely to occur in the future.

"Reinforcement is very familiar to everyone, but it is not used as often as it should be. In fact, if you master the use of positive reinforcement with [child's name], you will notice really dramatic improvements in behavior. The difficulty is in knowing how to use reinforcement and then in actually using it. Unfortunately, good behavior is normally ignored in most homes, at school, and at work. For example, most parents want their children to do what they are told. When children listen and do what their parents say, their behavior is usually ignored rather than praised. On the other hand, parents often reprimand and scream when children aren't doing the things they want them to. But this isn't going to work too well. Does this sound familiar? You work really hard on a project and put many hours into it and your effort goes unnoticed, but you come in late just once and you get written up. Now, there are some dangers we will talk about later in relying on punishment. If parents would praise specific behaviors they wanted and did this often, they would see behavior change a lot and in the way they wanted."

How to Observe and Count

"Before we work on changing your child's behavior, you must really watch the problem to see what the behavior is and how often the behavior happens. For example, some parents want to work on decreasing tantrums that occur twice a week, and other parents want to decrease tantrums that occur more frequently. Observing allows you to identify what behavior to work on and to see how often it occurs. This is especially helpful to do before starting a program to change a particular behavior, and later this information helps you evaluate whether the program is working.

"Observing means watching carefully to see if the behavior is happening. For example, if you wanted to reduce the amount of television your child watches each afternoon, you could *observe* to see if your child watches TV in the afternoon and then count the number of shows your child watches or the number of hours the TV is turned on.

"The amount of TV watching is easy to count. Other behaviors may be a little more confusing. Let's count *not minding*. When observing it, we need to count how many times a child does not do as told. Each time the child is asked to do something and does not do it, that is an instance of not minding. For example, Johnny's mother *asks* him to hang up his coat. Ten minutes later, she *asks him again* to hang up his coat. But later, when his mother comes back into the room, the coat is still on the dining room floor. How many 'not minding' behaviors should we record?" Help the parent if necessary. Provide examples until the parent clearly understands.

Recording Behavior and Helpful Hints for Observing

"When we observe behavior, we record how many times the behavior happens so we know whether the behavior is happening more or less often over a period of time. I'll ask you to observe and record one behavior for 1 hour each day. When we record behavior, it is very important to record behavior immediately after it happens. This means no recalling, guessing, or trying to remember, hours later, if a behavior happened. And remember, we can count something as a behavior only if we can see or hear it."

Weekly Observing Sheet

"We have gone over what a behavior is, how to define it, how to prompt a behavior, and how to observe and count behaviors. Earlier, we discussed how your child does not always listen. Practice is important here, so let's begin by having you observe [child's name]'s 'minding' and 'not minding' behaviors." If the parent indicates that not listening is not a problem behavior for this child, have the parent identify three problem behaviors and choose one of them for this exercise.

"At home, you will need to observe your child and record the 'minding' and 'not minding' behaviors. Let's pick a time when this behavior is most likely to be a problem, like dinnertime or bedtime.

"Now we are ready to fill out the weekly observation sheets you will be using at home." Show an observation sheet. "Remember that to learn a new skill, it is necessary to use the new skill. First, let's copy the behaviors and their definitions onto the sheet.

"Your hour to observe each day is from _____ o'clock to _____ o'clock. Each time the behavior occurs during that hour, put a tally mark in the box next to the definition. Where it says 'Actual Time Observed,' write the amount of time you actually observed. As we said before, 1 hour each day is ideal, but if that is not possible because you have interruptions or emergencies, write down the actual time you observed. Your observing and recording of these behaviors will be very helpful to us later when we are using techniques to increase the positive behavior and decrease the negative behavior. So, it is important for you to be as consistent as possible when you are doing these observations.

"Keep the observation sheet somewhere handy so you can get to it easily. If your child asks what the sheet is, explain briefly that you are curious about how often certain things happen, but don't get into too much detail. After you've explained, just drop the issue. When the behavior occurs during an observation period, be careful not to point it out to the child. For example, don't say, 'Oh, you didn't listen; that's one count.' Here are some helpful hints to help you use the observation chart." Show Chart IV and read slowly, emphasizing the need to record the exact time.

Chart IV: Helpful Hints for Observing

1. It is not necessary to hover over the child or drop what you are doing when you observe. Rather, when you observe, make a special point of watching the child out of the corner of your eye.

2. When you are first practicing how to observe, try to avoid unnecessary interruptions like visitors and phone calls.

3. Try to observe the same amount of time each day. If you are interrupted, note the actual number of minutes you spent observing that day.

4. Record a behavior only if you are certain of the behavior and only during your observation period. To avoid any confusion later, mark the chart immediately after the behavior.
5. Record a behavior as a minding behavior only if you have checked to make sure it was completed first.
6. Remember, record your child's compliant behavior as a minding even if he wanted to do it.

"Tell me whether you would record these on the observation chart." The therapist then reviews Chart V and clarifies any difficulty the parent may have. Show Chart V.

Chart V: Behaviors That Can and Cannot Be Recorded

While you are in the kitchen making dinner, you ask your child to get himself something to drink and he does. (Yes)

Just before going to bed, you *sort of* remember your child hanging up his coat after you asked him to when you were supposed to be observing. (No)

You ask your child to clean up his room, and 15 minutes later your daughter tells you he did it. (No)

While you are watching TV, you ask your child to take his feet off the table and he does. (Yes)

Assignment

Hand out the weekly assignment sheet and review it. "Next week we will be talking about positive ways to encourage your child to engage in more positive behaviors. To do this, we need to identify pleasant and enjoyable things that can be used for a program. So, before next week, we would like you to sit down with your child and discuss six things that are pleasant and enjoyable and that can be done on a daily basis. Examples could be staying with a friend, extra time staying up, extra TV time, going to the park, reading time, or special snacks or treats. Just jot these rewards down on the weekly assignment sheet. In addition to observing these two behaviors on the weekly observation sheet, I'd like you to define two problem behaviors [child's name] has and the positive opposites of these problem behaviors. This will give you additional practice at defining behaviors in terms of what you can see or hear. Please bring the sheet with you to next week's session."

"I will be calling you during the week to see how things are going and answer any questions you might have. When would be a good time for me to reach you? If you have no further questions [pause], that will be all for tonight and I'll see you on [day]. Please call if you have any questions. The number is on the card." Hand the parent an appointment card.

Positive Reinforcement
Point Incentive Chart and Praise

The goal of this session is to review the elements of positive reinforcement and teach the parent how it is applied to change behavior. The presentation begins with an introduction to designing a point incentive chart. Positive reinforcement is then applied to the home situation by designing a point incentive program. The parent also begins to practice how to praise her child.

Objectives

To review with the parent the elements of positive reinforcement.
To design a point incentive program to change the child's behavior at home.
To teach the parent how to praise the child for positive behavior.

Equipment and Materials

Handouts
- Four Types of Reinforcers
- Changes in Behavior Occur When . . .
- Helpful Hints to Make the Point Chart Work
- How to Make Your Praise Most Effective
- Point Incentive Chart/Time Out Chart/Attending and Ignoring Chart (Only the point incentive part is used in this session.)
- Weekly Assignment Sheet

Program Review

After welcoming the parent, the therapist says, "Before we start with today's material, let's review the weekly observation sheet I gave you last week." Praise the parent enthusiastically for any evident effort and progress in obtaining the data. Identify specifically the behaviors you are praising. Also, note whether the parent brought in the list of six rewards. "Although it may seem difficult or frustrating to complete the observations, getting clear information like these

273

observations is important before we can work on changing behavior. The more specific information we have about a behavior, the easier it will be to change that behavior."

Therapist Presentation

"Today we will focus on what positive reinforcement is and how to use it. During our sessions, we will develop reinforcement programs for you to use at home with your child. Today we'll work on setting up what we call a point incentive chart. It will help your child to strengthen positive behaviors and decrease problem behaviors.

"As you learned last week, positive reinforcement is the most powerful way to change behavior. Reinforcement is the procedure of increasing and strengthening behavior by following it with a reward or reinforcer. Remember, our goal is to increase your child's positive behavior. In most homes, in schools, and even at work, much attention is given to negative behavior. Any time you give attention (reinforcer), it increases the behavior, even the problem behavior. For example, let's say your children are playing cards in another room and they are getting along. You definitely want to go in and say, 'This is so nice! The two of you are playing together so well. I really appreciate it!' What usually happens in that scenario is that the good behavior goes unnoticed and the problem behavior gets all the attention. We'll show you how to handle the problem behavior later. Until then, practice *praising* your children for the positive behavior. We will help you do that with our point incentive chart.

"In developing a point incentive chart, it is really important to include a variety of reinforcers. Many things can function as a reward or reinforcer, and they all have one thing in common. When a behavior is followed by a reinforcer, it is increased or strengthened. There are four basic types of reinforcers that we will be using for your child." Show Chart I.

Chart I: Four Types of Reinforcers

1. Material Reinforcers: Tangible items such as toys, clothes, and candy.
2. Privileges or Activity Reinforcers: Time together with the parent, slumber party, staying up late, chore done by the parent.
3. Social Reinforcers: Your approval! A smile, a wink, a hug, and praise.
4. Token Reinforcers: Items given to your child that can be exchanged for more valuable reinforcers.

After discussing the four types of reinforcers, the therapist should ask for the parent's list of six rewards and then help the parent identify which type of reinforcer each item is.

Basic Rules for Selecting and Using Reinforcers

Discuss the basic rules for selecting and using reinforcers: "Here are some basic rules for selecting and using reinforcers." Refer to Chart II.

Chart II: Changes in Behavior Occur When . . .

1. The reinforcers increase the strength of the positive behavior. If they do not, you may need to choose different reinforcers.
2. The reinforcer should occur immediately after the positive behavior.
3. Your child must perform the desired behavior before receiving any reinforcers.
4. For new behaviors to occur, the reinforcer needs to follow the behavior every time.

Planning the Point Incentive Chart

"So far we have been talking about positive reinforcement in general terms. Now we are ready to design a reinforcement program to encourage your child to improve some behaviors. First, can you tell me a task or chore your child does well and fairly regularly?" Assist the parent in generating a behavior. "OK, good! Now let's think of a behavior or chore that is more difficult for your child and right now requires constant reminders, such as playing nicely, sharing, or dressing for school." Again, help the parent generate ideas for behaviors to improve. "Remember, we'll automatically work on 'minding.'"

Define Tasks

"The next thing we need to do is write a description or definition for each of these behaviors." Praise the parent's efforts. Mention the "stranger test," noted in PMT Session 1. The therapist should take an active role in coming up with clear definitions for the parent.

"We need to assign points for each behavior. When your child does the behavior, he will be rewarded with a specific number of points. These points are added up at the end of the day and exchanged for rewards."

Allow the parent to help decide how many points to assign to each behavior. The harder the behavior is for the child, the more points should be assigned to that behavior. "Let's start with 'minding.' Because there are so many opportunities for minding to occur, you can give your child 1 or 2 points. Now [difficult chore/behavior] is more difficult, so let's give it 8 or 10 points. This next behavior [an easier one] is an easier one for your child. We can make that behavior worth 5 points.

"OK, now that we have the behaviors and the point values, let's write down the rewards that can be exchanged for these points." Work with the parent in producing rewards for the menu and in assigning values. The reward that is difficult for the parent to give or the more expensive reward should have a higher price. Smaller privileges with the parent should have lower price values so that the child can "buy" those activities more frequently.

"Now that we have devised our point chart, here are some helpful hints to make the point chart work." Show Chart III.

Chart III: Helpful Hints to Make the Point Chart Work

1. Remember to praise and give points immediately after the desired behavior.
2. Review the chart with your child at the end of every day. This gives you a chance to praise the number of points accumulated that day and review all the positive things your child has done to earn the points. Also, when few points have been earned, it gives you a chance to handle it neutrally and encourage your child to earn more the next day.
3. Have some of the rewards available every day.
4. Give rewards as agreed. Once your child has earned enough points to buy a reward, he should be allowed to receive it regardless of anything else that may have happened that day.
5. Encourage your child to buy rewards each time. Remember, it is an opportunity to reinforce the behavior you are working on.
6. Bring the point chart to our sessions each week whether or not it is completed. That way we can track your child's progress.

Role-Playing Implementing the Point Chart and Praise

"Now let's practice using the point chart. This week, put the points on the chart and *praise* your child. When praising your child, it is very important to do the following." Show Chart IV.

Chart IV: How to Make Your Praise Most Effective

1. Deliver praise when you are *near your child*. When you are close to your child, you can be sure that the behavior you are praising is taking place. Also, when you are close, your child is more likely to pay attention to what you are saying.
2. Use a *sincere, enthusiastic* tone of voice. You don't need to be loud, but make sure that you sound thrilled about what your child is doing.
3. Use nonverbal reinforcers. Show your child you are pleased by smiling, winking, or touching. Hug your child, high five him, or pat him on the back.
4. Be specific. When praising your child, say exactly what behavior you approve of. "Wow, thank you so much for picking up your shoes and putting them in the closet." You want to be specific.

"OK, let's act this out! I'll be you, and you are [child's name]. Let's pretend that I am asking you to put on your jacket before you go outside. Remember this is a 'minding,' so I want to give you 2 points for this. '[Child's name], please put on your jacket before you go outside. This way you will be warm, and I can give you 2 points'" Evaluate your prompt briefly for the parent, and point out how clear and positive you are. "Great [walk over, touch]. I'm so glad you put on your jacket, and as soon as I asked, too! Thank you.' OK, I came over to you so I was *close*. I put my arm around your shoulder so I *touched*. I was *enthusiastic*, and I was *specific*.

"Now it's your turn." Have the parents role-play praising each of the behaviors on the chart. This may be difficult for them so it's important to praise their efforts.

When prompting them to do a better job, be sure to initially praise what they did do well. "Great, you got right out of your chair to praise me. Now remember to touch me and to tell me specifically what I did that you liked." After the second role play, work on making their responses even better. Praise what

---

they did well, and encourage them to include all components of praise. Push the parent to give a high-quality performance by repeatedly praising what she has done and prompting her to do more.

For two-parent families, the therapist encourages the parents to praise each other in an effort to develop a supportive environment and to help parents work as a team. "OK, Dad, how was Mom's praise? Was she immediate? Did she touch? How was her enthusiasm? And was she specific? All right! Go on over and give her a hug! Nice job, Dad, praising Mom!" If the significant other is at all critical, interrupt and ask what it was that the partner did well. "OK, we're only talking about what it was that _____ did that was great. Right, she was very enthusiastic! [To mother] Now, this time when you praise, remember to be immediate, touch, and be specific." The parents role-play again to give the significant other the chance to praise again. The therapist should always summarize the parts of the role play that were done well.

The therapist should also role-play what to do when the child does not listen. First model the desired behavior, stating, "I won't be able to give you any points now, but we will try again later, and if you follow my directions right away, I'll be able to give you points." The therapist could also model giving the child a choice: "You could either do it now and receive your points, or I could do it now and not be able to give you points." Explain to the parent that different situations call for different statements. Have the parents practice remaining calm and ignoring any potential tantrum. Again, have the parents praise each other.

Role-Play Explaining the Chart

It is extremely important for the parent to explain the point chart to the child so that the child knows what to expect and what to look forward to. The parent should begin with the rewards, which are more exciting and appealing to the child. The parent should let the child know how much each reward costs in terms of points and encourage the child by suggesting that the rewards will be easy to get by earning more points. The parent should then explain specifically what each behavior is, what the child has to do, and how many points each behavior is worth.

The therapist should first role-play explaining the chart; then the parent should role-play explaining the chart. In this way, the therapist models the desired behavior and then can shape what the parent does.

Assignment

"Your assignment for this week is to use the point chart that we have set up. Remember, each time your child engages in the behaviors we have on the chart, give points and praise just the way we practiced. I will make a copy of this chart. I'll keep the original and each week I will make you a new copy. This way I can see progress each week."

Time Out from Reinforcement

The third session teaches the use of time out as a specialized technique for managing problem behaviors. The therapist discusses and teaches parents the following points:

1. Correct explanation and use of time out.
2. Proper room selection for time out. Be sure the parents understand that the door should never be locked.
3. Role-playing time out with the child before using it.
4. Using time out immediately.
5. Using time out rather than threatening its use.
6. Telling the child what was done wrong before sending the child to time out.
7. Praising the child who goes to time out without having a tantrum.
8. Informing the child that he will lose privileges if he does not go to time out.
9. Correcting or cleaning up things broken or messed up on the way to time out or while in time out.
10. Giving *positive reinforcement* for desired behavior.

Objectives

To teach parents the elements of time out.

Equipment and Materials

Handouts
  • Damaging Side Effects of Physical, Verbal, or Prolonged Punishment
  • Effective Punishment Guidelines
  • Time Out Rules
  • Guidelines for Explaining Time Out to the Child
  • Variations of Time Out

- Point Incentive Chart/Time Out Chart/Attending and Ignoring Chart
- Weekly Assignment Sheet

Program Review

After welcoming the parent, review the point program and the praise program. Ask the parent to cite some examples of how they praised and rewarded the child over the past week. Role play should be used for selected situations when the parent is "explaining" how the programs are running.

Therapist Introduction

"At our initial meeting, we talked about defining, prompting, and observing behavior. Then we learned about positive reinforcement and designed a point incentive system. Today we'll add another skill to help you better manage your child's behavior, a skill called time out."

Time Out Presentation

"Effective discipline really begins with rewarding and praising positive behaviors. When you are faced with a problem behavior, mild punishment techniques can be effective, but only when they are paired with positive reinforcement for the positive opposite of the problem behavior.

"An example of an effective punishment technique is time out. When used consistently, time out has proven to be extremely effective in decreasing the problem behavior. It is a mild procedure that involves removing the child from the opportunity to receive attention or other rewards when he engages in undesired behavior. The child is sent to a boring or non-reinforcing place for a brief period of time immediately after a problem behavior occurs. Like the point program, some special rules will need to be followed for maximum effectiveness.

"First, let me give you an example of time out. A boy swears when his parent asks him to do his homework. The parent tells him he has to take a 5-minute time out for swearing by sitting in a chair. The child then sits on the chair until the parent tells him his 5 minutes are up.

"Many parents, teachers, and clinicians now use time out because it has been found to be very effective when used consistently. I have some guidelines to review with you. Perhaps the most important is: Do not use physical, harsh verbal, or prolonged punishment. Physical punishment is anything that causes the child physical pain. Harsh verbal punishment includes yelling, intimidation, and insults. Prolonged punishment is restriction or privilege losses for a week or more. As a general rule, punishment should be given only on the day of the misbehavior and not carry over to other days.

"Many parents disagree with this recommendation, but research shows that physical, harsh verbal, or prolonged punishment does not eliminate the behavior in the long term. Also, this type of punishment often has some very undesirable side effects on the parent–child relationship. The following are some repercussions that can occur with physical, harsh verbal, or prolonged punishment." Show Chart I.

Chart I: Damaging Side Effects of Physical, Verbal, or Prolonged Punishment

1. Physical, harsh verbal, or prolonged punishment leads to only short-term success. This type of punishment may work initially, but the negative behaviors continue and often increase.
2. Physical, harsh verbal, or prolonged punishment can cause emotional reactions in children such as crying, anger, or fear of the parent.
3. The child is likely to avoid the parent, and the parent–child relationship deteriorates. This means the child would not want to be with you. Some parents think a punishment was effective if their child becomes upset. There is no necessary relationship between the two.
4. Physical, harsh verbal, or prolonged punishment also may cause the child to become aggressive and hit you, other family members, or friends.
5. Physical, harsh verbal, or prolonged punishment sometimes decreases a child's aggressiveness in the home, but outside the home the child becomes much more aggressive.
6. Physical, harsh verbal, or prolonged punishment does not teach the child how to solve problems. If the child sees the parent become aggressive when angry, the child is likely to do the same.
7. Punishment alone does not teach new or appropriate behaviors. It teaches the child what *not* to do.

"Whenever time out is being used, it is extremely important to use it with *positive reinforcement.* By pairing these two, the effectiveness will be greater than with either one used alone." Show Chart II, which also shows effective punishment guidelines.

1. Remain calm.
2. Use time out immediately so that your child doesn't have the opportunity to become more aggressive.
3. If you need to take a privilege away, take it away for a short period of time, such as TV or phone privileges for an afternoon or an evening. How immediate and consistent the punishment is usually is more important than how big the loss is or how upset your child becomes.
4. Praise and reinforce your child's positive behaviors (positive opposites):
   - Temper tantrums versus handling problems calmly
   - Teasing others versus playing cooperatively with others
   - Talking back versus using your words calmly and respectfully
   - Physical aggression versus keeping one's hands and feet to oneself when angry

"Another way to make sure time out is effective is to use it consistently—every time the behavior occurs."

Many parents at this point may comment that they have tried sending their children to their rooms and this tactic hasn't worked. The therapist can point out, "Many parents have tried sending their children to their rooms. This is a form of time out, but to be effective time out must be done in a precise way. So now we will go over the rules for using time out effectively." Show Chart III. The therapist should then begin discussing the rules.

1. Be sure you can observe the behavior you want to stop.
2. Select a room that is away from people and without anything interesting to do. *Do not lock the door*!
3. Stay calm.
4. Before using time out, explain and role-play going to time out; the child will cooperate.
5. Use time out immediately. Don't wait until matters get out of hand.
6. Don't threaten time out. Use it!
7. Don't debate or argue. Tell your child what he did wrong and calmly tell him to go to time out.
8. If the child goes to time out without having a tantrum, give praise and tell him why you're providing praise (for example, "I asked you to go to time out, and you went right away. That's great!").

9. If your child won't go to time out right away, the time it takes your child to get there is added to the original 5 minutes. [Note to therapist: the original minutes in time out can vary from 1 to 5 minutes.]

10. Let your child know that time out starts when he is quiet and in the time out area.

11. If child absolutely refuses to go to time out, then use backup procedures such as restrictions, loss of privileges, or response cost. Make sure you let the child know ahead of time what will happen if he does not go to time out; for example, "You lose [privilege] if you don't go to time out." The child should be told of this when time out is first introduced. Also, if the child refuses to go to time out, he should be reminded calmly.

12. If child breaks something in time out, he needs to fix it. If child makes a mess, he needs to clean it up after time out.

13. Be sure to continue to *praise* appropriate behavior. In fact, this is the most important part of time out or any other punishment technique.

Explain again that whenever you use a punishment technique, you must also use positive reinforcement for the positive opposite.

Identify and Define the Problem Behavior

"Let's think of a problem behavior your child does that we can decrease with time out." Make sure the behavior involves only one child. Assist the parent in defining the behavior in specific terms. "Now, let's write the behavior and definition on the Time Out Checklist Form." The therapist fills in the time out behavior on the time out chart.

Identify and Define Positive Opposite

"The next step is to identify and describe the positive opposite of this behavior." Again, give assistance as needed. "Remember, it is very important to reinforce this behavior whenever it happens. In fact, punishment will not work very well unless the positive opposite behavior is rewarded." The therapist should fill in the positive opposite on the time out chart.

Role-Play Use of Time Out

"To show you how to use time out for [problem behavior], let's pretend I'm the parent and you're the child. We'll role-play how to use time out."

For all role plays, after modeling the correct use of the technique, the therapist should reverse roles with the parent, giving prompts if needed. Remember to praise any of the parent's correct behaviors.

The therapist should role-play how the parent should respond when:

1. The child goes to time out immediately.
2. The child takes excessive time to get to time out. (Add the time it takes the child to get there to the original 5 minutes.)
3. The child is noisy in time out.
4. The child refuses to go to time out. (Let the child know that he will lose privileges or will get extra chores if he does not go to time out.)

After modeling the use of time out for these situations, the therapist should reverse roles with the parent.

Role Play #1: Child Goes to Time Out Immediately

The parent performs the problem behavior, and the therapist then gives a time out. "This time, let's practice a situation when [child's name] goes to time out immediately without any problems. It's important to include a couple things when you're giving time out in order to make it the most effective. The first thing I'll do is make sure I'm very calm when I give the time out, and I'll tell [child's name] what he's getting the time out for and how long the time out is. I'll also praise [child's name] as soon as he sits in the chair and is quiet. Then, when the time is up, I'll go over and praise him for sitting in the chair and having a calm time out. It is very important to give very little attention for the negative behavior. 'OK [child's name], I want you to take a 5-minute time out for [problem behavior]. [Child sits in chair.] Hey! You did a great job of going to the chair as soon as I asked. I'll go set the timer. [Five seconds is sufficient for practice.] Wow! You did a great job of sitting in the chair for your time out.' Now, I'll be [child's name], and you be the parent. I'll [problem behavior], and you give me a time out. Remember to:

1. Stay calm.
2. Tell what the time out is for and how long.
3. Praise as soon as the child sits in the chair.
4. Praise when the time out is completed successfully by the child."

Have the parent give the time out to the child. Praise the parent for remaining calm, praising the child for going to time out and for finishing the time out calmly, and, if applicable, suggesting the positive opposite in a positive, encouraging way.

For two-parent families, the therapist should encourage the parents to praise each other in an effort to develop a supportive environment and to help the parents work as a team. "OK, Dad, how was Mom's time out? Was she calm? Did she remember to say what the time out was for and for how long? Yes! And she remembered to praise when you went to time out. Go on over and give her a hug! Nice job, Dad, praising Mom!" If the parent or significant other is at all critical, interrupt and ask what the first parent did do well. "OK, we're only talking about what it was that [significant other] did that was great. Right, she was very calm! [To mother] Now, this time, when you send your husband to time out, remember to tell him what for and for how long." The parents role-play again, giving the significant other the chance to praise again. The therapist should always summarize the parts of the role play that were done well.

Role Play #2: Adding Time to Time Out

"It's also important to stay calm when adding time to the time out. So let's have you be the child again and do [problem behavior]. Notice how calm and neutral I am when I add the time, but, when you eventually go to the chair, my praise will be just as enthusiastic and, of course, immediate. I will add 1 minute at a time up to 8 minutes; then for this role play, you will go to the chair. OK, here we go. '[child's name], I want you to take a 5-minute time out for [problem behavior].' Now complain as if you were [child's name]. Again, notice how calm I am when adding time: 'Six minutes [more complaining], 7 minutes [complaining], 8 minutes [complaining].' And then you go to the chair. 'Hey, thank you so much for going to time out. I'll set the timer for 8 minutes.' After the time is up, I will praise you for taking the time out. 'Good job doing your time out.'" Have the parent evaluate the therapist's administration of time out. "Now, I'll be [child's name], and you be the parent. I'll [problem behavior], and you give me a time out. Remember to:

1. Stay calm.
2. Tell what the time out is for and how long.
3. Look away as the child argues and debates.
4. Increase the time minute by minute (slowly).
5. Praise your child when he goes to time out.

Have the parent give the time out to the child. Praise the parent when they incorporate the above points into the role play.

For two-parent families, the therapist encourages the parents to praise each other in an effort to develop a supportive environment and to help the parents work as a team. "OK, Mom, how was Dad's time out? Was he calm? Did he remember to say what the time out was for and for how long? Yes! And he calmly increased the time as you argued! Go on over and give him a hug! Nice job, Mom, in praising Dad!" If the significant other is at all critical, interrupt and ask what the first parent did do well. "OK, we're only talking about what it was that he did that was great. Right, he was very calm! [To father] Now, let's do this one again. Remember to look away as your wife argues." The parents role-play again, giving the significant other the chance to praise again. The therapist should always summarize the parts of the role play that were done well.

Role Play #3: Child Is Noisy on the Way to Time Out or in Time Out

"If your child is noisy on the way to time out, complains, or talks back, it is really important to ignore those behaviors and praise him if he ends up sitting in time out. If your child is still noisy when he sits for the time out, then let him know that you cannot set the timer until he is quiet. If he continues to be noisy, then offer him the choice of either doing the time out quietly or losing a privilege. If he is quiet, praise him specifically, set the timer, and then walk away. If he becomes noisy again, then he automatically loses the privilege.

"If your child goes to time out quietly but becomes noisy after you have already set the timer, then offer the child the choice of either doing the time out quietly or losing a privilege.

"Now, I'll be [child's name], and you be the parent. I'll [problem behavior], and you give me a time out. Remember to:

1. Stay calm.
2. Tell what the time out is for and for how long.
3. Praise as soon as the child sits in the chair.
4. Stop the timer when the child becomes noisy, and offer the choice of either sitting quietly or losing a privilege."

Have the parents role-play these points. Repeat a given scenario to fine-tune their skills, if needed.

For two-parent families, it is important that the therapist encourages the parents to praise each other in an effort to develop a supportive environment and to help the parents work as a team. "OK, Dad, how was Mom's time out?

Was she calm? Did she remember to say what the time out was for and for how long? Yes! Go on over and give her a hug! Nice job, Dad, of praising Mom!" If the significant other is at all critical, interrupt and ask what the first parent did do well. "OK, we're only talking about what it was that she did that was great. Right, she was very calm! [To mother] Now, let's do this one again. Remember to offer a choice of either sitting quietly or losing a privilege." The parents role-play again, giving the significant other the chance to praise again. The therapist should always summarize the parts of the role play that were done well.

Role Play #4: Loss of Privilege Because Child Will Not Go to Time Out

"There will be times when [child's name] refuses to go to time out. After you have attempted to extend the length of the time out, you should offer a choice between the time out and loss of a privilege. The privilege should be lost for 1 day at most. If the time out is given at the beginning of the day, then the child should lose the privilege for half the day. The privilege should be significant enough that taking the time out is the obvious choice for the child. If the child refuses to go to the chair then he is automatically choosing to lose the privilege. Let's decide on two or three privileges that [child's name] might lose, just in case he does not take his time out." The therapist should assist the parent in generating some ideas for the loss of privilege so the parent is prepared in the event that the child does not choose time out. The therapist should ensure that the parent does not take away privileges, which are earned, from the behaviors on the point chart.

"Let's practice. You are [child's name], and I'll give you a time out for [problem behavior]. '[Child's name], I want you to take a 5-minute time out' [follow the procedures in Role Play #2, extending the time in the time out chair]. When [child's name] refuses to go to time out even after the time is extended, then you should say, 'OK, you can choose. You [loss of privilege], or you can take the 8-minute time out. It's up to you.' And drop the issue. [Child's name] might approach you later on and ask to have the privilege reinstated. All that needs to be said is, 'This time you chose to lose [privilege] instead of taking the time out.'" The parent should not get involved in bargaining with or reinstating the privilege for the child.

"Something else that might happen is that your child may decide to do the time out immediately after losing the privilege, to which you can respond neutrally, 'You chose to lose [privilege] this time. I hope next time you'll choose to do the time out instead.'"

"Now, I'll be [child's name], and you be the parent. I'll [problem behavior], and you give me a time out. Remember to:

1. Stay calm.
2. Tell what the time out is for and for how long.
3. Increase the time slowly as child refuses to participate.
4. Offer the child the choice of either sitting for the maximum time or losing the privilege.
5. Take away privilege."

Have the parents role-play these points. Repeat a given scenario to fine-tune their skills, if needed.

For two-parent families, the therapist should encourage the parents to praise each other in an effort to develop a supportive environment and to help the parents work as a team. "OK, Mom, how was Dad's time out? Was he calm? Did he remember to offer the choice of doing time out or losing the privilege? Yes! Go on over and give him a hug! Nice job, Mom, of praising Dad!" If the significant other is at all critical, interrupt and ask what the parent did do well. "OK, we're only talking about what it was that he did that was great. Right, he was very calm! [To father] Now, let's do this one again. Remember to take the privilege away rather than offer the choice again." The parents role-play again, giving the significant other the chance to praise again. The therapist should always summarize the parts of the role play that were done well.

How to Explain Time Out to the Child

In discussing how to explain time out to the child, the therapist should say, "We have some guidelines to follow when introducing this technique to your child." Show Chart IV.

Chart IV: Guidelines for Explaining Time Out to the Child

1. Select a time to talk when everyone is relaxed and in good control.
2. Calmly explain the procedure to the child. Don't debate and argue with your child about time out.
3. Be sure to incorporate the following:
   a. Time out behavior: Spell it out specifically (the stranger test). It is important that the child know exactly what behavior will result in a time out.
   b. Where the time out is.

  c. How long time out is.

  d. Time out starts when he is quiet.

  e. If he won't go to time out, the time it takes him to get there is added to his original 5 minutes.

  f. If he breaks something in time out, he needs to fix it; if he makes a mess, he needs to clean it up.

  g. If he refuses to go to time out, he will receive a backup punishment.

4. Ask the child to practice (role-play) time out with you, at a time when everyone is calm and relaxed. Be sure to praise your child afterward for cooperating.

5. When role-playing the procedure with you, the child need not stay in the time out. If your child refuses, don't make an issue of it.

Variations of Time Out

"We have discussed and practiced giving time out. There are some variations of time out that are also very helpful. One is using time out for problems that occur outside of the home, such as at another person's home, a store, a mall, or a restaurant." Show Chart V.

Chart V: Variations of Time Out

1. Time out for problem behaviors away from home, such as at another person's home, a store, a mall, or a restaurant.

  a. Before starting on an outing, clearly describe how you want your child to behave. This precaution will reduce the chances that a problem will occur.

  b. At another person's home, send the child to an uninteresting place in the person's home or take the child to the car for time out.

  c. At a store, require the child to sit or stand in a remote corner or aisle, or take the child to the car for time out.

  d. At a mall, use a bench as the time out site.

  e. At a restaurant, place the child at a nearby table or take the child to the car.

  f. When giving time out in a car, have the child sit in the back seat while you remain in the front seat or outside the car. Be sure to ignore the child while he is in time out.

  g. If you cannot give time out in front of others, give a delayed time

---

out; that is, send the child to time out immediately after returning home.

2. Time out from toys: removing toys from a child, which is useful for handling misbehavior when a child is playing with a toy or when two children
   are fighting over a toy or misusing a toy.
   a. Calmly remove the toy from the child for 15 minutes.
   b. Tell the child the reason for the toy time out.
   c. When 15 minutes are up, the child may retrieve the toy.
3. Time out from the parent. The parent leaves, goes to another room, and
   does not respond until the child is calm. This is useful when a routine time
   out has failed to stop a child's escalating physical or verbal aggression or
   the child has lost control.
   a. Separate yourself from the child, go to another room, and shut the
      door if necessary.
   b. Wait until the child is calm for at least 5 minutes.
   c. Praise the child for regaining a calm demeanor.
   d. If the child is calm enough to discuss the problem, then approach it
      again; if not, wait until a more appropriate time.

Assignment

"For this week's assignment, begin using time out as we practiced. Explain time
out to your child, and practice role-playing time out once or twice. The role
plays should be practiced when you and your child are both calm and in a good
mood. Make sure you really praise your child for practicing time out. Remember to reinforce the positive opposite."

Attending and Planned Ignoring

Objectives

The purpose of this session is to instruct parents in how to manage various minor problems (such as whining, complaining, pestering, failing to entertain oneself, being noisy, pouting, teasing, bickering with siblings, and crying) by using attending and planned ignoring. These behaviors may upset or irritate the parent but generally do not warrant time out or other serious consequences if the parent consistently uses attending and ignoring with them.

Equipment and Materials

Handouts
- Rules for Attending and Ignoring
- Attending and Ignoring Exercise
- Worksheet for Attending and Ignoring
- Common Problems to Ignore
- Point Incentive Chart/Time Out Chart/Attending and Ignoring Chart
- Weekly Assignment Sheet

Program Review

The therapist should review with the parents the programs set up the previous week and give specific reinforcement for the parents' behaviors and efforts.

"How was your week? Did you give any points? How many times a day did you praise? Did you have any problems running the programs this week? Wow, great job, keeping track of all these points and remembering to praise!"

Therapist's Introduction

"Today we will learn two new skills, attending and ignoring. These techniques are useful in decreasing irritating behaviors such as whining, complaining, and noisiness. First we will talk about attending, then about planned ignoring, and after that we will put the two skills together."

Attending

"Attending is noticing when someone is doing something desirable and then giving that person attention by praising, smiling, asking pleasant questions, talking nicely, hugging, or giving a pat on the back. When parents consistently give this kind of positive attention to their children when they are doing a desired behavior, these behaviors will increase. Many times what we do is pay attention to unwanted behaviors, and so we get an increase in these behaviors. Whenever we give attention to any behavior, it will increase. What we need to practice and become aware of is giving attention only to appropriate behaviors, ones we want to increase; essentially, we want to catch your child being good.

"Let's take an example. If you wanted your child to clean his room more often, you could use attending by praising, hugging, or smiling at him when you see him cleaning his room.

"For attending to be effective, we need to use it in a very specific way. There are three steps to follow when you are using attending:" Show Chart I.

Chart I: Rules for Attending

1. Define the behavior you want to increase: the *positive opposite*.
   - A good definition tells who, what, where, and when.
2. Decide on the type of attention to use.
   - Vary the attention and approval.
   - Specific praise is most effective when paired with attention and interest in the child and what he is doing.
3. Decide when to use it.
   - While the behavior is happening or immediately after its completion.

"Let's take an example of what usually occurs in households. We want two children to play cooperatively. We are sitting in the kitchen trying to get a few moments of quiet time before dinner. The children are in the living room playing in a cooperative way, but 5 minutes later they are arguing. We go in there to check on them and end up yelling at them or giving them attention when they are arguing. What happened is that we attended to the negative behavior (arguing) and ignored the positive behavior (playing cooperatively). Whenever we miss a chance to praise desired behavior, we lose a chance to increase the desired behavior. Let's go through this same example but use the rules for attending. If you want your children to play cooperatively, first of all you need to define *playing cooperatively*: 'playing in a calm, nice manner; sharing.' We also need to decide what kind of attention to use; you could praise, hug, and look at them, ask them questions about what they're doing, or give them high fives. Finally, you need to decide when to give attention—while they are playing cooperatively. This is a great example of using attention to increase a behavior.

"The points about attending and planned ignoring are the same for everyone, even adults. Can you think of an example of when attending and planned ignoring be used in your personal life? [The therapist should help with an example involving an adult spouse, friend, or parent.] That is an excellent example! How could you use attending and planned ignoring to change that behavior?" Praise the parent for coming up with a program.

Planned Ignoring

"The second skill we will talk about is planned ignoring, which is basically when you do not give any attention to a behavior. You deliberately ignore an undesirable behavior in order to decrease it. If you do not give any attention to a behavior, what do you think will happen to that behavior? That's right; it will decrease. To use ignoring, you do not look at the person, talk to them, or smile at them; instead, you turn away, talk to someone else, or just leave the room. When used consistently and in a specific way, planned ignoring is effective as a mild form of punishment.

"For example, a child complains when he is asked to do the dishes. His parent could respond by not looking at him or talking to him whenever he complained. If ignoring is used consistently each time the child complains, the result would be a decrease in that behavior.

"Often, parents use methods such as spanking or nagging to get their children to stop doing something. These methods may have short-term success, but they are not effective over time and do not teach the behavior we want them to do instead. So instead of spanking or nagging, we suggest that parents ignore. Let's go over the rules to follow when using planned ignoring." Show Chart I, the bottom half.

Chart I: Rules for Ignoring

1. Define the behavior to be ignored.
   - A good definition tells who, what, where, and when.

---

2. Decide what kind of planned ignoring to use when the defined behavior occurs.
   - Look away, move away.
   - No facial expression.
   - Do not talk with your child.
   - Ignore all requests.
   - Leave the room.
3. Decide when to use it. Set an acceptable limit of tolerance for the identified behavior.
   - Decide how much of the behavior you will tolerate; for example, ignore all whining after you explain once.
   - Use ignoring immediately after the limit has been reached.
   - Use it every time the behavior occurs.
4. Decide on what positive behavior (positive opposite) to attend to.
   - Planned ignoring will not work if attending is not used at the same time.

"Let's go over an example. Let's say your child whines when he wants something. We must first define what we mean by *whining*: "Asking for something in a whining tone of voice." Second, we have to decide what kind of ignoring to use—walk away from your child, look away, talk to another person? You also need to decide *when* you are going to ignore the whining, maybe after you have explained once why your child cannot have something. What is extremely important is that you attend to your child when he asks for something in a calm tone of voice.

"There are two potential problems when you use ignoring. First, the behavior you start to ignore may get worse before it gets better. If you start ignoring a child when he yells, then he might yell louder or for a longer period of time. The important point to remember is to make sure you keep on ignoring; the behavior will decrease if you continue to ignore. Second, another potential problem is that a child may engage in some form of aggressive behavior when you use planned ignoring. You should continue to ignore the behavior but make sure you either give a time out or take away privileges for any aggressive behavior, such as hitting, kicking, or cursing.

"Like all the other skills we have talked about, it is very important to use planned ignoring consistently. Every time the identified behavior occurs, you should ignore. Attending to the positive behavior is also very important while you are using planned ignoring. As you are decreasing a negative behavior by ignoring, be sure to attend to the positive opposite."

Hypothetical Exercise

"Attending and ignoring are also useful for everyday situations. Positive behaviors are often difficult to see because they do not draw attention to themselves; they are expected behaviors. Consequently, they may be ignored and therefore decrease or become a problem behavior instead. Problem behaviors draw attention, like the squeaky wheel that gets the oil, and unfortunately, that is why they keep recurring. To change a behavior, attend to the positive behavior when it happens. When you train yourself to do this, you will see positive changes in your child's behavior.

"Let's look at this example and apply attending and ignoring. Show Chart II. Let's identify the behaviors we need to attend to and also the behaviors we need to ignore. As you can see, the parent has a lot of possible ways to respond to the child. But there is only one way for the parent who wants to see more of the positive behaviors and fewer of the problem behaviors."

Chart II: Attending and Ignoring Exercise

Your child has a major report due for school. A few nights before the due date, you encourage your daughter to start her book report, but she complains and states, "I don't want to do it now, I'll do it later!" You calmly remind her that she can earn bonus points on her point chart for working on it that night. She gets her books and mumbles under her breath, "This is stupid, I hate this class and who cares about this topic?" She looks out the window for a few minutes and begins working again. After working on it for about 20 minutes, she looks up and yells, "This is all your fault. I wanted your help last week, but you were too busy!" Two minutes later, she pulls the book back and begins reading. As she continues her report, she looks confused and calmly asks her mother for help.

Behaviors to attend: _____

_____

_____

Behaviors to ignore: _____

_____

_____

Always attend to the positive behavior immediately!

Choose a Behavior to Ignore

"Now we are ready to work on one of your child's behaviors and set up an attending and ignoring program for you to use at home. Here is a list of common problem behaviors. Show Chart III. Which one would you like to start working on?" The therapist should assist the parent in choosing a behavior the parent is able to ignore. The parent should fill out the worksheet for Attending and Ignoring. Show Chart IV.

Chart III: Common Problems to Ignore

Whining

Bad table manners

Complaining

Yelling

Unable to play alone

Pleading to be bought things in stores

Crying

Swearing

Noisiness

Quarreling with siblings

Pouting

Teasing

Interrupting

Chart IV: Worksheet for Attending and Ignoring

General Problem: _____

_____

When my child does this (problem behavior):	*I will do this:*
_____	Ignore him/her
_____	Not look at him/her
_____	Not talk to him/her
_____	Not smile at him/her
_____	Turn/walk away
_____	Talk to someone else
_____	Attend to another child

And I'll do it every time!

When my child does this (positive opposite):	*I will do this:*
_____	Pay attention to him/her
_____	Look at him/her
_____	Talk to him/her
_____	Smile at him/her
_____	Praise him/her
_____	Ask questions
_____	Hug, kiss, or high five

And I'll do it every time!

"Great, now let's fill out this worksheet. Let's list examples of what your child does when he [problem behavior]. The next thing we need to do is write down the positive opposite, what we want your child to do instead or the attending behavior."

Role Play

"We are ready to start practicing attending and ignoring. Let's role-play when your child does the positive behavior and you attend to it, then let's practice ignoring the negative behavior, and finally we will put the two skills together and practice attending to the positive and ignoring the negative." The therapist should model each situation and at the end of the role play point out what the parents did that they should be aware of. Next, the therapist and the parent should switch roles. The therapist should praise the parent specifically and give corrective feedback where necessary. The therapist should also assist the parent in a self-evaluation of the parent's role play. The therapist should prompt the parent to alternate when to attend and when to ignore by switching between the positive and negative behaviors.

"OK, I'll be the parent in this situation, you be [child's name]. We are in the store. You ask me to buy you a treat, and I say no. For this, handle it calmly so that I can pay attention to you. 'Great job being such a big boy! I know you really wanted that toy. Maybe we can use it as one of your rewards that you can earn.' Notice how I paid attention to you and even praised you for being so calm. Now it's your turn." The parent then uses attending skill on the therapist. The therapist should be sure to praise the parent's efforts.

"Now, let's practice how to effectively ignore. Again, we are in the store, you ask me to buy you a treat, and I say 'no.' Here you want to whine and beg so that

I can show you how to ignore." The parent whines and begs, and the therapist turns around and walks away. "Now it's your turn." The parent then uses the ignoring skill on the therapist, and the therapist praises the parent's efforts.

"We are now going to put attending and ignoring together so that you can practice how it may play out at home. Let's pretend we are in the store. You are going to ask me for something, and I am going to say 'no.' This time I want you to whine so that you can see how I ignore, and then calm down so that you can see how quickly I attend to you." The parent asks for something, the therapist says "no," and the parent begins whining. The therapist turns around and walks away. The parent becomes quiet, and the therapist immediately attends and responds, "Great job of calming down. I know you really wanted that treat! Maybe you can earn it on your point chart. Now it's your turn." The therapist should switch back and forth between positive and negative behavior to exercise the parent's skill in attending and ignoring. Again, the therapist should fine-tune the parent's skills by praising what was done effectively and prompting for more if needed.

For two-parent families, the therapist encourages the parents to praise each other in an effort to develop a supportive environment and to help the parents work as a team. "OK, Dad, how did Mom do with attending and ignoring? Did she catch you when you were calm and pay attention to you right away? How about when she walked away from you when you started to get upset? Great! Go on over and give her a hug! Nice job, Dad, praising Mom!" If the significant other is at all critical, interrupt and ask what was done well. "OK, we're only talking about what it was _____ that [the other parent] did that was great. Right, she was very enthusiastic! [To mother] Now, see if you can turn your back when he becomes upset." The parents role-play again, giving the significant other the chance to praise again. The therapist should always summarize the parts of the role play that were done well.

Assignment

"I'd like you to keep track of every time you attend and praise (positive behavior). We want you to focus on attending to the positive behavior, because that is how you will get a change in behavior. You will not need to keep track of the ignoring, but make sure you are using it every time the problem behavior occurs. Each time you attend to the positive behavior, make sure you record it immediately on your point chart in the praise section.

"This is a handout on attending and ignoring that you can take home and read. Also, continue with your point and praise program for next week."

Shaping and School Program

The technique of shaping is introduced in this session, and then it is applied to an identified problem behavior at school. The therapist defines shaping, reviews the guidelines for its application, and demonstrates how it is used with some example behaviors. Prior to the session, the therapist will have discussed the child with the teacher and identified a problem behavior to work on in the classroom. During the rest of the session, the teacher information is discussed with the parent, and a shaping program is set up for the identified behavior. If the child has no reported school problems, then a shaping program should be designed for an academic task at home. If the therapist is unable to contact the teacher, then a home program should be set up until the teacher is contacted and a school program can be implemented.

Objectives

To teach the parents the components of shaping.
To review school-related problems.
To design a shaping program for a school-related problem.

Equipment and Materials

Handouts
- Guidelines for Shaping
- School Program Form
- Shaping Worksheet
- Guidelines for Homework Program
- Home Program
- Parent Guidelines for School Problems
- Guidelines for Building a Positive Relationship with Teachers and School Personnel
- Point Incentive Chart/Time Out Chart/Attending and Ignoring Chart
- Weekly Assignment Sheet

"Before we start today's new material, let's review how the programs are going at home. Great point chart, you have been putting on a lot of points! How is the attending chart? Let's go over how the time outs were this week. Did you get a chance to try it this week?"

Shaping

"Today we are going to discuss a technique called shaping, and then we are going to apply it to a behavior. First, I would like to talk about what shaping is and how we can use it, and then we will talk about how we can apply it to a problem so that we get more of the positive behavior.

"Many parents want their children to do certain behaviors, but they find they have difficulty getting them to do these behaviors. We know that rewarding positive behaviors will make them happen more often, but if your child never does a particular behavior, then we never have the chance to reinforce it. That is when we use shaping.

"Shaping is the process of teaching a new behavior by reinforcing small steps toward that behavior. It involves reinforcing minor improvements toward the new behavior in a step-by-step manner. With shaping, you break up a behavior or chore into smaller steps and then reinforce every step toward the complete behavior. You can use shaping with either a new behavior that your child may have difficulty doing or a behavior your child does not want to do.

"For example, a child may refuse to pick up all of his things. A parent could use shaping to change this behavior by reinforcing him for putting away one item that belongs to him. Every time the child puts away one item, he should be reinforced. After the child does this consistently, then the parent would reinforce the child for putting away two things, then three, and so on, until eventually the child is putting away all of his things.

"Let's go over some of the guidelines for shaping." Show Chart I.

Chart I: Guidelines for Shaping

Overview

1. Define the beginning behavior and the goal behavior in very specific terms.
2. Reinforce the beginning behavior until this behavior happens consistently. This step is going to take time.
3. Slowly increase the requirement for your child to get the reinforcement. Any small improvement toward the goal behavior should be reinforced.

4. If the behavior is not equal to or better than the previous attempts, then just acknowledge it.
5. The reinforcement should *consistently* be given after the behavior occurs.
6. Once the goal behavior has been reached, be sure to keep on reinforcing it every time it occurs.

Using Shaping

"Let's use these guidelines to encourage a child to clear off the table."

1. Define the beginning behavior (BB) and the goal behavior (GB):
   BB = the child carries just his own plate to the sink.
   GB = the child clears off his and his mother's setting.
2. Reinforce the beginning behavior until it occurs consistently:
   Every time the child carries his own plate to the sink, the mother reinforces this behavior by praising him and saying, "Great job putting your plate in the sink; now you can get your ice cream!"
3. Slowly increase the requirement for the child to receive the reinforcement:
   Once the child has been putting away his own plate consistently, then add another item, like his glass. Now the child has to put away his own plate and glass to receive your praise. Once these two items are put away consistently, then we would add a third item (silverware).
4. If the behavior is not equal to or better than the previous attempts, then do not reinforce it:
   If the child puts away just the plate when he had been putting away his plate and his glass, then you should not praise him, but you can acknowledge it. You might remind him about the glass, and if he does not put it away, then just put it away yourself while ignoring the fact that he did not.
5. The reinforcement should be *consistently* given after the behavior occurs:
   The child should be praised every time he clears off what he is supposed to.
6. Once the goal behavior has been reached, be sure to keep on reinforcing it every time it occurs:
   Once the child has reached the goal of clearing off both place settings, then you should praise him every time he continues to do this behavior.

In-School Program or Nonacademic Task

The therapist should work on the behavior that was discussed with the teacher and use shaping. The identified behavior may be broken down as a task, or the behavior may be expected only part of the day.

"Now we are going to talk about how to use shaping with a school-related behavior. I have talked to [child's name's] teacher about how he is doing in school. [Teacher's name] said he was doing a great job in [a subject]. The teacher also said that he was showing improvement in [a subject]."

"What [teacher's name] and I decided to focus on is to help [child's name] with [specific behavior]. We will set up a specific program for the school behavior. This will be a little like the program you already have at home that is based on positive reinforcement to develop new behaviors. We will start to work on [child's name] doing the positive opposite behavior, starting for 1 hour every morning. The teacher will monitor this behavior and check an evaluation box for how [child's name] did that day. [Child's name] is responsible for bringing the sheet home every day. If bringing it home becomes a problem, then points can be awarded for compliance. Each evaluation has point values (such as 0, 2, 4), and [child's name] will be awarded the points according to how the teacher has rated him."

"Let's discuss now how we are going to set up the reward program at home. We can either tie it into the existing point chart you are doing or set up a different school point chart. We can set up a point chart with different rewards, and that might actually be more exciting." Show Chart II.

Chart II: School Program Form

Child's Name: _____ Date: _____ Day: _____

Teacher Instructions: Please rate the child's degree of compliance with the following behavior in the classes listed here. Place your initials in one of the three spaces that *best* describes the child's behavior, and send the sheets home to the parents daily. Thank you.

Behavior: _____

Definition: _____

_____

Class: _____

Teacher's Initials:

(   ) Most of the time

(   ) Some of the time

(   ) Very little of the time

"As time goes on and [child's name] improves the behavior we are working on, then we can add more time or another behavior (depending on the identified behavior and how it was set up)."

Let's role-play how this is going to work at home. We will practice:"

1. Your child comes home with a good report.
2. Your child comes home with a medium report.
3. Your child comes home with a poor report.

Good Report (Most of the Time)

The therapist should play the role of the parent, modeling how enthusiastic the parent's praise should be. "OK, I'll be the parent, you be the child. Let's practice what to do when your child comes home with a 'most of the time' report. 'Look at this! You got a 'Most of the time!' Fantastic! The teacher said that you were able to stay at your desk most of the time! Great job! Let's go get your reward!' Now, I'll be [child's name] and you be the parent. Remember to be specific and enthusiastic."

Medium Report (Some of the Time)

Again, the therapist should play the role of the parent modeling the level of enthusiasm needed to praise a 'some of the time'. Praise should be moderate in enthusiasm but certainly not ecstatic. "This time when I praise you I am going to be a little less enthusiastic, but definitely pleased. 'Nice job. You got a some of the time. You must have sat at your desk some of the time. Good job. Here's your reward.' Now, I'll be [child's name] and you be the parent. Remember to be specific and moderately enthusiastic."

Poor Report (Very Little of the Time)

The therapist and parent role play how to handle a poor report. The therapist should play the role of the parent. "It's especially important that you stay calm when [child's name] comes home with a poor report. 'I see you had a hard time staying in your seat today. I can't give you your reward tonight, but let's try again tomorrow. I'm sure you'll have a better day.' Now, I'll be [child's name] and you be the parent. Remember to stay calm, let me know that I can't have my reward, and encourage me to stay in my seat tomorrow."

For two-parent families, it is important that the therapist encourages them to praise each other in an effort to develop a supportive environment and to help parents work as a team. "OK dad, how was mom's praise? Was she enthusiastic? Was she specific? Yes! Go on over and give her a hug! Nice job dad praising mom!" If significant other is at all critical, interrupt and ask what it was that she did do well. "OK, we're only talking about what it was that _____ (wife, girlfriend, etc) did that was great . . . Right, she was very enthusiastic! (To mother) Let's do this one again. Remember to tell me specifically why I got a 'Most of the time.'" Parents role play again giving the significant other the chance to praise again. Therapist should always summarize the parts of the role play that were done well.

The therapist should emphasize to the parent that if there is no report, then there is no reward given to the child. This serves as an incentive for the child to bring the report home. Also, the therapist should remember to prompt the parent's praise to be more enthusiastic for "most of the time" than it would be for "some of the time."

Nonacademic Task

Parents have the option to work on an academic task either at home or in school or to work on a nonacademic task at home, such as room-cleaning, going to bed, or getting ready in the morning. If parents choose to work on a task at home, the therapist should guide them through the shaping worksheet to establish the goal and beginning steps. Show Chart III.

Chart III: Shaping Worksheet

First Step: _____
_____

Reinforce this behavior until it occurs consistently (4–6 days).
The reinforcer I will use is: _____
Second Step: _____
_____

Reinforce these two steps consistently (4–6 days).
The reinforcer I will use is: _____
Third Step: _____
_____

Reinforce these three steps consistently (4–6 days).
The reinforcer I will use is: _____
Fourth Step: _____
_____

Reinforce these four steps consistently (4–6 days).
The reinforcer I will use is: _____

Last Step: _____

_____

Be sure to continue reinforcing this behavior consistently!

The therapist should role-play how this will work at home:

1. Completion of the beginning step
2. Refusal to do a step
3. Introduction to the next step

Completion of the Step

The therapist should play the role of the parent modeling how to praise the child for completing the beginning step. "Ok, I am going to play the role of the parent. Watch how enthusiastic I am when you put your pillow on your bed. 'Look at this! You put your pillow on your bed!! I am so proud of you! Let's go get your sticker!' Now, I'll be [child's name] and you be the parent. Remember to be enthusiastic and specific."

Refusal to Do the Step

In this scenario the therapist is going to play the role of a parent whose child has refused to do the step (pillow on the bed). "[Child's name], It's time to put your pillow on your bed so that you can get your sticker." Parent says, "No." Therapist then states, "'It looks as though you are having a hard time this morning putting your pillow on your bed. I can't give you your sticker but we will try again tomorrow.' Now, I'll be [child's name] and you be the parent. Remember to stay calm, remind me that I cannot get my reward, and encourage me to try tomorrow."

Introduction to the Next Step

In this situation the therapist is going to play the role of the parent who is going to introduce the next step to the child. "In order to introduce your child to the next step you have to be really enthusiastic. In this case, your child will be getting the same reward but you are requiring more from him. 'Johnny, you have been doing such a great job putting your pillow on your bed. I am so proud of you. Because you have been doing so well you are ready for a super challenge. Now to get your sticker, I am going to ask you to put your pillow and your stuffed animals on your bed. I bet you can do it. Let's try.' Now, I'll be [child's name] and you be the parent. Remember to sound upbeat and encouraging and tell me exactly what I have to do to get my reward."

Again, for two-parent families, it is important that the therapist encourages them to praise each other in an effort to develop a supportive environment and to help parents work as a team. "OK mom, how was dad's praise? Was he enthusiastic? Was he specific? Yes! Go on over and give him a hug! Nice job mom praising dad!" If significant other is at all critical, interrupt and ask what it was that she did do well. "OK, we're only talking about what it was that _____ (husband, boyfriend, etc) did that was great . . . Right, she was very enthusiastic! (To father) Let's do this one again. Remember to tell me specifically what I did that was great." Parents role play again giving the significant other the chance to praise again. Therapist should always summarize the parts of the role play that were done well.

Homework Program

With some children, behavioral or academic problems in the classroom are not identified, but there might be a problem with homework completion.

"I spoke to [teacher's name], who said that he is doing a good job in the class and with his class work. You mentioned that he has difficulty completing his homework and gives you a hard time doing it. We are going to set up a program to help [child's name] do better with homework. We are going to develop a specific program for [homework completion, bringing home the work, finishing homework, doing it neatly, or whatever the problem is] and use shaping. Let's go over the homework program guidelines." Show Chart IV.

Chart IV: Guidelines for Homework Program

1. Implement the use of a daily assignment sheet. Have the teacher review it and sign it at the end of each day.
2. Reward your child with praise and points for bringing home the assignment sheet.
3. Establish a place where the homework will be done without any distractions.
4. Establish a time when homework should start.
5. Reward your child for the behavior you are working on (such as starting it, getting materials ready, writing neatly, or staying seated until a break).
6. You can make certain activities contingent on completion of homework.
7. Implement a monitoring system whereby the teacher can let you know whether the homework was turned in.

"Now that we have reviewed the guidelines, let's set up a shaping program for homework. You mentioned that [child's name] has difficulty getting started with his homework, so let's break up this behavior, come up with a beginning behavior, and set up an incentive chart for this behavior."

A shaping program may be set up with respect to a time limit for doing homework, the number of prompts to do homework, getting materials together to start homework, the amount of time before a break (or the number of breaks), or remembering to bring the necessary materials home from school.

"Now let's role-play how to do this at home. Let's practice these situations:"

1. Your child does the beginning behavior.
2. Your child refuses to do the behavior.
3. Your child does part of the behavior.

When the Child Is Not in School

A school-based program may not be appropriate if the child is not in school (summer) or school is about to end and an intervention within the remaining weeks is not feasible. We still like to implement a school-related program in the home, given the significance of academic problems. A reading or studying program in the home can be implemented in which the child has periods of time for completing an academic task. There are several benefits for this program, such as developing periods of studying, improving reading or academic abilities, exposing the child to some of the rewards of reading and studying, and also changing some of the parent–child interactions in relation to reading and studying.

The home program should provide special points to the child for reading or studying (or any academic task) in a designated area for a brief period of time. The amount of time may be increased as time goes on, or the task may be increased, according to how the shaping program is implemented.

There are certain guidelines to follow when setting up the home program. Show Chart V.

Chart V: Home Program

1. The academic task should be something the child would like to do, such as reading a comic book or a magazine or doing enjoyable math tasks.
2. The child should help choose the materials needed.
3. The parent should monitor the academic task to be able to praise as the child is doing the task. The child should do the task alone and then have a few minutes to report about the reading or go over the math tasks.

---

4. Some changes may be made to the program as the child does the academic task consistently. Eventually, if this program is going well, different amount of points may be given for different types of and amounts of the academic task.
5. The Home Reading/Learning Program Sheet should be used to record the child's progress.

The program should be introduced to the parent in this following way:

"Because [child's name] is not in school right now, we are going to set up a home program with [child's name] doing an academic task for a limited amount of time each day, and then we'll set up a reinforcement program. We will focus on either a reading task or a math task. Reading is a skill that is central to everything else they do in school, including science, English, and even math. Also, improvements in academic areas such as reading or math may help to decrease disruptive and problem behaviors at school.

"What I would like to do is to develop a program that helps [child's name] become more involved in reading [used here as an example]. We will apply a shaping program to start off slowly and eventually either add more time or add more tasks. We can't start your child off with reading novels and encyclopedias, but we can build reading skills and interest in learning so that [child's name] will more be likely to enjoy these tasks in school.

"We will set up a few times a week for [child's name] to sit and read something in a designated area. He can read anything as long as you approve it, so it does not necessarily have to be a schoolbook. It can even be solving word puzzles or reading newspapers and magazines. We are going to keep track of the reading on this sheet (Home Reading/Learning Program Sheet), and we also have to set up the points and the rewards."

Assignment

At this point the therapist should give parents copies of their charts to do for the week. The therapist should also pass out the two handouts about building a better relationship with the school and discuss any problems the parent has with the school personnel.

"I would like you to continue the point chart, the time out chart, and the attending chart and also start the school chart for this week.

Review and Problem Solving

In this session, we review the techniques that have been discussed so far. We begin with a review of the existing programs and any adjustments that need to be made. Following a review of specific programs is a review of all the skills discussed so far in treatment. A review of parenting skills is then conducted with the Program Review Checklist (see end of this section). The checklist is then discussed with the parent, and the techniques are applied to hypothetical problems, which the parent has to solve with the therapist's help.

Objectives

To review programs and make necessary changes.
To review skills introduced so far in treatment.
To practice applying skills to hypothetical problems.

Equipment and Materials

Handouts
- Program Review Checklist
- Review of Techniques
- Before Beginning a Program
- Point Chart/Time Out Chart/Attending and Ignoring Chart/School Program
- Cards for Problem Solving
- Weekly Assignment Sheet

Review of Programs

"Before we get started today, let's review how the programs are going at home. Wow! This is great. You brought in all your charts, and you've been keeping track of the behaviors!"

Program Review Checklist

Hand out a Program Review Checklist for each parent to fill out. The therapist can either stay in the room or step out until it is done. Discuss it with the parents when they are finished, making sure you go through each item. Praise all items marked with an *A* or *U*, and then ask the parent to elaborate (*always* did this = A; *usually* did this = U). On items marked *S* or *N*, find out what some of the obstacles are and assist the parent in problem solving (*sometimes* did this = S; *never* did this = N). Ask the parents to discuss the situation—what the child does and what they do. Inquire about alternative solutions and make suggestions.

Therapist Presentation

The therapist should give the parent the Review of Techniques handout and review it with them. The following techniques should be discussed:

1. Defining and observing behavior, ABCs
2. Positive reinforcement: points and praise
3. Attending and ignoring
4. Time out
5. Shaping and school

"Let's review the skills that we have learned in our sessions up to now. Here is a list of techniques with definitions to assist you as a review."

Go over each technique, asking open-ended questions that encourage parents to talk about what they remember. This should be done in a nonthreatening way and include the following points:

1. A brief definition of the technique
2. How the technique is used
3. Examples of its use (include a role play)
4. When and for what behaviors it should be used

Defining and Observing

"Defining a behavior before beginning a program is very important. We must describe the behavior clearly and specifically. Observing the behavior means that we must watch and listen carefully to see how many times the behavior has occurred in a limited amount of time. Why would we want to define a behavior before we work on changing it? Why do we want to record how many times a behavior occurs? What should be given before a behavior and what should be given after?"

Positive Opposite, Positive Reinforcement, Points and Praise

"Positive Opposite is the positive behavior you want your child to do in place of the negative behavior they are engaging in.

"Positive reinforcement is a powerful technique we can use to change behavior. When we use positive reinforcement after a desired behavior occurs, will that behavior increase or decrease? That's right, it will increase or strengthen.

"There are four types of reinforcers: material, social, privilege/activity, and token. Can you think of examples of each? Let's go over some of the rules we follow when we are using positive reinforcement:"

1. What would happen to a behavior if the reward is effective?
2. Should a reward be given right after the behavior occurs, at the end of the day, or as the behavior is happening?
3. Should you use reinforcers every time the behavior occurs?
4. Can you give a reward if only part of the behavior has occurred?

"A point program is another skill you have been using to increase good behaviors by following them with points that your child can exchange for rewards. Let's review the rules that should be followed in using point programs."

1. When should you give points and praise?
2. Should you give points every time, some of the time, or every other time the behavior is performed?
3. If a behavior has not occurred, should you take away points?
4. The chart should be reviewed at the end of the day. True or false?

"Praise is a social reinforcer that is used to increase positive behavior. There are four things to do when you are praising effectively. Let's go over them:"

1. You should come up close, but not touch your child, when you are praising. True or false?
2. When you are praising, why should you be specific?
3. You should use a _____ tone of voice when praising.
4. Should you praise immediately after the positive behavior?

The therapist should have parents role-play their praise so that therapist can assess praise and give them feedback if necessary.

Attending and Planned Ignoring

"Attending is noticing when someone is doing a positive behavior and giving the behavior attention by looking at the child, talking to the child, hugging the child, and expressing approval. Ignoring is a form of mild punishment in which an undesirable behavior is not given any attention."

1. When you are attending, what do you do when the desired behavior occurs?
2. Does a behavior increase or decrease when you attend to it? How about when you ignore it?
3. When do you want to start ignoring a negative behavior?

Time Out

"Time out is a mild form of punishment. It involves removing the child from a reinforcing setting for 2 to 5 minutes when the negative behavior occurs. The parent should choose a safe and boring place for the child to sit during time out. The parent should also explain to the child what the time out behavior will be and how it will work. Let's review the following guidelines:"

1. Calmly tell your child what he did wrong, and tell him to go to time out.
2. If he participates in time out without having a tantrum, what should you do?
3. If your child does not go to time out immediately, should you convince him to go and debate with him?
4. If your child refuses to go to time out, you tell him he loses a privilege for a month. True or false?
5. Reinforce the positive opposite when it happens; otherwise, time out will not be effective.

The therapist should practice with the parent if time out seems at all unclear.

Shaping

"Shaping is the process of teaching a new behavior by reinforcing small steps toward that behavior."

1. When we are using shaping, what two behaviors do we define?
2. What behavior do you reinforce until it occurs consistently?
3. Would you add a new step if the previous step occurred once in a while?

4. Should you continue reinforcing once the goal behavior has been reached?

School- or Home-Based Program

"A school program is applying shaping to increase a positive behavior in school. You get in touch with the teacher and agree on what behavior to work on. The teacher monitors that behavior for a limited amount of time each day and sends home daily checklists. You reward your child at home according to the checklists."

1. Would you set up the time limit for the identified behavior for 1 hour, half a day, or all day?
2. What would you set up at home to reward the monitored behavior?
3. What would you say if your child brought home a not-so-good checklist?

Make sure you praise the parent along the way.

Problem Solving

"Now that we have reviewed the techniques, let's apply them to some problem situations. Before we start, I want to give you some important reminders. To change behavior, always start with a positive intervention first. The punishment techniques should be used only as a backup or with extreme behaviors (like physical aggression). Also, for a punishment technique to work, we have to use a positive reinforcement technique along with it to strengthen the behaviors we want. OK, let's start with the first card. I will solve this one and then we will role-play it. You can try the ones after this one."

Card #1: The Therapist Models

"Your child always leaves his toys around." (This initial statement is printed on a card presented to the parent. The same applies for each of the other "cards" used in this session and in a later session.)

The therapist suggests using a point incentive chart, as well as a shaping program. "This would be a great chance to use a point chart, praise, and shaping. If your child is always leaving his toys around, I would use shaping by focusing on a small period of time during the day. It could be the morning, afternoon, after dinner, or before bed. You would choose one of those time frames to ask your child to put his toys away. If he does it, you praise immediately and enthusiastically and then give him his reward. So for this problem situation, I have just used a point chart, praise, and shaping. If your child refuses to clean up his toys, you would let it go and put them away yourself. Your child would not get any points or praise. OK, let's role-play. You be the child. Let's pretend that I am working on you to get you to put your toys away after dinner. For this first role play, please cooperate, so I can model praising and giving you the points. Soon I'll show you what to do when your child doesn't listen. 'OK, it's time to clean up your toys. Remember, if you do this now, then I can give you your two points and a big hug!'" The parent plays the role of the child cleaning up the toys. The therapist then praises, "Great job putting your toys away! I am so proud of you. Let me give you your two points." To the parent, "Now let's practice what to do when your child refuses to put his toys away. I'll play the role of the parent. When I ask you to put your toys away, say no or ignore me. 'OK, it's time to clean up your toys. Remember, if you do this now, then I can give you your two points and a big hug!'" The parent says, "No! I don't feel like it. I'll do it later." The therapist then states, "It looks like you are having a hard time putting your toys away. I am not able to give you any points. I will give you a chance to try again later." To the parent, "Now it's your turn."

The therapist should explain to the parent that once putting toys away after dinner has been accomplished, then the parent could expand the time frame from after dinner to before and after dinner, and so on.

Card #2: The Parent's Turn

The card says, "Your child never goes to bed on time and is always grumpy in the morning. You are sick of arguing with him in the morning."

"Before you tackle this one, let's simplify this problem. We can assume that your child is grumpy in the morning because he is tired. What can you do to help your child go to bed on time?"

The therapist should assist the parents in coming up with a reinforcement program. This is the first time they are given the opportunity to devise a program, so the therapist should be very flexible. It is acceptable for the parent to suggest any positive intervention from a point chart to attending. A point chart with shaping is preferable, but many parents shy away from using shaping because they just learned it the week before. After the parent develops an acceptable reinforcement program, the therapist reinforces what the parent did correctly. Then the therapist can suggest other ideas: "What a nice way to reinforce your child to go to bed on time. You came up with a clear bedtime and a wonderful reward system for the behavior. You can also use shaping if you find that your child is still staying up late. It may be that the bedtime you have established is just too early for your child. You would use shaping by finding a time that is closer to when he actually goes to bed, but is still earlier.

"OK, on this next one I'll be the child. Choose one of the programs we just talked about, and let's role-play how you would explain it to me and then how it would work."

Card #3: The Parent's Turn (again)

"Your child refuses to change his clothes or take a bath each day."

"In this situation you want to pick your priorities. Decide which behavior is more important to you and go from there." The parent should select. Usually it is focusing on having the child bathe. The therapist should encourage the parent to use a positive reinforcement program first, preferably shaping. Perhaps the beginning behavior could be one bath a week with an immediate reward to follow. The second step could be two baths, and so on. The therapist should be sure to praise appropriate programs.

"OK, on this one I'll be the child. Let's role-play the program you just developed."

Assignment

"Continue doing your charts this week. We'll see you next week."

Family Meeting

The seventh session is a family meeting, which includes the parent(s), the child, and the therapist. The purpose of this session is to give the therapist an opportunity to observe the parent–child interactions and reinforce both parent and child for compliance with the programs.

The PMT therapist facilitates the session by generating discussion about the programs. The questions should address the child's understanding and opinions of the programs, as well as reveal how the programs are implemented and with what consistency. Any changes or departures from the recommended procedures often become apparent at this time. The PMT therapist uses the information to praise and reinforce the parent's and child's progress and to guide them in making changes and improvements. If the parent begins to report on the child's negative behavior, the PMT therapist should redirect the focus to what has been accomplished and what improvements have been made.

Objectives

> To observe how the parents and the child interact
> To reinforce parent compliance, consistency, and positive behavior
> To give the parents feedback on how they are doing
> To confirm that the programs are being carried out correctly

Equipment and Materials

Handouts
- Point Chart
- Time Out Chart
- Attending and Ignoring Chart
- School Program

Therapist Presentation: Family Meeting

"Welcome every one, I'm glad you're here. Today we'll be reviewing the programs, and we'll be doing a lot of role playing. You and I [to the parent] will have a chance to go over any questions or concerns you may have at the end."

The therapist should review the chart with the family and ask the child to explain the chart. This helps the therapist ascertain whether the programs are being done at home. Did the parent bring in a currently completed point program? Can the child describe any of the programs, how to earn points, and what time out is? The therapist can assume the parents are using the charts and programs if the child can describe the point chart and appears familiar with the praise, time out, and other programs. If not, the therapist should review the point chart with everyone and perhaps simplify it to make it easier for the family to use.

Also, the therapist should look for feedback from the child and try to problem-solve any issues with the parents there. If the parent appears hesitant to make any changes with the child there, the therapist should make a note of what the child wants, assess if it is reasonable, and speak with the parent privately at the end of the session. To the child, the therapist asks, "So tell us, are you still happy with your point chart? How are the rewards going? Are there any that you want to change or replace?" It is very important that the therapist quickly determine whether the child's request is appropriate. If so, the therapist should ask the parent, "How does that sound? Would it be OK to replace the amusement park with the movies?"

The therapist should review the behaviors on the chart with the family and determine if any are occurring consistently enough to be replaced. The child is told, "So it looks like you have been cleaning your room every day for the last few weeks! That's great, good for you!" The parent is asked, "Is there something else that you want to work on, since this behavior has become so consistent?" The parent may choose another behavior or may want to work on the old problem for a little while longer. If the parent chooses another behavior, then the therapist should be sure to role-play the child doing the behavior while the parent praises it.

Role Play

In this contact with the family, the PMT therapist should be standing next to the parent(s) and ready to praise at any given moment for any execution of a skill, such as prompting, praising, or even ignoring the child. Also, the therapist should be ready to prompt the parent for better use of the skill. Perhaps the parent's tone was punitive or the parent neglected to praise. Again, praise the parents once they have more adequately implemented the technique. Prompt and shape parent behavior as needed.

"Let's get up (parents are seated), and we'll work on this first behavior on the chart, minding. Your mother is going to ask you to do something. What will you be asking [child's name] to do . . . ok, putting your shoes away. If you can do that the first time asked then your mother can give you 2 points." The role play begins.

For two-parent families, it is important for the therapist to encourage them to praise each other in an effort to develop a supportive environment and to help parents work as a team. "OK, Dad, how was Mom's praise? Was she immediate? Did she touch? How was her enthusiasm? And was she specific? All right! Go on over and give her a hug! Nice job, Dad, praising Mom!" If the significant other is at all critical of the first role player, interrupt and ask for an example of something that was done well. "OK, we're only talking about what it was she did that was great. Right, she was very enthusiastic! [To mother:] Now, this time when you praise, remember to be immediate, touch, and be specific." The parent role-plays again, giving the significant other the chance to praise again. The therapist should always summarize the parts of the role play that were done well.

The session continues with repeated role plays by the parent, alternating parents if two parents are present. The role plays are repeated as the therapist uses prompts and praise to develop high levels of competence in each parent's delivery of prompts and praise.

At the end of the session, the therapist and the parent review the charts, and the parent is given specific feedback about the session.

Assignment

The parents are to continue the programs at home. There is no special assignment sheet for this session.

Low-Rate Behaviors

Working with children referred for aggressive and antisocial behaviors that are serious and severe can be very frustrating. Examples of such behavior are stealing, running away, shoplifting, breaking and entering, destroying private or public property, vandalism, assault, and arson. Beyond the harm or damage these acts cause, they pose an additional problem from the standpoint of managing behavior through the usual consequences.

Typically, a child is referred to the clinic for aggression. In addition to various high-rate behaviors such as fighting at home and at school, intake may reveal that the child has stolen from the local grocery store, broke into a neighbor's house, and, in the company of a friend, was caught riding a stolen motorbike. The parents are placed into treatment and taken through our initial core program. While improvement may be slow, enough change is evident to encourage them to continue treatment. Suddenly, everything goes awry. The child, with a friend, breaks into the school or is caught shoplifting. The school, police, and courts are involved, and the parents are again ready to give up on their child. Treatment is judged as ineffective, not treating the "real" problem, and a waste of time. The parents revert to the previously used harsh punishment and abandon the program and skills we have taught.

Given the likelihood of this scenario, one problem in working with children who have committed serious low-rate behaviors is the anticipation of their occurrence. Anticipating and stating to the parents the possibility of low-rate event occurrences does, ultimately, make the situation more manageable. In this session, we try to prepare the parents for the occurrence of these low-frequency behaviors of their child and provide them with the means to handle these behaviors when they arise.

Low-rate antisocial behaviors are always a possibility for our clinical population. Our preparation of the parents for these behaviors may differ slightly, based on the characteristics (e.g., age, specific behaviors) of the child. If the child has engaged in low-frequency behaviors (e.g., at least twice) in the 2 months prior to treatment, we may want to prepare the parents for low-frequency behaviors and how they are handled relatively early in treatment. In any case, we will address the problem of low frequency behaviors for all parents and families.

To prepare parents for occurrences of low-rate behaviors.
To provide parents with a means of handling these behaviors, should they occur.

Equipment/Materials

Handouts
- Low-Rate Behaviors
- Low-Rate Rules
- Low-Rate Behavior Worksheet
- Program Presentation Guidelines
- Commonly Asked Questions
- Point Chart/Time Out Chart/Attending and Ignoring Chart/School Program
- Weekly Assignment Sheet

Therapist Presentation

"Today we are focusing on low-rate behaviors, what that means, and how to decrease them. Low-rate behaviors happen less frequently than many of the other behaviors we have previously discussed, but they are significant because of their seriousness. By less frequent, I mean that they happen no more than once a week. If you find that the particular behavior happens more than that, then it is more effective to set up a positive reinforcement program. This category includes behaviors such as:" Show Chart I.

Chart I: Low-Rate Behaviors

Stealing and shoplifting

Firesetting and matchplay

Destroying property

Running away

Physical attack

Disobeying curfews and wandering

Alcohol and drug use

Inappropriate sex activity (early, promiscuous, inappropriate comments and/or gestures)

Truancy

Lying

Playing with weapons (guns or knives)

"Have these behaviors been a problem with your child? Often these behaviors appear in combination. Today we will design a program to deal with these behaviors before they occur to assist both you and your child. You'll be able to implement the program easily, and it allows both you and your child to be clear about the consequences for such behavior, suspected behavior, or clusters of behavior. This program is designed to take the burden of proof off you and place the responsibility for staying out of problem situations on your child. The child will receive a boring, tedious chore for such behaviors instead of the typical punitive response such as grounding, lectures, or physical punishment. When such behaviors happen in clusters, parents should provide consequences for only the initial behavior they are addressing. This is much more effective in decreasing the problem behavior so that it is less likely to be an issue in the future.

"For example, often a child denies stealing or fighting, even when the evidence is to the contrary. Parents are instructed to tell children that it is up to them to stay away from these situations because if they are associated with such problems in any way, they will face the consequences. Even if you only think your child might have done it, he still has to deal with the consequences.

"We are going to develop a special program for dealing with low-rate behaviors. To begin, let us look at some of guidelines for the program." Show and discuss Chart II.

Chart II: Low-Rate Rules

1. Be sure you can observe (strongly suspect) the behavior you want stopped.
2. Select a chore that is tedious, not something you would like him to do or that he would like to do on a regular basis.
3. Stay calm.
4. Before using a low-rate chore, explain to the child and role-play, if he will cooperate.
5. Assign the chore immediately, based on evidence or strong suspicion.
6. Don't threaten the chore; give it right away.
7. Don't debate or argue. Tell your child what he did wrong (or suspect he did wrong) and calmly give him the chore.
8. If he won't do the chore, calmly tell him you won't be able to start the time until he starts the chore.

---

9. If he still won't go, give him a choice of either doing the chore or losing a privilege.

10. If the child starts the chore but is angry, out of control, or purposely doing a terrible job, calmly stop the chore and take away the privilege.

11. Praise your child once he begins the chore *and* while he's doing the chore.

12. Continue to praise the positive opposite of the problem behavior.

A Program for Low-Rate Behaviors

"You said that [the low-rate behavior] is a problem behavior with your child. [If the child does not display any low-rate behaviors, use stealing as an example.] To develop a program to deal with low-rate behaviors, we have specific guidelines to follow. This worksheet will help us. [Hand out Chart III.] Notice that there are several behaviors with their suggested definitions to choose from. Defining the problem behavior is the first step toward developing a program."

The therapist should fill in the behavior on the low-rate behavior worksheet and review it. After the review is complete, the therapist should assist the parent in generating two sets of chores (30 to 60 minutes) to be used as the low-rate behaviors occur. Some examples are included on the worksheet.

Chart III: Low-Rate Behavior Worksheet

Program for _____

1. _____ is to be defined as: _____

_____

_____

Low-rate behaviors happen no more than once a week. If any of these behaviors happens more often than that, then a positive reinforcement program should be set up. The following behaviors and definitions are suggested, should any be a problem with your child.

Stealing: possession of anything that does not belong to him, or taking anything that he does not own. This includes items "found" and "borrowed." The burden of proving ownership is on the child.

Firesetting: playing with matches, starting a fire, playing with the stove, or being around, reporting, or even putting out fires.

Destroying of property (vandalism): breaking or damaging, using in a way it was not intended, handling in such a way as to risk damage to any

---

objects, including those owned by the family or by another child, the school, a business, or the community.

Running away: being in a prohibited area, not being where the child says he will be, not returning within 15 minutes of the time period.

Lying: telling something that isn't true, omitting relevant information in telling something (telling a half-truth), "shading" or "bending" the truth.

Physical attack: attempting to inflict injury on another person, such as by hitting, punching, kicking, or biting.

Disobeying curfew: returning home after specified time.

Alcohol or drug use: any suspected use of drugs or alcohol, including intoxication, finding drugs, alcohol, or other related evidence.

Inappropriate sexual activity: any evidence of sexual activity that is early or promiscuous, or inappropriate comments or gestures.

Truancy: any evidence that the child is not attending school or is skipping classes.

Playing with weapons: any activities involving guns, knives, or objects used as or like a weapon.

2. The parents alone decide whether _____ has occurred. They need not prove _____ beyond a reasonable doubt. Occasional false accusations will not undermine the program. Should it later turn out that the child was falsely accused and assigned consequences, a sincere apology should be sufficient. In no case should that mean backing down in the face of the next suspected _____.

3. Set two levels of consequences for _____: Depending on the child's age, half an hour's worth of useful but boring chores for suspected or less serious _____; 1 hour for founded or serious _____. Recommended chores, depending on the age of the child, are scrubbing floors, raking leaves, pulling weeds, cleaning, and straightening up the garage. Estimate how much time it would take to perform the chore if the child worked consistently and assign a task or tasks that equal the time earned. This avoids having to stand over the child urging him to do a 30-minute chore; that is the child's problem, not the parent's. No other consequence, such as lectures, humiliation, or spankings, should be used. The only exception is when some person or facility outside the family is the victim. In those cases, the child should be required to meet with that person and apologize. Restitution, when applicable (such as for stealing or property destruction), should be made, though the extent of it may be limited by the fact that a child is usually unable to repay extensive damages. In that case, partial restitution may be the only possibility.

4. When _____ occurs (or is suspected), the parents are to simply say: "According to the rules, you have _____ and now you must do your chore."

Should the child argue, the parent should remind the child that they cannot start the time until child is working on the chore. If the child refuses to do the chore, then a choice should be given between doing the chore or losing a privilege.

5. All occurrences of _____, even trivial ones, are to have consequences. Each _____ and consequence is part of the teaching process that _____ will be punished. To allow even small incidents of _____ to pass will slow down the learning process.

6. Positive reinforcement for periods of non _____ is difficult to use. Try to reinforce the positive opposite whenever possible. For example, if you are using this program for stealing, you want to reinforce your child every time he asks for something, waits to save for something, or tells you that he really wants something. If you are using this program for lying, reinforce your child every time he tells you the truth.

7. The program should remain in effect for at least 6 months after the last _____. At that point, the parents and child may renegotiate if applicable.

If the child is often unsupervised for long periods, he may engage in low-rate behaviors. It may be useful to institute a telephone checking system whereby the child phones in every hour or two to say where he is. The parent may need to hang up and call the number back to verify that the child is really there. Another monitoring procedure is a sign-out sheet for recording where and for how long a child will be out. A child is less likely to engage in these serious behaviors in a structured home.

Introducing and Monitoring the Program

Presentation of the program is straightforward. Hand out Chart IV.

Chart IV: Program Presentation Guidelines

1. Present to the child specifically, and carefully discuss exactly what is meant by _____.
2. Use lots of examples until the child fully understands how "tight" a definition will be in effect.
3. Practice discussing an incident of _____ and the assignment of a chore consequence. It is not necessary for the child to practice if he doesn't want to.

4. Here is an example of presenting the low-rate program for stealing. Note to the therapist: This is material to present already prepared for "stealing," but use as needed for another behavior.

"I know that there are times when you see things that you really want and you might just want to take it. There are times when I really want something, too, but instead of taking it, there are many other things you can do. When this happens, you can always ask for what you want or ask to borrow what you see and want, you can ask me to put it on your point chart, or you can save for it. Now you are already doing many of these things. However, when I find that you did take something that is not yours, or suspect you of that, even if you borrow something but forget to ask, I will give you a chore. If it is something small like taking a quarter off my dresser or borrowing your brother's shirt without asking, you will have a small chore to do. If it something bigger, such as taking money out of my wallet or bringing home a friend's toy, you will have a bigger chore. But you know what? I know you don't want to do any chores, and I don't want to give you any chores, so let's stay as far away from stealing as possible."

or

"I know that there are times when you want to _____. There are times I really [feeling or desire], but instead of [low-rate behavior], there are many things you can do instead. When this happens, you can always _____, _____, or _____. Now you are already doing many of these things. However, when I find that you did [low-rate behavior] or suspect you of that, even if you [trivial occurrence of low-rate behavior], I will give you a chore. If it is something small like _____, you will have a small chore. If it something bigger like _____, you will have a bigger chore. But you know what? I know you don't want to do any chores, and I don't want to give you any chores, so let's stay as far away from _____ as possible."

Have the parents role-play the presentation of a program. The parents present and state the several steps of the program with a careful discussion of what is meant by "stealing" or the other behavior identified. They should use many examples until the child fully understands how strict a definition will be in effect. Role-play the discussion of an incident of _____ and the assignment of the chore consequence. If the child is unwilling to role-play, simply state that it is not necessary to role-play, but that he should understand the new regimen that has been imposed.

"I would give many examples of the behavior until I am absolutely sure the child understands what I mean. I'll cite instances of it from the past without being punitive. If you do get the opportunity to praise for the positive opposite, then take full advantage. When presenting this to [child's name], it's really important to remember to praise him for sitting and listening and for accepting the program without any debate. You can also suggest role-playing the program with the child, but this is not necessary. However, if the child does complete the role play, much enthusiasm and praise should be used. Now, this program will be much more effective if you explain it to your child before the problem occurs, almost as a preventive measure."

The therapist should then act as the child and have the parent explain the program, looking specifically for a calm, nonpunitive voice and praise for accepting the program calmly after it is explained.

Remind the parents that during the regular phone contacts, you will be asking about the occurrence of _____ and the assignment of consequences. Then, during those calls, be sure to inquire about the matter, the nature of such events, and how well the appropriate consequences were applied.

Role-Play Use of Low Rate

"To show you how to use the low-rate program for [the problem behavior], let's pretend I'm the parent and you're the child. We'll role-play how to use low rate." For all role plays, after modeling the correct use of the technique, the therapist should reverse roles with the parent, giving prompts if needed. Remember to praise any of the parent's correct behaviors. For two-parent families, have each parent play the role of either the child or the parent.

The therapist should role-play how the parent should respond when:

1. The child accepts the low-rate chore immediately.
2. The child takes excessive time to do the chore, either quietly or with tantrums.
3. The child is unruly or out of control while doing the chore.
4. The child refuses to do the chore.

After modeling the use of low rate for these situations, the therapist should reverse roles with the parent.

Role Play #1: Child Is Given Chore for Low-Rate Behavior

The parent should perform the problem behavior, and the therapist follows this by assigning a chore. "This time, let's practice a situation when you suspect or know that [child's name] has had a serious problem and you have given your child a chore that he does immediately without any problem. It's important to include a couple of things when you're giving a chore. The first thing I'll do is make sure I am very calm when giving the chore, tell him why, and for how long. I'll also praise [child's name] as soon as he starts the chore, as well as while he is doing the chore. It is also very important to make sure you praise your child when he has completed the chore. Also, pay very little attention to the negative behavior. 'OK [child's name], I believe you have taken my $20 bill because it was missing from my wallet and I found it in your pocket. You need to go clean the shower and scrub the bathtub. [Child goes to perform the chore.] Excellent job, going right away to clean the shower and bathtub! This should take a half hour, so I'll check on you and let you know when the time is up.' I will make sure I go in and praise him every few minutes for continuing to work on task. [Chore has been completed.] 'Wow! What a nice job you did of cleaning the shower and tub; it's sparkling in here.' Now, I'll be [child's name], and you are the parent. Suspect me of stealing and give me a chore."

Remember to:

1. Stay calm.
2. Tell the child what the chore is for and for how long.
3. Praise as soon as the child starts the chore, as well as while he is doing the chore.
4. Praise when the child successfully completes the chore.

Have the parent practice giving the chore to the child. Praise the parent for remaining calm, for praising the child for doing the chore right away and for completing the chore, and for suggesting the positive opposite in a positive, encouraging way.

For two-parent families, the therapist encourages parents to praise each other in an effort to develop a supportive environment and help parents work as a team. "OK, Dad, how did Mom do? Was she calm? Did she tell you what the chore was for and for how long? Yes! Go on over and give her a hug! Nice job, Dad, praising Mom!" If the significant other is at all critical, interrupt and ask what it was that the partner did well. "OK, we're only talking about what it was that she did that was great. Right, she remained calm! [To the mother] Now, tell me what the chore is for and how long." The parent role-plays again, giving the significant other the chance to praise again. The therapist should always summarize the parts of the role play that were done well.

"It's also important to stay calm when your child refuses to do the chore or delays in doing it. Simply tell the child that you cannot set the time until he has started the chore, and then walk away if your child is still upset. If he has still not started the chore after approximately 5 minutes, then you give him the choice of either doing the chore or losing a privilege. By the same token, if your child has started the chore but is still upset, complaining, or doing a poor job, then offer choice of the chore or losing a privilege. If the child does do the chore, remember to praise!"

The therapist directs the parent to act as a child who complains about doing a chore. "OK [child's name], I believe you have taken my $20 bill because it was missing from my wallet and I found it in your pocket, so you need to go clean the shower and scrub the bathtub. [The child complains and refuses to do chore.] I won't be able to start the time until you start working on the chore." The child becomes angry and continues to complain. "At this point I will walk away and ignore my child. I will wait a few minutes. If I have ignored his complaining, chances are he will have started the chore. Once your child starts to work on the chore, you give him big praise: 'Great job for starting to clean the shower! I will let you know when your time is up!' If he has not started the chore after 2 to 5 minutes, then I will offer him the choice of completing the chore or losing a privilege. "[Child's name], either you scrub the shower stall for a half hour, or you may not play with your Game Boy this afternoon." If the child continues to complain, then you take the Game Boy away.

"OK, now I'll be [child's name]. Give me a chore for [low-rate behavior], and I will not go right away. Remember to tell me what I've done, what chore I have, and for how long."

Remember to:

1. Stay calm.
2. Tell the child what the chore is for and for how long.
3. If the child has not started the chore, let him know that you cannot start the timer until the child starts the chore.
4. If the chore has still not started, offer a choice between doing the chore or loss of a privilege.
5. Praise the child if the chore has been begun.

Again, have the parents praise each other if both are present. "OK, Mom, how did Dad do? Was he calm? Did he tell you what the chore was for and for how long? Yes! Did he say he couldn't start the time until he started the chore? Yes! Go on over and give him a hug! Nice job, Mom, praising Dad!" If the significant other is at all critical, interrupt and ask what was done well. "OK, we're only talking about what it was that he did that was great. Right, he remained calm! [To the father] Now tell me what the chore is for and how long." The parent role-plays again, giving the significant other the chance to praise again. The therapist should always summarize the parts of the role play that were done well.

Role Play #3: The Child Is Disruptive or Out of Control While Doing the Chore

"It is important to remain calm when your child becomes upset after being assigned a chore. You have just learned what to do if your child refuses to do the chore or remains upset after being assigned the chore. You know to tell him that you cannot start the timer until he starts the chore, and you know to give him the choice of doing a chore or losing a privilege. Now, let's discuss what to do if he has started the chore but is still out of control:"

1. Started to do chore calmly but became increasingly upset to the point that the child is out of control.
2. The child is out of control and starts to do chore.

The therapist directs the parent to act as a child who complains about doing a chore. "OK [child's name], I believe you have taken my $20 bill because it was missing from my wallet and I found it in your pocket, so you need to go clean the shower and scrub the bathtub for an hour. [The child complains and refuses to do the chore.] I won't be able to start the timer until you start working on the chore. [The child becomes angry and continues to complain.] At this point, I will walk away and ignore my child. I will wait a few minutes."

1. If your child decides to do the chore but then becomes upset to the point of being out of control, then you need to offer the choice of either doing the chore calmly or losing a privilege. "OK, you have a choice, either do the chore calmly (for an hour) or you may not watch TV tonight."
2. If your child is still upset and refuses to do the chore, offer the choice of either doing the chore or losing a privilege. "You can either do your chore (for an hour) or lose TV for tonight."

"OK, now I'll be [child's name]. Give me a chore for [low-rate behavior], and I will be difficult for you. Remember to tell me what I've done, what chore I have, and for how long."

Remember to:

1. Stay calm.
2. Tell the child what the chore is for and for how long.
3. Give the choice of either doing the chore calmly or losing a privilege.
4. Praise the child for doing the chore.

Again, have the parents praise each other if both are present. "OK, Dad, how did Mom do? Was she calm? Did she tell you what the chore was for and for how long? Yes! Did she tell you that she couldn't start the timer until she started the chore? Yes! Go on over and give her a hug! Nice job, Dad, praising Mom!" If the significant other is at all critical, interrupt and ask what it was that she did do well. "OK, we're only talking about what it was that she did that was great. Right, she remained calm! [To mother] Now give me the choice of either doing the chore or losing a privilege." The parent role-plays again, giving the significant other the chance to praise again. The therapist should always summarize the parts of the role play that were done well.

Role Play #4: Child Refuses to Do Chore

"If your child absolutely refuses to do the chore you have assigned, then you take away a privilege. Let's practice. You are [child's name], and I'll give you a low-rate chore for stealing. '[Child's name], I suspect you of stealing $20 from my wallet because it is missing and I found a $20 bill in your pocket. Now I need to ask you to scrub the shower and bathtub.' You as the child protest and complain about the chore. 'I cannot start the time until I see that you started your chore.' You, playing the child, continue to complain. I then give you the choice of either doing the chore or losing your Game Boy for the afternoon. If you have not started to walk toward the bathroom, then I take your Game Boy away."

Remember to:

1. Stay calm.
2. Tell the child what the chore is for and for how long.
3. Let him know that you cannot start the time until he starts the chore.
4. Offer the choice of either doing the chore or losing a privilege.
5. Take a privilege away.

For sessions with both parents, have them praise each other. "OK, Mom, how did Dad do? Was he calm? Did he tell you what the chore was for and for how long? Yes! Did he tell you that he couldn't start the timer until he started the chore? Yes! Go on over and give him a hug! Nice job, Mom, praising Dad!" If the significant other is at all critical, interrupt and ask what it was that he did do well. "OK, we're only talking about what it was that he did that was great. Right, he remained calm! [To the father] Now, after you have given the choice of doing the chore or losing the privilege, take the privilege away because he is not doing the chore." The parents role-play again, giving the significant other the chance to praise again. The therapist should always summarize the parts of the role play that were done well. After the role play review with the parents, answer any questions they may have. At this time, show and discuss Chart V.

Chart V: Commonly Asked Questions

1. What if my child likes to do chores? Young children commonly like to do chores along with their parents because it makes them feel like their big helpers. In the case of a "low-rate" punishment, the child does the chore alone, without the help of the parent. Also, your child will be doing a chore he normally wouldn't do.

2. What if I don't think my child's behavior should be punished? Because these behaviors are serious in nature, you want to ensure that they de- crease. The most effective way to do this is to give each incident conse- quences. This prevents the parent from becoming angry, lecturing and discussing at length, or issuing harsh or overly punitive punishment.

3. I don't want to accuse my child falsely. You won't be accusing your child of a problem behavior out of the blue. You suspect him of such behavior because of the circumstances, the child's explanation, and perhaps his fa- cial expression. Also, chances are your child has engaged in this behavior before, which gives you little reason to trust his explanation.

4. Will my child really learn from such a mild chore? Your child won't learn to do appropriate behavior from a punishment. Your child will learn to do positive behavior through positive reinforcement for _____. However, it is important to provide consequences for serious incidents with appropriate punishment techniques. When consequences are harsh, physical, or prolonged, many side effects will occur, such as increased oc- currence of behavior, increased aggression inside or outside the home, avoidance, and fear of the parent.

5. For behaviors that occur in clusters, does it make sense to just punish one of the behaviors and not the others? While you want to be clear about which behaviors are acceptable and which are not, you run the risk of using too much punishment. Excessive punishment always risks serious side effects. Using the low-rate program for an incident (which may in-

clude one or more problems) is much more effective than having them do a chore for breaking curfew, another chore for lying, another chore for stealing, and so on.

Assignment

The parent is to continue all programs and should be encouraged to introduce the low-rate behavior program and begin its implementation.

Reprimands

In this session the parents are taught the most effective way of using reprimands to reduce a child's undesirable behavior. Reinforcing the positive opposite behavior is the best way to change problem behavior. This process can be helped once in a while by adding very mild punishment, such as reprimands. Using reprimands for the inappropriate behavior, but only in combination with reinforcement for the desired behavior, promotes long-term changes in the child's behavior. Also, because parents commonly use reprimands, learning to do them correctly increases parents' effectiveness.

Objectives

To teach parents how to implement reprimands effectively.

Equipment and Materials

Handouts
- Rules for Using Reprimands
- Problem Behaviors Appropriate for Reprimands
- How to Give a Reprimand
- Point Chart/Time Out Chart/Attending and Ignoring Chart/School Program
- Weekly Assignment Sheet

Program Review

After welcoming the parent, review the low-rate program. Ask the parent if there was an opportunity to give a chore. Role play should be used for selected situations when the parent is explaining how the programs are running.

Therapist Introduction

"A reprimand is a form of punishment. It is usually a verbal expression of disapproval. However, gestures such as frowning, glaring, and head shaking also signal disapproval. The most powerful reprimand combines both a verbal statement and a gesture of disapproval.

"Many parents have used reprimands before but find they haven't been very effective. Parents have commented to us that reprimands may work at the time they are given, but the behavior usually continues in the future. However, we find that reprimands are not effective because they are not administered correctly. When using reprimands, most parents do not develop a reward program for the positive opposite or for appropriate behavior. Parents also fail to tell their children what behavior they desire. So whenever reprimands are used, the effectiveness of the reprimand depends on how much praise is given when the desired behavior occurs.

"Remember, always reinforce or reward appropriate behavior (relate this to the concept of positive opposite). Whenever we strengthen this appropriate behavior, we are ensuring that reprimands will be most effective. Another thing to remember is to single out a specific behavior to receive reprimands. If too many behaviors are reprimanded at once, the environment may become too aversive, and the child will try to avoid you. So to keep the environment as positive as possible, use reprimands for one problem behavior at a time, and be sure to reward the positive opposite behavior.

"Let's look at an example. A child is bouncing his basketball in the living room. His mother immediately walks up to him and in a firm voice says, 'John, stop bouncing the ball inside; something could break. I want you to take your basketball and play outside.' A moment later when John goes outside to play basketball, his mother praises John and says, 'Great job listening! I'm glad you're playing basketball outside!'

"Notice how praise was given immediately after John performed the desired behavior. We mentioned that a reprimand is a punishment, and it is intended and designed to weaken a behavior. However, unless reprimands are administered correctly, they will have little or no effect on decreasing inappropriate behavior. Therefore, it is really important to master certain skills so you can administer the most effective reprimands. The following rules have been taken from research that identified these parts to be present in reprimands that were successful in decreasing inappropriate behaviors." Show Chart I.

Rule #1: Always Praise Positive Behavior

1. Reprimands alone will not teach new or appropriate behavior.
2. Reprimands usually can reduce problem behavior more rapidly when a more desirable behavior is taught and praised. For example, "John, stop hitting the cat. You will hurt her. Play gently with her like you did yesterday." Then, as soon as your child complies, say, "I am pleased with how nicely you can play with your cat. You are being so gentle."

Rule #2: Use Specific Reprimands

All reprimands must specify three things:
1. What to stop
2. Why to stop
3. What to do instead

For example, "Joe, stop throwing your toys. You could break them. I want you to play gently with your toys or put them away." All three factors are present in this reprimand.

Rule #3: Use a Firm and Calm Tone of Voice

"You want to convey to your child that you are displeased by what he is doing. You also want to emphasize in a louder tone the key words, such as '*stop* throwing the ball indoors, because you could break something. Play with it outside.'"

Rule #4: Use Nonverbal Expressions of Disapproval

"Be sure to further indicate your disapproval with expressions or gestures such as a frown or a stare while delivering verbal reprimands. Be sure to *never* touch the child. *Don't grab or hit.*"

Rule #5: Deliver Reprimands When You Are Close to Your Child

"Be sure to move close to your child when delivering a reprimand. Reprimands are far more effective and have more impact when they are delivered as physically close as possible. It is easier to make better eye contact."

Rule #6: Do Not Ignore the Behavior If You Have Decided to Use Reprimands

"Do not ignore behavior that you have previously reprimanded. Remember the importance of consistency. You are teaching the child the connection between undesirable behavior and a reprimand. For example, hitting your brother = reprimand."

Rule #7: Physically Terminate Behaviors That Are Dangerous

"You must at times physically terminate behavior that is dangerous to the child or involves danger or risk to others. It is important to remember that we physically intervene *only* for the protection of the child or others. For example, your child is playing in the street, seriously attempting to hurt another, or destroying property—these are places to intervene immediately with something to remove the danger."

Rule #8: Back Up Reprimands When Needed

"When reprimands *do not* produce desired results, effectiveness can be helped by pairing them with procedures such as time out or loss of privileges but *never physical punishment*! For example, your child ignores your reprimand to stop teasing his brother. You must pair your reprimands with a loss of privilege. 'You can either talk nicely to your brother or you will lose TV tonight for not listening.'"

Rule #9: Stay in Control

"To be effective, you need only be firm, not out of control. Firm means your voice is controlled and your expression is serious. Remember, by staying in control you are modeling good control for your child, especially when he sees that you are really angry and still calm. Also, in the event a reprimand does not suppress the behavior, remember that you have several other things you can do."

Show and discuss Charts II and III.

Chart II: Problem Behaviors Appropriate for Reprimands

Playing ball in the house
Running in the house
Jumping on the furniture
Roughhousing
Playing too roughly with siblings or pets
Yelling or playing too loudly
Splashing water out of tub

Chart III: How to Give a Reprimand

There are many components to an effective reprimand. This chart lists the steps the parent should take for a reprimand to decrease the problem behavior.

The parent gives a reprimand: what to stop, why, and what to do instead.

If the child is compliant, praise the positive opposite.

If not, give a choice of positive opposite or loss of privilege.

If he chooses the positive opposite, praise the positive opposite.

If not, take the privilege away.

Role-Play Use of a Reprimand

The therapist should take the role of the parent and model the correct way to administer reprimands and praise desired behaviors. After each example is demonstrated, switch roles and have the parent demonstrate this skill. Prompts may be needed for the parent. Be sure to praise the parent's efforts. At least three role plays should be completed, including what to do when the reprimand is effective and what to do when it demands additional punishment (loss of privilege). For sessions with both parents, have each parent take the role of either the child or the parent so both parents are actively involved and not sitting in a chair.

The therapist should role-play how the parent should respond when:

1. The child complies with the reprimand.
2. The child doesn't comply right away, and the parent gives the choice of positive opposite or loss of privilege for not listening.
3. The parent takes the privilege away.

After modeling the use of reprimands for these situations, the therapist should reverse roles with the parent.

Role Play #1: Child Complies with Reprimand

The parent should perform the problem behavior, and the therapist follows this by giving a reprimand. "This time let's practice a situation when [child's name] is jumping on the furniture. It's important to make a couple of points when you're giving a reprimand in order to make it the most effective. The first thing I'll do is make sure I'm very calm when reprimanding, and I'll include what to stop, why to stop, and what to do instead. Once you follow the reprimand, I'll praise you for doing the positive opposite. '[Child's name], stop jumping on the furniture; it could break. I want you to sit on the couch or jump outside. [Parent should be directed to sit on the couch.] Great, you're sitting on the couch! That's excellent!' Now, I'll be [child's name] and you be the parent. I'll jump on the couch and you give me a reprimand. Remember to:"

1. Remain calm and firm.
2. Include what to stop, why, and what to do instead.
3. Praise the positive opposite.

Have the parent give the reprimand. Praise the parent for remaining calm and firm, for including what to stop, why, and what to do instead, and for praising the child for the positive opposite.

For two-parent families, it is important that the therapist encourages them to praise each other in an effort to develop a supportive environment and to help parents work as a team. "OK, Dad, how did Mom do? Was she calm? Did she include what to stop, why, and what to do instead? And did she praise the positive opposite? Yes! Go on over and give her a hug! Nice job, Dad, praising Mom!" If the significant other is at all critical, interrupt and ask what it was that she did do well. "OK, we're only talking about what it was that she did that was great. Right, she remained calm! [To the mother] Now tell me what to stop, why, and what to do instead." Parents role-play again, giving the significant other the chance to praise again. The therapist should always summarize the parts of the role play that were done well.

Role Play #2: Choice of Positive Opposite or Loss of Privilege

The parent should continue the problem behavior even after the therapist gives the reprimand but should choose positive opposite instead of loss of privilege. "This time, let's practice a situation when [child's name] is jumping on the furniture and doesn't stop right away. Again, it is really important to include a couple of points when you're giving a reprimand. The first thing I'll do is make sure I am calm and firm when reprimanding, and I'll include what to stop, why to stop, and what to do instead. As you continue jumping, I'll offer you a choice of either sitting on the couch [jumping outside] or losing a privilege for not listening. Now give me a hard time. Do what you think [child's name] will do when you give him a reprimand, but be cooperative before you lose a privilege. '[Child's name], stop jumping on the furniture; it could break. I want you to sit on the couch or jump outside. [Parent is directed to continue problem behavior.] Either sit on the couch or jump outside or lose your favorite show for not listening' [The parent is directed to sit on the couch.] 'Great job sitting on the couch!'

"Now, I'll be [child's name], and you be the parent. I'll continue jumping on the couch, and you give me a reprimand. Remember to:"

1. Remain calm and firm.
2. Include what to stop, why, and what to do instead.
3. Offer a choice of positive opposite or loss of privilege for not listening.
4. Praise positive opposite.

Have the parent give the reprimand. Praise the parent for remaining calm and firm, for including what to stop, why, and what to do instead, for offering the choice of positive opposite and loss of privilege, and for praising the child for positive opposite.

Again, in sessions with both parents, it is important that the therapist encourages them to praise each other in an effort to develop a supportive environment and to help parents work as a team. "OK, Mom, how did Dad do? Was he calm? Did he remember to offer the choice of either the positive opposite or the loss of privilege? Yes! Go on over and give him a hug! Nice job, Mom, praising Dad!" If the significant other is at all critical, interrupt and ask what it was that he did do well. "OK, we're only talking about what it was that he did that was great. Right, he remained calm! [To the father] Now, after you have given me the reprimand, remember to give me the choice of the positive opposite or a loss of privilege." The parents role-play again, giving the significant other the chance to praise again. The therapist should always summarize the parts of the role play that were done well.

Role Play #3: The Parent Takes a Privilege Away

The parent should continue the problem behavior even after the choice of positive opposite or loss of privilege. "This time let's practice a situation when [child's name] is jumping on the furniture and doesn't stop. Again, it is really important to include a couple of points when you're giving a reprimand. The first thing I'll do is make sure I am calm and firm when reprimanding, and I'll include what to stop, why to stop, and what to do instead. As you continue jumping, I'll offer you a choice of either sitting on the couch (jumping outside) or losing a privilege for not listening. Now give me a hard time. Do what you think [child's name] will do when you give him a reprimand. '[Child's name], stop jumping on the furniture; it could break. I want you to sit on the couch or jump outside.' [The parent is directed to continue problem behavior.] 'Either sit on the couch (or jump outside) or lose your favorite show for not listening.'

[The parent is directed to continue problem behavior.] 'It looks as though it is difficult for you to listen right now. You have lost your favorite TV show tonight.'

"Now, I'll be [child's name] and you be the parent. I'll continue jumping on the couch, and you give me a reprimand. Remember to:"

1. Remain calm and firm.
2. Include what to stop, why, and what to do instead.
3. Offer the choice of either the positive opposite or a loss of privilege.
4. Take the privilege away.

Have the parent give the reprimand. Praise the parent for remaining calm and firm, for including what to stop, why, and what to do instead, for offering a choice of positive opposite or loss of privilege for not listening, and for calmly taking a privilege away.

Again, in sessions with both parents, it is important that the therapist encourages them to praise each other in an effort to develop a supportive environment and to help parents work as a team. "OK, Mom, how did Dad do? Was he calm? Did he remember to offer the choice of either the positive opposite or loss of privilege? Yes! Go on over and give him a hug! Nice job, Mom, praising Dad!" If the significant other is at all critical, interrupt and ask what it was that he did do well. "OK, we're only talking about what it was that he did that was great. Right, he remained calm! [To the father] Now, after you have given me the reprimand, remember to give me the choice of the positive opposite or a loss of privilege." The parents role-play again, giving the significant other the chance to praise again. The therapist should always summarize the parts of the role play that were done well.

Assignment

The parent is to continue all programs and should begin using reprimands correctly for one behavior. Help the parent identify this behavior and use the tally sheet to mark progress.

Compromising
First Session

During this session, the parents are taught to discuss problem situations effectively with their child. The parents and therapist review and practice the techniques needed for successful discussion with their child. Assuming the parent reaches the session goals, the next parent session focuses on an actual situation the parent and child have argued over.

Objective

To teach the parents a strategy for resolving conflicts within the family.

Equipment and Materials

Handouts
- List of Negotiable and Nonnegotiable Issues for ages 7–8 and 9–13+
- Steps and Rules for Compromising
- Example of a Mediation Session
- Point Chart/Time Out Chart/Attending and Ignoring Chart/School Program
- Weekly Assignment Sheet

Program Review

Briefly review the programs currently implemented in the home. Remember to identify and reinforce positive parent behavior. Correct and, if necessary, role-play any changes that are made.

Therapist Presentation

"The purpose of today's session is to learn and try out a procedure to follow when there are problems among family members. All families have problems. How we manage those problems can make a big difference in how we get along.

This is not to promise that every problem has an easy solution or that everybody will be happy. However, we do feel it is better to try to work on problems at an early stage than to let them escalate and cause a major argument."

Presentation of the Child Bill of Rights

"In any home there are clear rules set out by the parent about behaviors or activities that are never allowed. As all parents know, each one of these rules will be constantly challenged by children as they grow up. As time goes by, the parent changes the 'nevers' in the rulebook to 'ask before you do it' activities. A good example is the rules for a 1-year-old child playing alone. It may be obvious to you that a 1-year-old child is never allowed to play alone. However, as the child gets older, it becomes OK to go into the backyard if permission is asked. And soon it is OK for your children to go to a movie and the mall as long as they ask their mom or dad first.

"Unfortunately, many changes in the rules happen because of an argument instead of a calm discussion where both the parent and the child are able to say their parts about what they don't like. What happens is that the child breaks the rules for a while and then gets punished for it. The child then gets the reward despite breaking the rules, so even when you tell him to be home by 8 P.M., he comes home at 9 P.M. and gets to stay out later. The most important guideline to follow when the rules are challenged is that all parties should always be given a fair chance to speak their opinions in a calm and understanding atmosphere. One of the best ways to teach children to respect others' opinions is to show them how to be respectful. You will also have the added benefit of knowing that they will be respectful when talking to you and that your opinions will be respected in return.

"Here is a list of issues [show Chart I] that we should take some time to review. Then we can label them as negotiable (acceptable) or nonnegotiable (unacceptable) for your child at this time. A Y means yes and that you can sit down and talk about it, and an N means no and that no discussion is allowed. Some of the acceptables and unacceptables will change in the future as your child gets older, like getting a driver's license. However, most of the items will be labeled with a Y because I'm sure you would be willing to at least sit down and calmly discuss the issue. Let's label some of these items on the list to get an idea of some of the things that might be negotiable."

The therapist with the parent should now label each of the issues on Chart I.

Please mark items with a *Y* for negotiable and *N* for nonnegotiable. *Y* means that it can be discussed, not necessarily allowed.

For ages 7 and 8

Having friends sleep over	When to do homework
Having a pet	Crossing the street alone
Dress style	Riding bicycle farther away
Bedtime	Walking to school alone
Snack time	Time to watch TV
What to have for snack	What to watch
Chores	Having certain toys
Having friends over	Taking the bus alone
Going to a friend's house	Allowance

For ages 9–13+

Having friends sleep over	Time on the phone
R-rated movies	Friends
Having a pet	When to do homework
Hair color, permanents	Dating
Curfew	Hairstyle
Going to concerts	Overnights with friends
Wearing makeup	Parties
Choice in music	Dances
Learning to drive	Tattoos
Piercing ears and other body parts	Allowance
Being sexually active	Spending habits
Chores	Privacy

"As we discuss the rules of negotiating and as you and your child get really good at settling disagreements, you will notice that many things that seemed nonnegotiable in the past are really issues both you and your child will be able to discuss calmly. For example." [The therapist should select a nonnegotiable issue the parent has identified and give an example of how the issue could be negotiated. It is important to identify an issue that a majority of parents would eventually negotiate with their children. The therapist should stay away from volatile issues at this point in treatment, such as smoking and being sexually active. The goal for this task is to teach the parent that when handled in the right way, very few issues will be cause for argument. Rather, the way the parent and the child discuss the issue is the important goal for the session.]

Presentation of Steps of Compromising, Including the Conflict Resolution Rules

"The process of compromising is a step-by-step method that requires flexibility according to each situation. [Show Chart II.] Here are the steps. I'll start by reviewing them and also some rules that I am sure will be helpful to you for compromising with your child. The first step is opening the session. That means you sit down with your child and express a willingness to discuss the situation as long as you are both calm. You should then take time to review the rules of compromising. Let's review them together now." The therapist should then review the rules of compromising with the parent.

Chart II: Steps and Rules for Compromising (First Session)

In Step 1, open the session and review the rules of compromising.

- Be calm. This is critical! However, you are human, too, and this is not always possible, so maybe leave the room or make a phone call, something that allows you time to get at least a little calm.
- Be as objective as you can. Go into all discussions with an open mind, and don't make any decisions until you hear all of the information from your child.
- Be a good listener. Good communication skills are essential to compromise and influence each step of the process. Often the problem is clouded by issues in the relationship or the situation, and sometimes these things can make it very hard to be a good listener. For example, you may be angry at your child for having broken a rule or feel you cannot compromise because the child will not follow the new rules either. When you are communicating effectively, you should acknowledge emotions and ask questions to make sure you understand the other's view of things.
- Be respectful. Both you and your child should treat each other with respect and understanding.
- Stay on the subject. Do not get sidetracked to other issues. Try to resolve one conflict at a time.
- Offer suggestions when you disagree. Don't just say no to a request. Try to offer an alternative, even if it is just a small step toward the child's goal.
- Focus on the present and what you would like to happen. Don't bring up the past.

Step 2 is gathering information. You want to calmly clarify each person's point of view about the situation. You should begin by gathering the information from your child and then summarize to be sure you have accurately heard the information. Then you should state your child's view of the issues and have the child summarize your point of view.

Step 3 is focusing on common interests. Some families focus on areas they disagree on, but there are also aspects of the issue that you and your child do agree on. It is important to focus on these issues. An example might be: "We both feel that you should be able to stay out later." One question that should be addressed is "What will happen if we don't try to resolve this?" The answer to this question is always "I guess we will continue to argue, and I will end up getting mad and so will you."

Step 4 is creating options.
- Say any ideas that come to mind.
- Do not judge or discuss the ideas.
- Come up with as many ideas as possible.

When we do Step 4, the most important thing to do is think of as many options as you can, even if they are only in your wildest dreams. The other thing to remember is that suggesting something or hearing a suggestion doesn't mean that suggestion will be the one that is chosen when the final agreement is written.

Step 5 is evaluating options and choosing a solution. Now you decide together which options you can really try in real life. Both of you will probably have some pretty clear ideas about the options you disagree with, so you both should decide which options on the list neither of you could live with and then eliminate each of those immediately. After that, you two can discuss which options would work in real life and then choose one together.

Step 6 is to write the actual agreement. You write down the solution you chose together and agree to work with it for 1 week. After 1 week, the agreement can be recompromised if it is not working for either you or your child.

Positive Changes of Communication Habits

Solutions are what we want from these sessions, but it is more important to show the best problem-solving behavior than to reach a solution. This session focuses on the skill of compromising, not the skill of working out every argument until you and your child agree.

In the end, it is more important to take the time to sit and talk politely than it is to force a solution to happen. When we are learning about compromising, the essential part is to stay calm and follow the rules and the steps of compromising.

Example of a Mediation Session

The goal for the hypothetical mediation session is to model and praise appropriate parent behavior. Any issues that would interfere with a successful mediation session should be addressed so that the discussion or redirection does not happen during the parent–child session. The most important goal for the therapist is to model appropriate behavior so the parent can guide the next session when the child is present.

"Now we are going to practice using the skills we just reviewed. The situation involves how a child dresses. [Give Chart III to the parent.] As you can see, this is a script with lines for each character. I will be reading the parent lines, and you read the child lines. Where you see the line of stars (asterisks), that's where I would like to interrupt to give a little feedback, so when you see that, I'll make comments that are not written on the sheets you have. Parts of this example, if not all, may seem unrealistic. However, the most important part about today's session is practicing the skills of compromising. If we can be prepared by practicing for negotiating or compromising, then we can best handle most situations that arise with children. I'll start reading."

Chart III: Example of a Mediation Session

Note: Parent reads all "child" lines and therapist reads all "parent" lines.

Step 1: Open the discussion (with the therapist acting as the parent).

Parent: I know that we both feel differently about the clothes that you are wearing. I would like to talk with you about this, and I think that if we both follow some rules, then we can discuss this without either one of us getting really angry. Let's review some steps and the rules. Step 1 is to open the discussion and review the rules of negotiating. Here we go.

Present and explain resolution rules sheet.

1. We need to be calm. We can take a break if we become upset.
2. We want to be objective and listen to the other person's point of view.
3. Let's be good listeners. We can't interrupt.
4. We want to be respectful. We can't call each other names.
5. We need to stay on the subject.
6. We have to offer suggestions when we disagree. We can't just say no.
7. We need to focus on the present. Let's not bring up the past.

*****Therapist: Did you notice the way I opened the discussion in a non-threatening way and stated the rules in a calm fashion? Now I'll go on to Step 2 and get information.

Step 2: Gather Information

Parent: Step 2 is when we gather information. That's when I get to say what I think and you get to say what you think. Let's see. We disagree because I told you that I wanted you to change before you went out of the house. Tell me why you honestly want to wear that out this evening.

Child: All of the kids dress this way. You just don't understand.

Parent: You are right. Maybe I don't understand. What are the kids wearing?

*****Therapist: Did you see how I was asking you for information instead of using my own possibly outdated information?

Child: You always complain about my pants being too baggy or too tight. Nothing is ever good enough for you. Also, you always say that I look sloppy because my shirt is not tucked in. I never comment on how you look. I would like to be able to wear what I want some of the time without having to worry about what you think or what you are going to say. You know I always try to wear something a little more conservative out to dinner with the family.

Parent: I'll summarize what you just said. It seems like you are saying that I very often don't compliment you on how you look and complain about what you are wearing. In particular, you feel that I say your pants don't fit or you look sloppy. What I worry about is what other people think of you. If you wear clothes that are sloppy, then people might not think you care about the way you look. I also think you should be able to choose what you want to wear some of the time without having to worry about any comments from me. However, it is important at certain times to be taken seriously. Now you get to summarize what I just said.

Child: Well, you want people to take me seriously, and sometimes the way I dress may make people think I'm sloppy with everything, not just my clothing.

Parent: That was nice. You are so calm, and you're really paying attention.

*****Therapist: Again, as the parent, I stayed calm instead of reacting to the situation. I praised you for calmly telling me you would like things different, and then I asked you to give me a summary of my viewpoint so I was sure you understood my viewpoint.

Step 3: Focus on Common Interests

Parent: Step 3 is when we get to look at the things we agree on. So what do we both agree on? It looks like we both feel that at times you should be able to wear what you want.

Child: I guess also we both care about what others think. I care about my friends, and you care about my teachers and other adults.

Parent: What will happen if we don't try to resolve this?

Child: I guess we will continue to argue. I'll end up getting mad, and so will you.

Step 4: Create Options

Parent: Step 4 is when we think of any options (solutions) to the problem. Let's come up with some ways that this can work. Let's put out all the ideas, and we'll evaluate them later. I'll start.

1. You wear what you want all the time.
2. I tell you what to wear all the time.

Child:

3. I wear what I want 50% of the time, and you tell me what to wear 50% of the time.
4. I wear what I want with my friends, and you tell me what to wear when we're with grown-ups.

Parent: Those are good ideas.

5. You can wear what you want to school as long as it goes by school rules, and we can discuss what you wear with grown-ups.

Step 5: Evaluate Options and Choose a Solution

Parent: Now that we both came up with some choices, let's evaluate these ideas. Number 3 (wearing what I want half the time), number 4 (wear what you want with your friends and wear what I want with grown ups), and number 5 (wearing what you want to school and talking about what to wear with grown ups) would be OK with me, but number 1 and number 2 would not work.

Child: Yeah, and I think number 4 (wear what I want with my friends, and wear what you want with grown ups) is OK, too.

Parent: Let's review the options we chose:

3. I wear what I want 50% of the time, and you tell me what to wear 50% of the time.
4. I wear what I want with my friends, and you tell me what to wear when we're with grown-ups.
5. You can wear what you want to school as long as it goes by school rules, and we can discuss what you wear with grown-ups.

[To child] Which one do you like the best?

Child: "I like number 4 (wearing what I want with friends, wearing what you want with grown ups). What about you, Mom?

Parent: I'll try that for a week as long as we can talk about this again in 1 week.

Child: OK.

*****Therapist: "It was really important to calmly evaluate all the ideas and not criticize any of them. Notice how calmly we discussed this situation.

Step 6: Write the Agreement

Parent: Now we are on the sixth step, writing the agreement. Now we need to write down what we both agreed on. Let's see, I said that you could wear what you want with your friends. What do I get to do?

Child: I said that you could pick my clothes out when we are with grown-ups.

Parent: The important point here is that we discussed this situation together so that in the end it was a calm discussion we were both participating in, instead of just two people yelling at each other. That was excellent.

*****Therapist: There are many things we got to practice today as a pretend parent and child, and I think you did a really good job of seeing how calm you need to be when two people are discussing a situation they don't agree on. Also, this was a mock situation that was resolved easily. It may be more difficult next week because it will be a more personal issue, and your child may generate some solutions you disagree with. To reinforce your child's participation, we have to encourage your child's solutions, even if they are sillier than you would like. Now when you come in next week with [child's name], I'll ask you both to generate topics you want from each other, either what you want from [child's name] or that he wants from you that he cannot have, and I'll probably pick the one your child wants. We do this because we want to help [child's name] discuss difficult issues in a calm, cooperative manner. Also, by choosing one of your child's topics, you are modeling how to negotiate in a positive, productive manner.

Assignment

"This week I would like you to continue all programs at home that are currently set up. I will continue to call you to see how things are going. Next week we are going to meet together with [child's name] so that we can practice a negotiating session. What I'd like you to do is think of some issues to practice compromising. It might help you if you took a look at the list of behaviors we labeled at the beginning of the session.

Compromising
Second Session

During this session, the child and parents are together to practice the skills learned in the previous session. The role of the therapist is to moderate and to guide, evaluate, and praise the parent and child through the entire communication process while they are working on a common solution to a problem.

Objectives

To teach the parent and child a strategy for resolving conflicts.
To guide them through appropriate communication about one problem area.

Equipment and Materials

Handouts
- Steps and Rules for Compromising
- Compromising on a Hypothetical Problem
- Compromising on a Real-Life Problem
- Two index cards
- Two pencils
- Point Chart/Time Out Chart/Attending and Ignoring Chart/School Program
- Weekly Assignment Sheet

Therapist Presentation of Session

"Today we are going to work on a skill needed when there are problems between any family members or even between friends. It is called compromising. All families have problems. How we manage those problems can make a big difference in how we get along. I am going to give you both a card, and I want you to write down three things that neither of you agrees on. Then we are going to select one of the six situations and try to discuss it calmly." Give out cards, and allow them a few minutes to write down situations. If there are problems, give some examples, such as some parents and children disagree on a curfew time, chores at home, friends, or living arrangements.

Collect the cards from parent and child. "It's great that you both came up with good ideas." The therapist selects one to work on during the session. It would be beneficial to choose one of the child's issues to work on because the primary goals for the session are to praise the parent for remaining calm, allow the child to discuss an issue, and make alternative suggestions when the child disagrees with what the parent is saying, or vice versa. "There are certain steps to follow when compromising, and when these are followed, people get along better. Your Mom [Dad] is really good at this and will help lead. [To parent] Here is a sheet [show Chart I] with the steps for compromising to help you both follow along. Mom [Dad], why don't you begin by reviewing the steps and rules with [child's name]? Sometimes examples help, so I may be interrupting." Have the parent review the rules and the steps with the child.

Chart I: Steps and Rules for Compromising

Step 1: Open the session and review the rules.
1. We need to be calm. We can take a break if we become upset.
2. We want to be objective and listen to the other person's point of view.
3. Let's be good listeners. We can't interrupt.
4. We want to be respectful. We can't call each other names.
5. We need to stay on the subject.
6. We have to offer suggestions when we disagree. We can't just say no.
7. We need to focus on the present. Let's not bring up the past.

Step 2: Gather information.
Step 3: Focus on common interests.
Step 4: Create solutions.
Step 5: Evaluate options and choose a solution.
Step 6: Write the agreement.

"Great, Now that you both have reviewed the steps and rules, we can go on to using them. The first thing we are going to do is practice working on a pretend problem. Here is the scenario." Give one copy of Chart II to the parent and one to the child. "You [to child] read the lines that begin with 'child'—they start on page 2—and [to parent] you read the lines that begin with 'parent.' The situation you will be reading about is a boy who wants to change his curfew, but his mother is concerned about his safety and so she has been pretty strict about keeping it early. When you are reading, listen carefully to the way the parent and the child generate options and then in the end come to an agreement about a different curfew time."

The therapist should allow the parent to guide the session with the use of the handout. The therapist guides and directs along the way, depending on parent ability.

Note to the therapist: During this entire session, your goal is to find and point out positive interactions between the child and the parents, especially to identify positive parent techniques that have been discussed and practiced during the last session. The therapist should interrupt ("Wait a minute! I have to stop you to tell you how well you are doing at . . .") to note positive interactions.

Hypothetical Problems

Chart II: Compromising in a Hypothetical Problem

Note: Parent reads all "parent" lines and child reads all "child" lines.

Step 1: Open the Session

Parent: I know that we both feel differently about your curfew. I would like to talk about this with you, and I think that if we both follow some rules, then we can discuss this without either one of us getting really angry. Let's briefly review the rules that are part of Step 1, opening the discussion.

[The parent should present the rules sheet to the child.]

1. We need to be calm. We can take a break if we become upset.
2. We want to be objective and listen to the other person's point of view.
3. Let's be good listeners. We can't interrupt.
4. We want to be respectful. We can't call each other names.
5. We need to stay on the subject.
6. We have to offer suggestions when we disagree. We can't just say no.
7. We need to focus on the present. Let's not bring up the past.

Step 2: Gather Information

Parent: Now we need to get some information so we can both know the other person's position. Let's see. We disagree because I said that you had to be in by 9 p.m. Tell me about what you honestly want in terms of a change in your curfew.

Child: Well, all my friends get to stay out till at least 10 p.m., and all I'm asking for is 9:30 p.m. because I know I have to come home at some point.

Parent: You are right; maybe I don't understand. Tell me more.

Child: Since everyone lives a little closer to my friend Jane, they can pretty much make sure they are safe later at night, but we live far away, which means I also have to leave earlier to get home. Of course, I don't want to be in danger.

Parent: Let me see if I understand your point. You think you should be able to stay out later because you have to leave earlier to get home on time. You really want to stay out and be with your friends. What I worry about is you being out and alone so late. That's why I have you come home at 9 P.M., because I'll be sure you're walking home by 8:30 P.M. at the latest. Now you get to summarize what I just said.

Child: I guess you feel that it might be unsafe for me to walk home any later than 8:30 P.M. and that's why you want me home by 9 P.M.

Step 3: Focus on Common Interests

Parent: Well, I guess we both agree that you should be able to have fun and hang out with your friends.

Child: And I think we both want me to be safe.

Parent: What will happen if we do not try to resolve this?

Child: I guess we will continue to argue, and I will end up getting mad and so will you.

Step 4: Create Options

Parent: Let's come up with some ways that this can work. Let's put out all the ideas and we'll evaluate them later. I'll start.

1. You could come home whenever you want.
2. You could never see your friends.

Child:

3. You could let me try to get a ride so I'll be safe.
4. You could let my friends come over.

Parent:

5. I could pick you up later.

Step 5: Evaluate Options and Choose a Solution

Parent: Now that we both came up with some choices, let's evaluate these ideas. Numbers 3 (getting a ride), 4 (having your friends come over), and 5 (picking you up later) would be OK with me, but 1 and 2 would not work. Which ones do you like?

Child: Number 3 (getting a ride) or number 5 (getting picked up later) would be OK, I guess.

Parent: So let's review our options:

3. Getting a ride
4. Having your friends come over

5. Picking you up later

[To child] Which one do you like best?

Child: Number 3, getting a ride home so I'm safe.

Parent: That's good. So if you get a ride, you can come home at 10 P.M. And until then your curfew is still 9 P.M. and that's OK?

Child: Sure, I'll ask someone for a ride tomorrow at school.

Step 6: Write the Agreement

Parent: Now we need to write down what we both agreed on. Let's see, I said that you could come home at 10 P.M. I also said that your curfew will be 9 P.M. if you don't get a ride.

Child: And I said you could let me get a ride home and be home by 10 P.M. And also that I will be home by 9:00 P.M. if I don't have a ride.

Compromising in a Real-Life Problem

"You both did a wonderful job with that problem. Now that we've really practiced the skills needed to use compromising, we'll take this issue [from problems generated by child and parent] and try to solve it so both of you can come to an agreement. Remember, the most important part of the session is to talk calmly to each other and to generate as many options as possible to solve the problem. Sometimes, it is really hard to come to an agreement after just one conversation, so maybe we won't have a final agreement, but I'm sure you will both try hard to practice the new skills you need to help solve problems in the future. An important part of what we are doing today is learning how to discuss an issue, so although it is nice to come to a common solution to the problem, it is more important to learn how to discuss issues calmly. That way you have a better chance of resolving the problem.

"What you [to child] suggested here about _____ sounds really reasonable." The therapist should fill in the first blank on Chart III. "Let's have your Mom [Dad] begin the compromise again, using these guidelines." Present Chart III to the parent.

Chart III: Compromising on a Real-Life Problem

Step 1: Open the Session

Parent: I know that we both feel differently about [write in topic selected]. I would like to talk about this with you, and I think that if we both follow some rules, then we can discuss this without either one of us getting re-

---

ally angry. Let's briefly review the rules that are part of Step 1, opening the session. [Present and explain rules sheet.]

1. We need to be calm. We can take a break if we become upset.
2. We want to be objective and listen to the other person's point of view.
3. Let's be good listeners. We can't interrupt.
4. We want to be respectful. We can't call each other names.
5. We need to stay on the subject.
6. We have to offer suggestions when we disagree. We can't just say no.
7. We need to focus on the present. Let's not bring up the past.

Step 2: Gather Information

Parent: Step 2 is when we each get to say our viewpoints. Let's see. We disagree because _____. Tell me about what you honestly want.

Child: You don't understand, I _____.

Parent: OK, let me summarize what you just said. _____.
What I worry about is _____. Now, you summarize what I said.

Child: Your opinion is that _____.

Step 3: Focus on Common Interests

Parent: Step 3, what do we both agree on? It looks like we both feel _____
_____
_____.

Child: I guess also that we both care about _____
_____
_____.

Parent: What will happen if we don't try to resolve this?

Child: I guess we will continue to argue, and I'll end up getting mad, and so will you.

Step 4: Create Options

Parent: Step 4 is when we create options. Let's come up with some ways that this can work. Let's put out all the ideas and we'll evaluate them later. I'll start.

1. _____.
2. _____.

Child:

3. _____.
4. _____.

Parent:

5. _____ .

Step 5: Evaluate Options and Choose a Solution

Parent: Let's evaluate these ideas. We have _____ options. I think #_____

and #_____ would be good but #_____ would not be so good. Now

we have _____ options (include child options). Which ones do you like?

Child: I think #_____ and _____ , and (if applicable) #_____ would work.

Parent: If you could choose one of those options, which one do you like the

best?

Child: I think that I would choose #_____ .

Parent: So let's try #_____ .

Child: OK, that sounds good.

Step 6: Write the Agreement

Parent: Step 6, now we need to write down what we both agreed on. Let's

see, I said that you could _____ .

Now what do I get to do?

Child: I said that you could _____ .

Assignment

"Wow, you both just did a wonderful job of compromising in that situation. You both came up with lots of options. For this week, what I'd like you to do is try to keep this agreement for 1 week, and when you come in next week, we will take a couple of minutes to review how the week went. If we need to make some revisions to the agreement, that will be fine, because sometimes it does take a little time to come to a final agreement. And, as we know, the rules may change again when you get older, and you are able to handle even more responsibility. I know your Mom [Dad] is really willing to sit down and compromise whenever you two don't agree on something. Good luck with your agreement this week.

"Also, take this situation [chosen from remaining five ideas generated by the parent and child at the beginning of the session] and practice using your new compromising skills. Here are some guidelines, and you can use them to write the agreement you decide on." The therapist gives the chart to the parent.

Skill Review, Practice, and Termination

This is the final session unless there are circumstances that require further meetings. During this session, application of skills and techniques to behavior problems continues. In addition, the therapist summarizes the parents' participation in treatment and emphasizes progress that both the parents and the child have made. Last, the topic of termination is discussed, and the parents are encouraged to provide feedback on the positive and negative aspects of treatment.

Objectives

To complete a final evaluation of all programs.
To practice applying techniques to manage behavioral problems.
To allow the parent to teach and train the therapist as part of role reversals.
To summarize parents' involvement in treatment.
To address any termination issues.

Equipment and Materials

Handouts
  • Positive Interventions/Negative Interventions
  • Problem Behaviors with Appropriate Interventions
  • Beginning a Program
  • Cards for Problem Solving

Role Reversals

A novel feature of this session is the different way the several role-playing vignettes are completed. With the role-play situations, there is a point at which the therapist takes the role of the parent and the parent takes the role of the therapist. The therapist involved in these role reversals has two simultaneous tasks and responsibilities, namely, (1) to prompt the parent to engage in appropriate "therapist" behaviors, if the parent requires assistance, and (2) to serve as a parent who is "learning" the techniques. Often the therapist whispers to the parent when serving in the former role and prompting the parent. The therapist then can use a normal speaking voice when playing a parent within the role-play situations. In this way, the two roles of the therapist (real therapist— whisper; pretend parent—normal speaking voice) are readily delineated to the parent in the session.

A special feature of the role reversals is that the therapist (when playing a parent) does not perform in an exemplary way. The therapist performs in a way that requires the parent to identify that the performance needs to be better. For example, the therapist playing the parent may praise a child in one of the role plays, but the praise may be missing a critical ingredient (perhaps less than enthusiastic, not specific, or not involving approaching and touching). Invariably, a parent (playing the role of a therapist) catches and corrects the mediocre performance, and the role play is repeated. The parent (serving as a therapist) and therapist (serving as a parent) repeat role plays to help shape the performance of the parent.

Throughout the treatment in prior sessions, a given role-play situation is repeated to help shape parent behavior. In this session, the parent playing the therapist repeats role plays with the therapist playing a parent to help develop the therapist's behavior. The session is enjoyable for parents and therapists as the parent administers prompts, praise, and corrective feedback. As the therapist sees the parent do this, the therapist can help with the fine-tuning of giving prompts, praise, feedback, and shaping more generally.

Status Report

Welcome the parent. Have the parent give a status report of the child's progress and activities. Review and make any necessary final changes in programs.

Presentation

The therapist should select two or three skills that have been difficult for the parent to grasp or use as a part of training and cover them briefly. If no specific skills come to mind based on this particular family, the therapist should briefly cover positive reinforcement, shaping, and time out. This can begin with a statement such as "OK, I know by now you understand the procedures we have discussed. But if I had to summarize some of the most important procedures they would be positive reinforcement, shaping, and time out.

"Probably positive reinforcement is the key procedure of what we do. You can get almost any behavior you wish, if you immediately and consistently reinforce it. Praise and points given on a regular basis can develop the behavior very consistently. Eventually, after behavior is stable, these may not be needed. But they really can get the behaviors you wish. Can you give me an example of this?

"Shaping is probably the next most important concept. If you wait to reinforce a behavior, the behavior may not occur at all, or it may not occur very often. Behavior can be developed gradually by reinforcing small steps and then larger steps. A child can learn to work on his homework for a long period. But this would not work very well if you just say, "Work for 1 hour, and you can go out and play." An hour is a lot to ask of someone who is not regularly doing homework. It would be better to reward a brief period, say, 15 minutes, and over a period of time build this to longer periods of time. Can you give me an example of this?

"Time out is a special form of punishment that is really effective. Because it is punishment, time out must always be used with a reinforcement program. For time out, you take the child out of the situation for a short period, usually just a few minutes. Time out is given immediately after the undesirable behavior. Can you give me an example of this?"

The therapist should also focus on any difficulty the parent may have had with any of the techniques throughout the program.

"Here are some handouts that summarize much of what we have been talking about. They may also be useful for the rest of today's session." Give out the three charts and discuss briefly.

Practice Problem Solving

"Today we will continue to apply the skills we have learned to develop programs for the problem situations on these cards. (The material reproduced here on 3- × 5-inch cards for ease of use in the session.) Remember, we want to use reinforcement programs. We will also continue to do role plays like we did last time. I'll start with this first card." The therapist models solving the situation on the first card and should try to get through as many role reversals thereafter as time permits.

Card #1: The Therapist Models Developing a Program

"You get a call from your child's teacher. She says that he talks out in class and won't stay in his seat. She adds that he has not brought in his homework four times in the past 3 weeks. OK. We want to change these behaviors."

The therapist suggests using a home-based school program: "This would be a good time to use a home-based school program. I would ask the teacher if she would be willing to work with me on a reinforcement program to help your child behave better at school and do his homework consistently. If the teacher is willing, I would develop a program to reinforce the positive opposites of the problem behaviors. For example, I would include raising his hand when he wants to speak in class, staying in his seat, and turning in homework. I would inform the teacher and your child what the program involves, namely, that each school day he will bring to school a special card that lists the behaviors we want to improve. The teacher will rate how the child did that day and sign the card. The child brings the card home and earns points and praise for the positive behaviors he has done. The points are exchanged for specific material, activity, or privilege reinforcers. I would stay in touch with the teacher, get feedback from her concerning the program, and find out if there are any other problem behaviors we may need to work on in the future. I would also let her know what she has done to help the program along and tell her I appreciate her taking the time and effort to work with us.

"OK, now let's try a role play. You be the child, and I'll be the parent. First, let's role-play explaining the program and then how the program it would be done." (Role play begins and is repeated as needed.)

"Now it is your turn. Here is your card."

Card #2: The Parent's Turn

"You want your two children to set the table before dinner and do the dishes afterward."

The therapist should assist the parent in coming up with a reinforcement program. One possible program could be the use of an individual point program. The parent can divide the tasks between the two children. One child is assigned to set the table; the other does the dishes. Each child receives points and praise whenever the task is done. After the parent develops an acceptable reinforcement program, the therapist reinforces what the parent did correctly. Then the therapist can suggest another way of setting up the program: "Another way we could improve these behaviors is by setting up a group contingency program. The children are told that on the days that the table is set and the dishes are done, the group receives praise and points that are exchangeable for reinforcers. However, if one or both tasks are not done, no points are awarded to the group, but praise should be given to anyone who did do their part.

"OK, on this one I'll be the child. Choose one of the programs we just talked about, and let's role play how you would explain it to me and then how the program would work."

Parent Serves as the Therapist

After card #2 is done, the therapist and parent switch roles. The therapist then asks the parent for advice for the problems on the cards (acting like a parent). The therapist and the parent should also switch chairs. "Now we are going to do something different. For the next card, I'm going to be a parent who comes to you for advice on how to handle a problem situation with her child. These situations may seem more difficult than the ones we just did, but remember, when you think of what program or techniques could be used, look for a way to reinforce positive behaviors."

Card #3: The Therapist Role-Plays a Parent as She Reads the Card

"I have a problem with my child. When he gets angry, he swears at me. I usually deal with it by hitting him, and that usually takes care of it. But now I'm not sure what to do because my child is getting bigger and recently he shoved me back."

After reading the card, the therapist states to the parent, "OK, here is a little hint: even though you want to get rid of some of the behaviors here, you won't want to emphasize a punishment program. Tell me what you think a good program would be to change behavior." If necessary, the therapist should prompt the parent for a reinforcement program for speaking politely. If the parent starts with a punishment program, interrupt and remind her that we always want to start with thinking about how we can get the behavior we want.

One possible program could be a point incentive program where the parent announces whenever the child becomes angry, "OK, the program starts now. You can earn points for discussing the problem calmly, without swearing." The therapist should, when necessary, point out that while a time out program for swearing can be combined with the point program, the focus is on reinforcing the child when he discusses a problem without swearing. As before, the therapist should reinforce the parent for any correct response and encourage the parent to model the positive intervention through role play. After card #3 is done, the therapist says, "Here's another card. I'm still a parent who comes to you for help."

Card #4: The Therapist Role-Plays a Parent as She Reads the Card

"My child never listens to me. No matter what I ask her to do, she does not do it. She either ignores me, or she does the opposite of what I ask her to do. No matter how many times I tell her, she does not listen. I've tried taking things away, but it has not worked. I've taken away her allowance and grounded her for weeks at a time, but no matter what I do, nothing seems to work."

Again, if necessary, the therapist should prompt for a reinforcement program and discourage a focus on a punishment program. One possible program could focus on reinforcing the positive opposite, listening. After a definition is obtained for listening, a point incentive program could be developed.

Card #5: The Therapist Role-Plays a Parent as She Reads the Card

"My child's teacher calls and says that he has not been consistently turning in his math homework."

Again, if necessary, the therapist should prompt for a reinforcement program and discourage a focus on a punishment program. One possible program could focus on reinforcing the positive opposite, turning in his math homework. Perhaps the teacher could complete a small monitoring sheet for the parent to state that she received the homework so that a reinforcement plan can be developed at home.

Card #6: The Therapist Role-Plays a Parent as She Reads the Card

"My child often continues to ask for something even after I've told him no."

Again, if necessary, the therapist should prompt for a reinforcement program and discourage a focus on a punishment program. One possible program could focus on reinforcing the positive opposite, accepting "no." In this situation, the parent can simply attend to accepting "no" by praising or interacting with child and then ignore the child when he has continued to ask for something.

Card #7: The Therapist Role-Plays a Parent as She Reads the Card

"My child often comes in past his curfew."

Again, if necessary, the therapist should prompt for a reinforcement program and discourage a focus on a punishment program. One possible program could focus on reinforcing the positive opposite, coming home on time. After a definition is obtained for following curfew, a point incentive program could be developed. Also, the parent could combine this reinforcement plan with a low-rate program for breaking curfew.

Card #8: The Therapist Role-Plays a Parent as She Reads the Card

"My child does not always tell me where he is going when he leaves the house."

Again, as necessary, the therapist should prompt for a reinforcement program and discourage a focus on a punishment program. One possible program could focus on reinforcing the positive opposite, letting the parent know where he is going. The parent can develop a reinforcement plan for calling or telling the parent where he is going. Also, the parent could combine this reinforcement plan with a low-rate program for wandering or leaving the house without telling the parent where he is going.

Discussion of Changes and Termination

The therapist should begin the discussion by reviewing what the parent has learned during the meetings. The therapist should praise the work they have done and all the progress they have made. "This is the final session, and you have come a long way. Let me ask you how you think you may have changed since we began this parent training program. What do you do differently now, compared with how you were before we started treatment?" The therapist effusively reinforces any evidence of behavior change that is referred to in the parent's comments.

"In addition to what you have said, I have seen a lot of other changes. It seems to me that now you are able to" (try to list things that the parent does differently or that have shown improvement).

"Let me ask you one really important question. What would you say is the most important procedure of all of the different ones we have discussed and practiced?" (The therapist should not prompt unless this is absolutely needed. Either shaping or reinforcement is acceptable as the correct answer. If shaping is given, say, "Yes, because shaping involves two important things, positive reinforcement and proceeding in a gradual way.")

The therapist should next ask for feedback from the parents on the sessions—what they liked, what they wish had been different. Allow the parents to discuss their feelings about termination and their expectations for the future.

Tell the parents that the staff will be in touch with them periodically to gather information. Also, they should feel free to call the therapist in the future if they need assistance.

Chart I: Interventions

Positive Interventions

Point program: used for any positive behavior you want to increase (focus on up to three behaviors at a time), such as minding, getting along with a sibling, talking nicely, doing any chore, potty training.

Praise program: used for increasing any behavior (which happens more than once a day), such as talking politely, playing nicely, helping out, and listening to instructions, solely through the use of your attention and praise.

Shaping: used with any behavior you can break down into smaller parts to reinforce the smaller parts individually, such as picking up toys, going to bed on time, feeding a pet, putting dirty clothes in the laundry, and getting dressed on time.

Attending: used in conjunction with ignoring (giving attention to the positive opposite of the behavior you are ignoring), such as any positive opposite of the ignored behavior.

Negative Interventions

Time Out: used with verbal or physical aggression, such as hitting, pushing, punching, talking back, or swearing.

Ignoring: used with mildly annoying behaviors that do not need to be stopped right away, such as whining, interrupting, complaining, having an attitude, or pleading.

Reprimands: used with behaviors that parents decide need to be stopped right away, such as jumping or running in the house, yelling, and being loud.

Low-rate program: used with behaviors that occur no more than two or three times a week and are serious in nature, such as stealing, lying, property destruction, wandering away, and playing with matches.

Chart II: Problem Behaviors with Appropriate Interventions

Problem Behavior	Intervention
Back talk, arguing	Attending to the positive opposite (praise)
	Ignoring
	Reprimands

	Time out
	Denial of privileges
Bedtime problems	Attending to the positive opposite (praise)
	Point program
	Shaping
Not doing chores	Attending to the positive opposite (praise)
	Point program
	Shaping
Cleanliness problems	Attending to the positive opposite (praise)
	Point program
	Shaping
Disobeying curfew	Attending to the positive opposite (praise)
	Point program
	Shaping
	Low-rate chores
Dressing problems, dawdling	Attending to the positive opposite (praise)
	Point program
	Shaping
Fighting, teasing	Attending to the positive opposite (praise)
	Point program
	Reprimands
	Time out
	Time out of toys
	Denial of privileges
Fighting with peers	Point program for positive opposite
	Low-rate chores
Not doing homework	Contacting teacher
	Attending to the positive opposite (praise)
	Point program
	Home-based school program
Property Destruction	Making restitution
	Time out of toys
	Denial of privileges
	Low-rate chores

Running away	Low-rate chores
School problems	Contacting the teacher
	Attending to the positive opposite (praise)
	Home-based school program
Stealing	Making restitution
	Low-rate chores
Lying	Low-rate chores
	Time out
Tantrums	Attending to the positive opposite (praise)
	Point program
	Time out
	Parent walks away from the child
Truancy	Contacting the teacher
	Low-rate chores
Whining, coaxing, crying	Attending to the positive opposite (praise)
Pouting, bickering	Ignoring
	Reprimands
	Time out

Chart III: Beginning a Program

1. Define clearly and specifically the problem behavior and the positive opposite in terms of what you can see or hear.
2. Be sure you can observe the problem behavior before starting the program.
3. Decide what positive intervention you are going to use.
4. Use the intervention immediately after the behavior and every time the behavior occurs.
5. Use a negative intervention only as a backup.

Positive Interventions	Negative Interventions
Point program	Time out
Praise	Planned ignoring
Attending	Reprimands
Shaping	Low-rate behaviors
School program	

Glossary

ABCs of Behavior   Parent management training focuses on the contingencies of reinforcement to change behavior. A contingency refers to the relationships between behaviors and the environmental events that influence behavior. Three components are included in a contingency, namely, antecedents (A), behaviors (B), and consequences (C), ergo, the ABCs of behavior. The notion of a contingency is important not only for understanding behavior but also for developing programs to change behavior. See also Antecedents, Behaviors, and Consequences.

ABAB design   An experimental design in which the target behavior of a subject or a group of subjects is assessed to determine baseline performance. The experimental condition is then introduced and remains in effect until the target behavior changes. A reversal phase follows, in which the experimental condition is withdrawn. Finally, the experimental condition is reintroduced. A functional relationship is demonstrated if the target behavior changes during each of the phases in which the experimental condition is presented and if it reverts to baseline or near baseline levels when the experimental condition is withdrawn. Also called a *reversal design* because during the design the conditions often are "reverse" (baseline is reinstated).

Acceptability of treatment   The extent to which those who participate in treatment (e.g., children, adolescents, families, clinicians) view the treatment as reasonable, justified, fair, and palatable. A dimension that can be distinguished from effectiveness and that influences the likelihood that a treatment will be sought, adhered to, and executed correctly.

Antecedents   Stimuli, settings, and contexts that occur before a behavior and influence the behavior. The influence could be in the likelihood that the behavior is performed or in precisely what behavior is performed. Prompts and establishing operations are the main types of antecedents used to change behavior.

Applied behavior analysis   The extension of operant conditioning principles and techniques to address clinical, social, educational, and other areas within everyday life. Compare with Experimental analysis of behavior.

At-risk behaviors   Behaviors that increase the likelihood of adverse psychological, social, and health outcomes. Examples include use of illicit substances, truancy, school suspensions, stealing, vandalism, and precocious and unprotected sex.

Aversive event   A stimulus that suppresses a behavior that it follows or increases a behavior that results in its termination.

Avoidance   Performance of a behavior that postpones or averts the presentation of an aversive event.

Backup reinforcer   An object, activity, or event (primary or secondary reinforcer) that can be purchased with tokens. A reinforcer that "backs up" the value of tokens.

Behavior   Any observable or measurable response or act. (The terms *behavior* and *response* are used synonymously.) Behavior is occasionally broadly defined to include cognitions, psychophysiological reactions, and feelings, which may not be directly observable but are defined in terms that can be measured by means of various assessment strategies.

Chain   A sequence of behaviors that occurs in a fixed order. Each behavior in the sequence serves as a discriminative stimulus (S^D) for the next response. Each behavior in the sequence (except the first behavior) also serves as a conditioned reinforcer that reinforces the previous response.

Chaining   Developing a sequence of responses. The responses can be developed in a forward or backward direction in which one response is added to the other until the entire sequence is learned.

Classical conditioning   See Respondent conditioning.

Clinical significance   Refers to the practical or applied value or importance of the effect of the intervention. The effects produced by the intervention should be large enough to be of practical value or have impact on the everyday lives of those who receive the intervention as well as those in contact with them.

Coercion   Sequence of interactions between the child and parent (or others) that includes actions and reactions that increase the frequency and amplitude of angry, hostile, and aggressive behaviors. Ultimately, one person in the interaction gives in or backs away from the interaction. In the process, increasingly high-intensity interactions are unwittingly reinforced (through negative reinforcement). Aggressive children can be inadvertently rewarded for their aggressive interactions.

Conditioned reinforcer   See Secondary reinforcer.

Consequence sharing   A contingency arrangement in which the consequences earned by one person are provided to both that person and his or her peers.

Consequences   Events that follow behavior and may include influences that increase, decrease, or have no impact on what the individual does. Positive reinforcers (praise, tokens) are primary examples of consequences used in parent training.

Contingency   The relationship among antecedents (e.g., prompts, setting events), a behavior (the response to be changed), and consequences (e.g., reinforcers).

Contingency contract   A behavior modification program in which an agreement or contract is made between a person who wishes behavior to change (e.g., a parent) and the person whose behavior is to be changed (e.g., a child). The contract specifies the relationship between behavior and its consequences.

Contingent delivery of a reinforcer   The delivery of a reinforcer only when a specified behavior has been performed. Contrast with Noncontingent delivery of a reinforcer.

Contingent upon behavior   An event (e.g., praise, tokens, time out) is contingent upon behavior when the event is delivered only if that behavior is performed.

Continuous reinforcement   A schedule of reinforcement in which a response is reinforced each time it is performed.

Delay of reinforcement   The time interval between a response and delivery of the reinforcer.

Deprivation   Reducing the availability of, or access to, a reinforcer.

Differential reinforcement   Reinforcing a response in the presence of one stimulus (S^D) and extinguishing the response in the presence of other stimuli (S^Δ). Eventually, the response is consistently performed in the presence of the S^D but not in the presence of the S^Δ.

Discrimination   Responding differently in the presence of different cues or antecedent events. Control of behavior by discriminative stimuli. See Stimulus control.

Discriminative stimulus (S^D)   An antecedent event or stimulus that signals that a certain response will be reinforced. A response is reinforced in the presence of an S^D. After an event becomes an S^D by being paired with reinforcement, its presence can increase the probability that the response will occur.

Escape   Performance of a behavior that terminates an aversive event.

Establishing operation   An antecedent that temporarily alters the effectiveness of some other event or consequence. Motivational states, emotions, and environmental events are establishing operations because they momentarily alter the effectiveness of the consequences that may follow behavior and influence the frequency of some behavior.

Evidence-based treatments   Treatments that have empirical evidence in their behalf. Most treatments used in the context of psychotherapy have not been evaluated in research. The delineation of treatments with evidence is a relatively recent movement in an effort to identify those that have been shown to be effective in rigorous studies. Other terms are also used, including empirically validated treatments, empirically supported treatments, evidence-based practice, and treatments that work.

Experimental analysis of behavior   The experimental area of research within operant conditioning that includes both human and basic animal laboratory studies. Compare with Applied behavior analysis.

Externalizing disorders or behaviors   Problems or behaviors that are directed toward the environment and others. Primary examples include oppositional, hyperactive, aggressive, and antisocial behaviors. Externalizing disorders dominate as the primary basis for referring children and adolescents to inpatient and outpatient treatment. Compare with Internalizing disorders.

Extinction   A procedure in which the reinforcer is no longer delivered for a previously reinforced response.

Extinction burst   An increase in the frequency and intensity of responding at the beginning of extinction.

Fading   The gradual removal of prompts such as instructions or physical guidance. Initially, developing behavior is often facilitated by prompts. However, in most situations, it is important to fade the prompt. Fading can also refer to the gradual removal of reinforcement, as in the progressive thinning of a reinforcement schedule.

Feedback   Knowledge of results of one's performance. Information is conveyed regarding how the person has performed.

Functional analysis   Evaluation of the behavior and of antecedents and consequences associated with the behavior. A functional analysis identifies the "causes" of behavior, that is, current conditions that are maintaining the behavior, by directly assessing behavior, proposing hypotheses about likely factors that are controlling behavior, and testing these hypotheses to demonstrate the conditions that cause the behavior. The information from functional analysis is then used to guide the intervention by direct alteration of conditions so that the desired behaviors are developed.

Functionally equivalent responses   See Reinforcement of functionally equivalent behavior.

Generalized conditioned reinforcer   A conditioned reinforcer that has acquired reinforcing value by being associated or paired with a variety of other reinforcers. Money is a generalized conditioned reinforcer.

Group contingencies   Programs in which the criterion for reinforcement is based on the performance of the group as a whole. The group must perform in a particular way for the reinforcing consequences to be delivered. Whether the individual child receives the reinforcer depends not only on his or her behavior but also on the behavior of others in the group. In parent management training, the group can be two or more siblings.

Home-based reinforcement   A reinforcement program in which behavior is assessed and evaluated in one setting (usually the school), but the consequences are provided at home. For example, a child may receive an evaluation on how well he or she did in relation to some behavior (e.g., classroom deportment, completion of assignments) at school. The performance earns points and backup reinforcers that are provided at home.

Incompatible behavior   A behavior that interferes with, or cannot be performed at the same time as, another behavior.

Inept child-rearing practices   A term used to summarize parenting practices associated with oppositional and aggressive behavior. These practices include attending to and reinforcing deviant child behavior, using commands to the child excessively, using harsh punishment, failing to attend to positive behavior, engaging in coercive parent–child interchanges, and failing to monitor children and their whereabouts.

Interapy   Psychological treatment that is provided through the use of the Internet. This is a computer-based way of delivering treatment without the necessity of face-to-face contact with a therapist. Treatment can be individualized to the family and to different clinical problems. Also treatment can be used by itself or as a supplement to other treatments (e.g., see Lange et al., 2003; Ritterband et al., 2003). Also referred to as internet-mediated therapy.

Intermittent reinforcement   A schedule of reinforcement in which only some occurrences of a response are reinforced.

Internalizing disorders or behaviors   Problems are directed toward inner experience. Primary examples include anxiety, withdrawal, and depression. Compare with Externalizing disorders.

Mediator   A factor that plays a role in explaining the basis for the change. In the context of therapy, a mediator is the mechanism or reason that change occurs.

Model   The person whose behavior is observed or imitated in observational learning.

Modeling   See Observational learning.

Moderator   A characteristic, variable, or factor that influences the effect of treatment. That is, treatment is differentially effective or varies in outcome systematically as a function of some other variable. Characteristics of the child (e.g., age, sex), parents and family (e.g., parent history of antisocial behavior, marital discord), and treatment (e.g., how many sessions) all might serve as moderators of treatment.

Multiple-baseline design   An experimental design that demonstrates the effect of a contingency by introducing the contingency across different behaviors, individuals, or situations at different points in time. A causal relationship between the experimental contingency and behavior is demonstrated if each of the behaviors changes only when the contingency is introduced.

Negative reinforcement   An increase in the frequency of a response that is followed by the termination or removal of a negative reinforcer. See Negative reinforcer.

Negative reinforcer   An aversive event or stimulus whose termination increases the frequency of the preceding response. The increase in frequency of the response that terminates or removes the aversive event is called *negative reinforcement.*

Noncontingent delivery of a reinforcer   The delivery of a reinforcer independent of behavior. The reinforcer is delivered without reference to how the individual is behaving. Contrast with Contingent delivery of a reinforcer.

Observational learning   Learning by observing another individual (a model) engage in behavior. To learn from a model, the observer need not perform the behavior or receive direct consequences for his or her performance. Also referred to as *modeling.*

Occasion   Presenting an S^D and thus increasing the likelihood that a response will be performed. Certain cues in the environment (e.g., music) occasion certain responses (e.g., singing).

Operant behavior   Behavior that is emitted rather than elicited. Emitted behavior operates on the environment and responds to changes in consequences (e.g., reinforcement, punishment) as well as antecedents (e.g., setting events, stimuli). Contrast with Respondent.

Operant conditioning   A type of learning in which behaviors are influenced primarily by the consequences that follow them. The probability of operant behaviors is altered by the consequences that they produce. Antecedents, too, are involved in learning as cues (S^D, S^Δ), become associated with different consequences, and can influence the likelihood of the behavior.

Parent Management Training   An intervention in which parents are taught social learning techniques to change the behavior of their children or adolescents. PMT is a specific treatment, rather than a generic approach of working with parents. The treatment is distinguished by (a) a conceptual view about how to change social, emotional, and behavioral problems; (b) a set of principles and techniques that follow from that conceptual view; (c) development of specific skills in the parents through practice, role play, and other active methods of training; and (d) integration of assessment and evaluation in treatment and treatment decision making.

Positive opposite   A behavior that is an alternative to and preferably incompatible with the undesired behavior. Suppression or elimination of an undesirable behavior can be achieved or accelerated by reinforcing a positive opposite. This is not a technical term but rather a useful way to approach the task of developing behavioral interventions. When the goal is to reduce or eliminate behavior, it is helpful to consider the positive opposite behaviors that are to be developed in its stead.

Positive reinforcement   An increase in the probability or likelihood of a response that is followed by a positive reinforcer. See Positive reinforcer.

Positive reinforcer   An event whose presentation increases the probability of a response that it follows.

Primary reinforcer   A reinforcing event that does not depend on learning to achieve its reinforcing properties. Food, water, and sex are primary reinforcers. Contrast with Secondary reinforcer.

Problem-solving skills training   Cognitively based treatment in which individuals are trained to approach interpersonal situations. Training focuses on the requirements of a particular task or problem, the behaviors that need to be performed, the alternative courses of action that are available, the consequences of these actions, and then selection of a particular solution. Individuals engage in self-instruction to guide themselves through the problem-solving approach.

Prompt   An antecedent event that helps initiate a response. A discriminative stimulus that occasions a response. Instructions, gestures, physical guidance, and modeling cues serve as prompts.

Punishment   Presentation of an aversive event or removal of a positive event contingent upon a response that decreases the probability of the response.

Punishment trap   A nontechnical term provided in this book to note that a parent (or teacher) is often trapped by a punishment contingency because use of punishment on the part of parents is invariably reinforced. This is *negative reinforcement*, which is defined as termination of an aversive state or situation contingent on some behavior. The aversive state or situation is something the child is doing or not doing (e.g., fighting with a sibling). The parents engage in some punitive action (screaming at or hitting the child). The aversive state ends immediately. This negative reinforcement of parent behavior (child cessation of the behavior) is immediate, contingent on the parent punishing of the child. Punishment is very effective in this instant in stopping the behavior. The difficulty is that the punishment does not usually influence the child's rate of behavior overall, even though the problem may have ended momentarily. The trap for parents is that this negative reinforcement controls their behavior and is likely to increase the use of punishment for child deviance in the future.

Reinforcement   An increase in the probability or likelihood of a response when the response is immediately followed by a particular consequence. The consequence can be either the presentation of a positive reinforcer or the removal of a negative reinforcer.

Reinforcement of alternative behavior Providing reinforcing consequences for a specific response that will compete with or is incompatible with the undesirable response, such as reinforcing cooperative play of a child with a sibling in an effort to reduce arguing and fighting. Cooperative play is incompatible with and opposite of arguing and fighting.

Reinforcement of changes in quality or characteristics Providing consequences for changes in intensity or characteristics of the behavior. A child may have very intense tantrums that include throwing things, hitting other people, crying, and screaming. Reinforcement can be provided by shaping less intense behavior. For example, the child may receive reinforcement for whispering rather than shouting or screaming.

Reinforcement of functionally equivalent behavior Behavior serves one or more functions. In this context, function means the consequences that follow the behavior. Functionally equivalent behavior refers to using the same consequences to support prosocial, positive behavior rather than deviant behavior. For example, tantrums, interrupting parents, and arguing receives attention from parents. With this schedule, the parents walk away from the child during these behaviors whenever possible but give attention and praise to the child when these behaviors are not going on. This closely resembles the other schedules but emphasizes use of the same reinforcer to support prosocial behavior.

Reinforcement of low response rates Providing consequences for a reduction in the frequency of behavior over time or in the period of time (e.g., minutes) in which the undesirable behavior does not occur. If a child engages in 10 episodes of some undesirable behavior (e.g., fights, throwing things, not complying), a reinforcement program is provided in which reduction in this number is shaped (gradually reduced). Tokens might be earned for reducing this to 8 per day; as this is performed consistently, the number is reduced. At the end of the program, 0 per day may receive tokens, with a special bonus for 2 or 3 days in a row with 0, and so on.

Reinforcement of other behavior Providing reinforcing consequences for all responses except the undesirable behavior of interest (e.g., praising the child any time he is not having a tantrum or screaming).

Reinforcement of positive opposites See Positive opposites.

Reinforcer sampling Providing the client with a sample or small portion of a reinforcer. The sample increases the likelihood that the entire event will be earned, used, or purchased. Reinforcer sampling occasionally is used to increase use of available reinforcers and hence the behaviors required to earn reinforcers. Reinforcer sampling is a special case of response priming in which the purpose is to develop or increase the utilization of an event as a reinforcer.

Resistance to extinction The extent to which a response is maintained once reinforcement is no longer provided.

Respondent Behavior that is elicited. Reflexes are respondents because their performance automatically follows certain stimuli. The connection between such unconditioned respondents and the antecedent events that control them is unlearned. Through respondent (classical) conditioning, respondents may come under the control of otherwise neutral stimuli. Contrast with operant behavior.

Respondent conditioning A type of learning in which a neutral (conditioned) stimulus is paired with an unconditioned stimulus that elicits a reflex response. After the conditioned stimulus is repeatedly followed by the unconditioned stimulus, the association between the two stimuli is learned. The conditioned stimulus alone will then elicit a reflex response. In respondent conditioning, new stimuli gain the power to elicit respondent behavior. Also called Classical conditioning.

Response See Behavior.

Response cost A punishment procedure in which a positive reinforcer is lost, contingent upon behavior. With this procedure, unlike time out from reinforcement, no time limit to the withdrawal of the reinforcer is specified. Fines and loss of tokens are common forms of response cost.

Response generalization Reinforcement of one response increases the probability of other responses that are similar to that response. Contrast with Stimulus generalization.

Response priming Any procedure that initiates early steps in a sequence or chain of responses. By initiating early steps, response priming increases the likelihood that the terminal response in the sequence will be performed.

Satiation Providing an excessive amount of the reinforcer. A loss of effectiveness that occurs after a large amount of the reinforcer has been delivered.

S^D See Discriminative stimulus.

S^Δ An antecedent event or stimulus that signals that a certain response will not be reinforced.

Secondary (or conditioned) reinforcer An event that becomes reinforcing through learning. An event becomes a secondary reinforcer by being paired with other events (primary or conditioned) that are already reinforcing. Praise and attention are examples of secondary reinforcers. Contrast with Primary reinforcer.

Setting events Antecedent events that refer to context, conditions, or situational influences that affect the contingencies that follow. Such events set the stage for behavior-consequence sequences that are likely to occur. See also Establishing operation.

Shaping Developing a new behavior by reinforcing successive approximations toward the terminal response. See Successive approximations.

Simulated practice Practice trials (opportunities) in role play or pretend situations in which the parent and child set up an artificial situation (e.g., at home) so the child can engage in the desired behavior. For example, the parent may say no to the child or say the child cannot go out and play. The child can receive consequences (praise, tokens) for engaging in prosocial behavior (acceptance of the parent's comment with mild frustration rather than the usual tantrum and screaming). The situation is preceded by the parent noting this is a simulated situation, that the child can earn tokens, and in the context of setting events in which the child is likely to be able to respond. The advantage of simulated practice is that it provides more opportunities for parents and children to engage in the behavior than might otherwise be available in the course of normal interaction.

Social learning theory   A conceptual framework within behavioral research that integrates the influence of different types of learning (respondent conditioning, operant conditioning, and observational learning) in explaining how behavior develops, is maintained, and is altered. Social learning theory emphasizes the significance of cognitive processes in mediating the influence of environmental events and performance.

Social reinforcers   Reinforcers that result from interpersonal interaction, such as attention, praise and approval, smiles, and physical contact.

Spontaneous recovery   The temporary recurrence of a behavior during extinction. A response that has not been reinforced may reappear temporarily during the course of extinction. The magnitude of such a response is usually lower than its magnitude before extinction began.

Stimulus   A measurable event that may have an effect on a behavior.

Stimulus control   The presence of a particular stimulus serves as an occasion for a particular response. The response is performed only when it is in the presence of a particular stimulus. See Discriminative stimulus.

Stimulus generalization   Transfer of a trained response to situations or stimulus conditions other than those in which training has taken place. The behavior generalizes to other situations. Contrast with Response generalization.

Successive approximations   Responses that more and more closely resemble the terminal behavior that is being shaped. See Shaping.

Target behavior   The behavior to be altered or focused on during treatment. The behavior that has been assessed and is to be changed.

Terminal response   The final goal of shaping or the behavior that is achieved at the end of training. See Shaping.

Time out from reinforcement   A punishment procedure in which access to positive reinforcement is withdrawn for a brief period contingent upon behavior. Isolation from a group exemplifies time out from reinforcement, but many variations do not require removing the client from the situation.

Token   A tangible object that serves as a generalized conditioned reinforcer. Poker chips, coins, tickets, stars, points, and check marks are commonly used as tokens. Tokens derive their value from being exchangeable for backup reinforcers. See Backup reinforcer and Token economy.

Token economy   A reinforcement system in which tokens are earned for a variety of behaviors and are used to purchase a variety of backup reinforcers. A token economy is analogous to a national economy, in which money serves as a medium of exchange and can be earned and spent in numerous ways.

Unconditioned reinforcer   See Primary reinforcer.

References

Adesso, V. J., & Lipson. J. W. (1981). Group training of parents as therapists for their children. *Behavior Therapy, 12*, 625–633.

Agency for Health Care Policy and Research. (1999). *Treatment of depression—Newer pharmacotherapies* (No. 99-E014; Evidence Report/Technology Assessment No. 7). Rockville, MD: Author.

Allinder, R. M., & Oats, R. G. (1997). Effects of acceptability on teacher's implementation of curriculum-based measurement and student achievement in mathematics computation. *Rase: Remedial and Special Education, 18*, 113–120.

American Psychiatric Association. (1994). *Diagnostic and statistical manual of mental disorders* (4th ed.). Washington, DC: Author.

Anastopoulos, A. D., & Farley, S. E. (2003). A cognitive-behavioral training program for parents of children with attention-deficit/hyperactivity disorder. In A. E. Kazdin & J. R. Weisz (Eds.), *Evidence-based psychotherapies for children and adolescents* (pp. 187–203). New York: Guilford Press.

Angold, A., Erkanli, A., Egger, H., & Costello, J. (2000). Stimulant treatment for children: A community perspective. *Journal of the American Academy of Child and Adolescent Psychiatry, 39*, 975–983.

Austin, J., & Carr, J. E. (Eds.). (2000). *Handbook of applied behavior analysis.* Reno, NV: Context Press.

Ayllon, T., & Haughton, E. (1964). Modification of symptomatic verbal behaviour of mental patients. *Behaviour Research and Therapy, 2*, 87–97.

Baer, D. M., Wolf, M. M., & Risley, T. R. (1968). Some current dimensions of applied behavior analysis. *Journal of Applied Behavior Analysis, 1*, 91–97.

Bagner, D. M., & Eyberg, S. M. (2003). Father involvement in parent training: When does it matter? *Journal of Clinical Child and Adolescent Psychology, 32*, 599–605.

Bank, L., Marlowe, J. H., Reid, J. B., Patterson, G. R., & Weinrott, M. R. (1991). A comparative evaluation of parent-training interventions for families of chronic delinquents. *Journal of Abnormal Child Psychology, 19*, 15–33.

Barkley, R. A. (1987). *Defiant children: A clinician's manual for parent training.* New York: Guilford Press.

Barkley, R. A. (1997). *Defiant children: A clinician's manual for parent training* (2nd ed.). New York: Guilford Press.

Barkley, R. A. (1998). Attention-deficit/hyperactivity disorder. In E. J. Mash & R. A. Barkley (Eds.), *Treatment of childhood disorders* (2nd ed., pp. 55–110). New York: Guilford Press.

Barkley, R. A., & Benton, C. M. (1998). *Your defiant child: Eight steps to better behavior.* New York: Guilford Press.

Barlow, J., Parsons, J., & Stewart-Brown, S. (2002a). Preventing emotional and behavioral problems: A meta-analysis of the role of group-based parenting programs for children aged 0–3 years. In *The Cochrane Library*, Issue 2. Oxford: Update Software

Barlow, J., Parsons, J., & Stewart-Brown, S. (2002b). *Systematic review of the effectiveness of parenting programmes in the primary and secondary prevention of mental health problems.* Oxford: Health Services Research Unit, Department of Public Health, University of Oxford.

Baskin, T. W., Tierney, S. C., Minami, T., & Wampold, B. E. (2003). Establishing specificity in psychotherapy: A meta-analysis of structural equivalence of placebo controls. *Journal of Consulting and Clinical Psychology, 71,* 973–979.

Benjet, C., & Kazdin, A. E. (2003). Spanking children: The controversies, findings, and new directions. *Clinical Psychology Review, 23,* 197–224.

Bierman, K. L., Miller, C. L., & Stabb, S. D. (1987). Improving the social behavior and peer acceptance of rejected boys: Effects of social skill training with instructions and prohibitions. *Journal of Consulting and Clinical Psychology, 55,* 194–200.

Boyle, M. H., Offord, D., Racine, Y. A., Szatmari, P., Fleming, J. E., & Sanford, M. N. (1996). Identifying thresholds for classifying psychiatric disorder: Issues and prospects. *Journal of the American Academy of Child and Adolescent Psychiatry, 35,* 1440–1448.

Brembs, B., Lorenzetti, F. D., Reyes, F. D., Baxter, D. A., & Byrne, J. H. (2002). Operant reward learning in aplysia: Neuronal correlates and mechanisms. *Science, 296,* 1706–1709.

Brestan, E. V., & Eyberg, S. M. (1998). Effective psychosocial treatment of conduct-disordered children and adolescents: 29 years, 82 studies, and 5275 kids. *Journal of Clinical Child Psychology, 27,* 180–189.

Brinkmeyer, M. Y., & Eyberg, S. M. (2003). Parent–child interaction therapy for oppositional children. In A. E. Kazdin & J. R. Weisz (Eds.), *Evidence-based psychotherapies for children and adolescents* (pp. 204–223). New York: Guilford Press.

Burns, B. J., Schoenwald, S. K., Burchard, J. D., Faw, L., & Santos, A. B. (2000). Comprehensive community-based interventions with severe emotional disorders: Multisystemic therapy and the wraparound process. *Journal of Child and Family Studies, 9,* 283–314.

Burns, D. D., & Spangler, D. L. (2001). Do changes in dysfunctional attitudes mediate changes in depression and anxiety in cognitive behavioral therapy? *Behavior Therapy, 32,* 337–369.

Capage, L. C., Bennett, G., & McNeil, C. B. (2001). A comparison between African American and Caucasian children referred for treatment of behavior problems. *Child and Family Behavior Therapy, 23,* 1–14.

Cavell, T. A. (2000). *Working with aggressive children: A practitioner's guide.* Washington, DC: American Psychological Association.

Cavell, T. A. (2001). Updating our approach to parent training. I: The case against targeting noncompliance. *Clinical Psychology: Science and Practice, 8,* 299–318.

Chamberlain, P., & Smith, D. K. (2003). Antisocial behavior in children and adolescents: The Oregon multidimensional treatment foster care model. In A. E. Kazdin

& J. R. Weisz (Eds.), *Evidence-based psychotherapies for children and adolescents* (pp. 282–300). New York: Guilford Press

Chambless, D. L., & Ollendick, T. H. (2001). Empirically supported psychological interventions: Controversies and evidence. *Annual Review of Psychology, 52*, 685–716.

Christophersen, E. R. (1988) *Little people: Guidelines for common sense child rearing* (3rd ed.). Kansas City, MO: Westport.

Christophersen, E. R., & Mortweet, S. L. (2001). *Treatments that work with children: Empirically supported strategies for managing childhood problems.* Washington, DC: American Psychological Association.

Connell, S., Sanders, M. R., & Markie-Dadds, C. (1997). Self-directed behavioral family intervention for parents of oppositional children in rural and remote areas. *Behavior Modification, 21*, 379–408.

Cooper, J. O., Heron, T. E., & Heward, W. L. (1987). *Applied behavior analysis.* Columbus, OH: Merrill.

Coren, E., Barlow, J., & Stewart-Brown, S. (2003). The effectiveness of individual and group-based parenting programmes in improving outcomes for teenage mothers and their children: A systematic review. *Journal of Adolescence, 26*, 79–103.

Cummings, N. A., O'Donohue, W. T., & Ferguson, K. E. (Eds.). (2002). *The impact of medical cost offset on practice and research: Making it work for you.* Reno, NV: Context Press.

Cunningham, C. E., Bremner, R., & Boyle, M. (1995). Large group community-based parenting programs for families of preschoolers at risk for disruptive behaviour disorders: Utilization, cost effectiveness, and outcome. *Journal of Child Psychology and Psychiatry, 36*, 1141–1159.

Dadds, M. R., & McHugh, T. A. (1992). Social support and treatment outcome in behavioral family therapy for child conduct problems. *Journal of Consulting and Clinical Psychology, 60*, 252–259.

Dadds, M. R., Schwartz, S., & Sanders, M. R. (1987). Marital discord and treatment outcome in behavioral treatment of child conduct disorders. *Journal of Consulting and Clinical Psychology, 55*, 396–403.

Dawes, R. M. (1994). *House of cards: Psychology and psychotherapy built on myth.* New York: Free Press.

DeRubeis, R. J., Evans, M. D., Hollon, S. D., Garvey, M. J., Grove, W. M., & Tuason, V. B. (1990). How does cognitive therapy work? Cognitive change and symptom change in cognitive therapy and pharmacotherapy for depression. *Journal of Consulting and Clinical Psychology, 58*, 862–869.

DiClemente, R. J., Hansen, W. B., & Ponton, L. E. (Eds.). (1996). *Handbook of adolescent health risk behavior.* New York: Plenum.

Dishion, T. J., & Andrews, D. W. (1995). Preventing escalation in problem behaviors with high-risk young adolescents: Immediate and 1-year outcomes. *Journal of Consulting and Clinical Psychology, 63*, 538–548.

Dishion, T. J., & Patterson, G. R. (1992). Age effects in parent training outcomes. *Behavior Therapy, 23*, 719–729.

Dishion, T. J., & Patterson, S. G. (1996). *Preventive parenting with love, encouragement, and limits: The preschool years.* Eugene, OR: Castalia.

Dishion, T. J., Patterson, G. R., & Kavanagh, K. A. (1992). An experimental test of the coercion model: Linking theory, measurement, and intervention. In J. McCord & R. E. Tremblay (Eds.), *Preventing antisocial behavior* (pp. 253–282). New York: Guilford Press.

Dumas, J. E., & Wahler, R. G. (1983). Predictors of treatment outcome in parent training: Mother insularity and socioeconomic disadvantage. *Behavioral Assessment, 5,* 301–313.

Durlak, J. A., Fuhrman, T., & Lampman, C. (1991). Effectiveness of cognitive-behavioral therapy for maladapting children: A meta-analysis. *Psychological Bulletin, 110,* 204–214.

Durlak, J. A., Wells, A. M., Cotten, J. K., & Johnson, S. (1995). Analysis of selected methodological issues in child psychotherapy research. *Journal of Clinical Child Psychology, 24,* 141–148.

Elliott, D. S., Huizinga, D., & Ageton, S. S. (1985). *Explaining delinquency and drug use.* Beverly Hills, CA: Sage.

Elliott, D. S., Huizinga, D., & Menard, S. (1988). *Multiple problem youth: Delinquency, substance abuse, and mental health problems.* New York: Springer-Verlag.

Evidence-Based Mental Health. (1998). (A journal devoted to evidence-based treatments and linking research to practice.) Volume 1, number 1.

Farmer, E. M. Z., Compton, S. N., Burns, B. J., & Robertson, E. (2002). Review of the evidence base for treatment of childhood psychopathology: Externalizing disorders. *Journal of Consulting and Clinical Psychology, 70,* 1267–1302.

Farrington, D. P. (1995). The development of offending and antisocial behaviour from childhood: Key findings from the Cambridge Study in delinquent development. *Journal of Child Psychology and Psychiatry, 36,* 929–964.

Farrington, D. P., & Welsh, B. C. (2003). Family based prevention of offending: A meta-analysis. *Australian and New Zealand Journal of Criminology, 36,* 127–151.

Firestone, P., Kelly, M. J., & Fike, S. (1980). Are fathers necessary in parent training groups? *Journal of Clinical Child Psychology, 9,* 44–47.

Flett, G. L., Vredenburg, K., & Krames, L. (1997). The continuity of depression in clinical and nonclinical samples. *Psychological Bulletin, 121,* 395–416.

Fonagy, P., Target, M., Cottrell, D., Phillips, J., & Kurtz, Z. (2002). *What works for whom? A critical review of treatments for children and adolescents.* New York. Guilford Press.

Forehand, R., & Kotchick, B. A. (1996). Cultural diversity: A wake-up call for parent training. *Behavior Therapy, 27,* 187–206.

Forehand, R., & Kotchick, B. A. (2002). Behavioral parent training: Current challenges and potential solutions. *Journal of Child and Family Studies, 11,* 377–384.

Forehand, R., & Long, N. (2002). *Parenting the strong-willed child* (2nd ed.). Chicago: McGraw Hill.

Forehand, R., & McMahon, R. J. (1981). *Helping the noncompliant child: A clinician's guide to parent training.* New York: Guilford Press.

Forgatch, M. S. (1991). The clinical science vortex: A developing theory of antisocial behavior. In D. J. Pepler & K. H. Rubin (Eds.), *The development and treatment of childhood aggression* (pp. 291–315). Hillsdale, NJ: Erlbaum.

Forgatch, M. S., & DeGarmo, D. S. (1999). Parenting through change: An effective prevention program for single mothers. *Journal of Consulting and Clinical Psychology, 67,* 711–724.

Forgatch, M. S., & Patterson, G. (1989). *Parents and adolescents living together. Part 2: Family problem solving.* Eugene, OR: Castalia.

Foxx, R. M., Bremer, B. A., Schutz, C., Valdez, J., & Johndrow, C. (1996). Increasing treatment acceptability through video. *Behavioral Interventions, 11,* 171–180.

Frank, J. D. (1961). *Persuasion & healing.* Baltimore, MD: Johns Hopkins University Press.

Frank, J. D., & Frank, J. B. (1991). *Persuasion & healing: A comparative study of psychotherapy.* Baltimore, MD: Johns Hopkins University Press.

Gershoff, E. T. (2002). Parental corporal punishment and associated child behaviors and experiences: A meta-analytic and theoretical review. *Psychological Bulletin, 128,* 539–579.

Glynn, S. M. (1990). Token economy approaches for psychiatric patients. *Behavior Modification, 14,* 383–407.

Gordon, D. A., & Stanar, C. R. (2003). Lessons learned from the dissemination of parenting wisely: A parent training CD-ROM. *Cognitive and Behavioral Practice, 10,* 312–323.

Green, C. W., Reid, D. H., Canipe, V. S., & Gardner, S. M. (1991). A comprehensive evaluation of reinforcer identification processes for persons with profound multiple handicaps. *Journal of Applied Behavior Analysis, 24,* 537–552.

Greenhill, L. L., & Ford, R. E. (2002). Childhood attention-deficit hyperactivity disorder: Pharmacological treatments. In P. E. Nathan & J. M. Gorman (Eds.), *A guide to treatments that work* (2nd ed., pp. 25–55). New York: Oxford University Press.

Gross, D., Fogg, L., Webster-Stratton, C., Carvey, C., Julion, W., & Grady, J. (2003). Parent training of toddlers in day care in low-income urban communities. *Journal of Consulting and Clinical Psychology, 71,* 261–278.

Hall, R. V., & Hall, M. L. (1998). *How to negotiate a behavioral contract* (2nd ed.). Austin, TX: Pro-Ed.

Hanf, C. (1969, April). *A two-stage program for modifying maternal controlling during mother-child interaction.* Paper presented at the meeting of the Western Psychological Association, Vancouver, BC.

Hembree-Kirigin, T. L., & McNeil, C. B. (1995). *Parent-child interaction therapy.* New York: Plenum.

Henggeler, S. W., Schoenwald, S. K., Borduin, C. M., Rowland, M. D., & Cunningham, P. B. (1998). *Multisystemic treatment of antisocial behavior in children and adolescents.* New York: Guilford Press.

Herschell, A. D., Calzada, E. J., Eyberg, S. M., & McNeil, C. (2002a). Parent–child interaction therapy: New directions in research. *Cognitive and Behavioral Practice, 9,* 9–16.

Herschell, A. D., Calzada, E. J., Eyberg, S. M., & McNeil, C. (2002b). Clinical issues in parent-child interaction therapy. *Cognitive and Behavioral Practice, 9,* 16–27.

Herzberg, A. (1945). *Active psychotherapy.* New York: Grune & Stratton.

Hibbs, E., & Jensen, P. (Eds.). (in press). *Psychosocial treatment for child and adolescent disorders: Empirically based strategies for clinical practice* (2nd ed.). Washington, DC: American Psychological Association.

Hinshaw, S. P., Klein, R. G., & Abikoff, H. B. (2002). Childhood attention-deficit hyperactivity disorder: Nonpharmacological treatments and their combination with medication. In P. E. Nathan & J. M. Gorman (Eds.), *A guide to treatments that work* (2nd ed., pp. 3–23). New York: Oxford University Press.

Hobbs, S. A., Forehand, R., & Murray, R. G. (1978). Effects of various durations of time out on the noncompliant behavior of children. *Behavior Therapy, 9,* 652–656.

Hollon, S. D., & Beck, A. T. (2004). Cognitive and cognitive behavioral therapies. In M. J. Lambert (Ed.), *Bergin and Garfield's handbook of psychotherapy and behavior change* (5th ed., pp. 447–492). New York: Wiley.

Hollon, S. D., Muñoz, R. F., Barlow, D. H., Beardslee, W. R., Bell, C. C., Bernal, G., et al. (2002). Psychosocial intervention development for the prevention and treatment of depression: Promoting innovation and increasing access. *Biological Psychiatry, 52,* 610–630.

Hood, K. K., & Eyberg, S. M. (2003). Outcomes of parent–child interaction therapy: Mothers' reports of maintenance three to six years after treatment. *Journal of Clinical Child and Adolescent Psychology, 32,* 419–429.

Horner, R. H., Dunlap, G., & Koegel, R. L. (Eds.) (1988). *Generalization and maintenance. Life-style changes in applied settings.* Baltimore: Paul H. Brookes.

Ilardi, S. S., & Craighead, W. E. (1994). The role of nonspecific factors in cognitive-behavior therapy for depression. *Clinical Psychology: Science and Practice, 1,* 138–156.

Jensen, P., Kettle, L., Roper, M., Sloan, M., Dulcan, M., Hoven, C., et al. (1999). Are stimulants overprescribed? Treatment of ADHD in 4 US communities. *Journal of the American Academy of Child and Adolescent Psychiatry, 38,* 797–804.

Jewell, E. J., & Abate, F. (Eds.). (2001). *The new Oxford American dictionary.* New York: Oxford University Press.

Kazdin, A. E. (1972). Response cost: The removal of conditioned reinforcers for therapeutic change. *Behavior Therapy, 3,* 533–546.

Kazdin, A. E. (1977). *The token economy: A review and evaluation.* New York: Plenum.

Kazdin, A. E. (1978). *History of behavior modification: Experimental foundations of contemporary research.* Baltimore, MD: University Park Press.

Kazdin, A. E. (1983). Failure of persons to respond to the token economy. In E. B. Foa & P. M. G. Emmelkamp (Eds.), *Failures in behavior therapy* (pp. 335–354). New York: Wiley.

Kazdin, A. E. (1995a). Child, parent, and family dysfunction as predictors of outcome in cognitive-behavioral treatment of antisocial children. *Behaviour Research and Therapy, 33,* 271–281.

Kazdin, A. E. (1995b). *Conduct disorder in childhood and adolescence* (2nd ed.). Thousand Oaks, CA: Sage.

Kazdin, A. E. (1996a). Combined and multimodal treatments in child and adolescent psychotherapy: Issues, challenges, and research directions. *Clinical Psychology: Science and Practice, 3,* 69–100.

Kazdin, A. E. (1996b). Dropping out of child psychotherapy: Issues for research and implications for practice. *Clinical Child Psychology and Psychiatry, 1,* 133–156.

Kazdin, A. E. (1997). Parent management training: Evidence, outcomes, and issues. *Journal of the American Academy of Child and Adolescent Psychiatry, 36,* 1349–1356.

Kazdin, A. E. (1999). The meanings and measurement of clinical significance. *Journal of Consulting and Clinical Psychology, 67,* 332–339.

Kazdin, A. E. (2000a). Adolescent development, mental disorders, and decision making of delinquent youths. In T. Grisso & R. Schwartz (Eds.), *Youth on trial: A developmental perspective on juvenile justice* (pp. 33–84). Chicago: University of Chicago Press.

Kazdin, A. E. (2000b). *Psychotherapy for children and adolescents: Directions for research and practice.* New York: Oxford University Press.

Kazdin, A. E. (2001a). Almost clinically significant ($p < .10$): Current measures may only approach clinical significance. *Clinical Psychology: Science and Practice, 8,* 455–462.

Kazdin, A. E. (2001b). *Behavior modification in applied settings* (6th ed.). Belmont, CA: Wadsworth.

Kazdin, A. E. (2002). Psychosocial treatments for conduct disorder in children and adolescents. In P. E. Nathan & J. M. Gorman (Eds.), *A guide to treatments that work* (2nd ed., pp. 57–85). New York: Oxford University Press.

Kazdin, A. E. (2003a). Problem-solving skills training and parent management training for conduct disorder. In A. E. Kazdin & J. R. Weisz (Eds.), *Evidence-based psychotherapies for children and adolescents* (pp. 241–262). New York: Guilford Press.

Kazdin, A. E. (2003b). *Research design in clinical psychology* (4th ed.). Needham Heights, MA: Allyn & Bacon.

Kazdin, A. E. (in press). Mechanisms of change in psychotherapy: Advances, breakthroughs, and cutting-edge research (do not yet exist). In R. R. Bootzin (Ed.), *Festschrift in honor of Lee Sechrest.* Washington, DC: American Psychological Association.

Kazdin, A. E., Bass, D., Ayers, W. A., & Rodgers, A. (1990). The empirical and clinical focus of child and adolescent psychotherapy research. *Journal of Consulting and Clinical Psychology, 58,* 729–740.

Kazdin, A. E., Esveldt-Dawson, K., French, N. H., & Unis, A. S. (1987). Problem-solving skills training and relationship therapy in the treatment of antisocial child behavior. *Journal of Consulting and Clinical Psychology, 55,* 76–85.

Kazdin, A. E., Holland, L., & Crowley, M. (1997). Family experience of barriers to treatment and premature termination from child therapy. *Journal of Consulting and Clinical Psychology, 65,* 453–463.

Kazdin, A. E., Holland, L., Crowley, M., & Breton, S. (1997). Barriers to Participation in Treatment Scale: Evaluation and validation in the context of child outpatient treatment. *Journal of Child Psychology and Psychiatry, 38,* 1051–1062.

Kazdin, A. E., Mazurick, J. L., & Siegel, T. C. (1994). Treatment outcome among children with externalizing disorder who terminate prematurely versus those who complete psychotherapy. *Journal of the American Academy of Child and Adolescent Psychiatry, 33,* 549–557.

Kazdin, A. E., & Nock, M. K. (2003). Delineating mechanisms of change in child and adolescent therapy: Methodological issues and research recommendations. *Journal of Child Psychology and Psychiatry, 44,* 1116–1129.

Kazdin, A. E., Siegel, T., & Bass, D. (1990). Drawing upon clinical practice to inform research on child and adolescent psychotherapy. *Professional Psychology: Research and Practice, 21*, 189–198.

Kazdin, A. E., Siegel, T., & Bass, D. (1992). Cognitive problem-solving skills training and parent management training in the treatment of antisocial behavior in children. *Journal of Consulting and Clinical Psychology, 60*, 733–747.

Kazdin, A. E., Stolar, M. J., & Marciano, P. L. (1995). Risk factors for dropping out of treatment among White and Black families. *Journal of Family Psychology, 9*, 402–417.

Kazdin, A. E., & Wassell, G. (1998). Treatment completion and therapeutic change among children referred for outpatient therapy. *Professional Psychology: Research and Practice, 29*, 332–340.

Kazdin, A. E., & Wassell, G. (2000a). Predictors of barriers to treatment and therapeutic change in outpatient therapy for antisocial children and their families. *Mental Health Services Research, 2*, 27–40.

Kazdin, A. E., & Wassell, G. (2000b). Therapeutic changes in children, parents, and families resulting from treatment of children with conduct problems. *Journal of the American Academy of Child and Adolescent Psychiatry, 39*, 414–420.

Kazdin, A. E., & Weisz, J. R. (Eds.). (2003). *Evidence-based psychotherapies for children and adolescents.* New York: Guilford Press.

Kazdin, A. E., & Whitley, M. K. (2003). Treatment of parental stress to enhance therapeutic change among children referred for aggressive and antisocial behavior. *Journal of Consulting and Clinical Psychology, 71*, 504–515.

Kendall, P. C. (Ed.). (1999). Special section: Clinical significance. *Journal of Consulting and Clinical Psychology, 67*, 283–339.

Kendall, P. C., & Chambless, D. L. (Eds.). (1998). Special section: Empirically supported psychological therapies. *Journal of Consulting and Clinical Psychology, 66*, 3–167.

Kessler, R. C., Merikangas, K. R., Berglund, P., Eaton, W. W., Koretz, D. S., & Walters, E. E. (2003). Mild disorders should not be eliminated from the DSM-V. *Archives of General Psychiatry, 60*, 1117–1122.

Ketterlinus, R. D., & Lamb, M. E. (Eds.). (1994). *Adolescent problem behaviors: Issues and research.* Hillsdale, NJ: Erlbaum.

King, G. F., Armitage, S. G., & Tilton, J. R. (1960). A therapeutic approach to schizophrenics of extreme pathology: An operant-interpersonal method. *Journal of Abnormal and Social Psychology, 61*, 276–286.

Kraemer, H. C., Kazdin, A. E., Offord, D. R., Kessler, R. C., Jensen, P. S., & Kupfer, D. J. (1997). Coming to terms with the terms of risk. *Archives of General Psychiatry, 54*, 337–343.

Krug, E. G., Dahlberg, L. L., Mercy, J. A., Zwi, A. B., & Lozano, R. (2002). *World report on violence and health.* Geneva: World Health Organization.

Kwon, S., & Oei, T. P. S. (2003). Cognitive processes in a group cognitive behavior therapy of depression. *Journal of Behavior Therapy and Experimental Psychiatry, 34*, 73–85.

Lange, A., Rietdijk, D., Hudcovicova, M., van de Ven, J., Schrieken, B., & Emmelkamp, P. M. G. (2003). Interapy: A controlled randomized trial of standardized treatment of posttraumatic stress through the Internet. *Journal of Consulting and Clinical Psychology, 71*, 901–909.

Lansford, J. E., Deater-Deckard, K., Dodge, K. A., Bates, J. E., & Pettit, G. S. (2004). Ethnic differences in the link between physical discipline and later adolescent externalizing behaviors. *Journal of Child Psychology and Psychiatry, 45,* 801–812.

LaVigna, G. W., & Donnellan, A. M. (1986). *Alternatives to punishment: Solving behavior problems with non-aversive strategies.* New York: Irvington.

Lerman, D. C., Iwata, B. A., & Wallace, M. D. (1999). Side effects of extinction: Prevalence of bursting and aggression during the treatment of self-injurious behavior. *Journal of Applied Behavior Analysis, 32,* 1–8.

Lewinsohn P. M., Solomon, A., Seeley, J. R., & Zeiss, A. (2000). Clinical implications of "subthreshold" depressive symptoms. *Journal of Abnormal Psychology, 109,* 345–351.

Lindsley, O. R. (1956). Operant conditioning methods applied to research in chronic schizophrenia. *Psychiatric Research Reports, 24,* 289–291.

Lindsley, O. R. (1960). Characteristics of the behavior of chronic psychotics as revealed by free-operant conditioning methods [Monograph]. *Diseases of the Nervous System 21,* 66–78.

Lochman, J. E., Whidby, J. M., & FitzGerald, D. P. (2000). Cognitive-behavioral assessment and treatment with aggressive children. In P. C. Kendall (Ed.), *Child and adolescent therapy: Cognitive-behavioral procedures* (2nd ed., pp. 31–87). New York: Guilford Press.

London, P. (1986). *The modes and morals of psychotherapy* (2nd ed.). New York: Hemisphere.

Long, P., Forehand, R., Wierson, M., & Morgan, A. (1994). Does parent training with young noncompliant children have long-term effects? *Behaviour Research and Therapy, 32,* 101–107.

Lonigan, C. J., & Elbert, J. C. (Eds.). (1998). Special issue on empirically supported psychosocial interventions for children. *Journal of Clinical Child Psychology, 27*(2).

Lonigan, C. J., Elbert, J. C., & Johnson, S. B. (1998). Empirically supported psychosocial interventions for children: An overview. *Journal of Clinical Child Psychology, 27,* 138–145.

Lovaas, O. I. (1987). Behavioral treatment and normal educational/intellectual functioning in young autistic children. *Journal of Consulting and Clinical Psychology, 55,* 3–9.

Lovaas, O. I., & Smith, T. (2003). Early and intensive behavioral intervention in autism. In A. E. Kazdin & J. R. Weisz (Eds.), *Evidence-based psychotherapies for children and adolescents* (pp. 325–340). New York: Guilford Press.

Markie-Dadds, C., Sanders, M. R., & Turner, K. M. T. (1999). *Every parent's self-help workbook.* Brisbane, Australia: Families International Publishing.

Martinez, C. R., & Forgatch, M. S. (2001). Preventing problems with boys' noncompliance: Effects of a parent training intervention for divorcing mothers. *Journal of Consulting and Clinical Psychology, 69,* 416–428.

Mash, E. J., & Barkley, R. (Eds.). (1998). *Treatment of childhood disorders* (2nd ed.). New York: Guilford Press.

Maughan, B. (2001). Conduct disorder in context. In J. Hill & B. Maughan (Eds.), *Conduct disorders in childhood and adolescence* (pp. 169–201). Cambridge: Cambridge University Press.

McEachin, J. J., Smith, T., & Lovaas, O. I. (1993). Outcome in adolescence of autistic children receiving early intensive behavioral treatment. *American Journal of Mental Retardation, 97,* 359–372.

Michael, J. (1993). Establishing operations. *The Behavior Analyst, 16,* 191–206.

Miller, D. L., & Kelley, M.L. (1994). The use of goal-setting and contingency contracting for improving children's homework performance. *Journal of Applied Behavior Analysis, 27,* 73–84.

MTA Cooperative Group. (1999a). A 14-month randomized clinical trial of treatment strategies for attention-deficit/hyperactivity disorder. *Archives of General Psychiatry, 56,* 1073–1086.

MTA Cooperative Group. (1999b). Moderators and mediators of treatment response for children with attention-deficit/hyperactivity disorder. *Archives of General Psychiatry, 56,* 1088–1096.

Nakajima, S., Liu, X., & Lau, C. L. (1993). Synergistic interaction of D1 and D2 dopamine receptors in the modulation of the reinforcing effect of brain stimulation. *Behavioral Neuroscience, 107,* 161–165.

Nathan, P. E., & Gorman, J. M. (Eds.). (2002). *Treatments that work* (2nd ed.). New York: Oxford University Press.

Neef, N. A., Mace, F. C., Shea, M. C., & Shade, D. (1992). Effects of reinforcer rate and reinforcer quality on time allocation: Extensions of matching theory to educational settings. *Journal of Applied Behavior Analysis, 25,* 691–699.

Newcomb, M .D., & Bentler, P. M. (1988). *Consequences of adolescent drug use: Impact on the lives of young adults.* Newbury Park, CA: Sage.

Nixon, R. D. V., Sweeney, L., Erickson, D. B., & Touyz, S. W. (2003). Parent–child interaction therapy: A comparison of standard and abbreviated treatments for oppositional defiant preschoolers. *Journal of Consulting and Clinical Psychology, 71,* 251–260.

Norcross, J. C. (Ed.). (2002). *Psychotherapy relationships that work: Therapist contributions and responsiveness to patients.* New York: Oxford University Press.

O'Brien, S., & Repp, A. C. (1990). Reinforcement-based reductive procedures: A review of 20 years of their use with persons with severe or profound retardation. *Journal of the Association for Persons with Severe Handicaps, 15,* 148–159.

Offord, D., Boyle, M. H., Racine, Y. A., Fleming, J. E., Cadman, D. T., Blum, H. M., et al. (1992). Outcome, prognosis, and risk in a longitudinal follow-up study. *Journal of the American Academy of Child and Adolescent Psychiatry, 31,* 916–923.

Orlinsky, D. E., Rønnestad, M. H., & Willutzki, U. (2004). Fifty years of psychotherapy process-outcome research: Continuity and change. In M. J. Lambert (Ed.), *Bergin and Garfield's handbook of psychotherapy and behavior change* (5th ed., pp. 307–389). New York: Wiley.

Owens, E. B., Hinshaw, S. P., Kraemer, H. C., Arnold, L. E., Abikoff, H. B., Cantwell, D. P., et al. (2003). Which treatment for whom for ADHD? Moderators of treatment response in the MTA. *Journal of Consulting and Clinical Psychology, 71,* 540–552.

Parrish, J. M., Cataldo, M. F., Kolko, D. J., Neef, N. A., & Egel, A. L. (1986). Experimental analysis of response covariation among compliant and inappropriate behaviors. *Journal of Applied Behavior Analysis, 19,* 241–254.

Patterson, G. R. (1965a). A learning theory approach to the treatment of the school phobic child. In L. P. Ullmann & L. Krasner (Eds.), *Case studies in behavior modification* (pp. 279–285). New York: Holt, Rinehart & Winston.

Patterson, G. R. (1965b). Responsiveness to social stimuli. In L. Krasner & L. P. Ullmann (Eds.), *Research in behavior modification: New developments and implications* (pp. 157–178). New York: Holt, Rinehart & Winston.

Patterson, G. R. (1976a). The aggressive child: Victim and architect of a coercive system. In L. A. Hamerlynck, L. C. Handy, & E. J. Mash (Eds.), *Behavior modification and families: Theory and research* (pp. 267–316). New York: Brunner/Mazel.

Patterson, G. R. (1976b). *Living with children: New methods for parents and teachers* (Rev. ed.). Champaign, IL: Research Press.

Patterson, G. R. (1982). *Coercive family process.* Eugene, OR: Castalia.

Patterson, G. R. (1988). Stress: A change agent for family process. In N. Garmezy & M. Rutter (Eds.), *Stress, coping, and development in children* (pp. 235–264). Baltimore, MD: Johns Hopkins University Press.

Patterson, G. R., & Chamberlain, P. (1994). A functional analysis of resistance during parent training therapy. *Clinical Psychology: Science and Practice, 1,* 53–70.

Patterson, G. R., Dishion, T. J., & Chamberlain, P. (1993). Outcomes and methodological issues relating to treatment of antisocial children. In T. R. Giles (Ed.), *Handbook of effective psychotherapy* (pp. 43–87). New York: Plenum.

Patterson, G. R., & Forgatch, M. S. (1987). *Parents and adolescents living together. Part 1: The basics.* Eugene, OR: Castalia.

Patterson, G. R., Reid, J. B., & Dishion, T. J. (1992). *Antisocial boys.* Eugene, OR: Castalia.

Pelios, L., Morren, J., Tesch, D., & Axelrod, S. (1999). The impact of functional analysis methodology on treatment choice for self-injurious and aggressive behavior. *Journal of Applied Behavior Analysis, 32,* 185–195.

Pfiffner, L. G., Jouriles, E. N., Brown, M. M., Etscheidt, M. A., & Kelly, J. A. (1990). Effects of problem-solving therapy on outcomes of parent training for single-parent families. *Child and Family Behavior Therapy, 12,* 1–11.

Pfiffner, L. J., & O'Leary, S. G. (1987). The efficacy of all-positive management as a function of the prior use of negative consequences. *Journal of Applied Behavior Analysis, 20,* 265–271.

Phillips, E. L. (1985). *Psychotherapy revised: New frontiers in research and practice.* Hillsdale, NJ: Erlbaum.

Prinz, R. J., & Miller, G. E. (1994). Family-based treatment for childhood antisocial behavior: Experimental influences on dropout and engagement. *Journal of Consulting and Clinical Psychology, 62,* 645–650.

Reid, J. B., Patterson, G. R., & Snyder, J. (Eds.). (2002). *Antisocial behavior in children and adolescents: A developmental analysis and model for intervention.* Washington, DC: American Psychological Association.

Reid, M. J., Webster-Stratton, C., & Baydar, N. (2004). Halting the development of conduct problems in Head Start children: The effects of parent training. *Journal of Clinical Child and Adolescent Psychology, 33,* 279–291.

Reimers, T. M., Wacker, D. P., Cooper, L. J., & DeRaad, A. O. (1992). Clinical evaluation of the variables associated with treatment acceptability and their relation to compliance. *Behavioral Disorders, 18,* 67–76.

Remschmidt, H. (Ed.). (2001). *Psychotherapy with children and adolescents.* Cambridge: Cambridge University Press.

Repp, A. C., & Singh, N. N. (Eds.). (1990). *Perspectives on the use of nonaversive and aversive interventions for persons with developmental disabilities.* Sycamore, IL: Sycamore.

Ritterband, L. M., Cox, D. J., Walker, L. S., Kovatchev, B., McKnight, L., Patel, K., et al. (2003). An Internet intervention as adjunctive therapy for pediatric encopresis. *Journal of Consulting and Clinical Psychology, 71,* 910–917.

Robinson, P. W. (1983). *Answers: A parents' guidebook for solving problems.* Canby, OR: Lion House Press.

Rogers, S. J. (1998). Empirically supported treatment for young children with autism. *Journal of Clinical Child Psychology, 27,* 168–179.

Roth, A., & Fonagy, P. (2005). *What works for whom: A critical review of psychotherapy research* (2nd ed.). New York: Guilford Press.

Ruma, P. R., Burke, R. V., & Thompson, R. W. (1996). Group parent training: Is it effective for children of all ages? *Behavior Therapy, 27,* 159–169.

Sanders, M. R., & Dadds, M. R. (1993). *Behavioral family intervention.* Needham Heights, MA: Allyn & Bacon.

Sanders, M. R., Markie-Dadds, C., Tully, L. A., & Bor, W. (2000). The Triple P-Positive Parenting Program: A comparison of enhanced, standard, and self-directed behavioral family intervention for parents of children with early onset conduct problems. *Journal of Consulting and Clinical Psychology, 68,* 624–640.

Sanders, M. R., Markie-Dadds, C., & Turner, K. M. T. (1998). *Practitioner's manual for enhanced Triple P.* Brisbane, Australia: Families International Publishing.

Sanders, M. R., Markie-Dadds, C., & Turner, K. M. T. (2000). *Practitioner's manual for standard Triple P.* Brisbane, Australia: Families International Publishing.

Sanders, M. R., Markie-Dadds, C., & Turner, K. M. T. (2003). Theoretical, scientific, and clinical foundations of the Triple P-Positive Parenting Program: A population approach to the promotion of parenting competence [Monograph]. *Parenting Research and Practice 1,* 1–24.

Sanders, M. R., & McFarland, M. L. (2000). The treatment of depressed mothers with disruptive children: A controlled evaluation of cognitive behavioural family intervention. *Behavior Therapy, 31,* 89–112.

Schrepferman, L., & Snyder, J. (2002). Coercion: The link between treatment mechanisms in behavioral parent training and risk reduction in child antisocial behavior. *Behavior Therapy, 33,* 339–359.

Serketich, W. J., & Dumas, J. E. (1996). The effectiveness of behavioral parent training to modify antisocial behavior in children: A meta-analysis. *Behavior Therapy, 27,* 171–186.

Shadish, W. R., Navarro, A. M., Matt, G. E., & Phillips, G. (2000). The effects of psychological therapies under clinically representative conditions: A meta-analysis. *Psychological Bulletin, 126,* 512–529.

Shiller, V. M. (2003). *Rewards for kids! Ready-to-use charts and activities for positive parenting.* Washington, DC: American Psychological Association.

Shure, M. B. (1997). Interpersonal cognitive problem solving: Primary prevention of early high-risk behaviors in the preschool and primary years. In G. W. Albee

& T. P. Gulotta (Eds.), *Primary prevention works* (pp. 167–188). Thousand Oaks, CA: Sage.

Skinner, B. F. (1938). *The behavior of organisms: An experimental analysis.* New York: Appleton-Century.

Skinner, B. F. (1953). *Science and human behavior.* New York: Free Press.

Smith, T. (1999). Outcome of early intervention for children with autism. *Clinical Psychology: Science and Practice, 6,* 33–49.

Snyder, H., Poole, R., & Wan, Y. (2000). *Easy access to juvenile populations.* Retrieved April 24, 2004, from: http://www.ojjdp.ncjrs.org/ojstatbb/ezapop.

Spivack, G., & Shure, M. B. (1982). The cognition of social adjustment: Interpersonal cognitive problem solving thinking. In B. B. Lahey & A. E. Kazdin (Eds.), *Advances in clinical child psychology* (Vol. 5, pp. 323–372). New York: Plenum.

Stoff, D. M., Breiling, J., & Maser, J. D. (Eds.). (1997). *Handbook of antisocial behavior.* New York: Wiley.

Strayhorn, J. M., & Weidman, C. S. (1991). Follow-up one year after parent–child interaction training: Effects on behavior of preschool children. *Journal of the American Academy of Child and Adolescent Psychiatry, 30,* 138–143.

Sturmey, P. (1996). *Functional analysis in clinical psychology.* Chichester, England: Wiley.

Sutton, C. (1992). Training parents to manage difficult children: A comparison of methods. *Behavioural Psychotherapy, 20,* 115–139.

Swanson, J. M., Arnold, L. E., Vitiello, B., Abikoff, H. B., Wells, K. C., Pelham, W. E., et al. (2002). Response to commentary on the Multimodal Treatment Study of ADHD (MTA): Mining the meaning of the MTA. *Journal of Abnormal Child Psychology, 30,* 327–332.

Task Force on Promotion and Dissemination of Psychological Procedures. (1995). Training in and dissemination of empirically validated psychological treatments: Report and recommendations. *The Clinical Psychologist, 48*(1), 3–23.

Thompson, R. W., Ruma, P. R., Schuchmann, L. F., & Burke, R. V. (1996). A cost-effectiveness evaluation of parent training. *Journal of Child and Family Studies, 5,* 415–429.

Tracy, P. E., Wolfgang, M. E., & Figlio, R. M. (1990). *Delinquency careers in two birth cohorts.* New York: Plenum.

Ullmann, L. P., & Krasner, L. A. (Eds.). (1965). *Case studies in behavior modification.* New York: Holt, Rinehart & Winston.

United States Congress, Office of Technology Assessment. (1991). *Adolescent health* (OTA-H-468). Washington, DC: U.S. Government Printing Office.

Wahler, R. G. (1980). The insular mother: Her problems in a parent–child treatment. *Journal of Applied Behavior Analysis, 13,* 207–219.

Wasserman, G. A., Ko, S. J., & Jensen, P. S. (2001). Columbia guidelines for child and adolescent mental health referral. *Report on Emotional and Behavioral Disorders in Youth, 2*(1), 9–14, 23.

Webster-Stratton, C. (1985). The effects of father involvement in parent training for conduct problem children. *Journal of Child Psychology and Psychiatry, 26,* 801–810.

Webster-Stratton, C. (1992). *The incredible years: A trouble-shooting guide for parents of children ages 3–8 years.* Toronto: Umbrella Press.

Webster-Stratton, C. (1994). Advancing videotape parent training: A comparison study. *Journal of Consulting and Clinical Psychology, 62*, 583–593.

Webster-Stratton, C. (1996). Early intervention with videotape modeling: Programs for families of children with oppositional defiant disorder or conduct disorder. In E. D. Hibbs & P. Jensen (Eds.), *Psychosocial treatment research of child and adolescent disorders: Empirically based strategies for clinical practice* (pp. 435–474). Washington, DC: American Psychological Association.

Webster-Stratton, C. (2000). *How to promote social and academic competence in young children.* London: Sage.

Webster-Stratton, C., & Hammond, M. (1990). Predictors of treatment outcome in parent training for families with conduct problem children. *Behavior Therapy, 21*, 319–337.

Webster-Stratton, C., & Herbert, M. (1994). *Troubled families—problem children: Working with parents: A collaborative process.* Chichester, England: Wiley.

Webster-Stratton, C., & Reid, M. J. (2003). The Incredible Years Parents, Teachers, and Children Training Series: A multifaceted treatment approach for young children with conduct problems. In A. E. Kazdin & J. R. Weisz (Eds.), *Evidence-based psychotherapies for children and adolescents* (pp. 224–240). New York: Guilford Press.

Webster-Stratton, C., Reid, J., & Hammond, M. (2001). Social skills and problem-solving training for children with early-onset conduct problems: Who benefits? *Journal of Child Psychology and Psychiatry, 42*, 943–952.

Webster-Stratton, C., & Spitzer, A. (1996). Parenting a young child with conduct problems: New insights using qualitative methods. In T. H. Ollendick & R. J. Prinz (Eds.), *Advances in clinical child psychology* (Vol. 18, pp. 1–62). New York: Plenum.

Weiss, G., & Hechtman, L. T. (1993). *Hyperactive children grown up* (2nd ed.). New York: Guilford Press.

Whisman, M. A. (1993). Mediators and moderators of change in cognitive therapy of depression. *Psychological Bulletin, 114*, 248–265.

Whisman, M. A. (1999). The importance of the cognitive theory of change in cognitive therapy of depression. *Clinical Psychology: Science and Practice, 6*, 300–304.

Wierzbicki, M., & Pekarik, G. (1993). A meta-analysis of psychotherapy dropout. *Professional Psychology: Research and Practice, 24*, 190–195.

Williams, C. D. (1959). The elimination of tantrum behaviors by extinction procedures. *Journal of Abnormal and Social Psychology, 59*, 269.

Windle, M., Shope, J. T., & Bukstein, O. (1996). Alcohol use. In R. J. DiClemente, W. B. Hansen, & L. E. Ponton (Eds.), *Handbook of adolescent health risk behavior* (pp. 115–159). New York: Plenum.

Woolfenden, S. R., Williams, K., & Peat, J. (2002). Family and parenting interventions in children and adolescents with conduct disorder and delinquency aged 10–17. (Cochrane Review.) In *The Cochrane Library* (Issue 4). Oxford.

World Health Organization. (2001). *The world health report: 2001: Mental health: New understanding, new hope.* Geneva: World Health Organization.

World Health Organization. (2002). *The world health report: 2002: Reducing risks, promoting healthy life.* Geneva: World Health Organization.

http://www.apa.org/divisions/div12/rev_est/pmt_child.shtml

http://www.cdc.gov/nch/fastats/druguse.htm

http://www.incredibleyears.com (for access to Webster-Stratton videos)

http://www.mhs.com/onlineCat/product.asp?productID=PARTAPE

http://www.parentingwisely.com

http://www.strengtheningfamilies.org/html/programs_1999/03_IY_PTCTS.html

Yates, B. T. (1995). Cost-effectiveness analysis, cost-benefit analysis, and beyond: Evolving models for the scientist-manager-practitioner. *Clinical Psychology: Science and Practice, 2,* 385–398.

Zanolli, K., Daggett, J., & Adams, T. (1996). Teaching preschool age autistic children to make spontaneous initiations to peers using priming. *Journal of Autism and Developmental Disabilities, 26,* 407–422.

Author Index

Abate, F., 64
Abikoff, H. B., 149–150, 177
Adams, T., 208
Adesso, V. J., 132
Ageton, S. S., 121
Allinder, R. M., 196
American Psychiatric Association, 6, 7
Anastopoulos, A. D., 177
Andrews, D. W., 30, 167, 179
Angold, A., 149
Armitage, S. G., 24
Arnold, L. E., 150, 177
Austin, J., 33, 160
Axelrod, S., 108, 220
Ayers, W. A., 16
Ayllon, T., 25

Baer, D. M., 26
Bagner, D. M., 132
Bank, L., 179
Barkley, R. A., 138, 148, 183
Barlow, J., 178, 183
Baskin, T. W., 170
Bass, D., 16, 194
Bates, J. E., 237
Baxter, D. A., 167
Baydar, N., 228
Beck, A. T., 165
Benjet, C., 93, 100
Bennett, G., 236
Bentler, P. M., 11, 178
Benton, C. M., 138
Bierman, K. L., 110

Bor, W., 144
Borduin, C. M., 151
Borowitz, S., 238
Boyle, M. H., 9–10, 240
Breiling, J., 170
Brembs, B., 167
Bremer, B. A., 241
Bremner, R., 240
Brestan, E. V., 183
Breton, S., 193
Brinkmeyer, M. Y., 141, 143, 176
Brown, M. M., 171
Bukstein, O., 10
Burchard, J. D., 152
Burke, R. V., 161, 179, 196
Burns, B. J., 152, 183
Burns, D. D., 165
Byrne, J. H., 167

Calzada, E. J., 141, 234
Canipe, V. S., 77
Cantwell, D. P., 150
Capage, L. C., 236
Carr, J. E., 33, 160
Carvey, C., 236
Cataldo, M. F., 61
Cavell, T. A., 138, 234
Chamberlain, P., 150–151, 164
Chambless, D. L., 15–16
Christophersen, E. R., 14–15, 138
Compton, S. N., 183
Connell, S., 144
Conners, C. K., 150

Cooper, J. O., 33, 160
Cooper, L. J., 240
Coren, E., 178, 183
Costello, J., 149
Cotten, J. K., 16
Cottrell, D., 14
Cox, D. J., 238
Craighead, W. E., 165
Crowley, M., 193
Cummings, N. A., 239
Cunningham, C. E., 240
Cunningham, P. B., 151

Dadds, M. R., 138, 144, 161, 171
Daggett, J., 208
Dahlberg, L. L., 181
Dawes, R. M., 163
Deater, Deckard, K., 237
DeGarmo, D. S., 167
DeRaad, A. O., 240
DeRubeis, R. J., 165
DiClemente, R. J., 10, 11
Dishion, T. J., 28, 30, 92, 138, 167, 179, 187, 229
Dodge, K. A., 237
Donnellan, A. M., 84
Dumas, J. E., 161, 183
Dunlap, G., 233
Durlak, J. A., 16, 171

Egel, A. L., 61
Egger, H., 149
Elbert, J. C., 15
Elliott, D. S., 12, 178
Elliott, G. R., 150, 177

Subject Index

ABCs of Behavior, 36–38,
45, 78, 80, 193,
199–202. *See also*
Antecedents; Behav-
iors; Consequences
Acceptability of Treat-
ment, 196, 240–241
Adherence to Treatment,
192–193, 220
Aggressive Behavior,
27–28, 92, 98, 107,
167–168
development of, 27–30,
167
Antecedents of Behavior,
36–45, 200–204
discriminative stimuli,
39
establishing operations,
39–41
prompts, 41–43, 78–79,
202–204
setting events, 38–41,
78–79, 81, 204, 207
Antisocial Behavior,
27–30. *See also*
Aggressive Beha-
vior; Conduct Dis-
order
Applied Behavior Analy-
sis, 25–27, 33*fn*, 160,
183
Assessment, 130
evaluation in PMT,
130–131
At-risk Behaviors, 10–11

Attention-Deficit/
Hyperactivity Dis-
order, 6, 15, 147–150,
177–178, 228
Attrition, 161, 175–176,
180, 193–194
factors that influence,
161, 171, 175
Aversive events, 49, 53–57.
See also Negative
Reinforcer

Backup Reinforcer, 51,
68–71, 78, 212
Behavior, 36, 45–48
chaining, 47–48, 63*fn*,
222–223*fn*
developing consistency
of, 210–211
knowing versus doing,
46, 71, 79–80, 125, 189
low-rate behaviors,
95–96
saying versus doing, 77,
131
shaping, 45–47,
204–206
target, 45

Chaining, 47–48, 63*fn*,
222–223 *fn. See also*
Shaping
Child and Adolescent
Disorders, 5–10, 227
anxiety disorder, 6,
8–9, 15–16

attention-deficit/
hyperactivity dis-
order, 6, 12, 15,
147–150, 177–178,
228
autism, 9, 24, 152–153,
178, 208
conduct disorder, 6, 12,
15, 21, 33*fn*, 147,
163–171, 174, 177–178,
183, 208, 235, 237
depression, 6, 8–15
impairment and, 5, 7,
9–10
mental retardation, 9,
24
oppositional-defiant
disorder, 15, 21, 33*fn*,
147, 153, 163, 174,
177–178, 183, 194, 235
prevalence of, 8–11
substance abuse, 7,
9–12
Child and Adolescent
Psychotherapy,
26–27, 180–181, 241.
See also Psycho-
therapy
Child Rearing, 21, 26–30,
40, 98, 111, 125, 150,
180–181, 190–191,
194, 229–230, 242
harsh, 100, 103–104,
118*fn*, 194
inept, 29–30, 167–168,
187, 229